Monash
&
Chauvel

ROLAND PERRY

Monash
&
Chauvel

How Australia's two greatest generals
changed the course of world history

ALLEN&UNWIN
SYDNEY•MELBOURNE•AUCKLAND•LONDON

First published in 2017

Allen & Unwin
83 Alexander Street
Crows Nest NSW 2065
Australia
Phone: (61 2) 8425 0100
Email: info@allenandunwin.com
Web: www.allenandunwin.com

Cataloguing-in-Publication details are available
from the National Library of Australia
www.trove.nla.gov.au

ISBN 978 1 76029 143 3

Maps by MAPgraphics
Index by Puddingburn
Set in 12.75/17.5 pt Adobe Garamond Pro by Midland Typesetters, Australia
Printed and bound in Australia by Griffin Press

10 9 8 7 6 5 4 3 2 1

To former Australian Deputy Prime Minister Tim Fischer AC,
who initiated the drive to make Monash a field marshal.

To Major General Jim Barry AM, MBE,
who increased the awareness of Monash's achievements
in the Great War.

Contents

PART 3: Amiens and Monash's Ascendancy

PART 4: Syria and Chauvel's Ascendancy

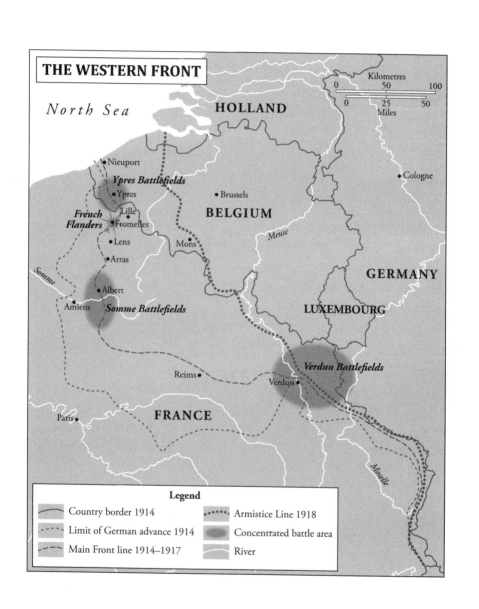

THE WESTERN FRONT

North Sea

HOLLAND

Kilometres
0   50   100
0   25   50
Miles

• Nieuport

Ypres Battlefields

• Ypres

• Brussels

BELGIUM

• Cologne

French Flanders

Lille
• Fromelles

• Lens

Mons •

Meuse

GERMANY

• Arras

Somme

• Albert

Amiens •   *Somme Battlefields*

LUXEMBOURG

Verdun Battlefields

Reims •

Verdun •

Paris •

FRANCE

Moselle

Legend

Country border 1914		Armistice Line 1918
Limit of German advance 1914		Concentrated battle area
Main Front line 1914–1917		River

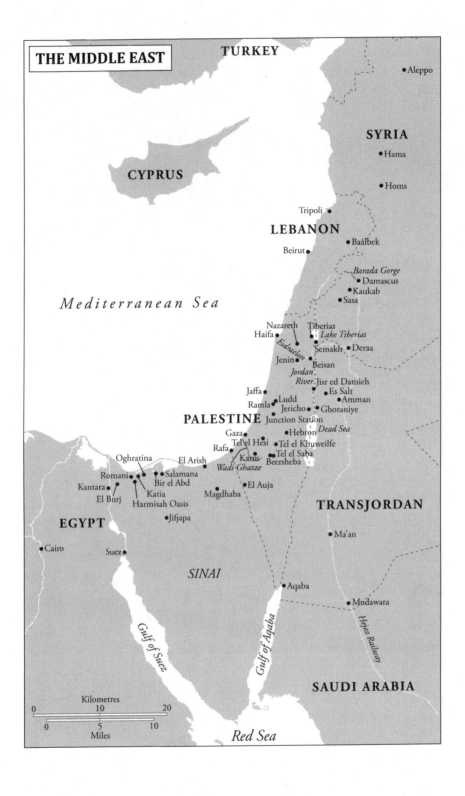

THE MIDDLE EAST

TURKEY

•Aleppo

SYRIA

CYPRUS

•Hama

•Homs

Tripoli•

LEBANON

Baálbek•

Beirut•

Barada Gorge
•Damascus
•Kaukab
•Sasa

Mediterranean Sea

Nazareth   Tiberias
Haifa•   *Lake Tiberias*
        Esdraelon Semakh• •Deraa
        Jenin•   Beisan
        Jordan
        River •Jisr ed Damieh
Jaffa•   •Es Salt
Ramla• •Ludd •Amman
PALESTINE Junction Station Jericho• •Ghoraniye

Gaza•   Hebron• *Dead Sea*
Rafa• Tel el Hesi• •Tel el Khuweilfe
Oghratina El Arish Karm• •Tel el Saba
Romani•   Salamana *Wadi Ghazze* Beersheba
Kantara•   •Bir el Abd
El Burj• Katia •El Auja
    Harmisah Oasis Magdhaba•

EGYPT •Jifjapa

TRANSJORDAN

•Cairo   Suez•   •Ma'an

SINAI

•Aqaba

•Mudawara

Gulf of Suez

Gulf of Aqaba

Hejaz Railway

SAUDI ARABIA

Kilometres
0   10   20

0   5   10
Miles

Red Sea

Introduction

One bullet from a Yugoslav nationalist on 28 June 1914 killed the heir to the Austrian throne and led to a billion more being fired over the next 53 months to 11 November 1918. In that time about 10 million combatants and 7 million civilians were killed in what became known as the Great War. When Archduke Franz Ferdinand was slain, nations lined up on two sides, almost in some cases as if they could not wait to fight. The Prince's death, it seemed, was a convenient excuse. Austria-Hungary delivered an ultimatum to Serbia. After a month, the Austro-Hungarians declared war on Serbia and invaded it. Russia mobilised in support of Serbia. The Germans were the most belligerent, having stepped up their preparedness over the previous decade with development and stockpiling of weaponry, particularly artillery. With victory in the Franco-Prussian War of 1870 fading from memory, it wanted fresh 'successes', conquests and territorial gains. Germany lined up with Austria-Hungary to form the 'Central Powers'. It invaded neutral Belgium and Luxembourg, before moving towards France. The United Kingdom reacted by declaring war on Germany.

These alliances drew in more nations as the war spread: Italy, Japan and the United States joined the 'Allies' (the United Kingdom and France), while the Ottoman Empire and Bulgaria joined the Central Powers.

The war had three interwoven explanations. First, it was a line-up of empires all searching for control and survival in a changing world. Second, there was conflict within a family of royals, the grandchildren of the United Kingdom's Queen Victoria: Kaiser Wilhelm II of Germany, Russia's Tsar Nicholas II and the United Kingdom's King George V. Wilhelm II was the belligerent of the three, who imagined that his two cousins, in fact most of the extended royal family, were against him. If these three had come to a rapprochement, war may have been avoided. But there was too much enmity between Wilhelm II and the others. There was no serious diplomatic will between them. They could not agree. Had Queen Victoria's son King Edward VII, the so-called 'peacemaker', been alive, events may have been different. But he had died in 1910. Their nations went to war.

A third factor was the old world of dictators and monarchies versus the growing, still fledgling new world of democracies. If the German military dictatorship won, the world would slip backwards into a dark period. If the British and French democracies emerged victors, then there was a chance that democracies would take a greater hold on progress.

The United Kingdom drew on the resources of its vast empire, including 650,000 Dominion (former colonial) soldiers, who would fight in Europe and the Middle East. In Australia 415,000 people (from a population of 4 million) were mobilised and employed in military service over the war's duration.

Among them were two outstanding battle commanders who would lead the most successful armies of the war. One was Harry Chauvel, who led the 34,000-strong Desert Mounted Column in the Middle East, which consisted of 75 per cent Anzac Light Horse. Chauvel was an empire man, who considered himself as British first, Australian second. His attitude changed over the course of the war as he realised that no matter what was achieved, he would receive more lasting recognition in his homeland.

The other great commander was John Monash on the Western Front in Europe, who at the peak of the deciding year of 1918 commanded the Australian Imperial Force (AIF). It had 208,000 soldiers (more than six times Australia's current defence force), and was the biggest single army corps of the twenty on the Allied side. He saw himself as Australian first and second. He viewed the war on the battlefields as that between two systems: military dictatorship and emerging democracy. His German lineage meant fewer ties to the British Empire and he had a real sense of Australia's needs as an independent fledgling nation. His background also made him more aware than any other Allied general of what was at stake.

PART I
1915 to 1917

Chapter 1

Monash

Australian generals John Monash and Harry Chauvel were poised with their armies early in 1918 to have a real impact on the two major battle areas of the Great War. At the beginning of that fateful year, Monash was running a division of 30,000 soldiers on the Western Front in northern France. Before mid-year, he would be commander-in-chief of the First Australian Imperial Force, the biggest of the twenty army corps on the Allies' side, when the nation's five divisions would come together as one fighting unit for the first time ever.

In the Middle East, Harry Chauvel commanded the Desert Mounted Column fighting the Turkish Army. It was made up of 75 per cent Anzac Light Horse and the rest variously from British cavalry, Indian Lancer and Jewish and West Indian contingents.

By mid-1918, he and his force were ready to attempt to push the Turks out of the Middle East after 400 years of sometimes brutal rule over the many Arab tribes.

Both these generals had strong records during the years 1915 to 1917. They came into contact with each other on Gallipoli in May 1915, when in the original Anzac force. Monash was a brigadier running 4th Brigade at Monash Valley above Anzac Cove. Chauvel's 1st Light Horse Brigade, without their horses, relieved it after three weeks of intense and bloody fighting. Monash stayed with Chauvel to help him adapt to the hideous, demanding conditions, leaving some of his brigade side by side with the Light Horsemen, who had not been trained for this kind of battle.

Chauvel then gained a healthy respect for Monash, who until Gallipoli was known as a 'citizen soldier'. In other words, he was not a regular army officer, and therefore not considered up to the challenges of war. But if ever an individual was underestimated, it was Monash. In 1915 he looked very much like a 'fat cat' from Melbourne's Toorak—at 100 kilograms and 180 centimetres—although within a year he had trimmed down. Monash, an engineer by profession, had a building business that had put up scores of bridges and other constructions around Australia. He was also one of the most successful barristers in Australia, with a 100 per cent win record in court battles over fifteen years, with one exception, when an opposition advocate bribed a magistrate. This was an unmatched record. But it had nothing in common, on the surface, with the business of commanding an army. What the Australian forces hierarchy and British High Command had little or no idea of was his record in the militia. Part-time soldiers had always been scorned, even if they had more than three decades' service, as Monash had. He joined the Melbourne

University Regiment in 1882 aged sixteen years and was forever showing friends or anyone who would watch how major battles in history were won, usually moving items such as salt shakers and cups around on a dinner table. It is unlikely than anyone in Australia, or possibly anywhere, had a better comprehension of the American Civil War or the Napoleonic Wars. Monash won a Gold Medal essay competition in 1912 for an outstanding dissertation, *The Lessons of the Wilderness Campaign*, on the Civil War.

Again, intellectual brilliance meant next to nothing to hardened professionals from the Sudan conflict in the late 1800s or the Boer War at the turn of the century. But Monash's military knowledge and experience went well beyond history books. He was a 'gunner', a first-class artilleryman, who knew all there was to know about weaponry, even to the point of creating his own— the Stanley Monash gun—that could pop up over parapets. He went on bivouacs and army exercises at any opportunity, usually with forty or fifty soldiers under his command and this way learnt much about the digger—the Australian fighting character—his foibles, weaknesses and strengths. Monash liked a drink and would socialise with those under him but he always kept a slight distance. He was never going to be a back-slapping 'great bloke' who would get drunk with the rank and file. Yet there was always respect for the man who would organise everything to the finest detail. Long before he received his high office, he was an efficient, experienced commander. There was nothing 'born to rule' about Monash; he was not seen early as a natural leader. But he was self-trained as a *commander* of men; someone who planned for one thing: winning. Monash had both eyes on how to stand out and be ahead of the pack in the upcoming conflicts. He went on a special course run in Sydney where field command was practised from a central bunker and where the officers were not permitted to actually venture onto the field of battle. This was revolutionary. Most officers educated under the British system believed in, if not leading from the front, then being near enough to it to give orders. Monash understood where the staging of war was heading. The cavalry charge that so motivated those in control of all the European armies in the early 1900s would diminish in importance. Monash was formulating how he would involve all arms at his disposal in a concerted effort. To him, a battle command was a lot like conducting a large orchestra, or building a bridge. It had to be meticulously planned and constructed. He believed that bridges should be built to stand up. The equivalent in battle was victory. And that was where Monash's obsessions lay.

Yet his grasp went far further. In 1901 he lectured at Australia's Royal Military College, Duntroon, and predicted the next major war would be a mechanised one with flying machines, armoured vehicles (tanks) and artillery predominant. He predicted that in a hundred years the use of machines would take over from humans, though not entirely. The reaction at Duntroon was disbelief; some treated Monash as a nutty professor. He was, even that early in his career, at 35 years of age, a military genius. This put him decades ahead of everyone else in his prescience, his vision.

As the Great War (1914–18) approached, he was a step ahead of every other general from all nations in several other ways. In keeping abreast of developments in weaponry he wrote, in German, to German manufacturers about their products. And, being innately polite, the arms makers wrote back to this educated fellow, fluent in their language, in far off Melbourne about where they were in the production of everything from machine guns and rifles to artillery and armoured cars. Consequently, Monash had a keen understanding of Germany's progress. Not only that, his Jewish parents were from Germany. He had studied the Prussian war machine, and he was well aware of where it was heading. He had toured the country of his forebears a few years before the war began and had a feel for its war footing. Monash also spent two years as a senior intelligence officer in Australia just prior to hostilities breaking out, which meant studying the Germans, as the likely enemy.

Monash, then, was in a strong position to contribute at the highest level to the Allied war effort. Yet when the war broke out he was a relatively unknown quantity to most. His unprecedented resources as a future battle commander were not understood and even if he impressed the British High Command, they would never be quick to promote someone from a former colony and a non-regular officer, not to mention having Jewish, and worst of all, *German* heritage. These, according to Sir Basil Liddell Hart, the foremost British historian of the era, were Monash's 'four handicaps of birth'. If ever someone would have to work hard to prove himself, it was John Monash. Even his appearance set him apart. He was handsome but not in the conventional, Anglo-Saxon sense. Sherlock Holmes's creator Arthur Conan Doyle was a journalist during the war. He was taken with the sheer power of Monash's presence. There was nothing of the swagger expected from some generals, nor the bombast about the Allies coming out victorious. Doyle found his 'comments' were matter-of-fact and convincing. Monash had an undemonstrative charm, which was not manufactured to impress; he was precise and articulate to the point of pedantry in the choice of the correct remark, yet his utterances were inspirational. Doyle found him the greatest of all the generals he met on the Western Front. He had 'an attractive aura' and a 'rare, compelling personality, whose dark flashing eyes and swarthy face might have seemed more in keeping with some Asiatic conqueror than with the prosaic associations of the British Army'.

These observations were made late in the war, when Monash had a brilliant record and reputation. In 1915, others may have just recorded his dark features, if anything.

His parents were immigrants, who worked hard, long hours in a country store to secure him the best possible education at Melbourne's Scotch College, which had an impeccable academic record. He was dux of the school in 1881. Monash went on to gain three University of Melbourne degrees in Engineering, Law and Arts. He spoke German fluently and French reasonably. All these academic achievements would mean something as the war progressed. The Great War would be primarily fought in France and his command of the language would be strong by the end of it; his German meant he would learn much from captured officers by personally interrogating them; his engineering capacities would be important in construction and re-construction of bridges and railways as the Australians fought, then pursued, the enemy. His understanding of the law would see him inducing commitments from his superiors that would stand up in court, if he were ever challenged for his sometimes daring battle plans. It would also see him helping engineers who needed advice on patents for innovative technical developments, inevitable during four years of concentrated war. But all this amounted to very little when he started out as a brigadier on Gallipoli in 1915.

Before then, Monash had no experience of actual battle, having declined to join the Victorian colony's Boer War expedition of 1899–1902. His reasoning said much about his political mindset.

He did not wish to be part of 'British Empire maintenance'. These were not views he aired in public. He wished Australia to develop independent of Great Britain, and in private spoke of a republic with its own army. After visiting New York in 1911 he saw a greater affinity with the United States. However, he did see the importance of fighting for the British Empire against Germany, primarily because he knew the Prussian mentality and how the Germans were preparing for war and world dominance, starting with Europe, but at the same time continuing to expand their colonial empire. The Germans already had bases in the Pacific and New Guinea. Monash was most aware that if Germany defeated Britain in the coming war it would take control of its main mineral-producing dominions—Australia and Canada. Therefore, apart from winning battle honours, which would be important to him, he had a clear idea of what was at stake.

Monash, in 1914, was married to Hannah Victoria—'Vic'— with one child, Bertha, and at 49 when war broke out, was ready to serve. He had made his fortune and believed he could delegate his construction and other business interests for a short time— perhaps a year or even two while he was away at war—without losing much income or control. (His business letter archive at the Baillieu Library, the University of Melbourne, demonstrates he was still running his operations during the war, sometimes sending missives and instructions during battle.)

Full-time regular soldiers were relatively inactive outside war years. There were only so many troop reviews, mock battles, field exercises, meetings, written papers and administrative duties a soldier could do before mental atrophy and doubts about a career path set in. Monash, by contrast, mapped his day by the minute between running his businesses, organising militia activities, family life, charity work and myriad other activities, including self-education in various fields, such as psychology and medicine. His leisure time was spent either reading, listening to music or playing the piano. Long before the description 'polymath' was in vogue, Monash was a classic example.

•

He was drawn to the conflict because of his comprehension of the German military's mentality and intent, which he predicted would develop quickly into a dictatorship. With his family history and recent professional experience, he fully understood the Germans. His family had escaped Germany's stifling environment in the middle of the nineteenth century. Monash was a product of the opportunities in a free and democratic society, begun and nurtured initially by the British. He felt he owed the country of his birth everything and was prepared to die for it.

Chapter 2

Chauvel

Harry Chauvel was different from Monash. His breeding and elite Anglo background developed not necessarily a born-to-rule but at least a born-to-achieve mentality. Given that his main career prior to the Great War was in the military, this expectation meant his ambitions lay in the United Kingdom, at the fulcrum of the British Empire. Australia was never going to be big enough for him. Chauvel's bloodline was French Huguenot, an aristocratic line of Calvinists or church reformers, who were forced to flee to England in the late seventeenth century. Chauvel's ancestors arrived in Australia as free settlers in 1838 and bought land in New South Wales. Born in 1865 (the same year as Monash), Chauvel was in a saddle before he could walk and a career in the Light Horse or cavalry was a strong possibility, if not predestined. Young Harry saw life through the prism of British military history, which was romanticised as all that was good and positive in life. Chauvel had a strong secondary education at Sydney Grammar. His working life with horses and cattle began in untamed country properties owned by his family, and he trained in the cavalry. His talent as a rider and his size—60 kilograms and 168 centimetres—saw him flirt with becoming a jockey, but his main aim remained to serve the empire, especially as Australia was still only a group of colonies. His chance arose in the Boer War in South Africa, when the British fought Afrikaner settlers to keep control of the region. It was an opportunity to break into the military mainstream and gain war experience. However, it was almost counterproductive from Australia's and Chauvel's points of view.

Had there been a stronger will from the various colonial premiers, especially in the pre-Federation fervour of the late 1890s, Australia could have sent an expeditionary force of soldiers under its own commander. This plan was on the table and needed quick consultation and ratification. But the British vetoed this, and the six colonies agreed to send their own small forces, which were destined to be sidelined or dispersed throughout the British Army, and used or even abused the way the empire wished. (This would have ramifications for the two big wars in the twentieth century. It was not until halfway through the final year of the Great War in 1918 that the Australian Army was formed as a unified fighting force. In World War II the Australians had to battle British Prime Minister Winston Churchill to retrieve Australian forces fighting in the Middle East and North Africa to prepare for a possible invasion by Japan. The mindset of the British, even after the Great War, was that Australian troops were there to fight for the British.)

Nevertheless, Chauvel gained good experience. He joined the Queensland Mounted Infantry (QMI), which in 1899 fought in South Africa, and later (after Federation) he was made a lieutenant colonel in the Queensland 7th Australian Commonwealth Horse, which arrived in Durban just before the signing of the peace treaty at Vereeniging on 31 May 1902. His contingent saw no action. But Chauvel had by then been on active service for five years and this had given him the skills to handle a mixed command. It had also shown him much about the importance of discipline, lacking on the South African veldt, and all the issues associated with horses and horsemen in a harsh country.

Despite Australia being federated as an independent nation in 1901, it was still controlled or managed in certain ways by the British, and this gave Chauvel a raison d'etre of sorts: to create an *Australian* defence force. He tried to gain secondment from the NSW General (Army) Staff in London but was rebuffed. It was a good thing for Australia. He was forced to make do with opportunities at home and he concentrated on lecturing about the things that had to be improved in his nation's soldiering. Chauvel endured a decade of relative inaction due to being out of favour with the army hierarchy, but was made the army's adjutant general in 1911. He moved with his family—his young wife Sybil and two children—to Melbourne, where he could do more to achieve a better armed force.

•

Monash, a battalion commander, and Chauvel, in charge of Australia's 1st Light Horse Brigade, had mixed experiences on Gallipoli. Early on, Monash was ordered to send his men into unwinnable trench battles, much against his own thinking and instinct. He put his case in each battle to his superiors, but was largely ignored. Monash was often frustrated, and once actually lost his cool demeanour after his men had been slaughtered in unacceptable numbers. He allegedly said, 'I thought I could command men!' It was hardly the exclamation of an unhinged commander, but C.E.W. Bean, the *Sydney Morning Herald* journalist, and Australia's official war historian, reported the utterance as if it was.[1]

Monash felt hemmed in at Anzac Cove in more ways than physically. He was allowed to voice his opinion to his immediate superior, General Alexander Godley, but he usually went unheeded. Godley was in command of the genuine 'ANZAC' 2nd Division, consisting of Monash's 4th Brigade, Chauvel's Light Horse contingent and the New Zealand Mounted Division. Monash's approach of meticulous planning and combining all weaponry in attacks—planes, artillery, machine guns—alongside the troops, could not be adhered to in full from the tiny beachhead of Anzac Cove. It didn't help his reputation for leadership that his brigade got lost on 6 and 7 August 1915 in a failed Allied attempt to attack and blast out the Turkish force in the heights on Gallipoli. But in general, he came away with good marks from his British superiors. Monash was a model officer, who would be looked upon favourably in the future. He had impressed Sir Ian Hamilton in late 1913 when that highly ranked British figure toured Australia. Hamilton found him the best soldier he met in the Dominions, saying he was 'a man of outstanding force and character'. He added that Monash had a necessary ruthless streak after viewing exercises that Monash had conducted in brutal bushfire heat at Lilydale outside Melbourne early in 1914.

Monash realised early on Gallipoli that he could not change the British mentality on how to fight on the Turkish peninsula. He decided he would wait for better opportunities to show his skills. Hamilton's headquarters during the Gallipoli battles was the battleship *Arcadian*, stationed off the coast at Imbros Harbour. In June 1915 Monash was invited on board for dinner with the commander-in-chief and a night away from the front. Monash's letters to his wife at the time show he was unhappy with his own progress and that of the British force, but he judged that airing his views to a set-upon commander would achieve nothing. Instead, he presented an optimistic demeanour that again impressed Hamilton. Monash was learning how to finesse and impress the people that counted in this war. He put aside his feelings about Australian independence and was very much a team player from the perspective of those running the war. This way, Monash hoped to gain as much power and responsibility as possible. He was relying on developing his abilities to command and run an army to be recognised over time. His reading of psychology informed him that the few windows of opportunity he had with people of intrinsic and real power had to be managed well. No point, he realised, in antagonising someone like Hamilton. Monash had made his arguments to Godley firmly, and repeating them to the top of the chain of command would not help his cause or that of his brigade. Consequently, Monash and Hamilton discussed music, Napoleon I and III and the Franco-Prussian War of 1870.

A few days afterwards, Chauvel was invited onto the *Arcadian*. He gave a frank, undiplomatic assessment of the conditions at the head of Monash Valley. Hamilton expressed his displeasure to Godley, who responded by saying he hoped Monash had not given Hamilton 'anything like the same idea'. Monash had not;

he appeared optimistic, but it was not simply to please the Chief. Monash was forever thinking about how to break out of Anzac Cove and defeat the Turks. He was incapable of sitting back and viewing a situation as hopeless. His life was about problem-solving in his work and leisure time. The drawback on Gallipoli for him was not being privy to battle plans or their design. There was no problem for him to solve. This left his military genius with nothing to tackle and he had only his sense of optimism, based on a confidence that he could extract himself from all tricky situations, if given the chance. Monash was powerless except in defensive tactics; these had proved successful in May 1915 when his positioning of machine guns had stopped the Turks from over-running Monash Valley and taking Anzac Cove. But he had no say in how the British force might take Turkish strongholds in the heights. He had to be a divisional or corps commander to see his views acknowledged and implemented, and this was not going to happen on Gallipoli where he and Chauvel were 'colonials' on trial. Chauvel's background in the Boer War and in the regular army put him ahead of Monash for any promotion. He was more in the 'British Club' than Monash because of his pedigree, both social and military.

Chauvel's pessimism was closer to realism about Gallipoli. He did not see any way out of a siege situation. Continual engagement was a waste of lives and time. Hamilton's response was to suggest to Godley that Chauvel be relieved from his command at the head of Monash Valley. Godley was irritated by Chauvel's lack of diplomacy but did nothing except to move him out of the main trench warfare 'hotspot' at the next opportunity, which had to happen anyway. Despite his lack of imagination and unreflective nature, Godley knew Chauvel's assessments were correct.

The expedition to the Dardanelles was a failure and a blight on Hamilton's illustrious career, as it was on that of its author, Winston Churchill.

•

Monash and Chauvel ended up back in Cairo after the disaster that was Gallipoli. From May 1916 Britain's General William Birdwood was in charge of all Australian operations in Egypt and Europe. He was inclined to promote Chauvel to a divisional command in Europe, but Chauvel himself was ambivalent. His ambitious, professional side saw there was a big chance of running a new Australian division, which eventually could lead to even higher command. But by nature he preferred to be with his horsemen, who would be reunited with their mounts after their unappreciated stint on the Turkish peninsula. There was only one divisional command spot to be filled in 1916—that of commander of the Australian 3rd Division, a new group of 27,000 volunteers, who would be joining the war in the full knowledge of what had happened at Gallipoli. Birdwood preferred Chauvel over Monash, whom he was reluctant to promote because of the lingering doubts about his German background. Some rumours even suggested Monash was a German spy. Yes, he could fight Turks, but how would he go against armies from the nation of his ancestors? But Hamilton, Godley and others sent good report cards about Monash to the British High Command and this allayed Birdwood's fears.

When interviewed, Chauvel's ambivalence meant he did not put his case either way, and this prompted Birdwood to appoint him commander of the Mounted Division; Chauvel would spend his war in the Middle East. This left the way open for Monash to take over the 3rd Division. He had increased his claim to big command after planning and commanding successful raids (future SAS-style) in mid-1916 into enemy areas in horrific circumstances on the Somme River in France.

Chapter 3

Romani

Chauvel settled easily into his new command post during the so-called 'phoney war' in the Sinai in the first half of 1916. Most contact was with Turkish scouting operations, before the Light Horse and British Army took on a 25,000-strong Turkish Army which marched into Palestine with the intention of crossing the Sinai Desert and taking Egypt. The Turks were confident after their successes against the Allies on Gallipoli and early in 1916 in Iraq.

Chauvel's job was to defend, against the odds, the wells at Romani from an attack by this enemy force. He had just 1700 horsemen to work with and could not rely on the garrison of British soldiers around Romani. They were not under Chauvel's command, and their generals were in Cairo, too far away to give assent to supporting the Light Horse if Chauvel needed them urgently.

The Turks were aiming to surround the entire British force, close in on it, strangle it and take the Romani wells. Without water in this harsh desert, which could see temperatures of more than 50 degrees Celsius, the big Turkish Army could not move forward to Cairo and take Egypt, mandated under British control. If the invaders succeeded, they would almost certainly take Egypt. If they failed to take the wells, the Turks would be stranded in terrible heat, with empty water bottles, dwindling ammunition and food supplies. The options then would be stark: defeat or retreat.

Chauvel did his reconnaissance and homework. Intelligence reports said the Turks would attack at night on 3 August 1916 and on into the morning of 4 August. His instructions were *not* to engage the Turks head on, as much as the troopers wanted to. His battle orders to his brigade were to withdraw on horseback gradually through the night. They would move back, dismount, entrench, engage in firefights, then mount up and repeat the exercise. The Turks were often nearly as close as they were in the fighting on Gallipoli. As Chauvel reminded his officers, this would take more discipline and as much courage as any encounter they would ever be involved in. And so it proved. A brutal protracted battle took place, with the troopers outnumbered about seventeen to one, but the controlled fallback proved decisive.

Midway through the fight, perhaps the most remarkable rescue and escape of the Middle East conflict took place, with Major Michael Shanahan, on his huge mount, the chestnut Bill the Bastard, managing to rescue four Tasmanian troopers who were stranded without their horses. Shanahan ordered the men up onto the three-quarter-tonne Bill, who dug his heels into the sand and pounded away from the front, thus saving the lives of the four troopers and Shanahan. This effort of man and horse exemplified the courage in this battle.

Chauvel's masterstroke was to hold back his 500-strong 2nd Light Horse Brigade until dawn. The attacking Turks had taken the heights in the massive, mountain-sized sand dunes, and they needed one last thrust to overwhelm the fatigued 1st Light Horse Brigade and take the wells. Chauvel himself took up a position at the head of the reserve force, which was watered, fresh and ready to fight. He wanted the enemy to see his rested troopers trotting forward in column formation on the sand. A gallop across the sand would have been futile and tiring, and this slow, deliberate movement, with a general at the head and a 110-kilogram commander (the brigade's 'Galloping Jack' Royston) behind him, dispirited the Turks. The psychology was straightforward. If the fatigued enemy attacked now it would most likely not overcome the fresh troops. The Romani wells were a struggle too far and they were out of water.

A firefight continued into the afternoon of 4 August, and while the British Infantry failed to support the troopers, other Anzac Light Horse brigades arrived in support. The Turks felt the heat in more ways than one, for most had abandoned their footwear in an effort to move over the sand in the night. The hot sand scalded their feet. Their tongues parched from lack of water, the entire enemy force withdrew to wells 20 kilometres away.

Chauvel modestly said the 'water bottle' had made the difference in the Battle of Romani but, at root, it was his tactics and planning that had prevented the Turks from taking the wells. The 'victory', in saving Egypt for the empire, did not receive the accolades it deserved, mainly because there was no British involvement at officer or rank-and-file level, and Chauvel himself was almost ignored for his efforts. He regarded this as his most important performance of the entire Middle East conflict, which was something for war historians to note. He placed it above the taking of Beersheba thirteen months later as a military exercise. First, it was a huge tactical victory. Second, it stopped the Turks and forced them to retreat for the first time in the Middle East war. Romani was Chauvel's line in the sand.

On reflection, it was one of the most important moments in his war.

Chapter 4

George V's Support

In the following month, on 27 September 1916, Monash also had a day to remember, but it wasn't in battle. In was on a dull, overcast morning at a parade ground, Bulford Field, on Salisbury Plain. Monash's newly formed and trained Australian 3rd Division lined up to march past him and the King of England, George V.

He was the least public, demonstrative or powerful of the three monarch grandsons of Queen Victoria. The other two were Kaiser Wilhelm II of Germany and Tsar Nicholas II of Russia. Wilhelm II was bellicose but losing influence as Germany struggled on in its third year of war with the French, British and Russians. The Tsar was even more autocratic, but in an increasingly dangerous revolutionary atmosphere. George V, by contrast, seemed on the surface to have no power, but in the arcane world of the British establishment, he had some influence over politics, where behind the scenes he might disapprove of a potential minister or even prime minister. He took a keen interest in the military, having spent twelve years in the navy, and he knew all the key figures in the three services. One of his best friends, Field Marshal Douglas Haig, was commander-in-chief of all British forces, and in effect, the most important Allied commander. The tall, broad-shouldered Scot, aged 55 and a graduate of the Royal Military College at Sandhurst, was an establishment man of empire. He fought in the Sudan in 1898 and the Boer War, and had held administrative posts in India. He had been in France since August 1914, running the British Expeditionary Force. In 1916 he committed masses of troops to the unsuccessful offensive on the Somme that had cost 420,000 British casualties.

Haig looked every centimetre a soldier. He was tall and handsome with a broad square forehead. His gaze was strict, even stern; his back ramrod straight. Haig presented a calm, 'in control' figure, not given to emotional outbursts. His thinking was not deep, but it had an inherent logic, and while he seemed reserved and, at times, severe on the surface, he had, according to those close to him, 'a warm heart'. Haig was religious and often in his diary referred to 'God's will', which at times was a useful explanation for mismanagement. He was not so much a complex character but a transparent one beneath a stiff demeanour. He was self-confident without bombast, and had developed over two decades a reputation as a talented, 'educated' soldier, within the prescription, limitation and scope of the military. His favourite reading was the monthly army review of books; he read few non-fiction books and disdained novels, which in his case was more than a hint of a lack of imagination. If he read a review, he didn't query the reviewer's skills, bias or motive. Nor was he motivated to delve further into the subject. His single-minded concentration as a military professional was both a strength and weakness. It led to an inflexibility that was hard to break. His fixed views were often made less pliable by a distinct incapacity to communicate clearly and concisely. Anecdotes were rife concerning this. A typical example occurred when Haig was giving out prizes at an inter-regimental cross-country race. He addressed the winning team: 'I congratulate you on your running. You have run very well. I hope you will run as well in the presence of the enemy.'[1]

The unintended result was a laugh from the audience. If he extemporised when speaking in public, he invariably got himself into a verbal tangle, and in his efforts to untie it usually became unintelligible and boring. But Haig himself always seemed unaware that he had presented something dull. He liked the sound of his own resonant utterances, even if they didn't make good sense. Haig wasn't alone in his lack of articulation. Field Marshals Edmund Allenby, William Robertson and (later) Archibald Wavell all carried the defect. It wasn't seen as a major blemish among army circles but it was when dealing with politicians. Prime Minister Lloyd George was set against Haig for representing all that was reactionary and outdated about the British Army. His incapacity to articulate gave Lloyd George more reason to denigrate him. The Prime Minister filled pages of his voluminous memoirs (*War Memoirs*) about Haig and his 'unthinking military mind'. In reference to Haig he wrote: 'Fluency is not a proof—nor a disproof—of ability, but lucidity of speech is unquestionably one of the surest tests of mental precision . . . Lucidity of mind ensures lucidity of expression. Power and light go together and are generated by the same machine . . . in my experience a confused talker is never a clear thinker.'

After two destructive years of war, Haig was in trouble. Politicians and the public, through the newspapers, were beginning to questions his methods. If it were not for his close mate the King, he would have resigned or been forced out of the command after the disastrous fighting on the Somme in mid-summer 1916. Many of his military cronies, including General Henry Rawlinson, Commander of the British Fourth Army and a veteran of the 1886–87 Myanmar Expedition, the 1898 Sudan Campaign and the Boer War, should have been removed from their posts after the calamity of 1 July when 20,000 Allied troops lost their lives in a total of 60,000 casualties. Monash, then still in charge of his beloved 4th Brigade (attached to Australia's 2nd Division in the Fourth Army), witnessed firsthand the folly of poor planning and the treatment of frontline soldiers as cannon fodder. Rawlinson was not equipped for such responsibility but he kept his position. His tactics and strategies had been approved by Haig. They would keep their commands as long as George V supported them. But even their jobs would be in jeopardy if there were any more massive failures when attacking on a grand scale. The fiasco on the Somme put the British High Command off trying to end the conflict in one mighty, concerted blow.

At that moment the King was looking for generals who could win, and was ready to meet any from the 600,000-strong force of dominion countries in his empire who might be able to help resist the German armies. The Bulgarians had been sitting on the sidelines watching the contest on the Somme, and had decided to come in on the German side. It was a fair indicator that the British could well lose the war, which would mean that

George V would be the monarch in place during the destruction of the British Empire and demise of the House of Windsor (formerly Saxe-Coburg and Gotha). He knew, too, that his belligerent cousin Wilhelm II would delight in deposing, even executing, him.

George V had heard about Monash from Sir Ian Hamilton before the war and Field Marshal Lord French, Commander-in-Chief of Home Forces, who had inspected the 3rd Division. On 27 September 1916, the King travelled down by train with his retinue and on arrival mounted a sleek, black Australian waler to take the salute as 27,000 diggers marched past. He met Monash, also on horseback, for the first time and there was an immediate rapport between the two. Monash had trimmed down to a fit and muscular 72 kilograms in a year, after a regimen of diet, walking and gym work. He now looked like a battle commander, but it was his comprehension of all things military and his forthright confidence that made a big impression on George V in the two and a half hours it took for the 3rd Division to march past. In that time, the King quizzed Monash on every aspect of the force, from the trivial, on such things as the diggers needing haircuts, to the profound, when he was asked for his thoughts on the use of artillery and machine guns.

At one point, the King spoke of his son David (the future King Edward VIII), who had been on Monash's staff in Egypt, and then he made the remark: 'If we win the war . . .'

Monash broke protocol, interrupted him with a determined smile and said: 'If we win?!'

The entourages of both men froze, wondering how the King would react. He threw back his head, laughed and said: 'Oh yes! We'll win right enough; nobody need make any mistake about that!'[2]

It was a telling moment. After the very recent events on the Somme, still ongoing but at their worst in July and August of 1916, no general could look the King in the eye and make such a comment. It had most impact because Monash had been on Gallipoli and in the thick of the Somme encounters. It was clear to George V that Monash's attitude was not that of a chest-beating, lightweight general wishing to please his King. Monash had experience. His remarks were made in the light of what he knew and expressed about the respective strengths of the opposing armies, their weaponry and personnel. He was already forming plans in his mind on how major battles should and would be conducted. Things unsaid, as much as said, registered with George V.

After the meeting, the King wasted no time in discussing him with Haig, who confused Monash, the engineer from Melbourne, Victoria, with Canadian General Arthur Currie, the real estate agent from Melbourne, Ontario. Not anymore. George V made it clear that he wanted Monash, of Victoria, and his division given every opportunity to show their capacities in battle. There was more than a hint in the King's advice that Monash should be elevated as fast as possible, and Haig took it seriously. George V rarely intervened with suggestions or comments, but when he did, Haig listened and acted.

In late November 1916, Monash and the 3rd Division had been in Belgium preparing for the Front only a few days when Haig turned up at their camp for an inspection parade. After it, Haig drew his horse close to Monash, put his arm around his shoulder and said: 'You have a very fine division. I wish you all sorts of luck, old man.'

From that moment, Haig insisted that their relationship should be on a first-name basis. Monash was surprised. Haig was not known for displaying emotion in public and the rushed parade had not been the best put on by the division. It was clear that the King's influence had been at work, and quickly. It manifested in several ways, including Monash being invited to big social functions where he would mingle with the British elite.

This was important in terms of his progress *off* the battlefield, but he was more preoccupied with the job he was expected to do on the Front itself. He continued conducting his speciality of raids behind enemy lines, but when these assaults began to look more like medium-scale operations than mere raids—he used nearly a thousand soldiers in one attack—the 3rd Division's continued successes began to come increasingly under notice.

Chapter 5

Gaza Failures

After the win at Romani, Chauvel and his Light Horse pursued the Turks. It took several encounters to push them right out of the Sinai and into Palestine. The enemy had no chance of attacking Cairo for the moment and instead decided to garrison themselves at the ancient, biblical stronghold of Gaza on the Mediterranean coast. By late October 1916 the Light Horse under Chauvel had done so well that he was able to go on 39 days' leave. After seeing his wife, Sybil, and children in London, he met with Birdwood, who was full of praise for Monash and his command of the 3rd Division. Chauvel told his wife of Birdwood's comments and she wrote to Vic Monash in Melbourne, telling her of her husband's increased 'standing' in the eyes of the man running the 1st AIF. Vic then wrote to Monash in France and he wrote back to her in January 1917: 'Glad to get extract from Chauvel's letter; this is the first indication I've had that Birdwood is really pleased, except what I was able to judge from his manner. I have heard that on his return to the Somme, after his recent visit to me here, he declared that my division is the best discipline of any of the five [Australian divisions]. If any of our divisions is to be broken up I feel sure it will not be the 3rd. Chauvel has done magnificently in Egypt.'[1]

Monash knew of the great work being done in Egypt, from personal accounts from Chauvel himself, but also from Birdwood and others. They had congratulated Chauvel during his well-earned break. This put Chauvel in a good frame of mind for the return train trip from Paris to Marseilles—until he read the French edition of the London *Daily Mail*. It carried the dispatch of the British Commander-in-Chief in Egypt, General Archibald Murray, concerning the Battle of Romani, which was now four months old. There was hardly a word about Chauvel or his troopers. He was not even mentioned in the lengthy list of honours for men who had been nowhere near the action.

Chauvel wrote a letter to Sybil: 'I cannot understand why the old man [Murray] cannot do justice to those to whom he owed so much. The whole thing is so absolutely inconsistent with what he had already cabled [about the outcome at Romani] . . . I am afraid my men will be very angry with what they see [in the *Daily Mail* report] . . .'[2]

With hindsight, Chauvel would later realise that the otherwise very capable administrator General Murray was not suited to running or winning a war. Murray was chief of staff for the British Expeditionary Force in August 1914 but suffered a mental breakdown during the distressing British retreat from Mons, in south-east France, after the Germans won the battle there. He was removed from his position in January 1915 and was tucked away in London in the Imperial General Staff for the rest of the year until he made a full recovery. Murray's administrative skills were recognised but he would not be pushed back into hotspots on the Western Front. Instead, in January 1916 he was made commander of the Egyptian Expeditionary Force and shipped off to Cairo, where the British were not expected to come under immediate threat from the Turks or Germans. But when the ebullient Turks did come, he and his staff stayed as far from the front (primarily in Cairo) as possible and so demonstrated a rare degree of incompetence in organising and running battles. Murray wasn't alone. Scores of generals and officers were on a good thing in Cairo before the conflict and he did not have the inclination or capacity to change things or venture near the front. Murray was most fortunate that Chauvel had been successful, but he had to hide his gratitude and preferred to take the credit himself. This approach was bound to have ramifications for the future.

In March 1917 Murray directed his force to take Gaza using 16,000 soldiers from two British Infantry Divisions. After the success in pushing the Turks out of the Sinai, it was decided that 6000 mounted troopers and cameleers would play a support role in the attack. Big artillery would play a key role. Now that the troopers were away from the sand dunes, it was thought by some that their role would be less significant. The mobile force would give way to the lumbering batteries of big guns.

The British Infantry bravely led the way, taking the fabled ridge Ali Muntar in front of Gaza, and Chauvel's Light Horse had the stronghold city surrounded. But then Lieutenant General Charles Dobell, 9 kilometres from the action, made the worst decision of the desert war to that point by ordering a retreat. He claimed to have intelligence that the Turks were reinforcing Gaza, but this was incorrect. The Light Horse had actually entered the outskirts of Gaza and was set to move in and secure it when the orders came through.

This major blunder was symptomatic of the problems created by High Command decisions being made too far from the battlefield. Had Dobell been at the front he would have been convinced by officers on the spot that Gaza was undefended and ripe for taking. Instead the force was ordered to fall back, which made it vulnerable to enemy attacks as the Turks learnt of the British retreat.

•

It was a bad time for the Allies. In Russia, mutiny had spread from the navy to the troops fighting the Germans on the Eastern Front. Thousands abandoned their posts and made their way back to Russia. They joined the workers, students and revolutionaries demonstrating in the streets. Trade unions were marching under their banners and calling for drastic reform and the abdication of the Tsar. Food was scarce in Russian cities. Soaring inflation meant prices were going up, while wages had remained static or had been reduced. St Petersburg was near revolt. Shops were looted and factories went on strike. The Tsar, isolated and out of touch, was praying that this was just an extension of the threat of revolution that had been ongoing for decades. Advisors were nervous about telling him it was more dangerous for him and his family than ever before. Much of the revolutionary propaganda was openly calling for the removal of the royal family.

It prompted Nicholas II to abdicate on 15 March. Then on 20 March, lawyer and revolutionary socialist Alexander Kerensky told the Moscow Soviet, the shadow city administration of Moscow, that 'Nicholas II is in my hands'.[3]

Kerensky added that he wanted to escort the Tsar to the dock and see him off in a ship to England, and show that the Russian Revolution was 'magnanimous'. Lenin, Trotsky, Stalin and the other more hard-line Bolsheviks were never going to be so generous.

In France, in April 1917, French General Robert Nivelle promised a decisive, war-ending victory over the Germans in 48 hours. His soldiers were euphoric as they entered the Second Battle of Aisne in northern France, the main action in the so-called Nivelle Offensive. When it failed it soured their attitude overnight. The will to attack was suddenly diminished and about half the French divisions on the Western Front were affected by the fall in morale. Over one million French soldiers had died since the war began.

General Philippe Pétain became the new commander. He talked to the men at the Front, told the press there would be no more suicidal attacks, and provided rest, home furloughs and recreation for exhausted units. Pétain promised a reduction in the severe, rigorous discipline that he admitted had been overdone in an effort to keep the troops in line. Having said that, he proceeded in secret with 3400 courts-martial, and 554 mutineers were sentenced to death. Perhaps because of his public pronouncements, more than 90 per cent had their sentences commuted. But the court action was kept from the public (and not revealed until the 1930s).[4]

•

General Murray in Cairo did not help overall Allied morale by claiming in reports to the War Cabinet in London that the First Battle of Gaza had been 'highly successful'. His excuses for Gaza not being taken were transparent and not credible. The High Command responded by demanding that the city be taken. Murray then assembled a larger force, but the Turks were now reinforced and the British lost the Second Battle of Gaza. Chauvel's Light Horse played only a secondary role in First and Second Gaza. In the first battle, a grand effort by the British soldiers, the troopers had fought well to surround the city, and had been ready to move in and take it over. In the Second Battle of Gaza, a superb rearguard action by Chauvel and his Light Horse saved the British Infantry from being slaughtered.

Chauvel wrote in detail about it to Monash, saying that in the wash-up of dismal results at Gaza and the many commander blunders, he expected to be given command of a mounted corps. Monash, delighted for his friend, wrote in turn to Vic in Melbourne on 15 May 1917: 'Have you heard how well Harry Chauvel has done? Reports say he saved the situation at Gaza, which was nearly a disaster for our arms. Rumour has it that he will be given command of mounted Corps in Egypt with the rank of Lieutenant General. Imagine an Australian rising to the rank of Corps Commander [!]'[5]

•

The monumental failure of Murray and his command had given the Turks back their confidence after their defeats in the Sinai and the failure to take Egypt. They began to dig in from Gaza to Beersheba, 70 kilometres inland, in the logical belief that if they could hold off two vigorous thrusts, then stronger defences and better trenches would make the line impregnable. In turn, Murray and his generals ordered the British troops to entrench but there was no talk of a third attempt to take Gaza. The region was in fixed-position stalemate. It had taken on the look of Gallipoli and the Western Front and there seemed no alternative in the waterless, rough terrain. Dislodging the Turks from the Middle East, for the moment, seemed a remote possibility. Major T.E. Lawrence, the British espionage agent later known as Lawrence of Arabia, had been using Arab tribes to terrorise the Turks on their railway in the Hejaz, the desert region running from Damascus deep into Arabia. But his operation would be reduced to harassing the one Turkish army in forts along the railway if the main British army could not move forward in Palestine against the two other Turkish armies in the Middle East. Murray's uninspired efforts at Gaza had left the entire desert war in limbo by May 1917. He was not going to change his defensive mindset into an offensive one after he had fudged his reports on Gaza, thus confusing the War Cabinet on the British position.

Chapter 6

Eyeing the Tank

The reputation of Monash's 3rd Division grew to where he was able to put up a battle plan to his immediate superior, General Herbert Plumer, to take the troublesome Messines Ridge, near Armentières and south of Ypres, held by the Germans throughout the war. Plumer was in command of the Second Army, to which Monash's division was attached. Plumer was a cautious, thoughtful commander, who, like Monash, cared about his men and was not going to be bullied into harebrained schemes from the High Command. Plumer admired Monash and his approach and approved the 3rd Division attack for 7 June 1917.

Monash's meticulous plan included the simultaneous blowing of 23 mines to collapse tunnels and trenches, the sound of which was heard across the English Channel. The 3rd's battalions then went over the top and quickly overwhelmed the Germans on the ridge's southern spur. This was midafternoon. By nightfall Monash had secured the entire ridge. Plumer, who had looked upon taking the ridge as a near impossibility, given previous efforts, congratulated Monash on his brilliant success. It was an Australian operation with New Zealanders in support, and boosted the morale of the 'new boys' on the block, whose division was the first of the Australian divisions to win a major battle. It was significant in giving Plumer's Second Army a huge success along its entire front.

Monash now had the King, Birdwood (after initial reluctance), Haig and Plumer supporting him, which was as strong a line-up as anyone could have on the Allied side. It didn't matter what observers on the outside felt about him now. Monash was in the important 'Club' of top British commanders on the Front in Western Europe. He had been fast-tracked by George V, but the King's faith in his selection had already been more than justified by performances in the field. Interestingly, despite Monash's basic philosophy about Australia's future independent development, he had managed to 'finesse' the upper echelons of the High Command, which in modern terminology meant he had shown remarkable EQ—'emotional quotient'—or the capacity to get on with people and compromise, to a point. His strong character, directness, succinct articulation and unmatched work ethic had come to the fore in the cauldron of the greatest war in history. His comprehension of new technology—tanks, planes, communications, artillery—and how to use them in combination was emerging at a critical time in the conflict.

He took a particular interest in the tank, and on 24 June, visited a tank battalion in IX Corps. The commander invited him to take a ride, and the value of these 'very wonderful and very terrible machines' was apparent to him. The weapon had not been in favour since its failure on the Somme in 1916; Monash probed the commander and his men with questions and then watched it in manoeuvres in formation and out of it. He timed them, interrogated the operators again and took copious notes. The Australians were sceptical about using the tank after the First Battle of Bullecourt two months earlier on 11 April when the 4th Division, under British command, had made an attack on German trenches east of the village of Bullecourt. In an attempt to surprise the enemy, the Australians went over the top without artillery support, but with the assistance of a dozen tanks. Nine of them failed to reach the German line. Despite this, the infantry seized two lines of trenches, only to be halted by further resistance, then counterattacks, which drove the diggers back. More than 3000 Australians died, and the tank was widely blamed.

Monash had studied the battle and now his observations of tanks had him formulating a different approach. He was convinced that the tank should be part of his armoury and he would never attack without giving his men adequate artillery support. Both weapons had to be incorporated, and with the consent of everyone, particularly diggers on the front line, who he envisaged moving forward beside the tanks after a massive artillery barrage.

Chapter 7

Allenby Meets
Lawrence and Chauvel

Chauvel's support from his British superiors took a positive turn when Murray was removed from his post and replaced by General Sir Edmund Allenby. Like Murray, Allenby was being 'dumped' after events on the Western Front and shuffled off to the Middle East, away from the main war in France. Allenby had been running the Third Army as part of a big British force in the Battle of Arras against the Germans in northern France and, as at Mons, a defeat meant scapegoats. Allenby, a rival to General Hubert Gough running Fifth Army, which, too, had been involved at Arras, was also a potential challenger to Haig as overall British commander. Arras had given Allenby's enemies within a chance to get rid of him.

Unlike Murray, Allenby was an aggressive commander, and he was in a bad mood when he arrived in Cairo. It didn't help when he discovered the disorganised way Murray had tackled the war against the Turks. But within a few weeks of arriving, Allenby found his mood was lifted by meetings with two vastly different but effective officers. One was T.E. Lawrence, who claimed that he could continue to hold the Turkish Army on the Hejaz Railway if he were given support in the form of advisors, weaponry and lots of gold, which would be used to bribe certain Arab leaders to the British side. The short, enigmatic, Oxford University-educated Arabist worked in Cairo's British-run Arab Bureau as an agent-runner, organising terror against the Turks throughout the Middle East. The bureau was a forerunner to World War II's Bletchley Park in England, but with more of a collegiate atmosphere. In Cairo, the technology of war was developed in three main intelligence areas: signals intelligence (Sigint); photographic image intelligence (Imint—used for tracking enemy movements); and agent-based intelligence (Humint). Each department knew what the other was doing and people such as Lawrence would wander into each other's offices and chat every day. In this respect it was more effective than Bletchley Park. Lawrence, the Middle East spymaster working Humint, made sure he built an expertise in the other two departments. His passion and certitude convinced Allenby that he should back him with more resources than Murray had given him; the other difference was in their intent. Murray wanted to avoid confrontation with the enemy; Allenby, if he sniffed any chance, would do his utmost to drive the Turks out of the Middle East, although that seemed more a distant dream than a possibility when he first arrived, feeling betrayed and despondent. Yet he saw that Lawrence's methods would increase the chance of achieving his aim of defeating the Turks, if a third to a quarter of their force was preoccupied with Arab attacks inland on the railway. It would mean Allenby could achieve something in the Middle East if he could defeat the remaining Turkish armies on the Mediterranean coast and in Palestine and Syria.

The other officer to lift Allenby's spirits in those first weeks was Chauvel, though not at their first meeting. The record showed that he had been by far the highest achieving general in the desert with his command of the Anzac troopers. Chauvel had been most responsible for repulsing the Turks and then pursuing them out of the Sinai, which even Murray in his retrospective analysis acknowledged by saying: 'The Light Horse is the cornerstone of victory in the Middle East.'

Chauvel had won every battle he had commanded in the Middle East. Even at Second Gaza, where his role had been marginalised for reasons Allenby did not quite comprehend, he did well. Chauvel's two brigades had fought two sharp actions against the Turkish 3rd Cavalry and had gained the ascendancy with relative ease.

Allenby was aware of his track record when he met the neat, tanned and lean Chauvel, who was also haggard-looking after two years on fronts from Gallipoli to Gaza. They were different characters. Allenby was big, brusque, bullying and restless. The diminutive Australian was cool, unruffled and thoughtful. In an attempt at intimidation, Allenby insisted that he (Allenby) should directly approach Australian Prime Minister Billy Hughes for more men and money. Chauvel resisted; he thought it better that General Birdwood should remain the conduit to Hughes, which was a way of keeping a vestige of Australian independence.

Even though Birdwood was English, he always seemed to have Australian interests at heart, and Chauvel wished to remain loyal to him. He went behind Allenby's back by writing to both Hughes and Birdwood to warn them of Allenby's aim.

There were other issues on which Chauvel stood firm rather than give in to demands concerning staff, and at first the new British commander-in-chief in the Middle East was displeased with him. But on reflection, and after consultation with other key officers and generals, Allenby realised that Chauvel represented his best chance of winning battles in Palestine and Syria. The infantry would play a role, but the war would be won or lost by the swift-moving mobile forces of cavalry and cameleers. His choice of field commander of the Desert Mounted Column would be the most important appointment of the Middle East conflict.

Chapter 8

Broodseinde 'Win'; Haig's Deadly Haste

Early in July 1917, Monash was on leave in London when King George V visited the front and wished to catch up with him again. Discovering Monash's absence, George V, accompanied by Haig and Godley, still insisted on seeing the 3rd Division's brigadiers to congratulate them on the win on Messines Ridge. He asked them to pass on his good wishes and thanks to Monash. It was George V's subtle way of reminding Haig and Godley that his support for Monash had been well founded. Godley got the message and when Monash returned from leave he left him as acting corps commander of the three divisions of II Anzac. It was the first clue as to who would be first choice to run the 1st AIF, *if* the five Australian divisions were ever to come together under one command. Haig did not favour this development. He preferred to have those divisions tacked onto British armies and therefore more under his control. Haig had already had trouble with the Canadians being uncooperative (in terms of doing what the High Command wanted) and he believed an Australian army would be just another headache. It was bad enough attempting to get cooperation with the French, let alone problem armies within the British force.

Haig believed that July–August 1917 was the time for the British to force home advantages. Any territorial gains or repulsions of the enemy would be important. After the shocking failure of the Haig/Rawlinson big push on the Somme a year earlier, the High Command had been shy about attempts at massive multi-army attacks. The Allies would proceed if possible by more modest thrusts, such as at Messines Ridge. But after Monash's crushing and quick win, Haig began to consider a big sweep of the ridges at Ypres, with his main target being Passchendaele, a 'ridge' rising to 60 metres in height over several kilometres. His crash-through approach was dangerous and ran contrary to Monash's cautious attitude, and need for near certainty. His approach was based on layered planning that took time and thought, and was clearly communicated to the officers and all ranks.

•

Another major indication of how much Monash was in favour with the powers-that-be in the British forces took place on 22 September 1917. Haig reviewed Monash's troops and invited him to dine at his HQ mess. Nothing remarkable about that, except that the other guests were General William Robertson,

Chief of the General Staff, and Major General Richard Butler, Deputy Chief of the General Staff. Haig and these two made up the central brains trust of the entire British force. They wanted Monash's opinions on upcoming strategies. Monash was unaware that he was the King's favourite general, and fast becoming Haig's too. Yet this invitation made him think that he would be in the running to command an Australian army, if the British would ever sanction it. Monash thought at first that his patronage by the King, who always sent royal relatives visiting the Front to see him, and that of Haig, was more or less what all the top divisional generals experienced. But when it became a regular occurrence, it began to dawn on him that this was not the case. He was the only Australian commander called upon this way. Not even British generals such as Godley, Gough or even Plumer, who Monash admired, were given the royal and top brass treatment in this way. His opinions were valued at the very peak of the British High Command.

By 27 September 1917, after several small victories at Menin Road and Polygon Wood, the British, spearheaded by Anzac forces, were in a position to make an attack on the main ridge in the area, at Broodseinde, 12 kilometres short of Passchendaele. It was the third operation directed by General Plumer as part of the Ypres Offensive and involved twelve divisions. The Anzac I Corps— 1st and 2nd Divisions—was moved north of Polygon Wood to a launching place. Then Anzac II Corps—Monash's 3rd Division and the New Zealand Division—were moved in beside them and in line. This caused a ripple of anticipation along the four-division front. It was the first time that such an antipodean line-up had ever occurred. The whole extension or revival of the Anzac experience from Gallipoli electrified the atmosphere over several kilometres. The soldiers were energised and ready for action.

The attack plan had very much a Monash/Plumer imprimatur, where the attacking troops' objectives were limited to a push of about 1500 metres into enemy lines. The advance before dawn on 4 October 1917 was preceded by a massive artillery bombardment, and a creeping barrage led the troops on to their objectives, and then protected them while they consolidated their positions. The Anzacs were shelled heavily on their start line and a seventh of them were casualties even before the attack began. When it did, the diggers were confronted by a line of German troops coming at them. By coincidence, the enemy had decided to launch their own attack on the exact same morning. It was something that not even the genius of Monash had factored into the planning. He had to rely on the courage of his shock troops as they forged on through the German assault waves and gained their objective along Broodseinde Ridge. This surprise enemy attack, along with its pillboxes, which were difficult to subdue, meant the Australian divisions suffered 6500 casualties in their biggest victory to that point in the war. Monash's 3rd Division had its second successive big win in two outings.

'The Germans were swept away in many individual combats by my Australians,' General Birdwood noted proprietarily and proudly. 'There could be no doubt as to the completeness and importance of our success.'

Monash wrote straight after the battle: 'Great happenings are possible in the near future . . . Our success was complete and unqualified. Over 1,050 prisoners taken, and much material and guns. Well over 100 dead enemy counted and many hundreds buried out of reach. We got absolutely astride of the main Ridge.'[1]

The Australians noted that they had seen 'the German teams hitching up their artillery guns and limbers [the carts that supported them] and galloping away. There were green fields and pastures, things we had never seen before in the Ypres sector.'[2]

Germany's commander-in-chief, General Erich Ludendorff, noted: 'The battle [at Broodseinde] of the 4th October was extraordinarily severe, and again we only came through it with enormous losses.'[3]

The official German monograph on the campaign spoke of this as a 'black day'. The descriptive colour of the 24 hours concerned was always recorded this way if the Germans lost or failed in an objective.

Bean gave very little credit to Monash but conceded: 'An overwhelming blow had been struck and both sides knew it.'

Broodseinde had brought a sudden change in confidence in observers. Bean was typical of reporters when he added: 'In view of three step by step blows [culminating at Broodseinde], all successful, [observers are asking] what will be the result of three more in the next fortnight.'

Haig wrote to Monash congratulating him on his part in the 'greatest battle of the war'. Broodseinde and Messines represented a clear breakthrough after all the indecisive, costly battles, large and small, until now. Haig's friend and military advisor, Captain John Chateris, wrote just after Broodseinde, and a day before Haig launched the big push at Passchendaele: 'With a great success tomorrow, and good weather for a few more weeks, we may still clear the coast and win the war before Christmas [1917]. It is not impossible but it is pouring again today.'[4]

Charteris's remark showed the optimism, bordering on unreality, that pervaded the High Command in the hours and days after Monash's spectacular victory. The commander-in-chief, following the mood of the moment, was keen to push on to Passchendaele.

His continuing belief, rather than reasoning based on hard intelligence, was that the enemy was demoralised, fatigued and weakened. This was as much wishful thinking as fact. Deep down, Haig was bothered by the thought of what was going on in Russia, which was facing revolution. If the Russians pulled out of the war, one million Germans would return to France to reinforce their troops and change the balance of the war. Monash agreed with pushing on hard, but under conditions that were right for his men. He did not want to attack when the weather was rotten. It rained on 4 October, too late to affect the Broodseinde battle. But now the rain had set in.

It was still pouring on 6 October when the 3rd was relieved by a British division. But the diggers' break would be brief. Haig and Plumer were now fully cognisant of their capacities and they wanted the diggers to be part of the big push on Passchendaele. But the rain came in torrents. Plumer, his Chief of Staff Major General Tim Harington, and Godley were all in favour of pushing on regardless of the weather. Monash was the most vocal against it, saying it would mean sacrificing thousands of soldiers in a huge bog and result in a probable loss. Better to wait three or four weeks until the weather improved. Monash was certain this would secure a win at Passchendaele. After some persuasion, Birdwood agreed with Monash but was not prepared to go against Haig. General Gough of Fifth Army was surprisingly ambivalent. His approach had been gung-ho on other missions and he always sided with his close mate Haig, but the destruction of ground in front of the main target ridge had created a quagmire. Progress through it would be nearly impossible, and glacially slow-moving. The cavalry would be at the biggest disadvantage.

Monash lobbied Gough and Plumer the next day, 7 October, and the two army commanders changed their minds as the rain set in again. But they did not have the nerve to approach Haig individually. Instead they put a joint proposal to him to end the campaign for the time being and wait until the weather picked up. Haig rejected it. He was now obsessed about taking the long, low, troublesome ridge.

Godley informed Monash that two British divisions, the 49th and 66th, would go in first on 9 October. The 3rd Division would follow, if those first two forces failed by 12 October. Monash spoke bluntly about attacking in the conditions; he believed that it would mean his men would be slaughtered. Godley, who had not softened his own attitude, told him it didn't matter. The commander-in-chief's mind was made up and that was that. Monash went over Godley's head to Plumer but received the same rebuff. Plumer didn't disagree, but Haig could be pigheaded, and this was a classic instance.

The rain was even steadier on 8 October. By the time Monash sent his troops over the top after the predictable British division failures, he had set up a thorough ambulance system to cope with the coming disaster. After eight hours of battle, Godley pulled the New Zealanders out. Monash was forced to do the same with his division, which took another two hours to extract its men.

Passchendaele, which should never have been attempted, was over. The 3rd Division had 3200 casualties out of the 5000 soldiers who went over the top. The New Zealanders fared even worse, with 3500 casualties. Each division involved had similar numbers. Haig's illogical, hasty directive had turned into an irrational obsession. In the end it was more of the mismanagement that had reached a zenith under Haig and Rawlinson on the

Somme in the previous year, unnecessarily costing the lives of thousands of men.

There was no more talk of 'winning the war by Christmas'. With the prospects of German reinforcements from the Russian Front a reality in 1918, thoughts turned gloomily to another realisation that was aired in the English press. This war could go on for several years yet.

On 25 October 1917, the radical-left Bolsheviks seized power in Russia and promised to make peace with Germany and withdraw from the 'capitalist, imperialist war'. Lenin claimed he would conquer other countries by revolution, not war. Haig was justified, at least in his mind, about his attempts to take Passchendaele. With the Russians now out of the war, those extra million Germans would soon be coming at the Allies.

The Bolsheviks began brokering deals with Germany. The fates of Poland, Finland, and the Baltic provinces of Lithuania, Latvia and Estonia and southern Russia would be in German hands within months.

•

Monash had long learnt to hide his feelings and look forward to better opportunities, but it angered him in private to experience such awful waste of his men, who had given him such strong and loyal service.

'Our men are being put into the hottest fighting,' he wrote to his wife, 'and they are being sacrificed in harebrained schemes, like Bullecourt and Passchendaele, and there is no one in the War Cabinet to lift a voice in protest . . . Australian interests are suffering badly. Australia is not getting anything like the recognition it deserves.'[5]

He began lobbying harder than ever for the Australian divisions to be brought together under Australian command in an attempt to avoid the British High Command's hideous follies. His division in II Anzac Corps was replaced at Passchendaele by the Canadian Corps, and for a short time was parked under its commander, General Arthur Currie, who impressed Monash as a 'very able man'. The feeling was mutual. According to Currie's biographer, A.M.J. Hyatt, the Canadians, Currie and the British High Command 'usually reckoned Monash as the most brilliant of [the Allied] Generals'.[6]

Currie had proved an outstanding battle commander at the Second Battle of Ypres in 1915 and Vimy Ridge in 1916, but he could be prickly and was not universally loved by his Canadian force. (He was so annoyed by ridicule of his name, originally 'Curry', when a schoolteacher early in his career, that he changed it to 'Currie'. It did not stop the jokes among the rank and file. He was dubbed 'Currie in a flurry' on occasion.)

His experience of the Canadians' independence was further confirmation for Monash that Australia should have its own army. Currie's corps made its own decision on when Passchendaele should be attacked. It resisted Haig's urging to go straightaway and waited until the weather had cleared and the ground in front of the ridge was not a lake. They went over the top a month later in dry conditions and took Passchendaele from the Germans. Currie predicted the casualties (nearly 16,000, with 4000 deaths), and had tried to talk Haig out of the attack altogether.

After this experience, the Canadians were confirmed in their determination not to take orders from the British High Command and decided to opt out of battles planned by the British in the future.[7]

Chapter 9

The Taking
of Beersheba

In the Middle East, the British faced another important battle, which, like Passchendaele, would lead to a better chance of winning the war. In this case it was against the Turks, who were being directed by German officers. This was to be the Third Battle of Gaza, an attempt to break through the strong enemy defences that had built up over half a year. In that time, Commander-in-Chief Allenby had created a careful plan, which included a major deception to make the Turks believe there would be a third, all-out assault on Gaza. This involved false plans being 'lost' by a British officer, which led the Turks to believe that the attack would be in late November (a month later than the actual plan) and nowhere near Beersheba, which would be the secret, main target. It held the wells, which, if taken, meant the British could plan for the final attack on Gaza.

The Turks, who had fallen for the ruse, prepared for an assault concentrated north of Gaza. They moved all their reserves up to the city. On the right flank of the British camp near Gaza, mounted Anzac patrols continued in front of Beersheba to accustom the enemy to their presence.

Allenby set the date of 31 October for a combined attack on Beersheba by XX Corps from the south-west and two brigades of Chauvel's mounted corps from the east and north-east. He chose the 3rd and 4th Brigades and two experienced, courageous and hardened commanders he knew from his Queensland mounted days, city lawyer Lachlan Wilson and Victorian grazier William Grant, to lead them. The XX Corps, commanded by Major General Philip Chetwode, was to creep off after dark towards Beersheba ready for the assault on the town. Chetwode moved into position south-west of Beersheba before dawn on 31 October. At 5.55 a.m. the muezzin heralded the new day from the minarets of the town and the infantry began its assault.

Chauvel placed his HQ on a high hill, Khashim Zann, 6 kilometres south-west of the town. He had what he called 'a dress circle view of the show', and could see most of his regiments advancing on the town, which gave him a good sense of how the battle progressed during the morning. He could see Chetwode's soldiers were doing well. To the east of the town the Light Horse from Anzac Mounted Division was being held up by a line-up of well-concealed machine guns at an outpost called Tell es Sabe. Troopers were being forced to dismount and inch their way forward. Heavy fire raked the plain. Shrapnel rained down.

Another problem was German aircraft, which flew uncontested above Beersheba, dropping their bombs on the soldiers and Light Horse. By 1 p.m. Chetwode's infantry had broken through Turkish trenches on the outskirts of the town but could not surmount the tighter, inner encirclement.

At 2.45 p.m. Chauvel, who had hardly put down his binoculars, had one eye on the clock. Allenby, 20 kilometres away, was sending frantic cables to him to attack. But Chauvel was waiting for the most propitious moment to strike. It was not to be a typical Light Horse attack, where the troopers would dismount close to the enemy trenches and then proceed on foot.

He made the decision to *charge*.

Chauvel knew that as the sun moved lower, the wells had to be taken, otherwise the Beersheba operation would not work and Gaza would fail to be taken for a third time. That scenario would lead to a failure by the British to remove the Turks from the Middle East.

Chauvel had to take advantage of the last hour of light before nightfall and there was method and psychology in his delay. He was gambling on a surprise. The German and Turkish officers in charge of the defence of Beersheba would see the Light Horse lining up and note the troopers' hats with tell-tale insignia of emu plumes. They would know how the Australians attacked and that they never charged right through. It was not their way. This, Chauvel hoped, would lull them into thinking they could defend against the troopers, who the enemy would expect to transform into riflemen on foot. The surprise, he anticipated, would turn into shock, allowing the Light Horse to make it past the trenches and into the town to secure the wells.

Both the British Cavalry and Chauvel's Light Horse wanted to make the charge and he had to choose one of them. So far, he had been fair and balanced in choosing English contingents, but in this instance he chose William Grant and his 4th Light Horse Brigade. Grant was to lead his 4th and 12th Light Horse Regiments, about 800 troopers.

Chauvel's thinking was accurate.

In Beersheba, the Turkish commander Ismet Bey had 4400 men and 28 artillery field guns, along with scores of machine gunners, snipers and planes dropping bombs, to hold off the two Light Horse Brigades after the British Infantry's push in the morning. But he was on edge. He did not believe this was a mere feint and that Gaza was the main aim of the overall attack. Ismet Bey asked his German commander General Friedrich Kress for reinforcements but was tersely rebuffed. This attitude created a strange mood in the town, with German officers convinced there would be no kind of mounted attack, and the Turks under them thinking there would be. Then the build-up on a hill 6 kilometres away was noted by all. The Germans maintained that the Light Horse activity was an elaborate manoeuvre, just another British ruse, a mere demonstration. But by midafternoon, the defenders began to have real doubts. They braced themselves for some form of attack, still thinking that they could withstand an Australian-style run at them.

'We did not believe,' one German officer said, 'that the charge would be pushed home. That seemed an impossible intention. [But] I have heard a great deal of the fighting qualities of the Australian soldiers. They are not soldiers at all; they are madmen.'[1]

The alleged insanity of their opposition was soon confirmed as the first squadron of Light Horsemen appeared in a line

1100 metres wide over the top of a ridge. It was 4.30 p.m. The sun was setting and would be out of sight in twenty minutes. Light was already fading fast. The Turkish officers barked orders at their artillerymen. As they saw the charge mount to a fast gallop forward, the Turks alerted their machine gunners to start raking the plain when the troopers reached 1.5 kilometres, halfway to the trenches and a quarter of the way to Beersheba. The German officers remained stubborn, believing they would destroy the oncoming front squadrons. The rest of the Australians would be forced to dismount in their traditional fashion, which would lead to a successful Turkish defence. But when the front of the charge bolted through the barrage and was within 400 metres, a chill ran through the command and the Turks in the trenches. The horses were not stopping. They could smell the water and were coming straight at the defenders. The Turks could hear the blood-curdling cries from the Australians in the brief lulls of artillery and machine-gun fire.

Ismet Bey and German officers turned and ran back towards the town. One officer was ordered to destroy the all-important wells, but he was captured moments before he could throw a demolition switch. The 400,000 litres of water in the wells was saved.

The charge was an overwhelming success. There were 31 troopers killed and a further 32 wounded; 70 horses paid the ultimate price and another ten had to be put down after sustaining injuries. In military terms, Beersheba was a big win. More than five hundred Turks were killed and another 1500 captured. Nine big guns were taken, along with a score of machine guns and a store of rifles.

Later (and for a century thereafter), Beersheba would be mythologised and Romani forgotten, except by a few serious military historians. Chauvel, who was the key commander at both battles, ranked Romani much higher from the point of view of a successful military action. He also placed it above Beersheba in terms of the outcome of the Middle East war. First, Romani stopped the Turks in their tracks, literally, en route to take Egypt from the British. Second, it was the turning point. From that battle on the Turks were being pushed back further and further.

Allenby, who had not been in the Middle East during Romani, was elated with the news of Beersheba, his first important win. He bustled into the town on the morning of 1 November, congratulated Chauvel and decorated Grant with an extra bar to his DSO. Later in the day he ordered the army corps at Gaza to attack. At 3 a.m. on 2 November it hit the city, which had been weakened by the movement of troops away to reinforce Beersheba. It was the second part of the one–two punch, and had the Turks reeling.

After a brief fight at Gaza, it was abandoned by the Turks. Before midday on 2 November 1917, it was under British control.

Allenby, rarely satisfied, did not think his infantry had done quite as much as he had hoped after the Australians' smashing of Beersheba. He urged Chauvel and the army commanders to drive hard against the retreating Turks of the enemy's Eighth Army. Within weeks Chauvel's Anzac-dominated Desert Mounted Column was at Jaffa, the ancient seaport on the Mediterranean 28 kilometres from Gaza.

Chapter 10

Emerging from the Pack

On 20 November Haig launched the last British offensive of 1917 when General Julian Byng's Third Army, led by 381 tanks, broke the German lines at Cambrai in northern France and penetrated 8 kilometres. In one day 4000 Allied soldiers were lost. This was typical of the death rate; the High Command was under pressure for its methods. Cambrai may have been seen as a 'success', which could have muted the growing press cries to fire Haig and the rest of the generals running the war, had the Germans not counterattacked ten days later and forced the British back to where they had begun, making the exercise, in essence, useless. No ground was gained despite the mass use of tanks in the operation and many deaths. The pointlessness of the entire war was beginning to impact on the British nation and empire.

Opposing sides in the war were approaching mental and

physical exhaustion after more than three years of belting each other like two huge heavyweight boxers. Both were nearly out on their feet but would not give in. A shortage of manpower was going to be a physical and political problem from now on. British Prime Minister Lloyd George could not get rid of Haig because of his closeness to the King, who believed he was still the best man to run the war. But Lloyd George could restrict Haig by not allowing him further reinforcements, or, as many were saying, *more cannon fodder.* This brought a reduction in division size from twelve to nine battalions. The British and Allied tactics, whether attempting big-scale crash-through advances or small-scale battle wins, were not gaining advantages that suggested they could win this protracted, terrible war. The Allies would have to strategise differently from any previous era in military history. Manpower, which was now an issue, would not be enough. New thinking had to emerge. Understanding how to combine all the new technology of war was now essential. Haig's mindset was still stuck in the era of the cavalry charge and he, Rawlinson, Gough, Butler and other generals were begrudging about the value and use of tanks, planes and 'modern' communications. The development of new weaponry was too fast for the High Command to grasp or be confident of using. Even the initial success of tanks at Cambrai did not convince its members or expunge the memories of their failures in 1916.

Only one key officer, Monash, kept abreast of every single weapons development as if he were in charge of each project. The conditions were set for him to rise to prominence. He was already being consulted by Haig on each major battle, although his views on the use of the advancing weaponry were not being countenanced.

He agreed with Lloyd George and Billy Hughes, who were appalled on behalf of their respective electorates, over the shocking loss of life already incurred, and the prospect of millions more deaths.

'I had formed a theory that the true role of the infantry,' Monash wrote in private, 'was not to expend itself upon heroic physical effort, nor to wither away under merciless machine gun fire, nor to impale itself on hostile bayonets, nor to tear itself to pieces in hostile entanglements.'

This was an indirect, yet clear, denunciation of the High Command mindset which saw the British commander-in-chief nicknamed in some quarters 'Kill More Germans Haig'. In other words, his philosophy was to expend so many Allied soldiers on the front that the German casualty numbers would be higher than the Allies'. This was a simplistic view, but Haig did not have a serious holistic approach to winning.

Monash added that he wanted his force 'to advance under the maximum possible protection of the maximum possible array of mechanical resources, in the form of guns, mortars, aeroplanes and tanks; to advance with as little impediment as possible; to be relieved as far as is possible of the obligation to fight their way forward'.

Monash's method was at odds with the High Command thinking. He wanted his soldiers to march on to the appointed goal or line. Then they would be important in defending and holding territory gained—'to gather the fruits of victory in the form of prisoners, guns and stores'.

The propaganda of heroic cavalry charges, that had been displayed in colourful picture books and dominated thinking in the nineteenth century, was not suited to the new warfare of the twentieth century.

Monash had become Haig's most admired general, and it was not only because George V favoured the Australian so highly.

His clear thinking and contribution on and off the battlefield was beginning to make its mark.

'Haig's relations with Monash were excellent,' Haig's biographer, John Terraine, noted. 'His admiration for Monash was noted after every meeting, perhaps the greatest volume of unmitigated approval for any one man in the whole of his diary.'[1]

But Monash was not going to have a grand-scale impact if he continued to run a division, and Haig was still not happy about another country, apart from Canada, having its own army. Furthermore, Monash was still no certainty to take the top commander's job if the five Australian divisions were formed into the 1st AIF, although he was the stand-out general. Bean was vitriolic in his opposition to him. Journalist Keith Murdoch, who acted as Hughes' proxy when the prime minister was not in Europe, was also against Monash, but not for the reasons of race that in some measure drove Bean. Monash did not trust Murdoch and the journalist felt uncomfortable with the general because he could not be manipulated. Murdoch loved the power he engendered as a newspaperman and his proximity to the prime minister, and it disturbed him not to be able to influence or gain the confidence of Monash. Murdoch had made his name by writing a report exposing the folly of the Gallipoli campaign, which had gone a long way towards having it called off. It was a sophisticated 'scoop' and he was always looking for another. He gained a similar 'rush' from his influence over Hughes, but political manoeuvring was less defined. Murdoch needed to have the top Australian generals as sources. When Monash refused to inform the journalist, Murdoch joined Bean's rickety bandwagon. Both journalists thought they were having an influence on the birth of the first Australian force. They wished to be the king-makers and have their say in the choice of the first commander-in-chief.

Should the 1st AIF eventuate, whoever commanded it would have the single biggest number of army corps on the Western Front under their control, with twenty corps and nearly two hundred thousand experienced warrior-volunteers. Whoever controlled these diggers, some of whom had come all the way from Gallipoli, was sure to have a considerable say in the outcome of the war, one way or the other.

•

The British Infantry and Chauvel's Light Horse pushed the Turks out of Jerusalem by 8 December 1917 and back to a line of defence covering Bethlehem 2 kilometres south of the Holy City. Refugees began pouring out. The enemy troops became a rabble, choking the Jaffa road into Jerusalem, which they preferred to pass through rather than run into Chauvel's horsemen. Memories and stories of their already legendary performance at Beersheba were still fresh. The Turks knew that if the Light Horse could charge heavily defended trenches, they would have no fear at all in coming at them in their isolated redoubts, trenches and posts, or on the roads around Jerusalem.

On 9 December 1917, after 674 years, Jerusalem again passed into the hands of a Christian power. British troops followed British Major General John Shea (commanding the conquering 60th Division) into the city, and he took the surrender. But the changeover of power did not stop the conflict, as the British 53rd Division continued to circle Jerusalem. They battled the Turks off the Jericho road and fought them at the Mount of Olives in the north-east. The 74th Division moved around outside the city's west and took the Nablus road.

Part of the Light Horse mission was to flank the infantry

divisions. Chauvel ordered the 10th Regiment to break off and join the 'event' inside Jerusalem, but the next morning it and fellow regiments were moving 13 kilometres along the Nablus road when they encountered heavy Turkish artillery fire. The enemy was not going to fade away without resistance.

The taking of Jerusalem pushed the reports of war on the Western Front off the front pages. Lloyd George was thrilled. He had wanted a diversion and a propaganda tool to wave at the enemies and the British public. The Middle East was a sideshow, but any clear victory was something to savour and perhaps inspire similar achievements elsewhere. Capturing Jerusalem, in the grand scheme of things, was next to meaningless. The breakthrough at Beersheba was more important, and taking Damascus, still little more than a possibility, would be bigger. Allenby's force had to tiptoe around the city, where there would be no actual fighting, in their drive to defeat the Turkish Seventh and Eighth Armies. Yet Lloyd George and his government milked it. They saw it as shoring up the Christian vote. Headlines about Christianity's cradle being in the 'right' hands abounded in the Western press. There was also the Jewish vote, with Jews everywhere ecstatic about access to the ancient homeland of 'Israel'. Then followed the so-called Balfour Declaration. This opened the way for Jews everywhere to migrate to Palestine which, it was expected, would be sooner or later under British control.

Christmas approached. The weather in Palestine worsened and supply problems increased. A few months earlier, Chauvel's Anzac troopers had been in extreme desert heat. Now the nights were freezing, the rain made it more miserable, and the Turks were not giving them any relief. Damascus, which Allenby wanted his army to take, and which T.E. Lawrence dreamt of the Arabs capturing, still appeared a long way off as winter closed down hard on 1917 in the Middle East.

PART 2
January to June 1918

Chapter 11

Ludendorff's Ascendancy

Monash and Chauvel were made Knight Commanders of the Order of the Bath on New Year's Day 1918, which was a positive and well-deserved boost for both. Chauvel knew that Allenby had made the recommendation, as the Australian emerged as his finest battle commander on the Eastern Front. His performances at Romani and Beersheba had ensured his elevation. Monash could not be sure who would have put him up for the honour, although he knew it would not have been Billy Hughes, with whom he had a prickly relationship. Monash did not suffer interfering politicians lightly and had presaged this in his 1912 award-winning essay on the American Civil War. The decision on the knighthood could easily have been made by the King himself, in conjunction with Haig, after his victories at Messines and Broodseinde. Field Marshal Plumer also held the Australian in the highest regard.

The two Australian commanders welcomed the extra kudos and prestige, especially as they were preparing for what they both expected to be the biggest year of the war, and perhaps their lives. Both were aware of the other's progress after their initial encounter on Gallipoli. They corresponded often and were familiar with the issues facing their respective wars, and the details of battles.

They sent each other congratulatory cables over the honours.

●

When Birdwood was on leave early in 1918, Monash took charge of the Australian Corps, and Major General Brudenell White was second-in-command. White was the mastermind behind the Anzac evacuation from Gallipoli and was highly regarded as an administrator, but he had never commanded in battle. Whenever they argued over issues, Monash won, not because of bombast or seniority, but because he'd had successful experiences on the battlefield and always prepared his positions as if he were in court. He did more homework than anyone, and White deferred to him. Monash had so far never lost a battle in which he had control over the plans and how to enact them, which was a formidable record unmatched by anyone on either side of the war. One example of this involved the issue of machine guns. Monash had long held that they should be used offensively, that is carried or placed forward by the troops, rather than by deploying them purely as a fixed defensive weapon, which was the position of White and many other officers in the Allied forces.

Instead of taking further leave early in January 1918, Monash went on a course at Camiers (80 kilometres south-south-west of Ypres) and was by far the most senior officer to attend. Monash, a weapons expert who knew how to take apart any gun and reassemble it, examined every piece of the machine gun and discussed its overall use in battle. He concluded that it was the most effective weapon in the Allied armoury next to artillery, and even placed it ahead of the tank in its capacity for devastation. Monash wrote a paper to this effect for his officers and explained how it should be used offensively and defensively.

Monash, White and other senior Australian officers had a full day's conference on the issue on 10 January. White conceded to Monash's position and Monash wrote of 'scoring heavily' over the issue, but this was not because of any damaging competition with his temporary second-in-command, for whom he had the highest regard as a soldier. Monash insisted on absolute consistency of thought and policy. He had deliberately studied every major battle that had taken place in the last thousand years, and concluded such discipline was a prime factor in winning. He wanted it in his 4th Brigade on Gallipoli and demanded it in his 3rd Division. Thinking of the future, he hoped for it in the 1st AIF. His mantra was simple but tough to enforce—perfect harmony of thought and policy from the commander down to the lowliest private. Differences had to be thrashed out. Monash was not a dictator, with an 'it's my way or the highway' philosophy. Differences had to be aired by intelligent discourse—as he did with White over the machine gun and many other issues. According to everyone who dealt with Monash in war, no one ever came better prepared to a meeting than he. He didn't always win, because the High Command was often inflexible. But if it got down to logical, rational argument, experience, comprehension, articulation and knowledge, he defeated all comers. His fifteen years' experience as a brilliant 'expert witness'—effectively acting in today's terms as a barrister—and a capacity to never lose a case, came to the fore. He intimidated everyone intellectually even before a conference or meeting began, and it sharpened and deepened discussion.

Monash's all-inclusive approach was to thrash out issues in minute detail after he had been the architect of the overall plan. This left the chance for challenges to tactics and structure. If an officer wanted to change something, he would have to prove its importance to Monash, not present simply a hunch, a whim or bravado.

·

Monash's family came from Krotoschin, Prussia (now Poland), which was near Poznan and the birthplace of the effective military dictator of Germany, Erich Ludendorff. The two leaders had the same year of birth, 1865: Ludendorff in April and Monash in Melbourne in June. There were other things the two had in common, which originated in their backgrounds. Monash's parents were struggling immigrants and his father Louis ran the general store at Jerilderie in the Riverina district of southern New South Wales. Monash was a brilliant student. While at the University of Melbourne, he joined its regiment and never failed to wear army uniform at least once a week until the Great War finished 36 years later.

Ludendorff was from an impoverished family of tradespeople. He entered cadet school at Holstein aged twelve. He was a good student who liked military history (the main subject of most history courses in Western schools of the time), mathematics and geography. Ludendorff was commissioned as a lieutenant at the age of seventeen, and served in several peacetime garrisons before passing into Prussia's well-respected Kriegsakademie. He reached the Great General Staff of the Army before becoming a major. Count von Schlieffen, the Chief of the General Staff, noted his capacities and selected him to join the 'second section' creating troop deployment plans. This was work for a devoted technocrat-staff man, just right for Ludendorff's rigid self-discipline. He then taught tactics and military history at his alma mater, Kriegsakademie, and returned to second section as its chief. This was the most important appointment. If war broke out he would be first choice as chief of operations, the number one post in the Germany Army.

Ludendorff's first wife Margarethe, who married him in 1909 when he was 44 and his habits were well formed, wrote: 'He was a man of iron principles. If work kept him up very late or we were at a ball or a party he still mounted his horse at seven the next morning, winter and summer.'

This could have been a quote from Monash's wife, Vic. Monash was never in bed after 6 a.m. and instead of horses, he had other exercise routines, which he stepped up during the war to bring his weight down. Both men had a thing about punctuality.

'Time was not reckoned in our house by hours, but minutes,' Margarethe said.[1] Monash went one better and often measured his punctuality by the second. Whether meeting the King for the first time, or visiting the dentist, Monash arrived at the appointed place as the second hand ran through the top of the minute. On eighteen occasions during the war, his arrival and departure scheduled to the second according to prior arrangement saved him from bombs, grenades and snipers' bullets. Consequently he became obsessed with promptness. Monash was an atheist. He had decided this at sixteen after about a year's thought, which meant he did not believe his survival was 'God's will' or even 'fate'. However, he did subscribe to providence, caution and plain dumb luck.

Neither he nor Ludendorff were always easy to live with, for different reasons. The German was given to mood swings and anger. Monash was often shut away in his study working, studying, listening to music or playing the piano. But this was the extent of their similarities. Ludendorff's 'natural' state was tense. He was a cold figure with 'a monocled, humourless eye staring from a heavily jowled red face as he barked orders in a high nasal voice, his second chin quivering from the effort'.[2]

The only hint of tension in Monash was his cigarette smoking, but even that was mainly a social habit of the era. He had a moustache like most officers, but he never wore a monocle, which was a pretension too far. By mid-war, Monash was lean-faced, and photographs showed an alertness in his eyes rather than the concern or suspicion that marked Ludendorff's expression. Monash was rarely heard to utter anything in anger, although he did stand his ground with forceful, clear comment. His voice was impressively deep and sonorous, which was a big part of his impact, along with his diction, when meeting others or addressing troops. Monash's guttural German voice as a youth was ironed out at Scotch College to something smooth. He never aped the British upper-class accent, but remained Australian and educated-sounding.

According to observers, Ludendorff was rigid and inflexible in thought, given to sudden rages, 'a table banger, frequently rude to subordinates, often tactless to superiors'.[3] Margarethe noted that he had not a spark of humour, and this was not just the view of a former wife. All who came in contact with him found he had no laughs in him.[4]

This granite figure was deliberately friendless and forbidding. He was hard to get to know, and not well liked. As he rode the power path as a technocrat of the German Army, there was not a trail of anecdotes or fond reminiscences in his wake. Ludendorff didn't rise without trace, but he hardly left a shadow.

By contrast, Monash was serious-minded because of the incessant application of his mind to learning, writing, studying and public speaking. But he liked a laugh, and appreciated a well-timed humorous remark. When he first presented his 3rd Division to Haig, an overweight Jewish colonel fell from his horse. A foot caught in a stirrup caused him to bump along the ground right in front of the British commander-in-chief. That night in the mess hall, Monash relayed, deadpan, the weather report: 'This morning during our parade, a heavy dew fell on the ground . . .'

At the beginning of 1918, both commanders were confident that their side would win. Monash was not yet in a position to have a dominant influence, but through 1917 Ludendorff had steadily cemented his control over the entire German force. He was more confident than ever about his nation's ascendancy, especially with the prospect of one million more troops, now being shipped back home to Germany, joining his force on the Western Front.

•

In 1916 the Kaiser made an urgent request for Ludendorff to serve as chief of staff of the Eighth Army on the Western Front, and appointed General Paul von Hindenburg to replace General Maximilian von Prittwitz, who had proposed abandoning East Prussia altogether. Hindenburg relied heavily on Ludendorff in planning battles; this pattern of influence continued when Hindenburg took over as Chief of the General Staff; he was the pliant, popular front man while Ludendorff ran the German war effort.

His vision, occasionally expressed in secret papers (and more vaguely in public), of a post-war world dominated by the German Empire was another reason for Monash's quiet determination to do what he could to oppose it. Ludendorff proposed massive annexations and colonisation in Eastern Europe. He planned settlements and Germanisation in conquered areas, which included Australia—indeed all dominions and colonies of the current empires of the British, French and Dutch. He saw resources from Eastern Europe and other nations being used for future wars against Britain and the United States.

Ludendorff's first act in this grand plan was to push the Russians out of the conflict. They had withdrawn outright in October 1917, but he wanted to judge the new ruling dictatorship of the Bolsheviks for himself. He participated in meetings with them that began at Brest-Litovsk in late February 1918 and ended on 3 March with a thrashed-out treaty. It assured Ludendorff that he could remove all his troops to the Western Front without impunity. The Russians gave assurances they would stay out of the 'imperialist war.' Lenin, in fact, was very happy to get out of it. He wanted the other powers to belt each other into submission, leaving economies in France, Germany and Britain impoverished and ripe for the further rise of communism.

Ludendorff, more instinctive than reflective, accepted the Bolsheviks' words at face value and turned his thoughts to what he could do with the large extra reserves of experienced soldiers. His mind was on the start of a big, fresh offensive, the first since the Battle of Verdun in 1916. Ludendorff and his under-commanders all knew, but would never admit, that the next effort had to be the one to break the Allies and win the war. His main aim would be to drive hard to take Paris. What the British would do after that would be anyone's guess but they, like their enemy, would be exhausted with fighting and probably ready to make peace in an armistice that would greatly favour the Germans. At least, this was the German hope.

Ludendorff was not going to rush things as Haig expected. He was prepared to reorganise his army and to train his additional force in the modern tactics and technology that had emerged since the war began in 1914. There was new armour to master, which had improved artillery barrages and increased accuracy, and had been trialled against the Russians at the Battle of Jugla. Ludendorff was most anxious to introduce the concept of 'stormtroopers' to break the trench deadlock. In other words, contingents of highly trained attack merchants who would rush a position and disrupt or take it over. Ludendorff may well have learnt this from his soldiers being hit by British 'raids' (a Monash speciality), which disrupted his lines in hits that fell just short of an all-out attack, and did not necessarily take new territory.

Ludendorff was the instigator of draft plans for Germany's 'final' offensives: Operation Michael, Operation Georgette, Operation Mars and Operation Blücher. He was in all but name Germany's dictator and commander-in-chief at the beginning of 1918. Hindenburg, looking more like a Prussian blimp as the war progressed, was now a mere figurehead. He deferred to Ludendorff, who was prosecuting the war at all levels. Kaiser Wilhelm II, with his withered arm and bravado to make up for it, began the war as King of Germany and Prussia, and by dint of the nation's ill-defined constitution, the most powerful ruler in the world. It allowed him to appoint and dismiss his chancellor, all federal officials, all army officers (except those in the Bavarian, Saxon and Württemberg contingents), and all navy officers. Wilhelm II had complete control of foreign policy. He could make or break treaties and alliances. He could declare war but was unlikely to do it (and didn't) without consultation with his key commanders. He was the 'supreme commander' of all the German imperial armies, and he didn't have to answer to the feeble parliament—the Reichstag. If a question concerning the vague constitution arose, he could interpret it as he wished or leave it to others. Wilhelm II could also end war by declaring peace, which could have been his prerogative in 1918. But in those early months it was clear that the Kaiser would be more reactive than proactive. At this stage, he was more often *told* what was happening on any issue of war, rather than consulted on it. Wilhelm II realised that he was way out of his depth in war when real experts running armies did their job. As Germany's situation became more complicated and contentious, he was increasingly paid lip-service or ignored, which accentuated his natural state of paranoia.

Chapter 12

Arab No-Show;
Setbacks Beyond Jericho

At Jerusalem's Barrack Square early on a bitterly cold March day, Chauvel stepped forward on a makeshift podium under the shadow of the Tower of David to be greeted by the smiling Duke of Connaught. The Duke pinned the gold and silver Knight Commander of St Michael and St George (KCMG) on Chauvel's left breast in front of an assembly of military personnel and local dignitaries. They shook hands. The Duke then pinned the Badge of a Companion of the Order of the Bath (CB) on the right of his chest and shook hands again. Chauvel turned to go. But there was more. The Duke found room on the General's 'bright breast' for a third decoration, the blue and yellow Order of the Nile, which had been instituted in 1915 by Sultan Husayn Kamil for 'service to the nation' of Egypt.

Chauvel saw the merit in such awards. He was a career soldier at the top, and they meant something, especially among his peers. It was a competitive business and part of the 'game' of soldiering, particularly among officers and especially among the generals. If Monash on the Western Front or other Australians doing well in the main war venue received a pretty new badge or ribbon, then Chauvel would want one too. But there was more to it than simply being a Battle of Baubles. Dominion commanders had to prove themselves much more than their counterparts among the British. The Australians had not been in the 'British Club'. But sheer performance was sorting all that out in the pressure cooker of war when abilities and shortcoming would out, one way or another. Chauvel rightly felt that in 1916 he had been ignored for honours (especially at the Battle of Romani). Anything he had pinned on him now would help make up for that. It was also recognition for his corps and the achievement of his mounted riflemen.

•

Lawrence led an Arab force in taking the town of Tafilah on Allenby's right flank. It demonstrated that perhaps the force of Prince Feisal of Arabia could do more than harass the Turks with hit-and-run guerilla tactics. However, the revolt was yet to have anything like the impact of Allenby's army, which into March 1918 was fighting crucial battles against strong enemy resistance. Chauvel did not take part, but provided his Anzac Mounted Division and Camel Brigade for Major General Shea of 60th Infantry Division (the Londoners) in an operation under General Chetwode. The horsemen would support the foot soldiers in the move to capture Jericho, famous in a biblical story for having been destroyed by Joshua, Moses' successor, in 1550 BC. In those ancient times, the town was penetrated by nomads and semi-nomads from the desert in the east travelling to the fertile lands closer to the coast. Jericho's positioning in the Jordan Valley at the foot of a passage through the Judean hills made it of strategic importance in history, and in 1918.

Major General C.F. Cox's 1st Light Horse and the New Zealand Brigade began from Bethlehem and eased down towards the Dead Sea on goat tracks and other paths through the yellow-brown, vegetation-free eastern slopes of the Judean hills. They could not always ride their horses on the narrow tracks. As they moved they could hear the battles occurring on the main hill road between the 60th Division and the Turks, backed by a German contingent. The infantry would take the brunt of the enemy force. The road to Jericho began to be studded with little crosses bearing the names of Londoners, poignant reminders of brutal clashes and quick burials.

Dismounted New Zealanders branched out on their own, attacking Turkish hill positions, while Cox's troopers edged down to the Dead Sea at the floor of the Jordan Valley, 400 metres below sea level. Unless there was a well-concealed enemy force hidden in caves or trenches, there seemed no opposition as the brigade approached Jericho. Cox sent out scouts, who reported that the town appeared deserted. He sent in a single troop of 32 horsemen to take it. They encountered about a dozen enemy soldiers, who were forced to surrender without much of a fight.

The troop was thrilled at the thought of acquiring such a well-known town, but the men were soon let down. It was one of the least prepossessing conquests of the long campaign. Squalid mud huts featured in a village dominated by a towering mosque and the unpopular Jordan Hotel, which endeared itself to none who stayed in it. Australian historian Henry Gullett, who had the displeasure of spending a couple of nights there during the war, remarked that he would rather have camped out. A cloying whiff of sewage prevailed. The food was inedible; the water undrinkable. The rooms were rat-infested, the beds flea-infested.

The main bulk of the Turkish force had retreated across the stone Ghoraniye Bridge, which they blew up. The raging, 30-metre-wide Jordan River could not be easily traversed. It gave the Turks temporary respite from the relentless pursuit by the trudging, fighting infantry and the sweeping, speedy Anzac horsemen who were so ready to use their bayonets or rifles.

The Turks consolidated in the light brown hills and the more jungle-like vegetation on the other bank, setting up their machine guns to cut down any brave soldiers who might attempt to swim the torrent.

•

Allenby now decided to push hard 65 kilometres east of Jerusalem to Amman which was on the Hejaz Railway. Its hoped-for acquisition would shore up the British right flank and support the Lawrence-generated Arab revolt, which was advancing north in parallel with the British on their left. This in turn would further isolate the Turks in the south. The Turkish Seventh and Eighth Armies, caught up in conflict in the Judean hills and closer to the coast, would be forced to assist with reinforcements on the eastern or right flank.

Allenby's main target was the 1200-metre-high Moab Mountain, which was held by the Turks. The two subsequent aims would be to destroy a rail tunnel and viaduct at Amman.

Before a force could come anywhere near those targets they had to cross the Jordan River, 25 kilometres from the Holy City. Chauvel rapidly trained an Anzac Light Horse engineering contingent for the challenging task of throwing a bridge across the river. They made an attempt at the site of the destroyed Ghoraniye Bridge, but water, scooting by at 12 kilometres and faster, along with machine-gun fire from the west bank, defeated their efforts. Heavy rains and turbulent waters delayed the mission three days until 22 March.

The engineers trekked south to the bank claimed as the place where John the Baptist baptised Jesus. This was the point of least resistance, considering the torrent and the enemy machine gunners. Australian and English engineers stripped down and hauled a raft load of soldiers across. The soldiers fended off attacks while the engineers worked hard through the night to build four bridges. They were made up of ten pontoons roped parallel to the banks with a wobbly wooden construction laid over it. Soldiers clamoured over them easily enough. But they were not safe for riding across. At first light, New Zealand troopers dismounted and led their horses gingerly over the bridges. They then rode out past the infantry and attacked the Turks, who were forced back 9 kilometres to the foot of Moab.

Allenby was relying on Lawrence and his Arabs coming up from the south to support the infantry and horsemen by cutting off any Turkish reinforcements coming north to help their brothers on

Moab. It was to be the second test of the hoped-for alliance with the Arabs, as the two forces headed inexorably towards Damascus. The earlier experiment with British Lieutenant Colonel S.F. Newcombe and his Arab contingent had met with mixed success five months earlier north-east of Beersheba. They had drawn off 6000 Turks from Gaza, but had been heavily defeated.[1]

The British force—the soldiers, horsemen and cameleers—began the march on the heavily defended Amman en route to Es Salt. The latter was to be taken by the 3rd Light Horse Regiment, and then held by British Infantry, but nature intervened on the night trek further south in the approach to Amman. Torrential rain made the going tough in the slush on the undulating goat trails. All were forced to go single file. Vehicles and artillery were abandoned. The horses coped, but the camels found it near impossible. Some were carried by the men, which slowed the camel contingent. The horsemen had to wait for them on a flooded tableland. After another freezing night in the wet, the whole attacking force linked up about 11 kilometres from Amman.

On the third night, the railway was destroyed. It was the signal for the thrust at the target, but it was protected by a half-circle of ridges harbouring 4500 Turks and Germans, who were being reinforced hourly by Turks arriving via the railway from the south, unhindered by Lawrence and his Arabs. The enemy used artillery and machine-gun fire to counter the attack by the courageous Londoners, who trudged through the mud. Sodden, they still moved unhindered in pace, direction and determination. But the barrage began to take its toll. Soldiers were cut down. The ranks thinned.

Binoculars remained trained on the horizon to the east and south in the hope of seeing the banners of the Arab force. But

Lawrence and his army were nowhere to be seen. Instead, German engineers were viewed reconstructing the railway, which would bring further Turkish reinforcements from the south. They began coming in midafternoon on the third day of action. After day six, the British had made no headway as the defending ranks built up.

A telling moment occurred when 96 horsemen from the 6th Light Horse made a bayonet charge. But it was not to be even a mini-Beersheba. All but one was brought down by intense machine-gun fire. It was the worst moment for the horsemen since the disastrous battle of the Nek on Gallipoli, and it had a similar impact.

Still the enemy numbers increased. Now they began flowing in by train from the north. If ever the Arabs were needed to show their importance to Allenby, Chauvel, Chetwode and the other generals, it was now. But apart from a token trickle who snaffled bully beef and bullets and then disappeared, never to be seen again, there was a 'no show' by Feisal's force. In those last three days, many men of the Egyptian Camel Corps froze to death. Chetwode called his venture off.

On 30 March, the British were ordered to withdraw. It took them two days to limp back with the wounded to the Jordan Valley. The British Infantry had 447 fallen officers and men. But the Anzacs and Camel Brigade fared worst, losing 671. Troopers were disgruntled at the abortive nine-day operation overall, and felt let down by the Arabs. Once more the Anzacs were downcast about leaving their fallen comrades on a battlefield with a mission unfulfilled. It reminded those who had been on Gallipoli of setbacks there.

Scapegoats were searched for in the failed mission. Fingers were pointed at Lawrence. He admitted he had failed to deliver and apologised to Allenby, which was not much use to the force that had depended on his assistance. No substantial reason was given for the Arabs not turning up, but they were known to prefer guerilla tactics to full-on battles. Excuses of lack of water and food were proffered. None were acceptable. But when Lawrence begged for another chance, Allenby granted it.

•

This was the first success for the Turks since Second Gaza. Much credit had to go to the 63-year-old Field Marshal Liman von Sanders, one of the oldest commanders of the war. He had been a key figure behind Turkish strategy on Gallipoli in 1915, after creating the Turkish Fifth Army for its defence. In 1916 and 1917, von Sanders had been based in Istanbul. Now, as the crisis in the Middle East escalated, he had taken command of the force in Palestine.

Von Sanders ordered General Erich Falkenhayn to concentrate a new Turkish force at Qatrani, on the Hejaz Railway between Maan and Amman, and just 40 kilometres from Tafilah. Much to Feisal's shock, this fresh enemy detachment took back the town and pushed the Arabs out, their first setback on the ride north. Putting on a brave front over the loss, Lawrence now claimed that Tafilah was 'not worth losing a man over'. Showing a remarkable tactical flexibility, he said that if the Turks kept a sizeable force there, they would weaken either the Maan or Amman garrison, which would work in favour of the British and Arabs.

Feisal remained disconcerted. Lawrence lifted his spirits by telling him Allenby was rewarding them for their drive to the Dead

Sea by placing 300,000 pound of gold 'to my independent credit'. The commander-in-chief had thrown in a train of 700 pack-camels complete with personnel and equipment. Gold, it seemed, not only talked in the desert war; it also strengthened resolve.

Chapter 13

Ludendorff's Mighty Attack

By mid-March 1918 on the Western Front, Ludendorff had 194 divisions, roughly 800,000 soldiers, at his disposal for one of the proposed 'Operations' in an attempt to win the war with one mighty attack. They included the highest-quality troops of the German Army—seven guard units, three Bavarian regular divisions and a marine division. He travelled the front like the good technocrat he had always been, and gleaned views on the operations from each army by weighing the evidence and arguing the possible outcomes. After much debate, argument and thrashing out of ideas, he finally decided on Operation Michael, in what became known as Kaiserschlacht, the Kaiser's Battle. Beginning on 21 March, its objective was to take the Cambrai salient

(160 kilometres north of Paris), along with a break-out towards Péronne (50 kilometres east of Amiens). While the left flank was held against any French intervention from the south, the attack would wheel northward to roll up the British armies. The overall plan was complicated, with numerous provisions for change and vague objectives. In this respect it was not unlike the plans of the British High Command and highlighted the deficiencies in the generals running both sides. The agonising build-up and the daily changes of mind typified problems when dealing with all the new accoutrements of war from tanks to planes, artillery machine guns and communications. The fuzzy aims would mean failed objectives and death for thousands of soldiers, which had been common to the opposing armies for the entire war.

The Germans arrayed three armies (the Seventeenth, Second and Eighteenth) and their guns outnumbered the British by a ratio of five to two and included a thousand weapons transferred from the Russian Front. The German troops and artillery were moved under the cover of darkness to conceal the point of attack from the British, who were unaware of the impending strike.

•

However, Haig and all his close confidants, including the King, Monash, Butler and Kidgell, were broadly alert to the prospect of a major German counteroffensive in the spring of 1918. Haig and his French counterpart, Field Marshal Pétain, had been more than jittery about it, but as the months dragged by and British intelligence reports had verified the movement of German troops from the Russian Front, they and others wondered if the attack would be in the summer. The Allied High Command was fortified in the knowledge that American troops were arriving in greater numbers, and would top a million men by midyear. In theory, this additional force would match the million extra enemy soldiers coming from the Russian Front. Yet this was a brutally practical war, not an academic equation, and everyone on both sides knew that the Americans would be untrained, and therefore unsuited for the kind of fierce, close trench warfare that had developed on the Western Front. The Allies were pleased with the extra numbers on their side. The French and British would include them in battles but park them in so-called 'quiet corners' until it was judged they were ready for useful engagement in the 'hot' zones.

The Allies were not fully unified in view, structure or purpose early in 1918 after the Versailles meeting in November, which had been an attempt to define these issues. Even commands within each nation's military could not see eye to eye. Pétain had little regard for his chief of staff, General Ferdinand Foch. Haig disliked his new chief of staff, Henry Wilson. US Commander General John 'Black Jack' Pershing could not stand his chief of staff, General Peyton March. It was less acrimonious but still problematic for the Allied commanders in dealing with each other. The French always distrusted British intentions, and redoubled their espionage activity to find out what the British High Command was really thinking. Haig respected Pétain but found him at times 'strident' and therefore unreliable. Pétain, in turn, did not like Pershing's insistence on keeping his growing number of divisions under his own command, which had caused a similar issue for Haig in dealing with the Canadians, and now the Australians who, with Prime Minister Billy Hughes the biggest nagger, were arguing for a stand-alone army. Hughes was supported by Murdoch, his proxy, and to a lesser extent Bean. Monash stayed out of the politics, but when asked by Hughes and Murdoch, made it more than clear that it was imperative Australia have its own force and command structure.

Pershing, perhaps through ignorance of the geopolitics of the battle terrain he had entered, was suspicious of Haig's strategic views. In part, the American was unclear because no one in the Allied High Command really had any major strategy except to not lose.

By mid-March 1918, the Allies' Western Front of 173 divisions was a collection of disparate 'princedoms' ruled by insular, self-serving commanders. In the far north of Belgium, King Albert's twelve divisions held a line running 38 kilometres. Albert's right flank linked with Haig's command, four armies that possessed another 200 kilometres, in which increasingly disgruntled Australian and New Zealand divisions were dispersed. The British right was connected to Pétain's biggest 'princedom' that defended a line of 500 kilometres. This consisted of General Franchet D'Esperey's three armies in the north, which held 112 kilometres; then General Noel Edourd Castelnau's four armies, which ran south (or right) all the way to the Swiss border. Pershing and his four divisions (equivalent in number to eight French or British) were being nursed along a near dormant line of 23 kilometres inside the Pétain-controlled Front. All 'princes' believed their fiefdoms would be attacked first by the Germans. Haig's intelligence on the likely strike was better. Operation Michael was aimed at his southern (or right) flank held by General Byng's Third Army on the left and by General Gough's Fifth Army on Byngs' right. German intelligence noted that the Canadians (refusing to be involved), and the Australian divisions (including Monash's 3rd) were on leave and not on Haig's front, which was an extra incentive, if not a defining factor, in deciding to attack the British first.

Haig refused to let an agreed central reserve (for all the Allies) have any divisions. Byng and Gough together had 30 divisions to defend their fronts but the numbers were misleading. Part of these forces had been hurt by the Passchendaele Offensive of October and Haig's overall reserves amounted to just eight divisions, five of them having been sent to Italy a few months earlier to counter any Austro-German attack, where they were still placed. There were still tens of thousands of troops in the United Kingdom, but Prime Minister Lloyd George, in his protracted and personal struggle with Haig, was only allowing him to have troops in small 'donations'. The prime minister was still smarting about the massive loss of life in Flanders in 1917 and the Somme in 1916. Haig was certainly stymied, especially concerning his desire to go on the offensive in Flanders again. This kept him on the defensive.

The lull in heavy encounters allowed intelligence reports to filter in, and one from the French noted a big concentration of Germans at Mézières, which Haig took as a threat to Amiens that would foreshadow an advance in force south-west at St Quentin more than an attack on Chalons. He ordered his French liaison officer to check the Allied defences at Amiens. This was a vital railroad junction of north–south and Channel traffic. Its loss to the Germans would split the British force and divide them from the French to the south.

Haig, and the French, even more pertinently, were aware that a quick breakthrough and the taking of Amiens, 120 kilometres north of Paris, would mean the Germans could drive on to

Paris and force the French to capitulate. After the nation's heavy losses and the mutinies in 1917, resistance would be low and the Germans would probably prevail. If he were a betting man, Haig would have put money on the Germans attacking the French. He had come to trust Pétain, although others doubted his integrity. Haig's problem was that he expected the French to be beaten and forced to defend, which had become Pétain's mantra. Pétain spoke often about 'falling back' and drawing on reserve divisions to shore up the French position. But Haig, too, was relying on 'defence'. Gough and his Fifth Army were told that if attacked they were not expected to maintain a 'static defence'. Instead they were told to make a 'fighting withdrawal' to the Somme, the usual cliché for avoiding a defeat or even a wipe-out.

Haig ordered an unrealistic 480 kilometres of trenches to be dug at the fortress city of Péronne (held strongly by the Germans) and along the embattled Somme. German intelligence was clear. The British sector was the most vulnerable. Its Third and Fifth Armies would be the main initial targets of Operation Michael.

•

Germany made its drive for a breakthrough victory at 4.40 a.m. on 21 March 1918 with the biggest artillery barrage in history to that point. The Germans had put most of their chips on artillery for this war and now was the time to cash in. They used just short of seven thousand guns, firing high-explosive and gas shells on a 70-kilometre front with 47 divisions on the move forward between Croisilles and La Fère. The quiet of a foggy, pre-dawn morning was shattered by the eardrum-splitting sound. The Germans pumped their shells for over five hours without a break.

The enemy was hell-bent on reducing everything in its way to rubble.

At 9.35 a.m. mortars opened up on forward British trenches. Pre-set charges were blown, ripping up Allied barbed-wire defences. After a final bombardment, the artillery opened up with 'creeping fire' as the guns were moved forward. It was the moment for the German special shock troops, the *Sturmtruppen* (stormtroopers), to make their push forward on foot. The specially trained soldiers, armed with automatic rifles, light machine guns, grenades and flamethrowers, burst through the forward British trenches. They were followed by bigger forces that did the euphemistic 'mopping up', which meant killing or capturing those not hit by the stormtroopers. German attack aircraft, armed with machine guns, flew low over the battlefield, strafing the area in front of the German soldiers.

The German assault continued into a second day, with General Oskar von Hutier's Eighteenth Army the main thruster, stomping over Gough's stunned Fifth Army to cross the Crozat Canal between St Quentin, on a loop in the Somme, and La Fère. Gough was forced into a retreat away from the Somme and to abandon an important bridgehead near Péronne. This collapse exposed the right flank of Byng's Third Army, already pulverised by General Marwitz's Second Army. Byng had to make a speedy fallback to close the gap with the British Fifth Army.

On day three, 23 March, the fronts of the two German armies were 24 kilometres inside British lines. The only 'straggling' attacking army was the Eighteenth, which still managed to penetrate 7 kilometres. The Germans also unleashed a 21-centimetre long-range cannon on Paris. This massive new gun spat out 264-pound explosive shells on random city targets. It was an impressive display of German weaponry, which would later (when captured) draw Monash's admiration. (Not so impressive was the gun's impact during the conflict. Before being captured in August 1918 it pumped out 283 shells that did not change the course of any battle.)[1]

Ludendorff was ebullient, although remained his cautious, nervous self. He was able to tell army group chiefs of staff at Avesnes that the main 'object was to separate the French and British by a rapid advance on both sides of the Somme'. Three of the German armies would thrash on against the British 'north of the Somme, in order to drive them into the sea. They [the three armies] would keep on attacking at new places in order to bring the whole British front to ruin.'[2]

After the attack was reported to the Kaiser, the three-day smash-through was being interpreted by him as the end of the war, with Germany victorious. At least this was his take after a visit to Avesnes. He exclaimed to anyone within earshot that 'the English have been utterly defeated!' It was a premature enunciation, which betrayed his hate for the British. He had bottled this emotion for decades, first against his mother, then his uncle, the late King Edward VII, and more recently let it loose in a bullying, irrational manner against his cousin George V. Wilhelm II had long been the detested 'outsider' in Queen Victoria's extended royal family. His complexes and inferiorities, as well as a confused sexuality, coupled with a self-loathing and probable untreated mental illness, had led to a bellicosity which played into the hands of the dominant Prussian ruling military class. Convinced, more publicly than any of the royals, that God was on his side, Wilhelm II had made a lot of noise prewar and in its first two years. Recently, he had been less secure in the face of determined British fighting, the introduction of Americans into the conflict and the realisation that he was a neophyte and mere frontman when compared to the hard-nut Ludendorff and his professional officers.

The sudden success of Operation Michael had caused his outburst. The Kaiser ordered flags flown and cannon salutes throughout the empire. Wilhelm II's euphoria was increased by a belief in his own publicity, which was put out in a joint communiqué by Hindenburg and Ludendorff. It told of 'our great victory under the personal leadership of his Majesty the Emperor'. In this moment of mutual admiration, the Kaiser bestowed on Hindenburg the Iron Cross with Golden Rays, which had not been awarded for 103 years, since Field Marshal Gebhard Blücher received one for his part in the Battle of Waterloo. Ludendorff, still unacknowledged as the real German Supremo, was handed the Grand Cross of the Iron Cross.

Ludendorff's aim of splitting the British and French armies and taking Amiens now seemed a strong possibility. The Germans had indeed shattered Gough's Fifth Army, and Byng's Third Army was in disarray. Unless Haig and his High Command moved fast, the war would be over before the summer of 1918. The French, with Pétain in command, were already preparing to fall back and defend Paris, but first Pétain gave Haig some relief by putting two armies under General Emile Fayolle on the British right flank. Yet Pétain rejected Haig's request for an extra twenty divisions around Amiens, which was obviously now Germany's main target. Pétain claimed the enemy was expected to attack in the south at Champagne, although there was no direct intelligence of this possibility. Haig met with him and was disappointed to find the French commander depressed. He feared that the British would be separated from the French and 'pushed into the sea', a regurgitation of German propaganda.

On day four, 24 March, the situation became critical for the Allies as Haig began calling on reserves and pushing them south just as French units reached Montdidier but found themselves unable to halt German advances. Pétain that night again met with Haig and was now 'very much upset, almost unbalanced and most anxious'; it was all becoming too much for the French commander. He had been unsettled first by the big gun bombing Paris, which was more a psychological blow that upset Parisians than anything else; but he believed it presaged an attack on the French capital. The possibility of an enemy attack in the Champagne area was another thing that stretched his nerves. It affected his decision-making, which resulted in some of his fellow French leaders and commanders questioning his judgement. For instance, General Fayolle, with his two stop-gap armies, was told that if the Germans advanced further he was to pull his troops back south-west to Beauvois in order to cover Paris.[3] This would leave Haig's British troops exposed on their right flank. Haig was more than disgruntled at this Pétain mantra of 'falling back' instead of making a stand. He wasted no time behind the scenes in attempting to replace Pétain with General Foch or some other French commander 'who would fight'.[4]

Haig's concern led, on day six, 26 March, to a high-level meeting of Allied commanders and politicians at Doullens, near the British Headquarters of X Corps. The gathering was given some urgency by the sound of artillery in the distance—and some heat by blunt exchanges. It became clear to all that Pétain was close to a breakdown and had lost his nerve. French Premier Georges

Clemenceau asked Haig: 'Do you intend to fight at Amiens, or continue to fall back?'

'We are doing everything we can to stop the Boche reaching Amiens,' Haig replied. 'What are *your* intentions?'

Pétain then came into the discussion, saying he was bringing up 24 divisions from the east at the rate of two a day. This caused a momentary lull; at that rate, everyone knew but did not say, the war itself could be over before the full contingent arrived. The interjection of 67-year-old General Foch, the pipe-smoking Gascon, with his acerbic manner and harsh voice, changed the mood again. He dominated the debate, stressing that he would never fall back.

'You aren't fighting?' he said with swift hand movements towards Haig and Pétain. 'I would fight without a break. I would fight in front of Amiens. I would fight *in* Amiens. I would fight all the time!'[5]

Foch's anger and exuberance was in part because he had been made a French scapegoat and then sidelined (until now) for the disaster on the Somme in 1916. He was a rebel of sorts with a religious fervour that gave him certitude about God being on his side, not the Kaiser's. This strong belief in God being an ally gave him a common bond with Haig. Foch had upset some in the French command because of his directive that officers should be educated and forced to read and think deeply, which excluded a lot of men in the armed services. His ebullience and spirit, along with well-credentialled military skills despite the Somme's deadly follies in 1916, were just what was needed, according to Haig, in the crisis. Foch could not be denied at this moment of need for his nation, which was bereft of aggressive military leaders. Pétain (as history would show) was a pessimist and defeatist who would be more likely to capitulate than fight. Foch was the opposite.

After the histrionics and bravado, with Foch presenting himself as the potential saviour, Lloyd George's representative Lord Milner met with Clemenceau privately and then announced there would be one Allied commander from then on. It was better late than never, and Milner, with Haig's consent, conceded that it had to be a Frenchman, and Foch was the best candidate. At least there was political consensus. Lloyd George was pleased, as he felt he had won another little victory over Haig. Pershing, who had held back his men because he didn't trust British leadership, immediately offered Pétain several American divisions that were currently in training. He then met Foch and offered him all his forces, with the proviso that they remained wholly American divisions under American command. This was a swipe at the British, who would not let the Americans fight as a stand-alone army. Haig and the British High Command stayed with their policy of control, which had caused the Canadians not to fight and the Australians to grumble about not having their own army. But Haig did have a point with the Americans. They had no experience of the way to fight trench warfare. He believed they had to be thoroughly trained before being let into the fray, for their own good. Pershing imposed conditions, especially that he would maintain full control of the 'tactical action' of all American forces. But the French, and indeed the British, did not bother too much about these conditions. The High Commands of both sides still could not rid themselves of the idea that having more numbers in the field than the enemy would give them the best chance of victory. There was not one general in a position of real power on either side that knew how to combine and harness all the modern technology beyond the use of soldiers in vast numbers.

Yet with all the huffing and puffing at the top, there still had to be generals on the Front with the soldiers, who would actually do the real fighting, rather than just talking tough and politicking about it.

Chapter 14

Blocking the Lunge

When Ludendorff's armies struck, Monash was enjoying some well-earned rest and recreation. He had been having a lovely fortnight in Paris, where he enjoyed the Folies Bergère revue and was seeing a lot of the lead dancer, whom he daily took to lunch at his favourite Paris restaurant, Café de la Paix. In a third week off, at Menton on the French Riviera, he had enjoyed a night at the opera and was lunching on 22 March at his hotel, Regina Palace and Balmoral, with one of his favourite Australian fellow officers Major General Sir Charles Rosenthal.

On 23 March, Monash received his recall order. He and his 3rd Division, now with the sobriquet 'crack', were told to move south from Boulogne to Doullens. The force and momentum of the German assault had changed the rules of the game; German troops were well inside the British lines and had left the trenches far behind. It meant Haig's British HQ at X Corps was a moveable feast; Monash and his staff had trouble finding it while driving around in the middle of the night of 25 March. They eventually discovered it near Doullens, after it had decamped three times in three days. It was disconcerting for the Australians when they came across defeated British soldiers from the smashed Fifth and Third Armies. They straggled into Doullens with stories of the 'Boche Cavalry' close behind.

Monash was relieved that, minutes after he arrived, Rosenthal and a battalion of his 9th Brigade came in by train. Taking no chances, Monash ordered them to guard against an eastern advance of the Germans towards Doullens, while they waited for another 4000 diggers to arrive. Monash then drove on to Mondicourt and greeted the 1st Battalion of the 3rd Division's 10th Brigade. Monash ordered its commander, Brigadier Walter Ramsay McNicoll, to defend the station and its surrounds, with instructions to commandeer any British soldiers and demand that they assist in holding the new lines of defence. Not surprisingly, most of the British agreed to fight with the 'fresh' Australians, knowing their reputation for determined action. Next, Monash took over a chateau with a good telephone exchange at Couturelle. The owners, a middle-aged couple, were more than grateful for the Australians' arrival.[1]

On 26 March he set out by road again, and ran into thousands of people retreating with their possessions. Most were French civilians fleeing the Germans, but some of them were soldiers, hauling their equipment, from the now utterly defunct British Fifth Army. Monash made contact with General Ewen Sinclair-Maclagan and his 4th Division at 4 p.m. Together they arranged for a string of outposts in a line towards the south-east and the advancing German divisions. The enemy had taken Albert—a major military town throughout the war—and opened a breach of 60 kilometres in the British lines. They were only 30 kilometres from Amiens and very close now to taking it, in the first of a quick one–two punch, with Paris planned as the second strike, to finish the opposition and win the war.

The Germans had briefly held Amiens in 1914, and after it was retaken had hit it hard with aerial and artillery bombardment over three and a half years. The French had garrisoned Amiens until 1916 when the British took over and based their hospitals there, along with their recovery and recreational activity. Most of the British supplies came to Amiens via the coastal French city of Le Havre.

Amiens was now, in this massive March offensive, the real target. Most citizens had been evacuated, but a handful of priests were still present, looking after the mighty Notre Dame Cathedral. The Pope had even written to the Kaiser asking him to desist from shelling the cathedral. But the latter had not responded, believing he had the hotline to God, not the Roman Catholic Pope.

At 9 p.m. on 26 March, Monash learnt he had been switched to the VII Corps of the temporarily 'down' British Third Army at Corbie, where its HQ had been just an hour earlier. The VII Corps was now on its way to Montigny.

'Had I failed to find General Congreve, the Seventh Corps Commander, *that same night*,' Monash noted with emphasis, 'it is almost certain that my Division would have arrived on the Somme too late to prevent the capture of Amiens.'[2]

Monash started out from Corbie at 10 p.m. accompanied by a staff of four—including his bodyguard nephew, the

194-centimetre Captain Paul Simonson—with two cars and two motorbikes. The blackness was made worse by unfamiliar roads and a flood of refugees coming the other way, and the small entourage did not reach Congreve at his base in a chateau in Montigny until after midnight. He found Congreve in the corner of a bare saloon seated with his chief of staff at a small table. They were examining a map by the light of a flickering candle. Congreve was direct: 'At four o'clock to-day my Corps was holding a line from Albert to Bray [west of Amiens], when the line gave way. The enemy is now pushing westward and if not stopped to-morrow will certainly secure all the heights overlooking Amiens.'[3]

Congreve wanted Monash to deploy his division across the German path. The valleys of the Ancre and the Somme offered good points on which the division's flanks could 'rest'. But if stopped, the diggers should occupy a 'good line of old trenches . . . running from Méricourt-l'Abbé towards Sailly-le-Sec'.[4]

The Congreve briefing finished at 1 a.m. and the little Monash cavalcade drove to the Couturelle chateau and snatched a few hours' sleep before getting up at 5 a.m. and driving with Simonson to an elevated position above the town of Franvillers. They alighted from their vehicles and used binoculars to look east to the Ancre River. They could see the German cavalry and advance guard near Malancourt forcing back scattered British troops. Simonson looked to Monash to see his reaction. He calmly lit a cigarette and remarked: 'The Cavalry are moving about slowly, almost as if they seemed puzzled about their success in getting that far and finding no one to challenge them.'

'But they'll be on us in an hour or two,' he added, his expression showing concern for the first time, 'before long we won't be able to intercept them.'

Simonson spotted several German armoured cars sending up dust as they sped in their direction. Monash and he departed just as speedily back to Franvillers.

'At that very moment,' Simonson noted in his diary, 'we were the only ones standing between Amiens and the German advance.'[5]

Monash sent out orders from his HQ. He was relieved at 8 a.m. to see 60 double-decker buses, seconded from London, beginning to arrive with two battalions from Brigadier James Cannan's 11th Brigade on board. They were followed by troops from McNicoll's 10th and then Rosenthal's 9th. This eased Monash's concerns. He had trained these diggers and officers and had faith in their courage and capacities. They'd had little sleep for two nights but nevertheless were spirited and wanted to take on the enemy again. They were assembled and company after company were directed down the steep, winding road to the little village of Heilly, then across the Ancre River. From there they were deployed on Monash's selected line of defence.

'The spectacle of that Infantry will be ever memorable to me,' Monash wrote, 'as one of the most inspiring sights of the whole war. He was the Third Division—the "new chum" Division, which, in spite of its great successes in Belgium and Flanders, had never been able to boast, like its sister Divisions, that it had been "down on the Somme"—come into its own at last, and called upon to prove its mettle.'

This was the moment that the diggers believed 'they were going to measure themselves, man to man, against an enemy who, skulking behind his field works, had for so long pounded them to pieces in their trenches, poisoned them with gas, and bombed them as they slept in their billets'.[6]

Monash reminded his troops that there was a new level playing field where artillery would not have such a big role. The men were ready, despite the warnings from British soldiers of the crushed Fifth Army coming from the opposite direction.

'Gerry will "ave your guts for garters!"' was a common cry. The French villagers had a different attitude. The men shook their hands; the women kissed them and gave them flowers. Their homes, their way of life, their lives were at stake. The diggers could see the fear, hope and gratitude in the faces of the locals. The Australians were inspired further. It was another reason to justify them coming so far to fight for people of another country.

'*Fini retreat, Madame! Fini retreat, Monsieur!*' was a French phrase every digger had learnt, as well as '*Fini retreat, beaucoup Australiens ici!*'

At 11 a.m. on 27 March, two battalions of the 3rd had relieved the spent British Infantry of the depleted 35th Division and sections of the 9th Scottish Division that had defended stoutly in the triangle between the Ancre and the Somme rivers. Some of the Scots had to be persuaded to go, and others insisted on joining the Australians, especially when it was learnt that the British 1st Cavalry Division on the front line was in part being shifted to help fragments of the Fifth Army south of the Somme. There seemed more than hope now of a fightback.

Similarly, north of the Ancre, two battalions of Sinclair-Maclagan's 4th Division relieved more of the beleaguered Scottish 9th, who were at the foot of a hill on the vital Amiens to Albert railway. Soon the four Australian battalions—two from the 3rd Division and two from the 4th—were in the front line alongside the cavalry and some Scots, who were adamant they could hold the Germans now.

By the night of 27 March, the nucleus of a good, mainly Australian defence stretched from Hébuterne to the Somme. For the first time since 21 March, the German advance had been halted. The stormtroopers had run out of steam; the German machine had run into a wall of fighting, defending diggers who were not going to be dislodged. Battles were in stalemate. Yet there was much more to be done south of the Somme, where the north flank of the French Army was being pushed south-west in line with Pétain's tactics of 'defence first'. Elements of the British 1st Cavalry, along with a ragbag of other British and Scots contingents were stretched thin in an ever-widening gap between the new Australian position and the French to the south of them (on the diggers' right flank).

Monash, as ever, was on top of all developments, with intelligence from dispatch riders and others running continually to him at his chateau, along with perpetual phone messages. He conferred with Congreve on the night of 27 March before sending Rosenthal and his 9th Brigade south to form a thin, extended line between the new digger positions and the French. The diggers soon confronted the Germans flowing into the gap and blocked their advance. It is doubtful that any other division on either side could have achieved this with greater speed, efficiency and precision. The Australians had on occasions appeared rough and undisciplined to British troops. But that was away from the battlefield. On it, as Monash stressed when defending the reputation of his men, there were no more disciplined, better-drilled, tough or courageous soldiers than his diggers.

The Australian front now stood between the Germans and Amiens, which had become a target too far for Ludendorff, who so desperately wished to take it. His mighty army had been brought to an abrupt halt in this part of the Somme. The Germans began moving up more artillery and intensifying fire. It was not going to budge the long Australian front but it put everyone, including Monash, in greater danger. The diggers counterattacked and caused the first German retreat.

•

Ludendorff then turned to Operation Mars. Nine German divisions struck at Arras, at the northern extremity of the British defence line. The British held their ground so firmly that by 5 p.m. on 28 March, the German effort faltered, then halted and incurred heavy casualties. The clear weather coupled with the excellent vantage point of Vimy Ridge allowed the British artillery to play a part.

Ludendorff cancelled Operation Mars that evening. Coupled with the unexpected resistance of the Australian 3rd and 4th Divisions, the German commander-in-chief suffered the reality of two major setbacks inside a day. Operation Michael had been expensive. The Germans suffered 160,000 casualties, and a further 90,000 of its soldiers were captured. A quarter of a million men would have seemed worth the struggle of the operation had it broken through the Australians on the Somme and taken Amiens, or even defeated the British at Arras. But in late March, Michael could not be judged a success. However, Ludendorff had some satisfaction from learning that the British had replaced General Gough of the Fifth Army for its failure to resist the Germans. He was replaced by Henry Rawlinson, who would hardly have upset enemy generals. Their analysis was that he was very much under the thumb of Haig and not an independent-minded commander of any strength.

Lloyd George was not happy about Gough's dismissal. It made the British prime minister more determined than ever to get rid of Haig, as the state of the war appeared to be even worse than they had been for the British in 1916. Yet again there was unacceptable loss of life. They suffered 160,000 casualties during Operation Michael, including 70,000 troops captured as prisoners of war, which meant more agony for families throughout the British Empire as they worried about the fate of their loved ones. (The French, despite their inclination to fall back and ultimately protect Paris, had 70,000 casualties.) A frustrated Lloyd George was in a mood to defy his king and move against Haig, but could not find anyone with the capacity to replace the commander-in-chief who, despite the horrors of his strategies and tactics, still had the respect of top Allied generals as 'the boss' of the British forces.

•

Monash was moving about the battlelines more than he did at Flanders and Gallipoli because the bigger, changing fronts demanded it. He was proving to be a dynamic commander in the fluid conditions, always sharp and yet calm. He continued to cheat death. Once a bomb hit a spot in a field near Corbie a half-minute before he got there. On another occasion, artillery fire hit a hut he had just come from a minute after he had departed.

Much to his discomfit, he was ordered by the High Command to hand over Rosenthal to reinforce the British 61st Division, which was in real trouble near the town of Villers-Bretonneux, and still further south. Villers-Bretonneux was some 8 kilometres east of Amiens and had to be defended, but it irritated Monash and upset his planning. It meant he would have to rearrange his entire division to cover the loss of the hard-hitting, well-led 9th Brigade. But he remained on top of every situation. He likened the problem in front of him to one of the tough mathematics puzzles sent to him by English and Australian professors. Monash would remain cool, work his way through them methodically and always reach a solution. This meant that on the battlefield, no matter what he was confronted with, he was confident of finding a way through the revised logistics. Yet this was not the issue that peeved him. He hated the High Command plucking out part of his Australian 3rd Division—in this case about 20 per cent of it—to plug holes caused by other nations' armies. His annoyance was not because he objected to assisting others. The issue was that Australian divisions had been tacked onto other armies and they were not allowed to be part of a cohesive army in its own right. Instead they had been cannibalised throughout the war to suit the High Command's whims and will. At times like this, Monash would feel the frustration of not being able to carry through his detailed planning.

He resolved to push hard for a stand-alone Australian army, like Canada's, that could not be dictated to by the British High Command. It was one major issue in which he was in full accord with Prime Minister Hughes, and journalists Murdoch and Bean. He wasn't their pick for commander, but Monash was not concerned about who controlled it, as long as it was an Australian general with a proven record. He was the stand-out commander, but he had high regard for others, who he believed could do justice to the job: Rosenthal, Sinclair-Maclagan, Talbot Hobbs, Thomas Glasgow (a Queensland grazier with a German wife) and Pompey Elliott. Monash also had great respect for White, whom he regarded as an outstanding staff officer and administrator and was only lacking experience as a battle commander. Until he or one of these six top-class soldiers was chosen and the army was formed, it would remain a point of contention, and in this case, exasperation. He had to plug the hole left by the 9th Brigade's departure by requesting Pompey Elliott's 15th Brigade from the Australian 5th Division to fill it. Monash was not one to play favourites, but whereas Victoria Cross (VC) winner Albert Jacka was his first choice as a frontline fighter, the brilliant, forceful and fearless Elliott was his number one battlefield commander.

The exchange of these brigades was complete by 30 March, when two German divisions moved up their growing and considerable artillery. Monash found that he was dodging shells all day as he moved between planning conferences and visits to his brigade commanders, making sure he held on to the small but strategically important section of the Ancre. The Germans bombarded Monash's line (from Buire to the Corbie–Bray road) and over it, hitting his Franvillers HQ 2 kilometres away so hard that Congreve ordered him to take his staff to a new HQ location at St-Gratien. Monash by now had a good eye for a decent sleepover place with a good telephone system, and he found a fine Louis XI chateau. It belonged to the Count de Theilloye, who was only too happy to make the Australians comfortable. Monash's manner always impressed the French. He was polite and deferential, but firm about his need to second private homes. Yet he was self-assured, studious and clearly in command of all his staff. The fact that his French was clear and grammatical helped. Monash had no more than a schoolboy comprehension of the language when he began fighting on the Somme with his large-scale 'raids' in mid-1916. But in less than two years, he had mastered it. He always carried a grammar book and a French–English dictionary, and often managed to find a moment in his day to dip into them. He also engaged locals, French officers and anyone in the British forces who spoke the language well in conversation. Monash insisted that while in France, he would speak the native tongue at every opportunity. And this was not just to appease his insatiable appetite for learning. He believed that clear understanding of the environment, from street signs to newspapers, was part of his armoury. If he did not understand a French argument or comment, he persisted in the other person's tongue until he had comprehension, and if that failed he resorted to writing it down.

He had great appreciation, even a definite love, for the French, especially the women, and their culture, but felt at times there was a breakdown in communications. The educated French, unlike educated Germans, tended to get their English understanding about half or three-quarters correct. He didn't attribute this to French arrogance, as many did, but to their being too polite to admit they did not know what was really being said. His perfection made a pedant out of him in English, German and, by 1918, French. It paid off on the road, with the simple things, such as trying to find an HQ, or the important ones, such as the exact location of the enemy. It was more than useful in meetings when thrashing out the positions of French officers on battle plans. Less importantly, it aided in his pursuit of charming female company, whether it be the stunning lead dancer at the Folies Bergère, or the women at parties arranged by the shrewd Baron de Gail. De Gail had been assigned to Monash's staff as the 'token'

Frenchman or liaison officer. He was really there to spy. All Allied armies had their agents embedded in the staffs of fellow armies to keep tabs on their real intentions. De Gail worked out early that Monash liked the company of attractive women, physically, intellectually and culturally. The Frenchman worked assiduously to meet these needs, calculating that Monash would most likely have a huge role in the outcome of the war. He wanted to know what his deeper aims and plans were, and believed he could glean more 'intelligence' using women for pillow talk. De Gail had a good sense of what he believed the Australian was thinking. There is evidence from Monash's diaries that a dancer from the Folies Bergère, introduced to him by de Gail, was a companion whenever the general went on leave in Paris. He would visit the Folies at night and lunch with her the next day at his favourite French restaurant, Café de la Paix.[7]

Chapter 15

Parry, Push and Pull at the Front

Monash believed always in attack first, rather than defence, wherever it was possible with minimum risk to his troops. Instead of digging in on the night of 29 March, despite his suddenly changed circumstances on losing 9th Brigade, he advanced the left of his line 1800 metres from south of Heilly along the Ancre River to east of Buire. The right of his line pivoted south and cut off the Germans 'from valuable vantage ground' along the main road from Corbie to Bray. It ran equidistant between the Ancre to its north and the Somme to its south. The road split the apex of the triangle formed by the rivers.

Monash's aggressive and surprise move meant that the Australians had taken the initiative. They tackled the Germans, killing 3000, captured prisoners and took up positions on this new line.

'My Artillery were firing over open sights,' Monash noted, 'and had never in their previous experience had such tempting targets.'[1]

Although the enemy had been halted in this part of the Somme by the end of March, the artillery shelling of all ranges continued, and put everyone in danger. On 1 April, Monash arrived at 11th Brigade minutes after shelling had killed three officers. His luck was still running. But instead of dwelling on it, he kept up his appointments and went on with his duties.

In the comparative lull in the first few days in April, Monash organised 'town majors' to gather up goods, produce and live-stock, such as cattle, sheep, wool, wheat, oats, bran, wine and furniture, which would otherwise die or rot in the war zone. It was a case of waste not, want not. He totted up its value with typical exactitude—94,472 pounds, 13 shillings and 6 pence—and made sure it was passed onto the French authorities. He also allowed his men to relax when off the front line, with the best of what the French countryside could offer. They could carouse in the green fields of abandoned farms in the early spring sunshine. They enjoyed the local champagne and wines, along with any pork, chicken or crops they could transform into meals.

•

Sporadic heavy fighting continued until 4 April, when the Germans hit with force south of the Somme at the village of Hamel, defended by a fatigued British division, which had been routed after being sent the night before. This offended Monash's neat and militaristic sensibilities.

'This success gave the enemy a footing upon a portion of Hill 104, and brought him to the eastern outskirts of Villers-Bretonneux [to the south-west],' he wrote, miffed that this tiny salient, or bulge of territory, south of the Somme was in German hands. On the same day a British division was beaten into a retreat, leaving his flank exposed again. He was more than irritated.

He kept his thoughts to himself and one or two confidants on his staff but let loose in letters to his wife, telling her that the British divisions were the 'absolute limit'. He was critical of the poor troops, staff and commanders. Monash was also scathing about the collapse of the British Fifth Army. He believed it had been avoidable, and he put it down to a 'gross lack of leadership and efficiency'. As on Gallipoli, he did not think the British lacked spine. On the contrary, he had respect for the fight in them, particularly the Scots. But he had no time for their inept officers and commanders, whom he had plenty of time to assess as Australian and British brigades were rotated under his control in anticipation of further German assaults.

The Germans attacked again on 5 April. The enemy now hammered battalions of the 4th Division that were defending the high ground north of the Ancre and the all-important railway to Amiens. The fighting was heavy as the much smaller band of diggers attempted to hold positions in what became known as the Battle of Dernancourt, after the village on the Ancre. If the Germans made it through, the 3rd Division would be trapped by the enemy in the river-bound triangle to the east, north and south. Monash monitored the battle through the day, aware that if Sinclair-Maclagan's 4th Division cracked, he would have to withdraw the 3rd fast, which would leave the way forward for the Germans to go for Amiens. The Germans gave their assault everything, rotating three divisions over twenty hours of intense fighting, but could not break through. For the moment, it spelt the end of the heavy attacks that had gone on for a fortnight on this section of the front.

'The great German blow against the important railway centre of Amiens had been parried,' Monash noted with caution, 'and from this time onwards interest in this sphere of operations rapidly waned . . . North of the Somme, his activity quickly died down, and the attitude of both combatants gradually assumed the old familiar aspect of trench warfare, with its endless digging of trenches, line behind line, its weary trench routine, and its elaborate installation of permanent lines of communication and administrative establishments of all descriptions.'[2]

Also on 5 April, the Australian 5th Division came into the line at last, relieving Monash's division and the British 1st Cavalry Division on a 4.5-kilometre front. On seeing this last of the Australian divisions, he was once more reminded of the importance of pulling all five together. He believed that the sum of them all fighting under the same flag would double in effectiveness with the right leadership. As fatigue and frustration deepened, Monash admitted to himself, if no one else, that he was the correct man for the big job. He felt, without expressing it, that he was by far the best equipped of all the generals to make the new force work cohesively and to design plans to win every battle. But Monash was not going to urge for more than the formation of the First Army. He knew who opposed him in the government and media, but was hoping that his rapport with the King, Haig, Plumer, Butler and others would see him put in charge. Even Godley, who had been Monash's nemesis on Gallipoli in 1915 and Flanders in 1917, had fallen in with his support. Apart from Monash asserting himself in debate or hot argument, and then in producing the goods on the battlefield, Godley noted how Monash was treated by the commander-in-chief and an intermittent stream of European royals, who had been directed by George V to 'go and meet General Monash' if they wanted confirmation that the Allies would come out on top.

There was no other Australian who had the skills, unbeaten record, the experience and the strong connections to the top of the British High Command, and beyond. Monash had no time for politicking and even if he had, he was a long, long way from Whitehall and London. He was preoccupied minute by minute with holding back the German thrust. He believed very much in the science of logic, and this dictated that he would be elevated, if the Australians were to have their own army.

Seeing the 5th Division march into the line also made Monash anxious to have his mighty 9th Brigade back under his control. But it had been whisked away from the trenches north to Flanders and Messines, near Ypres, which under Monash it had played a strong part in taking only ten months earlier. It had linked up with the 5th Brigade of the Australian 2nd Division. This meant further annoyance for Monash. How could he or anyone fight a coordinated battle if part of his force was continually being disrupted, not by the enemy but superiors moving pieces around on a board, pretending to know what they were doing? And how on earth, he wondered, did the British manage to put themselves in a position to possibly lose Messines Ridge, which his troops had once secured?

The 1st British Cavalry Division and the Australian 5th Division were under the control of the British III Corps run by General Butler, which had been beefed up to fill the gap between the Somme and the sagging French Army. By now the British High Command was rushing divisions to any point where the German attack was greatest, thus splitting the Australian corps, which in theory had formed but in practice was a long way from one command and coordination. The emergency of the huge German push of 21 March aside, the British High Command was paying only lip-service to the concept of the new, functioning formation.

Even the 1st Division, which was on its way to join the 2nd Division at Villers-Bretonneux, was hurriedly turned around and moved back to Flanders just in case the build-up of enemy troops east of Ypres meant a new enemy push there. Operation Michael was now judged as a strategic failure, thanks in large part to the Australian 3rd and 4th Divisions' efforts. Ludendorff was only left with the option of shelling Amiens, which would do no more to end the war than the massive weapon—known as the Kaiser's Gun—would in its unfocused firing on Paris. The Germans found themselves with an extended, thin front facing Amiens, which was a reverse of their stated aim in 1917 of short-ened lines. Extended lines meant more troops committed to 'position', that is, trench warfare, which Monash detested and the Germans now loathed because it meant more resources devoted to defending the salient. It was already being hammered by Allied guns and aircraft.

Meanwhile, the new Allied commander-in-chief Foch was having to deal with three egos that were almost as large as his own: the well-manicured, inarticulate Haig, who despite his intellectual deficits was determined, and not a bad partner to deal with; the rumpled, negative-minded Pétain, who was becoming more shrill with every meeting; and the slim, overly self-assured, jut-jawed Pershing, whose unblinking ignorance about his force's capacities in the conditions was exasperating. Foch could have filled some holes in the front line with the American's untrained divisions but Pershing was stubbornly refusing to release them unless they were under American command. Understandably, Haig had his eye on protecting the channel ports if the British were crushed. Monsieur 'fallback' Pétain was equally concerned with looking after Paris. The fragility of the French Army was not giving Foch enough confidence to test it under Pétain. Foch still believed Amiens remained the biggest danger area and so denied the red-cheeked, irritated Haig extra divisions north, but he did allow four to go into reserve positions west of Amiens.

•

Ludendorff would never admit that his darling 'Michael' had failed, but he was forced to turn to another offensive: St George. This was against 80 kilometres of British front around Ypres, which would eventually converge on the rail junction at Hazebrouck with the aim of wheeling north to cut off and destroy the British and Belgium armies in that area.

Ludendorff had correctly judged that Haig had weakened his northern armies to meet the Michael offensive. But the German command also had to compromise, and aimed for a major strike between La Bassée and Armentières, with complementary attacks to the north, which caused a dry-witted staff officer to change the codename 'St George' to 'Georgette'.

The new plan was given over to General Ferdinand von Quasts's Sixth Army, which would attack General Sir Henry Horne's First Army; General Sixt von Arnim's Fourth Army would go after Plumer's Second Army. Quast attacked on the morning of 9 April and flung vast volumes of mustard gas and tonnes of high-explosive shells along Horne's front. Four hours later the stormtroopers moved out. This was followed by six German divisions striking at the weakest link in the Allied chain: one division of Portuguese soldiers holding 9 kilometres of front. It was soon easily flattened, which was wonderful news for Ludendorff, who was celebrating his 53rd birthday at a lunch given by the Kaiser. The two men disliked each other intensely. The commander thought Wilhelm II was a 'loud-mouthed clown and odd-ball'. The Kaiser, forced to eulogise his top commander at the lunch, privately referred to him as 'sergeant'.

After the strained celebration, reports came in that the British were putting up stiff resistance, yet by evening Ludendorff was relieved to learn the Germans had advanced 9 kilometres to the River Lawe, which they crossed on the morning of 10 April. By the evening they had pushed across the River Lys. In the north, von Armin's Fourth German Army had done even more damage to the Allies by recapturing Messines and Ploegsteert. Armentières fell to von Quast's Sixth Army the next day. By 12 April, Quast was less than 8 kilometres from Hazebrouck.

•

Monash and all the Australians resented the news that Messines, Armentières and Ploegsteert Wood had been lost after all the work they had done to win and hold them.

The losses created some ill feeling among the diggers, who had long been the butt of British gibes about lack of discipline, and more importantly had suffered under what they saw as incompetent British officers. The disgruntled Australians now felt they had a right to lash back. The diggers began circulating derogatory stories about the 'Tommies', as the English were called, and their commanders. It was clear they were performing far, far better on all fronts than their British counterparts.

Monash stamped it out fast. He was more aware than most of the amount of fighting the two nations would have to do side by side and in combination. Yet his private correspondence showed that he agreed with the crude criticism. He vented his thoughts to friends whose sons had been killed. Yet in public, he put on a different face. He had to keep up the morale of his force.

•

Haig delivered a superfluous, cliché-riddled 'backs to the wall' order of the day concerning the renewed Ypres fighting, but he need not have bothered. The British, reinforced by the Australians, had been fighting as hard as they could for four days, with many casualties. They were supported by effective and disruptive air strikes. Plumer, calm, sensible and conservative, brought his lines back almost to Ypres, thus giving up ground that in the autumn of 1917 had cost more than 250,000 British casualties. Yet his method had merit. He shortened his lines and waited until fresh French troops arrived. By 19 April, Operation Georgette was at a standstill.

•

Enemy morale was further dampened on 21 April when the much-lauded 'Red Baron' fighter pilot was shot down by two of

Monash's machine gunners—relieving cooks—near the Somme. They had spotted the easily recognisable red-painted German Fokker triplane making its 80th 'kill' the day before. Now they had it in their sights, tailing a cumbersome British RE8 artillery spotter from 2300 metres down to 50 metres. The gunners waited until the Fokker was overhead and opened fire. The bullets ripped the fuselage; the engine faltered. It flipped and crashed into the next field. Aware that the Red Baron was down, the Germans maintained artillery fire in a circle around the plane for half an hour, while a formation of Fokkers circled overhead. The German planes flew off when it was clear no one was going to emerge from the plane wreck.

The cooks-turned-gunners and other artillerymen reached the plane and took the body from it. Papers on the pilot confirmed it was the fabled Red Baron, Manfred von Richthofen. Monash was notified. He rushed to the plane and collected 'a tiny piece of the red fabric of Richthofen's machine' and a piece of its wooden propeller. Monash, a memorabilia collector, sent the fabric home to Melbourne but kept the propeller piece with him.[3]

The British instructed that von Richthofen be buried with full military honours. Monash had his No. 3 Australian Flying Squadron place a wreath on the grave. Later the RAF dropped the dead hero's personal effects over the German lines, with a message of condolence. The Australian gunners added their condolences too. No one else who had personally killed so many Allied fighters was given as much respect. In the rarefied activity of war, utmost recognition was given to the man who had created so much carnage in the air. The news of the gunners' kill boosted the 3rd Division's spirits, while it was a blow to the Germans, who had promoted the Red Baron as invincible.

Soon after the strike, another German Fokker was hit, and it crashed not far from where von Richthofen went down. 'The pilot was wounded but the officer observer [who had been in the plane's rear seat] was quite all right,' Monash wrote. 'He was brought to me; I gave him a glass of wine, and he talked freely. He told me that the German Flieger Corps much appreciated the placing of the wreath on the Red Baron's grave.'

Monash's perfect German was important when interrogating enemy officers. In this case, the goodwill between the two was evident, but Monash always took the opportunity to glean even the minutest detail about enemy activity, to add to his mighty store of information. Monash never missed the nuance of a response, and his quiet, strong manner, which included plenty of pregnant pauses, often intimidated his German opposite numbers into divulging more than they wished.

Two days later, on 23 April, the 9th Brigade was retired from the front line at Villers-Bretonneux; it had held the Germans back for three solid weeks. While it was rested, the British 8th Division took over. This seemed to be the signal for the enemy to strike hard and it hit with four divisions, which captured the town. An important avenue to Amiens had been opened.

The Germans showered the area with heavy gas shelling, coming dangerously close to Monash's new HQ at the handsome, 17th-century Bertangles Chateau, 8 kilometres north-west of Amiens and just 2 kilometres from the village of Villers-Bretonneux. They also cut his communications, but he found ways to communicate with the British III Corps. Its commander requested that Pompey Elliott's Australian 15th Brigade and the 13th Brigade under Major General Glasgow make an attempt to take this strategically important village. The counterattack was set for before dawn on 25 April, the third anniversary of the Gallipoli landing. It galvanised the weary outfits for a supreme effort. They attacked with ferocity and caught the Germans by surprise.

'They advanced 2700 metres in the dark without artillery support,' Monash wrote with pride. '[They] completely restored the situation, and captured 1000 prisoners. I can see the prisoners pouring past the Chateau as I write this letter. It was a magnificent performance.'[4]

He had the highest praise for the drive and courage of Elliott and Glasgow. The diggers' effort put a blunt stop to the German thrust that had been going for 35 days. Had the enemy held Villers-Bretonneux, they could have regrouped, pushed up their artillery and gained breathing space for a grand assault on Amiens from north and south. Instead, the Germans were forced to pull back in disarray, and many soldiers were captured in one of the most decisive, quick battles of the entire war.

Monash was in no doubt that the Anzac spirit had inspired his soldiers. He had been the first commander to commemorate Anzac—on 25 April 1916 in Egypt. He believed this date was the moment that the true spirit of Australia, then only a nation of fourteen years, was born. He made sure there were ceremonies each year to remember the more than eight thousand Australians who died on the Turkish peninsula in the hope they and their experience would never be forgotten.

The energy generated to win at Villers-Bretonneux, Monash believed, had been caused by the date's importance to every member of the 1st AIF. And it was a significant win, not because of its size, which in the context of the war was a minor battle. Its true 'weight' had to be seen in the context of the war's *outcome*. Hindenburg admitted later that it was a turning point.

Chapter 16

Hamel Attack Rejected

The Australian Corps HQ was now at Bertangles, with its attractive grounds and spacious parks. For the first time the divisions were acting in some unison, with three in the line and one in reserve. Monash's 3rd Division still occupied the sector between the Ancre and the Somme, where it had been since it was won on 29 March. He kept a dynamic in the 3rd Division's activities, rotating their operations and devising small battles to keep them 'interested' and avoid boredom. He kept up the pressure on positions east of the Somme but had less flexibility in the south because of the major 'sore' of a problem in the form of the Hamel village, which the Germans had occupied since 5 April.

'I was in possession of much of the higher ground,' Monash noted, 'and was able to look down, almost as upon a map, on the enemy in the Hamel basin'. He could see their concealed artillery, which could hammer the exposed valley next to his HQ and was dangerous for the Australians if they moved into it. This irritated Monash and offended his sensibilities concerning a neat plan that had been formulating in his mind for months. There had been a lot of talk about a counterattack, a grand-scale full-on British/French push. Haig, in a broad sense, had a taste. Rawlinson, now commander of the Fourth Army, which carried the Australian Corps and the British III Army Corps, had no desire for it. He had been shaken to the core by the failure on the Somme in July 1916, and was not prepared to take the initiative for another big Allied attack. Rawlinson would leave another decision of that scale to Haig; he was preoccupied with trying to up the number of soldiers on the Front. He was even considering disbanding the Tank Corps to release more personnel for the front line. Britain's manpower shortage, maintained by Lloyd George, was beginning to bite. The new Fourth Army Chief had no faith in the tank and no idea how they might be used to better effect than in 1916, or even 1917. He had not kept abreast of the new models, which were superior to the early versions that had failed and dispirited the foot soldiers alongside them.

Monash, by contrast, was cogitating on the sort of scale that would end the war. He believed the timing was just about right for a big counterpunch, especially given that the German forces had been fought to a standstill in northern France and Flanders. More important than anything else, he believed he could devise a plan to make a decisive breakthrough. But first he would need to give the High Command a taste, a preview of what could be done with precise planning.

Taking back Hamel was part of his grand strategy.

Monash put the plan to Birdwood, who was the commander of the Australian Corps, which was then more an administrative entity than a proper corps. Birdwood rejected it, not once but four times. He looked at the maps, and could not see the issue over Hamel, but that was because Monash was not going to explain his grand plan for a counterattack using several allied armies. He knew it would have been presumptuous. Monash was not in a position to air such an ambitious scheme. Birdwood reminded him that Rawlinson would not bother with it, and certainly not if Monash envisaged using tanks, which he did. So Birdwood vetoed the plan. Monash mentioned it to Brudenell White, who also would not support it. White argued that Hamel had originally been thought of as a useful feint for another bigger attack elsewhere. If it was not anymore a location for a feint, why should manpower and equipment be wasted on taking it now? White was surprised that Monash should be so fixated by a village of little or no importance. But again, Monash was not about to reveal his bigger idea to end the war. It would seem immodest, over-ambitious and unrealistic for a mere divisional commander to come up with a concept that should, by rights, be left to Haig and his High Command. After all, massive counterattacks were now not the real flavour of the war. The British had failed with one in 1916; the Germans had just exhausted themselves with their version, and it had not delivered a coup de grâce. No one on either side was thinking anywhere on Monash's grand scale.

This instance highlighted further critical differences between Monash and those close to him at the top of Australian corps command. White had shown outstanding skill in managing and planning the Anzac withdrawal from Gallipoli. But it was a finite project and not a battle. White was an excellent administrator with plenty of time to air his vision on how the Allies should proceed, which he did but without the clout, gravitas or record to gain credence for implementation of his views. Birdwood was popular with the diggers and a good administrator, but he too was not a battle commander with the sort of vision, experience and ambition for a big gesture or a knockout blow to the opposition. Rawlinson was a career soldier with friends in the right high places, but his competence was below the level required for the scale of fighting and thinking required. He had been stunned, then numbed by failure, rather than shell-shocked like the tens of thousands of soldiers his pathetic plans had debilitated or killed. Rawlinson was not a corrupt or bad leader. He was simply a career soldier way out of his depth in comprehending what was needed for victory.

At this moment in 1918, Monash's ambition, urgency and vision were beginning to stand out. His ubiquity and activity impressed everyone with whom he came in contact—not to mention the clear success he had just achieved with his 3rd Division. Within the AIF, he was taking shape as the number one general in the force. His reputation with the French, Canadian and British top brass was already high. His name was synonymous with competence, a frightening level of planning, sheer brilliance of mind, and most important of all for those who fought under and around him, a conscious drive to protect the lives of others, especially those doing the real fighting. His mind, which was broad as it was deep, was in essence unrestricted in ideas. Hamel, for instance, was part of a much bigger scheme that was more than a dream. Removing the town as a problem was just the first step in realising it.

Monash differed from White, Birdwood, Rawlinson and others in one other vital way: by nature he had an attacking mindset. He had an unfathomable self-confidence, partly born of his exceptional, hungry, eclectic intellect and partly because of his three decades of achievement in so many walks of life. He had a belief that he could take on the Germany Army and win.

There was a lot of talk about the enemy having 'come to a standstill' and the need for a huge counterpunch, but Monash recognised that both sides would have to re-energise and refresh. The Germans' main offensives of Michael and Georgette had failed, yet still they had accomplished a great deal. Ludendorff had turned the tables on the Allies in more ways than just psychologically. Germany had seized the initiative, and it had not just gained a few hundred blood-soaked metres. The great five- to six-week push had taken more square kilometres than either side had managed in three years. Breaking the trench gridlock in those 40 or so days had led to bigger gains—some 80 kilometres behind the former Allied lines. The British had 236,000 casualties, including 9500 officers, in a period of defensive fighting. French casualties numbered 75,000, plus the loss of 15,000 prisoners. The British had 59 divisions and only six of those had not seen action. Twenty-five had been tossed into the fray multiple times. Ten of them were judged as 'fatigued', and five had been broken up, which left 38 fit to fight on immediately and another six ready to go but without any experience on the battlefield. It was not the hoped-for German crash-through and total victory that had been heralded early and exalted by the Kaiser prematurely, but it had given Ludendorff extra credibility and power, despite his own force being exhausted and suffering 250,000 casualties. Where Haig had been driven on by the thought of a million extra Germans arriving in 1918 from the Russian Front, Ludendorff had been mindful of the American build-up to about 650,000 by the end of April. He had not panicked. In fact, he was a little blasé about the impact the Americans would have, given that they had to be trained and equipped by the French and British.

The Americans first performed in combat on 20 April at the village of Seicheprey between St Mihiel and the Moselle River, a quiet sector held by 26th (Yankee) Division. Early that morning they were tested by the attack of 3200 stormtroopers. In a two-day battle, the Americans had 634 casualties, including 160 dead and 136 taken prisoners.

'The Americans fought well,' Ludendorff said patronisingly, 'but our success had nevertheless been easy.'[1]

The German High Command believed it could win the war before the Americans were fully acclimatised and battle-ready on a grand scale. Monash did not expect a renewed enemy attack before August. It was another reason he wished to strike on a massive scale, with a battle to take Hamel as a precursor. But he had been denied this opportunity. It had thwarted, too, for the moment, his quiet intent to involve the Americans in fighting with his diggers, which he'd planned for Hamel. Monash had a grand vision for Australia's future that was predicated on more reliance on the United States than England. It was radical thinking at the time. Most Australians were tied to the 'mother country' but his background gave him a broader global and futuristic view. Monash had huge admiration for the Americans as the democracy Australia should aim to be most like, given their roughly similar origins. He had been inspired on a visit to New York in 1911 when he noted the city was 'electrified', industrious and progressive. So Monash was watching the American troops with a keen interest.

Chapter 17

Of Agrarian Gods, and Sheep

Turkish confidence in the Middle East was high after the failed attempts in March by the British and Lawrence to get beyond the Jordan Valley. Turkish hopes rose even more after the massive attack by the Germans on the Western Front. The consequences for Commander-in-Chief Allenby's campaign were dire. The British in Belgium and France needed reinforcements fast and he was asked to supply them. Like his predecessor, General Murray, he responded by offering to send 60,000 troops over the next three months. Unlike Murray, he was not prepared to sit back and wait until something happened or he could obtain more troops, which was dependent on events on the Western Front. Murray had asked for and was promised the Indian Cavalry in

France. Allenby was also promised Indian Infantry, but they had to be trained. That process would not be completed for half a year.

Before he could recover and continue after the huge German assault from 21 March, he had a mighty reorganisation and training program to instigate.

Chauvel remained the most unscathed by the transfer of troops, in terms of the force under him. He did lose the yeomanry (cavalry), which were replaced by the Indians. Despite their experience in France, they still had to be trained in the different conditions, which would delay his corps being more or less at full strength until after April.

With the infantry in disarray until reconstructed, Chauvel would have to provide the main attack focus for the Eastern Expeditionary Force campaign. Allenby boosted the mounted/cavalry force in a reorganisation that saw Chauvel's corps increase to four divisions. It was to be bigger than any other mounted/cavalry force in modern history.

Yet it would be months before it was properly organised, providing there were no setbacks. In the meantime, by late April the British and Arabs had put out of action 130 kilometres of the Hejaz Railway. Seven stations were in their hands. The force of Lawrence and Feisal had now made impotent the Turks' operations in Arabia's Medina, which had troubled the planning of Murray, then Allenby and Feisal, for so long.

•

The success on the railway encouraged Allenby, who was under pressure to act fast or be forced to sit out the rest of the 1918 spring and summer until the next propitious moment for a further big push to Amman, Deraa and Damascus as late as the next autumn. He put a plan to Chauvel. It was in three stages. First he had to capture two enemy strongholds at Es Salt, where the Turkish Fourth Army had its HQ with a thousand men, and nearby Shunet Nimrin where there was a garrison of 5000. Second, once his forces consolidated in the area, he had to take Amman. Third, he told Chauvel that as soon as his operations had gained the front Amman–Es Salt, he was to at once prepare for operations northwards, with a view to advancing rapidly on Deraa.

Deraa was a local capital 104 kilometres north-east of Jerusalem, which acted as the rail junction between Damascus and Amman. (Amman was connected to the Hejaz Railway running south to Maan and on to Medina.) It was the point where the Hejaz Railway threw out its western branch, crossing the Jordan River south of the Sea of Galilee.

Allenby knew Deraa would take a big operation to win. Yet once it was taken, Damascus would be the next important Syrian city to fall, and a less difficult proposition.

•

One risk among several came in Allenby's assertion that the Arabs in the area east of Jerusalem, the Beni Sakhr, would come to Chauvel's aid. 'The closest touch must be maintained with them,' Allenby directed. Perhaps he had been influenced by Lawrence's optimism concerning the Arabs, despite the let-down in late March in the assault on Amman. But it was not simple. The Arabs had to be wooed and won everywhere by any means possible. The British force in general still distrusted the Arabs, who to them seemed to drift with the wind. If it blew for the Turks, they would stay with them. If it blew for the British, they *might* go with them. But the distrust was mutual; the Arabs distrusted all 'invaders'. Unless they were persuaded by Lawrence himself, they were most unlikely to do the bidding of the British, and he was not called on to help out. Nor was his liaison officer with this tribe; Hubert Young was an Arabist Lawrence first met at Carchemish before the war (and the man he had nominated as his replacement should he be 'incapacitated', which was a euphemism for killed). Allenby's HQ representatives had been heavy-handed in dealing with the tribe. They had not communicated their plans and what was expected of it. Young later reported the British envoys had 'perplexed and frightened' them.

The envoys wrote to Allenby that the Beni Sakhr tribe would only help out before early May while their sheep were still grazing in the area. After that, they would have to move on to other pastures. It sounded like a 'thin' restriction (and in reality an excuse for *not* helping out) that would never have been put to experienced Arabists Lawrence and Young. Nevertheless, Chauvel was informed that the Arabs would march on the village of Naur, 14 kilometres east of Shunet Nimrin, cut the Turkish communications and attack them as they withdrew.

Allenby put a time constraint on Chauvel, saying that the spring wheat and barley harvest on the plains west of the Jordan would be important to the Turks. For these reasons, Allenby claimed, it was imperative to strike before the beginning of May 1918.

The commander-in-chief, then, was giving the impression of being dictated to by the agrarian gods and the eating habits of a flock of sheep. It was out of character. He could see his grand plan to take Damascus and defeat the Turks slipping away. There was not quite the whiff of panic in Allenby's directive. But it was rushed and over-ambitious. There were more risks than most pragmatic generals would accept.

Chetwode was asked to 'demonstrate' against Shunet Nimrin to make the Turks think the British were going for Amman first. In private, he thought this a 'stupid' plan (and said so later). Why alert the Turks to something big with a feint that would have them prepared for a sizeable attack? This took away the element of surprise, especially for the mounteds, whose advantages over the infantry included speed of attack, and shock.

Chauvel did not like the 'feint' proposal either. It worried him that the 5000 well-entrenched, forewarned Turks were waiting for his force to attack. At a conference with Allenby on 24 April he asked for an infantry division to help out. He was granted the 60th Division, minus one brigade of three, which was to sit in reserve with Chetwode. But Chauvel felt he needed a full division. He became uneasy about the entire scheme. He was a diligent planner, who left little to chance and there were too many 'what ifs' in this scheme. On top of that, intelligence reports informed him that German infantry would most likely be enlisted to come from Amman. The enemy would have a big supply of artillery and machine guns.

He used the legitimate yet convenient excuse that his transport capacity would only stretch to Es Salt. He wrote to HQ and asked that plans two and three be 'postponed'. Allenby was perhaps aware that he had suffered from a rush of blood over the three-part plan, or maybe his staff gently disabused him of it. Whatever the influence, he agreed to Chauvel's request.

This still did not make the first aim any easier, although it did relieve Chauvel of worrying about the improbable logistics beyond it.

●

He sent the two brigades of the 60th Division across the Jordan at 5 a.m. on 30 April and on another 8 kilometres to tackle Shunet Nimrin. The Londoners fought with their usual tenacity, but they were up against a powerful force of fire from artillery, machine guns and rifles. They needed that third brigade.

Despite repeated thrusts, they could not make a breakthrough.

●

At first light, Chauvel sent out one of his favourite attack commanders, 47-year-old Brigadier General William Grant, who had been prominent in the attack on Beersheba. He was to strike further north with his 4th Brigade up west of the Jordan. If he made it across the plain of Mafid Jozelle, he was to swing across the Jordan and aim for Es Salt, which was 16 kilometres northeast of Shunet Nimrin. The 4th would be followed by more Australian Light Horse.

The Light Horse swept 15 kilometres north and brushed aside Turkish posts en route to the plain, despite big guns firing on the stream of mounted riflemen. By 8 a.m. the 4th Brigade's 4th Regiment had reached a small tributary to the Jordan another 10 kilometres further north. A squadron of the 11th Regiment was aiming to reach a crossing on the river at Damieh. But the Turks had a string of big gun emplacements and were making the passage difficult. They attempted to pulverise the oncoming horsemen, who were forced to disperse.

Grant brought up his own considerable artillery in the hope of clearing a way for his riders. Chauvel's troopers were about to continue their relentless drive against the Turks.

Chapter 18

Es Salt Assault

At 6.30 a.m. on 30 April 1918 Brigadier Lachlan Wilson, the 'retiring' Queensland city lawyer, arrived with his 3rd Brigade on the Mafid Jozelle plain. He and Grant had a quick conference. Grant informed him that his men had cut the telegraph wires at Damieh, which meant that the Turks at Es Salt might not know of the impending assault from the north. Grant thought he could hold his ground and at the same time cover Wilson and his riders, who would make for the Damieh Crossing.

Wilson made his move, leading the horsemen over the crossing and then on to a plain and a winding climb of 23 kilometres south-east towards Es Salt. The road became a narrow, dangerous track as it left the plain. It rose so sharply for 2 kilometres that the men dismounted and led their horses single file. No transport could make it, but a train of 360 camels, not used to acting like mountain goats, scrambled up. Twenty-nine camel cacolets for the wounded were included. Some carried the six guns of the Hong Kong and Singapore Mountain Battery and their ammunition. Each man carried 230 rounds of ammunition. For every Hotchkiss gun there were 3100 rounds; for each machine gun there were 5000 rounds.

Wilson sent Scott out ahead with the 9th Regiment. They were surprised to see nothing of the enemy, especially as the track past the steepest part was surrounded by hills where snipers and machine gunners would have strong vantage points. Enemy scouts could have warned the Turkish Fourth Army base at Es Salt.

So far there was no opposition.

Scouts for the 9th came across their first three Turks 6 kilometres from Es Salt. They crept up on them, shooting one and capturing the other two. The next encounter was with a Turkish cavalry troop of 32. The Australians rushed them. The enemy fled on horseback and foot across the rocky ground. Wilson's brigade had come 17 kilometres in a climb of 1200 metres and were on a tableland.

The third confrontation came about 800 metres further on. The Turks had set up small fortifications on a high ridge running for a kilometre to the left of the track and on hills either side of it.

Wilson was determined to take Es Salt by nightfall after he intercepted a radio message from Chauvel saying it had to be done. The slow camels were holding up Wilson's advance. With the afternoon wearing on, he did not hesitate to take on the Turks in the hills and on the ridge, sending his men on foot. The horsemen revelled in their mission. They were aided by broken ground, which allowed them to close in on the Turks, who would have been unnerved to see how the Australians did not hesitate to go into action. Wilson let loose three of the Hong Kong battery guns with twelve of the machine guns, which softened up the enemy.

The Light Horse-turned-infantry attacked in three directions. The machine-gun fire and shells kept coming until the horsemen were almost at the Turkish sangars. Many of the enemy soldiers were still crouching when the Australian attackers, armed with revolvers or bayonets, came over their fortification at them. German officers tried to make their Turkish charges stay and fight. But the stories of the Australians at Beersheba had filtered back to the entire army. This assault had something of the intensity of that historic charge, again brought on by the urgency of reaching their objective before nightfall. Some of the Germans in the defence stood and fought, but they were soon overwhelmed.

•

Wilson could see this first battle going his way. He ordered Major Herbert Shannon to prepare for a mounted dash of 3.5 kilometres to Es Salt itself. By the time the 8th's squadrons were ready, Wilson gave the signal for them to take the town. The 250 horsemen trotted off. They ignored fire from the hills and broke into a gallop but then met intense fire from sangars 2 kilometres further on. They were forced to stop and take on the 60 Turks by the road. Shannon ordered his troopers to flank and break the opposition, which was done in less than twenty minutes. The Light Horse regrouped and continued on the approach through several small valleys flanked by stony hills. They met occasional opposition, which necessitated troopers thrusting in bursts at the enemy, whose lines were soon broken.

Shannon and his men were now galvanised to take the town at a rush. This was their moment. Every trooper lived for these isolated chances to be part of a hot-blooded charge.

•

Lieutenant Charles Foulkes-Taylor, a 28-year-old London-born West Australian, led the first troop into Es Salt. The town was at the head of a valley on a hill dominated by a medieval castle. Its basalt houses and buildings rose one above the other on the hill slopes. On its western and southern sides it was protected by a system of steep terraced hills.

Preferring the revolver to the bayonet, Taylor fired at some of the 300 Turks and Germans still left in the Fourth Army HQ as he charged down the cobblestone lanes, startling inhabitants and enemy alike. Most had evacuated in the last hour knowing that the Australians were coming. The remaining soldiers were under orders to fight.

Taylor saw a German officer in a courtyard trying to rally some Turks to make a stand. He spurred his horse at them, aiming his revolver at the German. Taylor pulled the trigger and found he was out of ammunition. He kept coming, still aiming his weapon and with bluff, forced his quarry to hand over his own revolver.

With the town under control, Taylor gathered eight troopers and tracked down transport leaving the town on the road to Amman. They overtook them on a narrow track beside a steep slope into a valley.

'The Light Horsemen forced teams and carts over the edge of the roadway,' historian Henry Gullett wrote in his official history, '. . . they tumbled into the deep-bed of the water-course.'[1]

Taylor had lost two men wounded and was down to six. He ploughed on, only to be pushed back by intense machine-gun fire 4 kilometres along the road. He was forced to retreat. Yet this small band with their reckless drive had captured 200 armed enemy troops, weaponry, food, water and other supplies.

Taylor was soon reinforced by other troopers from the secured town. They turned back to Es Salt, satisfied with their afternoon's 'work' and haul. (It would earn this newly commissioned officer the Military Cross.)

German radio traffic was intercepted after the town was taken.

'Es Salt had been captured,' it said, 'by the reckless and dashing gallantry of the Australian cavalry.'

A German officer noted that the 8th Regiment's rush on Es Salt featured troopers galloping their horses in places where 'no one else would have ridden at all'.

Documents captured later in Nazareth confirmed that the Es Salt action had caused more problems between the Germans and Turks running the war. The shock debacle at Beersheba had begun the rift; Es Salt had deepened it. Von Sanders was most unhappy about the way Djemal Pasha, one of the more brutal Turkish commanders and a former Syrian governor, conducted the operations east of Jordan even before Wilson's fierce attack from the river to Es Salt. The German commander condemned Djemal's 'failure' to guard against the ride up the Jordan Valley and the taking of Es Salt. Von Sanders believe the town should never have changed hands. The Turks, he claimed, should have held it at all costs.

The battle was far from over, but enemy faultlines were already exposed.

•

The town was soon covered by the regiments on the routes north and east. A spirited search for 'booty', always the consequence of a new town acquisition, was carried out. It didn't have the intensity or intent of the local Arabs' looting. Nevertheless, the Australians were buoyed by their finds, especially five lorries, six German cars and 28 new machine guns yet to be unpacked. There was also a tonne of ammunition and small arms.

One captured German officer spoke a little English.

'Well,' he said to a 10th Regiment officer, 'and how long are you going to make the war with us?'

'Until we lick you,' the Australian replied.

'Lick? Lick? What do mean lick?'

'Until we beat you.'

'Oh,' the German said, shrugging his shoulders, 'then it will be a very, very long war!'[2]

•

The 10th Light Horse Regiment found the night sky over Es Salt strange. It was pitch black by 6 p.m. except for the odd flickering of a primitive oil lamp in some of the stone buildings. By 9 p.m. the moon forced its way through a dark bank of clouds and threw fitful light on the wet cobblestones. Here and there the ghostly shapes of naked, dead men in the streets were visible and then the glimpses were gone as the moon or the clouds moved on. They had been stripped in the Arab scavenging tradition that none of the Australians could come to terms with.

The silence was broken by the groans of the wounded and dying, somewhere in a lane or a back alley. The helpless sounds were overridden by the howls of stray dogs.

'Occasionally a rifle shot reverberating through the basalt piles,' the 10th Light Horse Regiment's Major Arthur Olden wrote, 'told of the native [Arab] making trial of his new-found toy—probably improving the happy circumstances of our presence in his domain by settling longstanding grievances with his neighbour.'[3]

There was a disturbance in a courtyard in the town's centre where 800 Turks were being guarded by the 8th Regiment. Prisoners were caught looking up to a building high on a hillside. Regular lamplight flashes were seen at a window. The guards watched. The code being signalled was not an Allied one. The enemy had to be sending the signals. An Australian marksman fired at the window, shattering it. The lamp stopped flashing. But half an hour later signals began again from another window. The same sniper fired again. The light went out once more. This happened several times, and the Australians were now alerted to this suspected espionage activity. A volley of shots from several trooper snipers snuffed out the light, and most likely the agent, for the night.

•

Wilson was satisfied with the day, but there was no call for cele-bration. The yeomanry and the 5th Mounted Brigade had not been as quick or successful as the 10th and were not going to be at Es Salt until the next morning. At last he made direct radio contact with Chauvel. The revised plan was to pursue the enemy 11 kilometres along the Amman road to Hill 2900. Wilson complied with this but not with the force he would otherwise have used if the others had arrived overnight. He sent out 37-year-old dentist Olden with two squadrons and four machine guns. Olden covered 9 kilometres in the moonlight by midnight before encountering stiff opposition. Olden encamped and remained on watch. His orders were to meet up with the Beni Sakhr west of Hill 2900.

The idea was that they would combine to stop any counter-punch by the Turks from Amman towards Shunet Nimrin, where Shea's 60th Division and the Turks in the fort there had battled to a stalemate. But the question as always was, would the Arabs cooperate?

Chapter 19

'Failure Be Damned!'

During the night the Turks threw a new bridge over the Jordan opposite the Mafid Jozelle plain. The next morning Chauvel sent the Camel Brigade to attack and destroy it, but it was too late. Von Sanders was annoyed about the loss of Es Salt. He realised that Shea's 60th Division had not been able to take Shunet Nimrin and was in trouble. The German sent more troops of the Eighth Turkish Army to the town.

At the same time, the Beni Sakhr tribe failed to show west of the town. Had they done so, the reinforcements of enemy troops and supplies from Amman would have been cut off, or at least held up, perhaps enough to have had an impact further east at Shunet Nimrin. It was the second time in a month that the Arabs had failed in their support of the British. Lawrence was not to blame this time. But the pattern disturbed the British officers and rank and file. The distrust from earlier incidents, beginning with the Arabs (in the pay of the Turks) massacring of British Yeomanry in the Sinai in April 1916, was maintained. If the Arabs were to play a significant part in the capture of Damascus, as Lawrence hoped, more leadership and determination had to come from them. Questions were raised about their value and their allegiances, although they could not be left out of Allenby's overall plans. They were a political necessity, no matter how poorly they contributed in combined operations. Besides this, they were doing well coming up through Jordan.

·

Early on 1 May Chauvel sent up air reconnaissance to find the Beni Sakhr, but they had dispersed. He ruled them out of his wider force and concentrated on options without them. Reinforced Turkish Infantry and Cavalry attacked, outnumbering Grant's 4th Light Horse forces by four to one.

A mound called Red Hill on the west Jordan bank was held by just one squadron of Grant's 4th Brigade and it was soon overwhelmed. The Turks were now either side of the Jordan and threatening to march south. Chauvel felt Grant's communications were now under threat. He ordered him to dispose his artillery so that if he were forced to withdraw he could take the big guns with him. But events were happening too fast for such rational plans. Grant, who had expressed his concerns to Chauvel on the previous afternoon, when the latter visited him at the front, decided on a hasty withdrawal. He did not think he had time to take his big artillery pieces with him. Nine of twelve were lost to the enemy, along with other weaponry and supplies.

There was a danger now that the Turks would overrun his retreating force. But the experienced troopers fell back with typical discipline over broken ground and steep slopes.

•

Chauvel sent Major General Edward Chaytor with a regiment of the reserve brigade and part of the New Zealand Brigade to protect Grant's retreating flank as the 4th Light Horse slipped back down the territory east of the Jordan. Chauvel ordered Shea to push harder against Shunet Nimrin, preventing pressure on the horsemen, who with Chaytor's reinforcements were soon repelling all Turkish attacks. Meanwhile, Englishman Major General Henry Hodgson commanding the Australian Mounted was pressing on with the plan to attack Shunet Nimrin from the rear. Yet there were concerns that with all tracks held by the Turks, except the one he had arrived on, he too might be cut off.

On 2 May, Chauvel directed more air reconnaissance. A huge number of enemy troops were photographed arriving at Amman. Already outnumbered by the Turkish forces in combat, and with ammunition, water, food and medical supplies a growing problem, he made contact with the Australian Mounted. It was under pressure from the north and east. Chauvel decided on a general withdrawal.

He had to consult Allenby first and the Chief visited Chauvel's battle HQ 4 kilometres south of the front on the Jordan at Ghoraniye. Allenby examined all the evidence. He concurred with Chauvel, without showing real emotion either way about the situation.

At 4 p.m. on 3 May, the order went out for the entire force to pull back.

•

Wilson and his 3rd Brigade had the longest trip, from Es Salt, but their passage along the tracks back to the Jordan was helped by the Australian Flying Corps' No. 3 Squadron. It piled up its planes with bombs and rolled them out on the Turks on the trail of the horsemen and followed this up with machine-gun strafing.

By midnight on 4 May the last of the Light Horse brigades crossed to the Jordan's west bank. The four-day enterprise, more than a raid and less than a breakthrough, was over.

•

Chauvel expressed his disappointment about the failure to Allenby.

'Failure be damned!' a surprisingly ebullient Allenby responded. 'It has been a great success.'[1]

Chauvel, the realist, was unsure about this response. The casualty figures were one way of giving the outcome of Es Salt a positive 'spin'. His force had 1649 casualties—split two-thirds infantry, one-third Light Horse; the Turks had more than 2000. Chauvel's force brought back nearly a thousand prisoners, and normally in this type of more-than-a-raid mission that would constitute a near win. Yet Chauvel factored in the loss of those big guns and the withdrawal. He would never claim it as a victory, even when Allenby later circulated a congratulatory message to all the troops which referred to the 'unity which led to success'.

In the compulsory post-mortem, the Chief was mildly critical, the way he would be even in a clear-cut victory, such as at the last Beersheba–Gaza battle. Chauvel was rapped on the knuckles for not strengthening Grant's Red Hill flank, when that officer had called for reinforcements. Chauvel was further taken to task for not directing Grant to tighten his defence. It was considered too dispersed. The report concluded that this led to the big guns being lost, which provoked some pertinent questions from the War Office in London.

Allenby's overall rosy assessment would have been in part because he wished to bury his own blunders. His 'demonstration' on 18 April that alerted the Turks was a fundamental mistake. He erred over his decisions relating to the Beni Sakhr. If he had called for Lawrence to liaise with the Arabs, or if he had ignored them and waited two weeks for another British infantry division, the outcome may well have been different. Again, the Arabs' 'no show' at a pivotal point in a battle was critical. It led to Turkish reinforcements moving from Amman towards the Jordan without opposition just when Chauvel's combined infantry and trooper dispositions could have tipped the scales his way. This was especially so after Wilson's sensational taking of Es Salt by nightfall on the first day.

Another factor was the rushed planning by Allenby and his staff. He had been clutching for a big breakthrough before he could be forced to hold his positions and feed off his troops to the Western Front. Every part of the plan had to work for this to come off, and it did not. This left the Eastern Expeditionary Force in limbo until events unfolded in Europe.

Allenby and his staff called this second attempt at victory over the Jordan a 'raid' to further diminish its significance.

•

Chauvel decided to sit out the summer 10 kilometres east of Jericho in the lower reaches of the Jordan River valley and endure the terrible heat and dust rather than move into the hills. This meant denying the Turks' occupation of the river lowland from the Dead Sea to 25 kilometres north.

•

The lull in fighting from May to September 1918 allowed time for ceremonial events and some medal-giving. Allenby decided to award decorations for the battles around the Jordan and chose a parade area near a road 5 kilometres north of Jericho. The Anzac Mounted Division lined up. Chauvel, Brigadier General E.F. Trew and Allenby were chauffeured to the division's HQ and switched to horses for the trot up the road to the parade. Allenby mounted, twisted around and belted the stallion on the rump. The waler, Bill the Bastard—the impressive horse involved in the rescue of Australian troopers at Romani—was not used to this.

'He put his head down and pig-rooted into the bush and dust,' a witness, Lieutenant Colonel Sir Michael Bruxner, said.[2]

Chauvel took off after the Chief, praying he would not fall off, reached him and reined in the indignant horse and the startled Allenby. As they trotted back, Chauvel saw that Trew on the other side of the road was also in trouble with his waler, who had reacted when Bill bolted. Chauvel galloped after Trew, settled his waler and drew him up with Allenby. The three riders proceeded to the parade ground to receive the salute and carry on with the ceremony.

Not a word was said about the incident. But all who witnessed it knew who the gifted horseman was among them. Rumours spread later that the famous balladeer Banjo Paterson, who ran the mounted's huge remount operation at Moascar, had deliberately assigned the aggressive Bill to Allenby. This was said to be revenge for the British decree that no horses would be returned to Australia after the war.

•

Summer hit hard and early. By the end of the first week in May, the heat was wicked and the flies vile. The temperature climbed a fraction each day until 40 degrees Celsius was considered cool. The heavy traffic needed to service Chauvel's mighty corps of men and horses (the 2000 camels had been 'retired' from this region) ground up the fine dirt, which became dust. Within weeks the whole area was covered in a light bed of powdered clay.

•

Even though major action had died down for a few weeks, by mid-May 1918 on both the major Great War fronts, the opposing forces were gearing up for final thrusts that would attempt to end the conflicts in their respective zones.

Chapter 20

The Commander's Top Picks

On the Western Front in France, Monash's whole outlook changed on 12 May when Birdwood was appointed to take charge of the new British Fifth Army and Monash would now command the Australian Army Corps. This had been decided by the British War Council, which behind-the-scenes meant George V and Haig in consultation. Monash's big part in stopping the German Michael assault and his exceptional work over the five-week period had convinced Haig and the council, with the King's ready acquiescence, that Monash was the man for the Australian command. It would be a huge leap in responsibility and mean a corresponding jump in independence for the Australian force which, with 166,000 Australians in it, along with other divisions from different countries parked with it, would mean a corps of more than 200,000 soldiers at any one time. This would make it the biggest single 'functioning army' ('corps') under one command of the twenty on the Allied side on the Western Front. There was nothing quite as big among the German force either.

If Monash was worn out from the previous two months buzzing around his part of the Front, it was forgotten with this exhilarating new opportunity. And if there was one man on either side who could take advantage of this strong new working entity, it was him. It would allow him to exercise his big-thinking tactics and strategy. Monash now had some of the tools and machinery he needed to build a bridge to Allied victory. He had yet to lose a battle that he had both planned and commanded, and this inspired him to work as fast as possible towards ending the war.

His first act was to make appointments. He dumped the British regulars and gave 1st Division to the tough-minded Major General Thomas William Glasgow, a Queenslander and Boer War veteran; 2nd Division went to another favourite, Sydney architect Charles Rosenthal; Scot Ewen George Sinclair-Maclagan, with Indian and Boer War experience, retained 4th Division; and Perth architect Talbot Hobbs held the 5th. These four were not Monash clones, but they all had an aggressive mindset. They would never have a 'fallback' mentality or crack under pressure. They were all cool-thinking, intelligent men. That left one further appointment: commander of 3rd Division, which was dear to him. It proved problematic. Monash was offered James Whiteside McCay, a 'rival' from his school days at Scotch College, Melbourne, who beat him to dux of the school in 1880. (Monash was dux the following year.) But McCay was not popular with his superiors or those under his command. He was too 'abrasive' and had upset Birdwood, who offered him to Monash for 3rd Division knowing full well that Monash would not appoint him. McCay had felt the strain of command and was once rejected for the commander-in-chief role of 1st AIF himself. After then being passed over for the 3rd Division, he was effectively demoted to being a depot commander. It gave Monash no joy to reject him, but left open the position, which Birdwood and White suggested should go to White's good friend Major General Sir John Gellibrand. He had displayed heroic leadership, notably at the failed Battles of Bullecourt in April–May 1917, in which 10,000 Australians died, due largely to British General Hubert Gough's impetuosity, coupled with poor planning. But Gellibrand, like McCay, was prickly with those above and below him in rank. Gellibrand had not endeared himself to Monash while in Egypt by raising questions about his suitability to command because of his German background. After much persuasion from Birdwood and White, Monash accepted him with reservations. One of Monash's greatest characteristics was putting himself above the innuendo, rumour and false accusations about his allegiances. His one recorded complaint was in an ironic aside in a private letter to his wife. He rode the bumps of vilification with finesse, strength and self-confidence to a point where no one, except Bean, now even remarked about his German-Jewish background.

Monash's only concern was for the men in 3rd Division, who would have to wear Gellibrand's at times rough and rude manner. It quickly became an issue when he clashed with Brigadier (later) Sir Walter Ramsay McNicoll, who complained to Monash that Gellibrand was bombastic and overbearing. Gellibrand countered by saying that McNicoll's 10th Brigade was slack and undisciplined. Monash was soon in mediation. McNicoll wished to resign or transfer to another division but Monash would have none of it. He had a high regard for the brigadier, who was one of the better and more courageous combat leaders, and did not want him to leave. Monash played peacemaker and got the two to attempt to work together. It was not an ideal situation. Gellibrand remained harsh in manner and McNicoll kept out of his way as much as possible.

McNicoll had the highest regard for Monash's abilities as a commander and always accepted his toughness and demands on the battlefield. He knew from experience that Monash was a master of tactics and decisions in the heat of combat. But aggression was one thing; Gellibrand's bullying and bluster in tense moments was another. Monash asked him to give Gellibrand a chance and quietly ordered the new commander to soft-peddle on the brigadier, reminding him that combat leaders of his calibre were not thick on the ground. Monash had some doubts about Gellibrand's will to win, but he respected his capacities enough to accept this command 'inheritance' or political appointment.

The new-look AIF commandership was now more or less in Monash's image: Australian with a voluntary citizen-soldier flavour. His own staff members were mainly his own appointments, although it is a moot point if he wanted or inherited his chief-of-staff, 34-year-old drover's son, Brigadier General Thomas Blamey, a former teacher from Wagga Wagga in New South Wales. He had a good record on Gallipoli. But his reputation for working and playing hard had preceded him. His leisure pursuits included a penchant for heavy boozing and careless 'womanising', particularly when on leave in Paris's Pigalle. Ambitious, sharp-minded 'Tom' was not alone in these predilections, and Monash could hardly reprimand him for them. Perhaps the only difference in their desire for female company, or the generic womanising, when not at the front, was in *class*. Monash preferred the company of the best-presented, most cultured French courtesans, especially his friend at the Folies Bergère; Blamey enjoyed being entertained at brothels. Monash kept his dalliances discreet but for elliptical hints, written in pencil in his little red Collins notebooks, which meant they could be erased easily. Blamey was often seen at houses of ill-repute frequented by front-line soldiers. Some of them were pleased to see a leading staff man near the top of the Australian command lowering himself to the level of the diggers, whose means, if they were so inclined, only allowed them to dally with street prostitutes or those in the lesser brothels. Other soldiers were not impressed with such rustic, off-hand behaviour from someone setting the standards and rules of discipline in the 1st AIF.

Within reason, Monash cared only for Blamey's capacity for hard application to the toughest of jobs. The commander found his new chief of staff 'had an infinite capacity for taking pains', which when translated meant Blamey worked to meet Monash's demands without complaint. There were reservations about Blamey being a regular soldier, who had been trained at the prestigious British Quetta Staff College in India. Monash noted this background with a hint of disdain but added that, despite this, Blamey was 'not a pedant'. It was a mild, backhanded compliment. Monash, the most broadly educated and experienced of soldiers, had himself not been through Australia's Duntroon or any British formal army training. He had contempt, to a point, for those who were not lateral thinking, or who had not had the raw experience of the battlefield, or command. But in some ways this was what Monash wanted. He said also that Blamey was 'thoroughly versed in the technique of staff work, and the minutiae of all procedure'.[1]

This was a prerequisite by the new commander, who crossed all t's, dotted all i's and demanded deep communication and understanding of battle plans. It was apparent from early on that Blamey would carry out his boss's directives to the letter. And Monash soon found that his new man was a 'head-kicker' who would carry out the unpalatable role of 'bully boy' if required. Monash soon realised, too, that Blamey was fearless in his work. It did not matter whom he confronted on the corps' behalf. He did what had to be done without reflection.

Monash accepted Blamey, but was not happy with his new administrative head, the 'charming and amusing' British Brigadier General R.A. Carruthers, a close friend of Birdwood, who, at this early stage as head of the AIF administration, had the power of such appointments. Carruthers would be in place to keep a close eye on Monash for Birdwood, who needed a 'spy' in the staff ranks. But Monash found Carruthers lazy and wanted him replaced by the outstanding soldier and army 'manager' Major General Bruche from Melbourne. Like Monash, he had a German background, and Birdwood said he didn't want this 'issue' revived, which was a most limited argument for omitting a top staff man. Monash was furious and wrote in private that he felt like reminding Birdwood of King George V's background. Monash was only too well aware that Bruche was extremely unlucky. In 1916 soldiers with his background, perhaps as a result of the kerfuffle over Monash's origins, were not allowed to serve on the battlefield overseas, although they could be used for staff work. This 'incredibly stupid' ruling, Monash remarked, had robbed Australia of an excellent staff man and commander.

Monash had no such qualms about his only other senior British officer, Brigadier General L.D. Fraser, a commander of heavy artillery, whom he regarded as the best in the business. This was an area of Monash expertise and on their very first discussion, these two 'gunners' had a rapport. Another capable assistant was the urbane, 26-year-old Australian Major R.G. 'Dick' Casey, who was from a new generation. Overall this left Monash with an AIF staff that had a blend of maturity and youth, volunteers and regulars, Australians and a smattering of experienced British officers. It was an excellent pool on which the new commander could draw for ideas, inspiration, experience and intelligence, Carruthers notwithstanding.

Chapter 21

Birdwood's Bolstering

Haig and co. had chosen Monash for many reasons, the first being his brilliance, accepted by all. He was also believed to be a team player; someone who would be more compliant with British and Allied wishes than Currie had been with the Canadians and Pershing was with the Americans. In effect, he was seen as already inside the 'British Club', almost as if he had come through the British system, with the culminating anointment of the King of the Club, the former British Navy sailor George V. Monash was expected to bring his own ideas and plans but not to 'rock the boat' and give the British High Command further headaches.

But Monash, from the day of his appointment, was not planning to be a passive operator like the competent, popular but unimaginative Birdwood. Monash was bursting to bring all five divisions together under his control, never again to be farmed out to British commands in losing battles. He could have been given 100 divisions and the entire Allied force and it would have made no difference to his outlook. It would have been a challenge but not daunting. For the moment, however, more than 200,000 soldiers—80 per cent of them his beloved diggers—would do.

The British appointment of Monash was not a fait accompli. It had to be 'sold' to Hughes, and while he understood Monash's reputation, he was miffed that he was effectively being 'told' of the appointment rather than being asked for his choice. Hughes, whose complexes and inferiorities were only matched by his ego and cunning, was suspicious.

Birdwood, who was well liked by Hughes, was asked by Haig to write and explain the selection to the Australian Government. Birdwood made it clear to Haig that he would have preferred to maintain the job he had, rather than take on the new British Fifth Army. Instead of a warrior force, he would now have to train and encourage novices, who would never reach the level of experience, drive and fighting ability of the diggers. Nevertheless, Birdwood accepted the High Command's decisions and delivered a clever, yet direct, letter to Hughes. Birdwood felt there were only two real candidates, his own deputy Brudenell White, and Monash. He adored White, who was the administrative brain behind him, and did all the 'heavy lifting' in the boring paperwork with diligence and thoroughness. But Monash was White's senior. He had commanded in battle; White had not. Birdwood believed that White would be malleable with his masters in the British High Command, whereas he felt certain that Monash would go his own way and aim to make the AIF a powerhouse, and although he never expressed it to Haig, might be as unmanageable as Currie and Pershing. But then again, Birdwood knew that Haig and the King wanted Monash, and in turn he knew that the Australian would impress and finesse them to his way of thinking, or at least put forward a compelling, well-researched case on every single occasion.

Birdwood wrote: 'Monash has commanded first a brigade then a division in this force without a day's intermission since our training days in Egypt in Jan. 1915 to the present time. Of his ability, there can be no possible doubt, nor of his keenness and knowledge. Also, he has had almost unvarying success in all the operations undertaken by his division, which has, I know, the greatest confidence in him.'[1]

This declaration of certitude was a far cry from early 1916 when Birdwood dithered over whether to recommend Monash for command of the 3rd Division. Birdwood had been influenced by some ignorant thinking and rumours about Monash's dedication to the Australian force and the British cause. This had not been helped by C.E.W. Bean's dislike for him, which augmented the racism that had made rumour-mongers wonder if he was perhaps a German spy. Birdwood addressed this, saying: 'This [the rumour-mongering] has, I think, been entirely lived down, as far as the AIF is concerned, by his good work.'

This 'work' was defeating Germans. Gone were the feeble fears that Monash might baulk at fighting them. Birdwood concluded: 'I do not think we can in justice overlook in any way his undoubted claims and equally undoubted ability to fill the appointment.'[2]

Hughes knew Monash well enough to make his own call. The prime minister's only real issue was that he had an inferiority complex concerning this highly educated, high-achieving individual. Keith Murdoch had also created doubts after first being given the hint by Haig as early as March that Monash was favoured. Hughes had inherited Murdoch from former prime minister Andrew Fisher after his commission of the journalist to assess Gallipoli. Murdoch had been Hughes' agent in pushing hard in English elite circles for the formation of the Australian Corps, and had become a strong political player in his own right. Now the AIF was shaping to be a strong entity operating under the control of Rawlinson's Fourth Army but with its own Australian command, Murdoch wanted to cap his influence over its formation with his choice of its commander. He had no outstanding candidate himself and was here influenced by Bean urging that his good friend Brudenell White should be the man. These two journalists were now stepping well outside their roles as 'observers', by attempting to create history themselves. This was not unusual (and isn't today, with the even greater influence of the media) and they may have achieved their aims if the choice had been simply down to the prime minister. But the decision was being made by those running a world war. It had critical ramifications, especially as the sizeable new entity was likely to have a real impact on the running of events, and perhaps the outcome of the war itself.

Murdoch and Bean were making the case that the British High Command was trampling on Australian sovereign rights by choosing the commander. This played to Hughes' inferiorities and struggle to be heard or have influence on the world stage. Bean's anti-Monash vitriol could be traced back to Monash ticking him off for his lack of reporting on 2nd Division activity, particularly the gutsy efforts of his 4th Brigade, on Gallipoli. The English-educated, thin-skinned Bean was not used to being corrected, especially by someone with Monash's background. It didn't help that Monash showed disdain for his 'pedestrian' reporting compared with that of the United Kingdom's Ellis Ashmead-Bartlett, whose writing showed far more flair. But Bean was going to fight someone he described as a 'pushy Jew' running the most important Australian post, and under the circumstances of the Great War, a position with greater influence and importance than the prime minister's. Racism was a common proposition during the era, yet Bean had taken it to a new, articulated level. A further factor was that he and Murdoch believed that Monash would be under the thumb of the British High Command, which demonstrated they had no real comprehension of his mentality. No choice could have had Australian interests more at heart. It was subtle but obvious from all Monash's public utterances and messages to the troops.

Bean first heard the news of Monash's appointment on 16 May from Birdwood, who said he would be taking White with him to the Fifth Army as his chief of staff. Birdwood would still be head of AIF administration. Bean began creating rumours and innuendo that Monash had self-advertised for the job and that such immodesty was not befitting the post he coveted. But not even Murdoch backed up this fabrication. Monash did not have to promote himself; the people that counted knew his record and manner. He was recognised as driven and ambitious. His inexhaustible work ethic had ruffled feathers, but it was this that had gone a long way to his achievement.

However, Bean and Murdoch kept their two-man cabal going by trying to manufacture support for White and to denigrate Monash. At an official reception for Hughes, Andrew Fisher, who had been High Commissioner to London since 1916, showed contempt for Monash. Birdwood told him bluntly that he was completely ignorant of the issue and of the new commander's capacities. Murdoch overheard the heated exchange and asked Birdwood: 'Do you really think Monash is fit to command the corps?'

'Of course,' Birdwood snapped back, 'he can do it better than I.'[3]

Birdwood later went out of his way to express his confidence in Monash to Hughes, telling him that Generals Plumer and Rawlinson had great faith in him. He also informed Hughes that the support went even higher than that, without saying he meant Haig and the King. It was a way of telling Hughes that Monash had the support of the people who counted in the British cause. It did not really matter if the Australian prime minister, or a couple of meddling journalists, were not among them.

•

On 28 May the US 28th Regiment of the US 1st Division went into action for the first time in attack (rather than in defence), on the Aisne River, 160 kilometres north-east of Paris in the French sector. They targeted the German salient around the village of Cantigny, 6 kilometres north-west of Montdidier. It was a modest operation on a front of 3 kilometres, which they penetrated 1.6 kilometres and captured. It was a start. On June their 2nd Division took up a second-line position to support the defences of Chateau-Thierry. A day later, a machine gun battalion went into action in that sector. On 6 June the 2nd Division counterattacked at Belleau Wood, to the west of Chateau-Thierry. These were minor forays that ended in significance when on 25 June they lost more than 2000 men in taking this German stronghold. It stamped the Americans as involved and committed. It was doubtful the Americans would have a major impact in the big, critical battles before September. But the psychology was important. The Germans would be aware of, but not yet alarmed about, the further Allied intervention. Monash, too, looked on, and called for American battle reports, which he studied with his usual detailed application. Now he had a free hand to plan battles without major initial interference, apart from 'edits' from his superiors. His mind was once more focused on how to integrate the Americans with his own expanded force.

Chapter 22

The Rise and Rise

Monash was exhilarated by the challenge of his new command. There would always be problems with Hughes, but if he could be parried or kept at bay, there were now only three superiors in the Allied force that he would have to sway to have his battle plans implemented. He was like a marathon runner with a new lease of energy as the last few kilometres were in sight and only a few runners in front of him. Monash was about 'winning'—1918 and the north of France was the background for the challenge of his life.

His immediate 'boss' was 54-year-old Rawlinson. Rawlinson's Fourth Army Chief of Staff Archibald Montgomery-Massingberd was the second party Monash would have to surmount, or persuade to his thinking. The third was Haig, who was already more than amenable to Monash, but Monash would have to find ways to make sure the commander-in-chief saw what he was presenting, which was not all that difficult. Montgomery-Massingberd and Rawlinson knew that Haig always wanted to know Monash's thoughts and positions on everything.

Monash already had a strong understanding of the three of them: their motives, fears and aspirations. He had learnt their characters, foibles, strengths and weaknesses. They were all army careerists without Monash's broad education, or comprehension of all the accoutrements of modern war. Now they were bowing to his experience as a battlefield commander, and as one who had the support of all those who worked with him, including Generals Butler, Plumer and Godley. They would not bend to his will, but they would give him a proper hearing on anything he wished.

Monash was one of the very few in the British Army that had not voiced an opinion on a big counterattack now that the Germans appeared to have run out of steam after their own mighty thrust from 21 March. Instead, he was putting his thoughts on paper in the form of a grand plan to end the war. He did not believe the rumours and comments from enemy prisoners, whom he personally interrogated, that the Germans were ready for a further large-scale attack. He felt it was the Allies that now had to make their own gigantic push. But first he had to demonstrate on a small scale what he had in mind. The village of Hamel was to be the setting.

•

Before he could implement his scheme for Hamel, he had to impose his will, a 'moral ascendancy', over his force, starting at the top with his staff. He wanted them to think as one, and he set the tone. Monash refused no one their ideas yet there had to be a single administrative and tactical policy. He did not act like a dictator. He first made all methods and decisions clear through consultation. He insisted on intense conferences, something Birdwood had avoided. He encouraged the flow and free exchange of ideas that led to the final battle plans. Monash was then prepared to go on the offensive with confidence, knowing that he had created a well-oiled machine.

He then turned his mind to Hamel to start his campaigns as a corps commander. The plan centred on the speedy 90-minute surgical removal of the German force there. Once that was achieved there was no immediate impediment for pushing his big, war-ending plan that was evolving every day. The village sat neatly on the other side of Vaitre Wood, just over 2 kilometres north-west of Villers-Bretonneux and his Bertangles HQ. Monash used his binoculars to monitor Hamel and could see German soldiers wandering around. The ground in front of them was not undulating—just right for a tank attack. He jumped in his Rolls-Royce, a perk he appreciated, with Blamey, and drove 30 kilometres for a meeting with Major General H.J. Elles, the commander of the British Tank Corps attached to the Fourth Army. Elles was excited by Monash's interest. There had been rumours that his Tank Corps would be disbanded. Here was a general with a big reputation who wanted to have a closer look.

They were shown the latest models: the Mark V and Mark V Star. They appeared similar to their predecessor, a tank that had let the Australians down at Bullecourt. But there were big differences. The Mark V only needed one pair of hands to drive it, instead of four. Monash observed that the special gears, the greater power and 'improved balance of its whole design, gave it increased mobility, facility in turning and immunity from floundering in ground even of the most broken and unclear character'.[1]

The more powerful engines rarely broke down. A reinforced armour shell could take anything short of a direct hit from a field gun. They were quicker too, or at least not as slow, at 5 kilometres an hour. Until now, the tank had been viewed as a defensive weapon, one that formed a mobile shield for infantry. Monash wanted to know if they could be used as offensive weapons. Elles was adamant that they could. He spoke effusively about it leading raids and causing havoc behind enemy lines. A direct artillery hit would be near impossible if the tank rolled into an enemy camp and smashed up an HQ. That made the vehicle nigh-on unstoppable in surprise attacks. Haig would allow this next year, Elles informed them. Monash was not interested in 1919. His Hamel trial run and then the proposal for a huge counterattack to finish the Great War were more immediate ambitions.

Was it possible now? Monash asked. Yes, was the positive reply.

Monash and Blamey returned to Bertangles with a daring possibility to consider.

'I proposed an operation for the recapture of Hamel,' Monash wrote. It was conditional on the use of tanks, a small increase in his artillery and an addition to the AIF's 'air resources'.[2]

Tanks dominated the first draft plan of attack. But he needed to win over the allegiance of his men, who were no lovers of these oversized mechanical slugs. They had heard only bad stories about them. Those who had experience of them directly were no fan either. There was another pertinent factor. Tanks would usurp their role in the battle. These men hadn't come to fight on the Somme as second-stringers to armoured vehicles. Monash arranged for the participants to bus to Vaux, a little village tucked away in a quiet valley north-west of Amiens, where they spent a day with Elles's Corps. The show turned into a party. Groups of soldiers rode around in them. Their forward- and reverse-gear flexibility was demonstrated.

Mock machine-gun nests were constructed. The tanks rolled and backed over them. The soldiers examined the result. It was as if a boot heel had been brought down on a beetle. The drivers and the infantrymen worked on special manoeuvres and ways to communicate.

They left Vaux pleased at the thought of having this powerful new weapon with them in an attack. Monash could now sit down and plan Hamel with tanks prominent. He took in comments from his battalion commanders, who nevertheless still didn't wish their infantry to play an inferior role to this new weapon.

Monash thrashed out an arrangement with the flexible Brigadier General Anthony Courage of the 5th Tank Brigade. Courage, like Elles, was thrilled to think that a commander such as Monash was now not just inspecting his weapons, but was set to use them. As a result he was most agreeable to almost all of Monash's proposals.

First, he allowed the infantry commanders to be in charge of his tanks. Second, he agreed that his vehicles would advance level with the infantry. And third, he was willing to risk the tanks coming in close with the infantry behind an artillery barrage, the danger being that the taller tanks, at nearly 3 metres in height, could be hit by shells falling short.

Monash knew that the tanks would be the main weapon, even if just as intimidation. The infantry would back them up by attacking strong enemy positions that the tanks might find difficult to overrun. The soldiers would also 'mop up and consolidate the ground captured'. This was military jargon for destroying or capturing anything or anyone the tanks missed. It also had a special 'Monash-speak' tone about it. He was always thinking about how he would protect his men and it was logical that the tanks would in reality be the lead 'weapon' in any attack, despite the soldiers being made to feel they were still taking the brunt of the enemy response. It was Monash's subtle way of letting the technology do the heavy hitting while preserving his men at every possible moment.

There would be three waves of about 8000 infantry—eight battalions—in total, and tanks: 15 machines in the first, 21 in the second and nine with the 'mopping up' infantry. This request, for 55 tanks to deal with Hamel, was met by raised eyebrows all round. Birdwood and White did not think the battle was necessary; Rawlinson and Montgomery-Massingberd had for months put the idea of tanks well out of their thoughts, except to take men from the tank corps and put them on the front line as soldiers because of the shortfall of men. This had been necessitated by Lloyd George in his ongoing behind-the-scenes struggle, so far unsuccessful, to get rid of Haig, or at least restrict him so much that he stepped down.

Monash wanted to use one of his conjuring specialties, cannisters of flavoured smoke. They would be fired every morning for five days at the proposed zero hour just before dawn to accustom the enemy to the smoke. This incorporated two Monash innovations. First, on the day of the attack, it was hoped that the smokescreen on the flanks and across the entire 6-kilometre front, with the left flank on the Somme, would hide the attack. Planes would be used along with the artillery to provide noise to hide the squeal of the advancing tanks. Second, the enemy would have no idea if the smoke was harmless or a deadly gas. They would don their gasmasks.

'This would obscure his vision,' Monash predicted, 'hamper his freedom of action, and reduce his powers of resistance.'[3]

Monash added battery emplacements on the Villers-Bretonneux plateau to hit German anti-tank guns (and tanks if the enemy had any).

Rawlinson received the plan on 21 June. In the end, Monash's arguments for taking Hamel and using a modest number of tanks won through. Haig ticked off on them both without a second thought, with the attitude that if Monash wanted to experiment, there had to be something good and positive in it. Four days later, Monash felt a little surge of satisfaction and power with this approval for the first major battle plan of his corps commandership.

Chapter 23

The Confrontation: Monash vs Hughes

Bertangles and the surrounding areas were swamped on 30 June with conferences for the Battle of Hamel. Monash had inculcated a culture of communication and clarity from the moment he created the 4th Brigade in 1914. Now he had control of the entire AIF, his style of management was developing in all divisions. Officers and commanders from brigades and battalions who may have been uncomfortable with articulating their thoughts, or lazy about putting them on paper, were rehearsing their speeches or re-drafting their ideas to impress, please and fulfil the corps commander's demands. Soldiers and officers who had no idea about the operations of the other arms of the AIF military now had at least a superficial comprehension of all of them. Cross-fertilisation of ideas between artillery, machine-gun, infantry, tank, flying and ambulance corps, and other officers was rife as they sought to plan their coordination in battle.

Monash held the biggest conference. It lasted four and a half hours and 250 officers attended, sitting through the ticking off of his 133 items on an agenda that ranged over everything from the supply of gasmasks and water to reserve machine guns. Nothing raised and unresolved before the conference was missed. Every key officer had to explain his plans. The others were encouraged to air opinions, opposing views and problems. Monash hated late changes. He wanted to walk away from the meeting with final decisions and proposals fixed and in place.

The conference marked the end of the planning stage. Monash was as happy as he could be that every major or minor issue had been ticked off and tied up.

The battle was set to commence before dawn on 4 July 1918.

•

Early in July Monash had two VIP visitors. He was happy to see the first, Haig, who was impressed with the arrangements and, as ever, praised the new corps commander. But Monash protested to Birdwood about Prime Minister Hughes' plans to turn up the next day. 'The whole business is extremely awkward,' Monash said.

With three days to go before Hamel, the commander's mind was immersed in the battle plans, and 'Mr Hughes has chosen a time which could hardly be more inconvenient.'[1]

But Birdwood didn't need to remind Monash of the continuing plot to replace him. And earlier, Monash himself had implored

Hughes to visit the front and see his AIF in action. Reluctantly, the commander had to set aside vital time for the visit.

Hughes came with his deputy Sir Joseph Cook, the Navy Minister, late in the morning, along with a retinue of pressmen and photographers. They were both unaware of the secret plan for Hamel. Monash decided the only way he could handle the visit and keep abreast of the build-up to the battle was to let them in on the secret plan. This way Hughes became aware of the impact and power of the man he was thinking about firing.

'Monash told me his plans for battle,' Hughes said on reflection after the war. 'He was no swashbuckler nor was his plan that of a bull at a gate. It was enterprising without being foolhardy, as was to be expected of a man who had been trained as an engineer and had given profound study to the art of war. Monash always understood thoroughly the ground he was to fight on. Maps lived for him.'[2]

Hughes asked him what the battle would cost in casualties.

'He had made his plans so that they would be as low as possible,' the prime minister commented. 'His estimate was about 300, including walking cases. This stamped him, in my mind, as an outstanding figure of World War One. He was the only General with whom I came in close contact who seemed to me to give due weight to the cost of victory. He said: "This is what we want to do; this is the way to do it with the least cost in human suffering."'[3]

While Hughes was forming a positive impression of Monash, Bean and Murdoch were powering on behind the scenes to undermine him. Bean had primed White for taking over by lying to him about Monash being on the brink of accepting a bribe to leave the corps to become a full general. Murdoch had built his false propaganda about Monash being unpopular with his key officers into a major deception for Hughes' consumption. The prime minister until this moment had been set to announce Monash's replacement by White. But White, honourably, had let Monash know in a letter that he wasn't supporting the move. He had washed his hands of the plotting and plotters. If Monash agreed to leave the corps then, White told him, the basis for his resisting the Bean/Murdoch scheming would be 'knocked from under' him. This was a polite way of pressuring Monash if he were contemplating 'retiring', which Bean had been peddling to White as a strong possibility.[4]

Hughes had not put anything to Monash by midday on 2 July. He was too busy being thrilled by the meetings and the activity at Bertangles and in the valley beyond it. He lunched with General Hobbs and his 5th Division staff (which included Bruche) and then had a private discussion with Hobbs about Monash. Hobbs recommended him as corps commander without equivocation and gave him a strong endorsement. He invited Hughes to speak with Bruche, who was effusive and said that Monash would prove to be the finest general of the war. Hughes then met with Rosenthal who told him that Monash was without doubt the out-standing man for the job. The prime minister was reminded that making any changes at this critical moment before a battle would prove a major problem for all officers.

At 2 p.m. Monash laid out the broad Hamel plan and had officers, who were coming to update him, brief Hughes and Cook as well. There was much poring over maps and viewing of the proposed battlefield with field glasses from vantage points.

In the early afternoon, Monash took them to inspect eight battalions of soldiers who were parading in full battle-gear in preparation for moving off to the assembly positions from which, on 3 July late at night, they would march into battle.

Both politicians were caught up in the electric atmosphere of anticipation. Monash invited them to address the troops.

At about 5.30 p.m., with the sun throwing long shadows, Hughes mounted a gun carriage in front of a West Australian battalion in full battledress, and began a speech.

'There was a major by my side,' Hughes recalled later. 'I found the shells flying overhead a little disturbing to the necessary flow of oratory.' He turned to the major and told him it was too noisy.

'Couldn't you let up a little?' Hughes asked him, 'I won't be long.'

'I'm sorry sir,' the major replied, 'but I can't do anything about it. That's the other fellow.'

The Germans were aiming their shells at Monash's HQ at Bertangles Chateau a kilometre away.

'Only a little flattening of the trajectory was needed to carry me out of France and into the next world,' Hughes noted. 'I finished my sterling oratory in short order.'[5]

'The stirring addresses,' Monash wrote, 'did much to hearten and stimulate the troops.'[6]

Hughes, in particular, was excited and in awe of his own power, in theory; this impressive volunteer force, whose divisions had built reputations, and which as a unified Australian Army in all but name, promised much.

Monash seized the moment. When they were alone for a few minutes at about 6 p.m., he told Hughes that he wanted to discuss the crisis over his commandership. Hughes thought it would be better to talk about it 'later'.

Monash wanted to address it then.

'I am bound to tell you,' he said eyeballing the prime minister, 'that the arrangement which would involve my removal from the command of this Corps would be in the highest degree distasteful to me. I would regard any removal as a degradation and a humiliation . . .'

Hughes broke in and, putting his hand on Monash's shoulder, said: 'You may thoroughly rely upon your issues in this matter receiving the greatest possible weight.'

It wasn't enough for Monash.

'I want you to know,' he said, 'I will not voluntarily forgo this command.'[7]

Hughes would have felt the full impact of Monash's intent. The commander was on *his* territory on the Western Front with *his* men. They were on the fringe of an important battle in Australia's history, set up by the man Hughes had come to confront. It was a long way from a safe politician's office in Melbourne. Even an expedient, at times brazen, politician like him knew that he could not remove a commander on the brink of a battle. There would be no sacking that day.

Monash would have been aware that he had stepped right into the controversial issue that he discussed in his 1912 essay, *The Lessons of the Wilderness Campaign—1864*: the conflict between a politician and a military commander over who should have the power over whom. Monash held the view that commanders should not be interfered with by politicians bending to 'public opinion'. In this case, Hughes seemed about to buckle to two journalists who had no claim to any opinion but their own, based on categorical falsehoods. Monash made it clear to Australia's prime elected official that he would not accept his order to go. Was it a bluff? How far would Monash go?

Soon after the discussion that never was, Monash penned a quick note to Birdwood, telling him of the Hughes meeting. He added a postscript for White, reassuring him that he trusted him.

After the strong endorsement of Monash by Hobbs, Bruche and Rosenthal at lunch, Hughes made a point of asking in private the remaining corps divisional commanders and several brigade leaders for their opinions of Monash, and if White should replace him. They all favoured Monash. Only the temperamental Gellibrand didn't give him a strong endorsement, yet even he acknowledged him as the best commander in the AIF. Hughes realised that Murdoch had not been straight with him about the feeling of these 'officers' he claimed opposed Monash.

That night, Hughes confronted Murdoch and demanded to know the names of the anti-Monash faction. The journalist had no response.

'Well, I haven't met a single one of them who thinks as you do,' Hughes said. 'They [the commanders] all say the same thing. You tell me there are men who think the other way [who want White]—where are they?'[8]

Murdoch remained mute. The prime minister set aside any decision, unless Hamel proved a disaster.

On 3 July, Monash took a few minutes to write a more considered note to White. He repeated his trust in him, but said he thought White's recent warning letter had been cryptic. There had to be something behind it. Then Monash put aside all the distractions. The timing of Hughes' visit had proved fortuitous. Monash was relieved that he was still at Bertangles and in charge.

Hamel now took his complete attention.

Chapter 24

Hamel: Rawlinson, Pershing Denied

There was one unforeseen problem that needed Monash's full concentration and nerve, otherwise Hamel would be called off. Monash had chosen 4 July, American Independence Day, in deference to a US contingent—2000 soldiers in eight companies—under his command in the battle. The Americans had been drawn from two divisions of ten training with the British in the areas behind the front. Because of secrecy, it wasn't until late on 2 July that the American commander, General Pershing, was informed that his men would be in the battle of Hamel. He objected. No American soldiers had ever fought under a foreign commander. Pershing didn't want the unusual distinction of being the first American general to allow it. Taking his troops away from him also threatened his dream for the US Army to enter the front line as a massive contingent and destroy the Germans in their section of the front line, which would lead to increased influence for US President Woodrow Wilson. Pershing also did not wish to break up the steady stream of US arrivals by filling up depleted Allied units. He compromised with Rawlinson, saying he would allow the equivalent of one battalion—1000 men—to fight. The other 1000 had to be withdrawn. The American officers and soldiers were incensed about the decision. They had been in the reserve areas undergoing training and were ready to fight. Monash had to redraw his plans with the assault leader, Sinclair-Maclagan.

Pershing grew unhappier in the next 24 hours with *any* of his troops taking part. Monash was at the HQ of the 3rd Division at Glisy, when Rawlinson notified him by phone of the new decision that there should be no Americans in the battle. It was 4 p.m. on 3 July, barely twelve hours before the battle was set to begin.

Monash was angry. He refused at first. Rawlinson said it *had to be done.* Otherwise there could be an 'international incident'. Monash was prepared to stand up to his superiors. He had done it on Gallipoli and in Egypt. Now he told Rawlinson that he had better come to the HQ and explain it all to Sinclair-Maclagan, who was also most unhappy with this sudden troop reduction. At 5 p.m. Rawlinson arrived with Chief of Staff Montgomery-Massingberd.

Rawlinson, and then Montgomery-Massingberd, insisted the Americans had to be withdrawn. Monash stood his ground. His dealings with Rawlinson so far had found him flexible to the point of indecision, which may have been attributed to his recent years of battle failures. Monash had heard one story about

Rawlinson, which confirmed his own experience. At an army commanders' conference with Haig earlier in the war there was discussion about whether to go around a wood or through it. Rawlinson had said at once, 'Certainly, I would go around it.' After a discussion, the majority thought it best to go through the wood. Rawlinson then said, 'Certainly, I should go through it.'[1]

Monash saw some softness in the army commander. He picked the moments to attempt to drive through it. This was one of them. He pointed out that his soldiers were already on their way to battle stations. The artillery would soon, under cover of darkness, be arriving at positions in the battle zone and setting up.

'Even if orders could still with certainty reach the battalions concerned,' Monash told them, 'the withdrawal of those Americans would result in untold confusion and in dangerous gaps in our line of battle.'[2]

Rawlinson became agitated. He spoke again of an 'international incident'. Monash responded that there could well be such an incident between the Americans en route to the battlefield and their fellow Australian combatants if they were to pull out now. The first 1000 Americans taken out had been unhappy. The others could become hostile.[3]

Rawlinson and Montgomery-Massingberd would not accept this. Monash summed up his position. First, it was too late to pull out the Americans. Second, the battle would have to go on with them, or not at all. Third, unless Monash was ordered by Haig to abandon the battle, Monash intended to go on with the original plan. And fourth, unless he received a cancellation order by 6.30 p.m. the battle could not be stopped anyway. As he spoke, the preliminary stages were beginning.

Rawlinson repeated that Monash had to obey Haig's order.

'The Commander-in-Chief could not have realised that his order [to withdraw all the Americans] would mean the battle had to be abandoned,' Monash said.[4]

Rawlinson's sympathy for Monash's position had evaporated.

'You cannot disobey an order,' he insisted.

'But *you* can,' Monash, the lateral-thinking lawyer, said, putting his case with logic. 'As the army commander, it is open to you to disobey in light of what you know.'

Rawlinson was a little rattled.

'Do you want me to run the risk of being sent back to England?' he said. 'Do you mean [defying the order] is worth that?'

'Yes, I do,' Monash replied. 'It is more important to keep the confidence of the Americans and the Australians in each other than to preserve an army commander.'[5]

The comment wouldn't have endeared him to Rawlinson. Yet he was riding on Monash's determination to fight. If the Battle of Hamel were to be a success, Rawlinson would receive needed credit. Monash's firmness and rationale swayed him. He agreed to make a decision by 6.30 p.m. Rawlinson couldn't contact Haig until 7 p.m. Haig agreed with Monash that the Americans should *not* be withdrawn.

The attack, the commander-in-chief directed, should go ahead as planned. If it failed, Rawlinson, who had felt the pressure, would be more likely to help Bean, Murdoch and Hughes get rid of Monash.

If it succeeded, Rawlinson's shaky commandership would be strengthened.

•

Whatever the result, Hamel would go ahead. Success depended on the start. If the Germans knew the Australians were coming they could position their artillery and machine guns along the 6-kilometre front and pick off the thin line of attackers before the tanks could wreak havoc. At 2.45 a.m. the 7000 Australians and 1000 Americans were lying on the grass and crops in the fields on the start line. The RAF night-fighters began their daily swoop over the German lines ahead of the familiar pre-dawn artillery bombardment. The Germans on front-line duty put on their gasmasks and braced themselves for nothing more than the usual strafing, shells, smoke and interminable noise from their loud opposition across the low-gradient valley.

There was one difference that fateful fourth of July 1918. A thick fog, rare for the middle of summer, descended on the area like a huge blanket. This made it difficult for commanders and officers to make observations. Guidance was tougher. But it had the overriding use of making the attack more of a surprise. With the noise drowning the sound of the tank movements, by the time the Germans knew they were being invaded, the vehicles were just metres away, emerging from the fog like monsters. The enemy soldiers who didn't freeze and let themselves be captured were flattened, chased or fought by the tanks and the supporting infantry.

There were some pockets of resistance from well-fortified machine-gun emplacements and artillery that belatedly defended. But it was a rout.

The Battle of Hamel, on which Monash had staked so much, was over in just 93 minutes. But he was not 100 per cent satisfied. There was an 'overrun' of three minutes. In typical style, he would work out why.

•

It was a modest encounter in the context of the war, but the rapidity of the victory, with much gain and little cost, meant an immeasurable lift in the confidence of the Australian Corps and the entire Allied command. The British Tank Corps at last had something to celebrate. This precedent would be the model for every British attack using tanks for the rest of the war.

The Australians, in their first action as a corps, had won a near perfect victory. Monash revelled in the sense of harmony achieved by his infantry, the Tank Corps, the Royal Artillery and the RAF. It had worked the way he planned it and had gone the way he had always dreamt perfectly prepared battles should go. He counted 800 casualties in his force, but most were walking wounded and would see action again. Monash's aim to have the machinery protect the infantry could not have been better executed. The tanks came through far better than ever before and well above expectations. Only three were out of action, but even they would be repaired to fight again.

The Australians were happy to collect 1500 prisoners, a huge haul for such a small battle. Monash was pleased that around half of them were wearing gasmasks, which was evidence that his smoke trick had worked. Another 1500 Germans were killed or injured. The booty—always a useful boast in war—was impressive. It included two field guns, 26 mortars and 171 machine guns. Territory gained—another military measure of success—was four times that achieved by any other force of a division or less in 1917, when the last British offensives happened.

Another aspect of Hamel was the American involvement. It was the second time they had been in an offensive battle in the war, and Monash was keen to increase this relationship.[6] There were no negative repercussions from his decision to insist on them fighting despite their commander-in-chief ordering them out. In fact, Pershing revelled in the afterglow of the Hamel victory, and the men who fought had a status that other US divisions envied.

Monash's other notable innovation, apart from strong support for the much-maligned tank, was the use of planes to drop ammunition to the machine gunners. When done on foot, it required two men to carry a box holding 1000 rounds, which one gun could fire off in less than five minutes. It was heavy, dangerous work for the carriers, often under fire. Now that risk to soldiers had been reduced. Time had been saved; efficiency was increased.

It was a small advance, but when put in the context of how this lifted the proficiency of machine gun use as an offensive weapon—another Monash edict—it increased his faith in the technology and his capacity to incorporate it effectively. It had all worked, from the use of smoke and every latest artillery projectile to combining machine guns and planes.

Monash and his force had set some sort of standard, recognised by the British Army, who sent out a staff brochure on the operation to all officers. This brought him much kudos, but he was more interested in his survival as a commander. A clue to his fate came from a long, effusive telegram from Hughes who, after visiting Bertangles and the AIF, had moved on to an Inter-Allied War Council meeting at Versailles outside Paris. It included a message from Haig to Hughes:

'Will you please convey to Lieutenant-General Sir John Monash and all Ranks under his command, including the Tanks and the detachment of 33rd American Division, my warm congratulations on the success which attended the operation carried out this morning, and on the skill and gallantry with which it was conducted.'[7]

This was the endorsement Monash wanted. He hoped Hamel had bought him time. Yet he would not rest on this achievement. Even late on the day of the victory, he ordered Sinclair-Maclagan and Hobbs to start patrolling into enemy territory. In reality it was raiding. While adhering to the doctrine of the 'limited objective', where territory was gained and held, Monash never stopped planning aggressively. Even as the tanks were bringing back the cheering, waving soldiers, including the wounded, he was leaning over his maps in the war room at the chateau. Some of his officers may have been opening champagne and unwrapping fat cigars, but Monash, smoking a pipe, was busy with the tireless Blamey putting down coloured paper, and using a cue to move around miniature infantry markers.

Monash was a realist. He sensed that the near-faultless Hamel success was mainly due to his strategic skills. Despite the massive reinforcements that had all now arrived from the Russian Front, the enemy was stunned and defending. It endorsed his instinct, based on intelligence coming in all the time, that now was the time to shake up the German defences even more, and to push hard for a massive counterattack.

Chapter 25

Clemenceau's Glow

The next day, 5 July, Monash asked Rawlinson to reduce his expanded front of 18 kilometres. It was too big for his four divisions, even on rotation, to maintain. Some of his brigades needed a long rest. Monash began to visit his men, inspiring them to be prepared for more hard work and battles. Everywhere the Rolls-Royce with the prominent Australian flag appeared, Monash received spontaneous applause and cheering. Ever since Gallipoli, his popularity had increased. There was always a good response for chatty, ebullient Birdwood, or the muscular leadership of the inspiring Pompey Elliott, or the fearless drive of Cannan. But Monash's reputation had been built on a solid foundation of training, planning, detail and performance. His attention to the little things that affected every soldier filtered down to them. His preference for control and decision-making from the expanding engine room at

HQ rather than being seen at the front had developed a mystique based on solid, reliable performances from the 'old man'. The name 'Monash' was now associated with not only a strong organisation, but with winning. Nothing would please him more than for it to be equated with victory. It was the way, too, he articulated the soldiers' success and what it meant in the bigger scheme of things, that endeared him more and more to every man in the corps. The men at the front appreciated his directness.

Monash read the mood of his men with certitude. He wanted to fuel the AIF's huge and hungry appetite for the fight. One way was to push Rawlinson and Haig for the return of the 1st Division. The AIF spirit was on such a high that he wanted to build on its morale by having all five divisions together. Monash was confident that if he could arrange this, then he could create a huge psychological advantage and sense of invincibility in the force. This feeling was important to his leadership. He had studied the attitudes of Napoleon and Wellington and their belief in being 'winners'. This mindset created an aura of invincibility, which built the confidence of his soldiers, and destroyed the morale of the opposition. Hamel had been the first step. Monash's aim, like that of Wellington, was to build the feeling that no matter what the position on the battlefield, his force could always find a way to win. His own interrogation of German prisoners confirmed that the enemy was already more than wary about tackling the Australians. One of Monash's aims, indeed themes, in discussions with officers and commanders, was to build on this, even if it meant bluffing the enemy.

After repeated requests it was agreed that the 1st would join the rest of the Australian Corps and be in reserve for the start of the next major engagement.

•

The result at Hamel was firming up the attitudes of others too. Monash received a letter from White. Now White made it clear his friends—Bean and Murdoch—were not conspiring at his 'suggestion' or with his 'approval'. This did not mean that White didn't covet the corps commander's job. He was just making clear to Monash that the frenetic, persistent plotting had nothing to do with him. But White still hadn't confronted his friends. He had not yet told them he was not a competitor for Monash's position.[1] Then again, he was now in London away from the action, and had not had a chance to speak to the peripatetic Murdoch and Bean since before Hamel.

White's distancing of himself from the conspirators, along with the positive reaction from Hughes and Haig, and the news that the French Premier Monsieur Clemenceau was on his way to congratulate the Australians, all buoyed Monash on 6 July when he met with Murdoch at Bertangles. With his guard down and his confidence up, Monash told the journalist what he had not been able to write earlier: when he had won battle honours, he would be happy to take up the administrative role in London.

This gave the plotters hope. But Monash did not specify what battle honours would satisfy him. Would he be content with another Hamel and then leave? Or would he want to push on into 1919 and be part of the actual victory, if it were to come the Allies' way?[2]

When Murdoch told Bean what was said at the meeting, the historian urged the journalist to advise Hughes not to give Monash time. But the prime minister was not ready to oppose him straight after Hamel. White, too, was in a different mood. His refusal to lobby against Monash was justified. In a face-to-face meeting on 12 July, White attacked Murdoch for 'impropriety, ignorance and dangerous meddling'.

The journalist didn't like the rebuke, especially after Hughes' rebuff over his concocted sources. But these minor setbacks had not diminished his view of his role as a powerbroker who would get his way.

From that moment, Murdoch was not a White supporter anymore. He now fell back on a jingoistic argument and viewed White as politically naïve and 'subservient' to England. White had been the plotters' choice because he had *not* been the British selection. But now that he showed no inclination to unseat Monash, Murdoch branded him an English lackey. It was a weak argument. The Bean/Murdoch position now seemed brittle, but they were nothing if not tenacious.[3]

Bean thought differently from Murdoch, although their aims were the same. Unlike Murdoch, who saw issues in terms of politicking and how he could manipulate the main players, Bean viewed everything in terms of what was right or wrong, *as interpreted by him,* in historical terms. But here he was completely out of touch with the importance of the Hamel win. He was desperate and carried away with his self-importance. Bean wrote to White imploring him to step forward and ask Hughes to appoint him corps commander. Bean saw it as perhaps 'the major job in his [Bean's] life' to ensure that Monash was made administrator in place of Birdwood, and that White got the Corps. It was a revealing comment, which would dictate the historian's writing and commentary from then on, especially after the key players were dead. He was the one and only source for negative comment about Monash. For instance, he alleged in the 1930s that Rawlinson made a racist remark about Monash after the war. Rawlinson, who died in 1925, and Monash, who died in 1931, were both gone when Bean reported the comment. The British General most likely never made the comment.

•

Monash was pleased to welcome the French Premier, the cultured 76-year-old Georges Clemenceau, on 7 July. He was the most influential Allied political figure, and a few months earlier had managed to persuade other government heads to place Ferdinand Foch as sole military commander, ahead of Haig. Monash admired the journalist/statesman Clemenceau for his single-minded determination to defeat the Germans and his declaration that he would wage war 'to the last quarter hour, for the last quarter hour will be ours'.

Monash assembled a large contingent of the soldiers who had participated at Hamel, and who were resting at Bussy. He was looking for every means to keep his fighters buoyant and willing. He couldn't think of a better person—the top representative of the country for which AIF soldiers were primarily fighting and dying—to speak to them. Monash was aware that 'Old Georges'—one of France's foremost political writers, and a lover of the Impressionists, especially Monet—would himself make a deep impression with his heartfelt words.

Clemenceau addressed the Australian volunteers in English, speaking about the attitude to freedom in Australia, England, France and Italy:

That is what made you come. That is what made us greet you when you came. We knew you would fight a real fight, but we did not know that from the very beginning you would astonish the whole Continent with your valour . . . I shall go back [to Paris] to-morrow and say to my countrymen: 'I have seen the Australians; I have looked into their eyes. I know that they, men who have fought great battles in the cause of freedom, will fight on alongside us, till the freedom for which we are all fighting is guaranteed for us and our children.'[4]

It was the right stuff, especially as the AIF was expected to be the spearhead of future battles. Every soldier understood why Clemenceau was nicknamed 'Le Tigre'. It was just the sort of inspiration Monash was looking for as his eager troops waited for more and bigger challenges.

Chapter 26

Re-enter, Mustafa Kemal

One of the first people to congratulate Monash on his elevation and his quick success at Hamel was his friend Chauvel, who was not surprised that he had ridden to the very top of the 1st AIF and done so well, so quickly. He reminded Monash that Australia now had two corps commanders on the two biggest battlefronts of the Great War. The two had exchanged letters and confidential information since they had gone their different ways in 1916. Their distant mutual admiration had grown over the years as they kept each other informed of their respective experiences. It had reached a point where Monash would surprise senior members of the High Command, such as Haig, Butler and Rawlinson, and British Cavalry officers, with his 'inside' comprehension of the Middle East war. He was able to correct them on the real reason for British victories at battles such as those at Romani and Beersheba, and the failures at Gaza.

Chauvel wrote about the lull before an expected late summer or early autumn push against the stubborn Turks, who still ruled most of the Middle East, and would continue to do so unless there was a concerted effort to remove them.

In the meantime, Chauvel had to deal with troopers suffering in the heat of the Jordan Valley, which was close to 45 degrees and occasionally closer to 50 degrees. This brought out scorpions in plague proportions, black spiders bigger than most of the Australians had ever seen at home, and snakes. A variety of insects joined the myriad flies, including the biting variety, and mosquitoes to disconcert the troopers. Many of them swore that taking on the Turks in rain and sleet would be far preferable to the conditions they now faced in the breath-choking atmosphere.

•

Cox's brigade of Chauvel's Desert Mounted Column was moved into the hills in late June 1918, and then in early July had a wonderful break in the Jewish settlement at Wady Hanein where the climate was hot but pleasant, and the fruit and wine appreciated. The New Zealanders and the 2nd Brigade, commanded by New South Wales politician and former heavyweight boxer Major General Granville Ryrie, were sent to a camp near Bethlehem, where Chaytor had his HQ in a Carmelite monastery.

Training in the use of the sword in the olive groves near the coast also lifted many of the troopers from their lethargy. By late July, the 3rd, 4th and 5th Light Horse Brigades had been trained and were waiting to use their newly acquired skills. Grant was next to be trained with his 4th Brigade. He and Wilson had been keen to take up the tradition. Chaytor had not. He and his men preferred the use of rifle and bayonet.

The Australians took to the new weapon with zeal. It brought a focus to their work as they waited for orders to move out on another mission.

Historian Gullett noted the joke that abounded in the villages near the sword-training camp: 'Not a wild dog has been left alive' in the region.[1]

This was repeated in the Jerusalem bazaars so that Turkish spies would pass back the chilling propaganda: *The horsemen of Beersheba and Es Salt now have long swords.*

•

The men not on rotation for rest or sword-training faced the growing dust and grime of midsummer in the valley of dreariness and death. More and more men fell sick, mostly with malaria, recurrent fevers and stomach complaints. The corps was at its lowest point during the entire campaign so far. The troopers still had to contend with shellfire and snipers. The losses may not have been heavy but they kept a steady pressure on Chauvel's force. Those that were wounded would end up back in the line after treatment when they otherwise may have been invalided out. There were no troopers to replace them. The bulk of these volunteers wished to tough it out with their mates no matter what the battle or conditions. But sometimes 'retiring' because of illness, injury or wounds was in their interests no matter what they viewed as their obligations to mates or the corps.

In the tight manpower months of mid-1918, hospitals far away in Cairo and elsewhere were not options.

•

Mustafa Kemal was appointed by the Turkish Sultan, against German wishes, as commander of the Turkish Seventh Army— one of the three about to face a British onslaught. Kemal, who would later become the creator of modern Turkey, was born on the fringes of the Ottoman Empire in the Macedonian seaport of Salonika. His mother was a barely literate peasant; his father was an unsuccessful merchant. Salonika had its own cosmopolitan flavour enriched by a variety of nationalities. The docks had their share with workers speaking more than six languages. Half the city's population was Jewish. The other half was mainly split between Turks, Greeks, Armenians and Albanians. Western Europeans dominated the trade and commerce, and reflected the domination of the ailing Ottoman Empire.

Kemal was not enamoured with Islam from his early years. He thought it and its leaders were 'a poisonous dagger which is directed at the heart of my people'.[2]

When a student in Constantinople, he was appalled at the way the Holy Men worked a crowd to hysteria. Kemal saw it as nothing more than primitive fanaticism.

'I flatly refuse to believe,' he wrote before the War, 'in the luminous presence of science, knowledge and civilization in all its aspects, there exists, in the civilised community of Turkey, men so primitive as to seek their material and moral well-being from the guidance of another sheikh.'[3]

He was broadly educated in mathematics, politics and French

literature, when at nineteen years of age he won a place in the Turkish Infantry College in Constantinople. He then found himself in a grander form of cosmopolitanism, which he adapted to easily after Salonika. The Turkish capital was less than half Muslim. The rest of the population was a mix of Sephardic Jews, whose ancestors had escaped from Christian Spain centuries earlier; Polish patriots fleeing Tsarist rule; Orthodox Armenians, Rumanians, Albanians and Greeks. The Greeks, as ever in the city, dominated commerce. Europeans controlled industry. More and more concessions were being given to foreigners, who did not pay taxes, as the Ottoman Empire crumbled.

Kemal studied and played hard, frequenting the city's salubrious brothels. (The foreign influence, good, bad and enjoyed, would later cause him to make Ankara the nation's capital.) He was typical of the young officers who supported modernising and making the empire stronger, as well as backing the attempted revolution of 1908 (which failed). The Ottoman Empire began to be dismembered. In 1908 Austria annexed Bosnia and Herzegovina. Bulgaria declared its independence in the same year. In 1911 Italy seized Libya. After the Balkan Wars of 1912 and 1913, Albania, Macedonia and part of Thrace, including Salonika, were lost. The latter stung the young Kemal more than anything.

By 1914 the European part of the empire, which at one time stretched into Hungary, was restricted to Thrace, a tiny enclave on Bulgaria's southern border. The Ottoman influence in Europe had dissolved in six years.

Kemal was having a good time as a diplomat in Bulgaria when war broke out in 1914. He was offered the command of a new division to defend Gallipoli, and it was the handling of this appointment that brought him to national and international prominence.

With this further appointment in 1918 to take charge of the Seventh Army, Kemal was the only Turkish commander who had not experienced defeat. He had an aura of invincibility after his mighty leadership on Gallipoli, which had seen the Allied forces stopped in April 1915 and then defeated into an evacuation later in the year. Kemal was no great strategist or tactician. He was more than that. He had inspired his troops to defend Turkey and they had succeeded. His late appointment was welcomed by the Turkish troops. Yet there was an ongoing friction between Kemal and General von Sanders, the German head of his country's military mission in Turkey for five years.

Von Sanders often overruled the Turks. He had not agreed to Kemal's continued demands through 1916 and 1917 to amalgamate the three Turkish armies in Palestine and Syria. Kemal thought his disparate force was undernourished, listless and ripe for demoralisation and defeat. By coordinating the three armies, he believed he could focus them on winning. The fact that a Turk put up such a radical plan meant it was going to be rejected. Yet Mustafa Kemal's brilliance as a battle commander and staunch leadership in defence of his nation was recognised even by his German superiors. His actions on Gallipoli in repulsing the Allied invaders made him a legend to the Turks. His efforts would be the springboard for other exploits, both military and political, which would make him the most notable Turk of the twentieth century. However, during the war he became a concern for von Sanders and others, who saw him as a threat. The Germans preferred a policy of keeping the Turks divided and while not conquered, at least under control. Had Kemal been given command of the three armies, historians have postulated that the outcome of the Middle East conflict from 1915 to 1918 would have been different.

When the pressure from Chauvel's corps mounted on the Turks in 1917, they had the added problem of the Arabs' revolt and the harassment of the Turkish forts along the Hejaz Railway, which ran from Damascus right through to the Muslim Holy City of Medina. Kemal was appalled to learn that other Turkish and German commanders were thinking of abandoning Medina. It was difficult, Kemal was told, to keep the trains running and supplying the Medina garrison of some 3000 Turks. Troops, equipment and supplies would be better sent to the main Turkish front in southern Palestine.

He was presented with a compelling logic. If the Turks lost Palestine, they would lose Medina anyway. Better to give away that remote garrison and move the forces to Palestine. But this was a rationale for lesser men; commanders without his great capacity to inspire soldiers. Kemal refused to go south to supervise the dumping of Medina in 1917.

He had waited until German General Erich von Falkenhayn arrived in Damascus to take command. The German had a complex plan, which seemed at best ambivalent about Medina. Kemal did not think it could work. He resigned in late 1917 and headed back to Constantinople, where he had the sympathetic ear of the Sultan. The Muslim spiritual leader cried at the thought of the Holy City of Medina being lost to his influence.

King Hussein, his sons, Princes Feisal and Abdullah, Lawrence and the ill-disciplined Arab force would have been no match for Kemal mustering his army in the Hejaz. But he had not been there. Nor was he in southern Palestine taking on the British and

Anzac forces once more. The best Turkish commander had been sidelined at a critical moment.

Now he was back in charge of one army in desperate times. Was it too late? Kemal did not think so.

•

Chauvel, who had learnt through intelligence that Kemal was commanding the Seventh Army, was very keen to defeat him after being part of the failed British campaign on Gallipoli. Without making propaganda through the ranks, he quietly informed his senior officers of Kemal's appointment, just to add an alertness and dedication to their efforts to win. Chauvel had learnt the art of patience in war. He now went into a 'quiet time' of two months as Allenby and he prepared the biggest attack of the Middle East conflict. This time, they determined there would be no repeats of the fiascos of First and Second Gaza.

PART 3

Amiens and Monash's Ascendancy

Chapter 27

A Problem with Pétain

Monash's divisional generals had to be content with nibbling at the enemy's forward positions for the rest of July. Rosenthal led the way with his 2nd Division, which advanced the Australian line by 1 kilometre on the eastern side of Villers-Bretonneux by taking Monument Wood. It had been thick with Germans. This rid that part of the town from the fear of being machine-gunned by the enemy, who could otherwise peer into the streets.

By early August, Foch and Haig had concluded that there would be no more big German pushes into Allied-held territory in the Somme Valley. The enemy was thought now to be purely on the defensive. The German Second Army, astride the river, was now the target and ripe for a massive attack. Monash began drafting a battle plan based on the strategies and tactics he had used at Hamel.

He had not been satisfied with the French XXXI Corps of General Marie-Eugène Debeney's army being positioned on his right or southern flank. He was at pains to explain it wasn't because the two forces didn't get on. A strange common vernacular—dubbed 'Francalian'—had even developed between them, and they fraternised well. But Monash was worried by the real language differences, which counted in the heat of battle, the gap in the style of fighting tactics, and the 'divergent temperaments'.

'The French are irresistible in attack as they are dogged in defence,' he said diplomatically, 'but whether they will attack or defend depends greatly on the temperament of the moment. In this they are unlike the British or Australian soldier, who will at any time philosophically accept either role that may be prescribed for him.'[1]

In other words, the British and Australians were better disciplined and drilled, making them more reliable under pressure. Besides that, even if Monash applied his improved French in an attempt to charm his hosts, he couldn't get them to push back the Germans in the French force's allotted territory. After Hamel, the front line had a nasty bump in it where the Australians had pushed forward, but the French had stayed put. This made the AIF's right flank vulnerable.

Monash knew they weren't weak but he was baffled by their intransigence. He wanted that front line bump free and straightened out. But because of a different policy, or sheer French bloody-mindedness, he worried about them in forthcoming 'much more serious undertakings'.

His concerns were exacerbated when he visited Field Marshal Pétain.

'If the Boche attacks,' the French leader told him, 'we'll fall back.'[2]

This was Monash's first personal experience of Pétain's mantra to defend at almost all costs, if the situation looked bad. Monash had been told about it by Haig, but hearing it himself made a difference. After the, at times, heated meeting with Pétain, the only Frenchman with whom Monash did not get along, he feared he would be vulnerable on both flanks if the French were there. The meeting, conducted in French for Pétain's benefit, ended abruptly with Monash standing and telling Pétain that he (Monash) had to see Haig about solving the problem.

He now wanted the French replaced by the Canadians. This was a huge request, which meant a big and problematic movement of troops in and out of the right flank. Monash spoke to Currie, with whom he got on extremely well, and understood the Canadian's attitude about not fighting under the British unless allowed absolute autonomous control over plans and battles. This had kept the Canadians out of the war in 1918. Monash used his linguistic and legal skills to tell Currie that this would be a 'Dominion operation'.[3] Monash would be the architect of the plan and Currie could put forward his needs long before the battle commenced. In other words, he and Currie, two Dominion commanders, would have most say on when, where and how the battle ensued. Currie agreed.

With this in hand, Monash asked Rawlinson for the Canadians to replace the French on his right flank. Rawlinson, as ever, demurred over such an important decision. He said he would have to ask Haig. Monash managed a private meeting with the commander-in-chief and the subject came up. Haig then informed Rawlinson he was to let the biggest late-decision switch of armies of the war take place.

It demonstrated that Monash was having the dominant say in the design of the battle and who should be in it, although he did not believe he would get things all his own way. With the Canadians now to replace Pétain's French on the right flank, Monash was left with another worry to deal with—the British III Corps led by General Butler on Monash's left flank.

Again, Monash was nervous about the British commanders, whom he did not think were up to the difficult task north of the river. But there was nothing to gain by airing this. Instead of complaining about Butler and his staff, he told Rawlinson he wanted his force to be 'astride' the river. Against his will, Monash was forced to wait until the battle to see if the problem unfolded as predicted.

There were other issues out of Monash's control in the build-up to the AIF attack. Although the Germans were not attempting infantry retaliation, they had no compunction about drenching the AIF front with mustard gas, fired by their artillery. On many nights, the Germans would think nothing of expending 10,000 shells on the half-ruined and partly deserted Villers-Bretonneux, or in the woods surrounding the town where the Australians sheltered.

The soldiers dreaded it. In its pure form this chemical weapon was colourless and odourless. But the Germans had given it a whiff by adding a mustard-smelling impurity. It increased fear. When that smell hit an area, soldiers were alarmed. Its symptoms and consequences could be horrific. It often began as itchy skin, which in a few hours led to blisters. It made the eyes sore; the eyelids would swell. In mild cases it led to conjunctivitis; in some it caused blindness.

Mustard gas had a rotten habit of not going away. The smell might disappear in the early morning, but when the warm August sun rose, invisible or brown-coloured pools of it, scattered over several kilometres, would form a vapour and strike unsuspecting soldiers. On hot days, concentrations were higher. Soldiers who inhaled it had bleeding and blistering in the windpipe and lungs. An end result could be pulmonary oedema, or even cancer, which could strike early or take decades. (Many an ageing digger would complain of lung problems that began with mustard gas. If it didn't get them on the battlefield it struck them down over time.)

The French, not the Germans, first used gas in August 1914. They fired tear-gas grenades (xylyl bromide). But the Germans were the first to study the development of chemical weapons and to use them in strength. They began in the capture of Neuve Chapelle in October 1914 with a formula that caused sneezing fits. The Germans often found French soldiers convulsed and clutching handkerchiefs in the trenches. It gave the Germans hope they could win the war by making all their enemies literally sneeze themselves to capitulation or death.

Inspired by the French experience in the early spring, they loaded up their 15-centimetre Howitzer guns with this gas on the Russian Front at Bolimov in the middle of winter. But none of the Russian soldiers were seen grabbing their noses, or making violent head movements. The gas failed to vapourise in the freezing conditions.

Disappointed that they couldn't win the battle of the sneeze, the Germans used the first poisonous gas—chlorine—in April 1915, at the start of the Second Battle of Ypres. It choked its French and Algerian victims, destroying their respiratory systems.

The British were quick to condemn the Germans, while rushing to develop their own chlorine bombs delivered in artillery shells.

The Germans stayed in front by developing something even more insidious than chlorine—phosgene. This horror was subtler. It caused less coughing and choking, but more of it was inhaled. Its effect was delayed. Apparently healthy soldiers would collapse two days later.

The French used prussic acid to make nerve gas, which they introduced now and again. Mustard gas, the worst of the lot, was used first by the Germans against the Russians at Riga in September 1917.

'This form of attack,' Monash recorded, 'and the constant dread of it, made life in the forward areas anything but endurable.'[4]

In the lead-up to the Battle of Amiens (the actual fight would be 10 kilometres east of it), the diggers scrambled on their gasmasks as soon as a bombardment hit to avoid becoming a casualty before the whispered big battle began.

Chapter 28

The Inventor's Invention

Haig and Rawlinson had considered a massive counterattack in May but were not confident about the unconvincing plans on the table. They abandoned them after another distracting German offensive on 27 May. The two discussed it again in June. But still no thoroughly thought-out plan was put up.

That all changed at Hamel. Monash's 'win' was based on the unprecedented harmonious use of tanks, air force, artillery and ground troops. Just at the moment when the Allies needed to be shown the way, Monash's solid ideas emerged out of the pack of concepts put forward by the 25 commanders under Haig, and it proved successful. From 1 July—three days before Hamel—for the next three weeks, Monash pushed hard for the instigation of his blueprint for a massive counterattack, based on the tactics he used at Hamel. He met every day from 4 July with Rawlinson. With Haig's more than tacit prodding, the veteran officer was now more willing than ever to consider the 'Dominion' commander's plans. So was Montgomery-Massingberd. They were to acquiesce with Monash on every major detail, and if they did not, it was to be reviewed by Haig for approval or not. Though nothing was official in July 1918, Monash had more power than his official masters in the Fourth Army. Aware of this, he was careful to show them all his work in progress and urged them to take the initiative now while the enemy was vulnerable.

The day after Hamel, Monash was convinced that he could drive through the German defences 8 kilometres or more, if he had that promised Canadian support on his right (southern) flank. It was not at that stage set in concrete. There was much hard work to do before Haig and Rawlinson would be confident about any huge counterattack.

At a meeting on 13 July, Montgomery-Massingberd asked for some specific proposals.

'Reduce my front [to more concentrate his Australian force], return 1st Division [from Flanders in the north assisting the British at Hazebrouk] and use the Canadians [on his southern flank],' Monash responded.

He again spoke to Rawlinson and Montgomery at length about the overall scheme on 14 July.

He said his position 'was analogous to an inventor who conceives a new scientific idea, and who talks it over with his colleagues and friends. They all make suggestions, which are discussed, some being adopted and others rejected, so that ultimately the new idea takes a definite form and substance.'[1]

Monash's 'friends and colleagues' were his staff, divisional commanders, Haig, Rawlinson and Montgomery-Massingberd. He redrafted it for several weeks, incorporating all their useful input (apart from a few key points that he would argue in future meetings) until his plan had 'form and substance' and broad consensus—a critical point in coordinating a military operation this big.

•

Monash put the fine-tuning on every aspect of the battle, from the use of tanks, aircraft and artillery to deception methods such as smoke and noise screens. His request to Montgomery-Massingberd for the 1st Division was motivated, too, by a desire to unite and direct all five Australian divisions in a battle for the first time ever. Monash had been a colonel in charge of the 4th Brigade at Gallipoli. He was proud of the courage, fortitude, resilience, endurance and fighting abilities of his men and all the Australian force that invaded Turkey in 1915. Then, he and his fellow commanders had been handicapped by poor planning from the British High Command, a very narrow beachhead on which to fight, and severe lack of resources and support. Now Monash would be given all the resources he wished. He had a much wider front on which to operate. And he had what he considered the best fighting force in the war to direct as the arrowhead—the 'shock troops'—for the Allies.

Monash had instigated the recognition and commemoration of Anzac Day. Now he was determined to advance the sense of nationhood an important notch beyond Gallipoli. He wanted victory. The move towards this would begin by presenting the German Army with its biggest surprise of the war.

•

On 15 July Monash briefed Rawlinson in detail about his 'counteroffensive' plan, and the next day presented it to Douglas Haig when he visited Bertangles. It focused on the role of the AIF, but incorporated a broad strategy for four attacking corps, running from left to right (or north–south) facing the enemy: the British, the Australians, the Canadians and the French. Pétain's soldiers were now pushed to the far right, where they could make their much-mentioned 'fallback' towards Paris, if necessary. The Australians and the Canadians would form the point of the arrowhead. The British on their left and the French on their right were meant to guard the flanks of the main attacking corps. Monash had not been part of any failed plan on the Western Front apart from the battle of Passchendaele, which he was more vocally against than any other British force commander. Now, with the architecture of his plan intact, he was keener than any of Haig's army or corps commanders to seize the chance to smash through the German lines. His aggressive attitude, based on his confidence in his own detailed planning and intelligence, saw him emerge in these critical days of mid-1918 as the most forthright leader in Haig's pack.

Haig's position had been strengthened in March 1918 when he helped dislodge his superior, French General Robert Nivelle, supreme Allied commander on the Western Front, in favour of his friend, Foch. Haig and Foch proved an amicable combination. The Scot got his way much more than he had under Nivelle. He could now exercise full tactical command of the British armies (including the Australian and Canadian forces), which Nivelle had never allowed.

Haig's brutal reputation had been tempered by his role in helping to stop the German offensives of March and May a few months earlier. Monash was giving a further enormous boost to Haig's status. Mindful of the King's appreciation of Monash, Haig was now paying him more attention than ever.

Monash's plans were also attractive for another reason that would enhance Haig's image and modify his reputation. They were structured for a minimum of casualties. It was a novelty in July 1918 and, with the manpower shortage, a necessity.

•

Haig sat in the Chateau Bertangles' piazza and read this most recent blueprint for victory against the Germans. He pronounced it 'very good indeed' and made some other favourable remarks without any suggested changes. The British commander reminded Monash that he had to be patient. He also mentioned that he couldn't 'authorise it without consulting Generalissimo Foch'.

Monash asked how long that would take. Haig thought two weeks. He said he was going to take a break 'in Torquay to play some golf'. Haig suggested Monash also take some long overdue leave, but in London rather than Paris. It would be easier to contact him. Monash thought he would go. Haig told him to 'tell Henry [Rawlinson] I recommend it'.[2]

Monash suggested they both put out press releases concerning their plans to take leave. This would deceive the Germans into thinking that no counterattack was being contemplated.

Chapter 29

Monash's Master Plan Takes Shape

Rawlinson received Monash's written plan for the Battle of Amiens late on 16 July. The army commander, who was admired more for his fluent French and skills as an artist than his capacities as a strategist, the next day submitted formal proposals to Haig. They incorporated 'edits' of Monash's master plan for an AIF thrust, with refinements for the other three corps.

Rawlinson didn't like Monash's 'artificial' boundary between the British Corps and the Australians. Rawlinson put back the Somme River as the boundary. He also put the first objective 'finish line' in the attack short of the German artillery. Monash wanted to take the artillery in one hit. Past experience taught his command that not doing this left the advancing force vulnerable to the enemy regrouping and using it against them.

Rawlinson also drew up plans for the cavalry that Monash had ignored. He thought horses were superfluous in the planned encounter, except for 'mopping up' after the main conflict. But Rawlinson was still rooted in warfare techniques from the previous century and was wary of tanks after the failures in 1916. Besides, Haig insisted that the cavalry be in the fight. There was nothing like the odd charge on horseback to spice up a battle. Monash thought it wasteful and a nuisance to have horses and tanks attacking together. The equine speed was considerably faster than that of the crawling, creaking armoured monsters. But it didn't matter. Haig wanted them in, so they were in.

Rawlinson agreed with Monash's request to reduce his front from 17 kilometres to less than 7 kilometres. He also allowed the Australian 1st Division to join the corps from where it had been fighting in Flanders.

This was an enormous boost for Monash and the AIF.[1]

•

From 18 to 22 July, news came through of a successful counter-attack by the French, led by General Charles Mangin 90 kilometres away to the south-east at the city of Soissons, and supported by France's Sixth Army. They went in with 2000 guns, 1100 aircraft and 478 tanks in support of 24 divisions, including just two from the United States. Both the French and British commands, and indeed Pershing himself, were nervous about the Americans being involved when they did not have full training on the wholly new experience of trench warfare. The mainly French force of

400,000 soldiers took 400 guns and 1500 prisoners. It came two weeks after Hamel, where Monash's force of 9000 soldiers took the same number of prisoners and a similar amount of booty, which for military experts, demonstrated on several levels the startling superiority of Monash's tactics.

The French-led Soissons assault, using ten times the number of tanks that had been used at Hamel, saw 107,000 casualties (95,000 French and 12,000 Americans) while the Germans suffered 168,000 casualties. The object was to eliminate the salient aimed at Paris and it ended with the French recapturing most of the ground lost in the German Spring Offensive earlier in May.

•

On the same day as the Soissons encounter, 18 July, the Germans began a two-pronged attack with 52 divisions on the cathedral city of Reims, 50 kilometres east. They were met by a smaller, predominantly French force of 34 divisions, including nine American, two Italian and a further two British divisions arriving just in time for the encounter. This 'Second Battle of Marne' followed one in 1914. The French and British had long experience of fighting in this area but it was a grim early experience for the Americans. They had shown determination to win through the German trenches or perish. But in the process, the battlefield was strewn with bodies in American uniforms. The fresh army was now learning the hard way what its allies had been through on the Somme in 1916 and Passchendaele in 1917, and in the long siege of Verdun in the heroic but failed attempt under French General Nivelle in Champagne.

Yet again this morbid, sad sight was proof that the Americans were in this grotesque war, and were committed to whatever it took to see victory.

•

The two blows at Hamel and Soissons, and the failure to deliver a victorious strike at Reims, exposed enemy vulnerability. But overall it was nothing near the knockout needed. It did, however, speed the Allies' plans and in particular Monash's grand battle counterattack design. Haig approved the plans on 19 July. Two days later, Rawlinson called a meeting of all the key commanders for this new offensive—to be known as the Battle of Amiens. It was set for 8 August.

•

The rendezvous location was the village of Flexicourt on the Somme, obscure enough for there to be little fear that an enemy spy would notice the unusual, pretentious motorcades arriving on the lawn in front of an elaborate white mansion. Rawlinson had commandeered it for the beautiful, still summer's day. The black and red flag of the British Fourth Army commander hung over the mansion entrance. Monash, punctual as ever, was looking at his watch as he arrived in a Rolls-Royce with the Australian flag prominent. General Currie, the Canadian commander, rolled up, his flag flying too. He was following General Butler of the British III Corps, General Kavanagh of the cavalry, senior representatives of the tanks and air force, and some American commanders representing a couple of regiments held in reserve that would be at the Fourth Army's disposal if needed.

Rawlinson outlined the complete attack scheme, which was Monash's creation.

The commanders sorted out the broad plans for the attack. Rawlinson imposed no limitations on what they did within their own boundaries, as long as they met their objectives and didn't let the other corps down. Monash's aim was to advance 9000 yards (8 kilometres). One of his goals was to take Chipilly Spur, a dangerous German-held vantage point just over the Somme.

Currie was happy with his plans, which Rawlinson had refined at the margins after he had seen Monash's proposals. Tanks were an additional item in the Canadian operation. Monash didn't think he had enough of them after their unprecedented success at Hamel. After a lengthy debate, in which Monash put his case for a tenfold increase, Rawlinson increased his quota to nearly 500.

The use of this number of tanks was an important breakthrough. After the startling taking of Hamel, and the more modest success at Soissons when so many more were used, Monash had a strong argument. The Allies, with Foch more encouraging about 'attack' than his predecessor had been, created bigger thinking in the overall command, although power (or numbers and size of arms) was preferred over technique. But now Monash was urging and influencing both. He had the tactical skills and know-how to implement his ideas and, most importantly, coordinate all the weaponry. The Allies had witnessed it all at Hamel on a small scale. They had belief in his planning and were ready to back him on a bigger mission.

The Fourth Army Chief agreed to the upscale of arms, without his usual reliance on Haig for arbitration or a final decision.

•

Monash was concerned about the confusion surrounding transmission of urgent messages from the front. There was no certainty of finding a phone terminal, and even then messages were transmitted too slowly for effective response at HQ. There was also a problem with the speed of transmitting up the chain of command from battalions to brigades and divisions. By the time messages reached HQ—often more than twenty minutes later—the battle conditions most likely had changed. Responses would be late. Monash proposed the use of planes for reconnaissance and message transmission. He was granted nearly 800, each one carrying a pilot and observer, from the No. 3 Australian Squadron. Monash expected to cut the time he and his staff received messages and intelligence from the front to around ten minutes. Again he had engineered a vital and enlarged scope for Australia in this most important battle of the war to date. (The French on the far-right flank had a further 1100 planes, although Monash would not rely on them except to expect them to buzz around early the first day of battle to confuse the enemy.)

The corps commanders were happy with their 2000 artillery guns. Yet there was concern about the numbers held by the enemy. Monash objected that Rawlinson had not approved German gun positions as being a target in the first of the three-phase attack, which would cover 3500 yards (3 kilometres). The Australian troops had complained that in earlier battles, if artillery was not taken or smashed in the first phase, in the pause before the second phase the Germans retreated with it and used it against them later.

Rawlinson changed his mind and consented to this.

Monash was also unhappy to see that Rawlinson had again made the Somme a northern boundary for the Australian Corps operations. Monash wanted at least one Australian brigade (4000 soldiers) over the Somme so that he controlled both sides of the river. He thought it was an unnecessary boundary.[2]

'It creates a divided responsibility [between him and the British commander in charge of the corps north of the river],' he told Rawlinson. Monash suggested that this would make it harder for him and the British commander to cooperate. His real worry again was Chipilly Spur's rocky ridge beyond some terrace meadows just north of the river, stoutly defended by Germans because of its vantage point. The Somme meandered as a boundary to those somnolent fields, then encountered the steep, wood-covered slope, which ran for several kilometres. The Germans would find easy targets among the Australian troops moving forward in the meadows, and be tough to dislodge from their dominant position. The spur offended Monash's obsessive dedication to ironing out all problems before any attack. It continued to dog him because the British Generals, particularly Butler, wanted British soldiers to attempt to take it.

There had already been fierce fighting there. Monash wanted to command the attack on Chipilly Spur, fearing that his left flank would be exposed if the British conscripts couldn't take it. Butler objected.

Rawlinson supported Butler, saying that this target remained with the British III Corps. Monash was uneasy. He suggested that Butler had to take Chipilly Spur. He had to keep attacking until he secured it. This suggestion caused some tension, but Rawlinson agreed. A disgruntled Butler was under instruction now to make Chipilly Spur a priority.

Monash was still not happy. He had little confidence in Butler and his staff. During a break, Monash told Sinclair-Maclagan to prepare a defensive flank in case the British failed. He knew how fluid matters could become once a conflict began. He would continue to urge for control of the operations north of the Somme.[3] For the moment he had to be content with his prescribed boundaries, marked to the north by the river and the south by the railway. The countryside in between—the Australian Corps' battleground—was flat, open and dotted with woods and villages. It was less difficult terrain over which to attack.

•

At the end of the meeting, Monash obtained Rawlinson's approval for leave in London as long as he was 'prepared to return at very short notice'.

Rawlinson also arranged that Monash would receive a coded phone message via the War Office at Whitehall, London, when he had to return.

•

Monash took off from Bertangles on Tuesday 23 July (a day after learning of the French victory at Soissons), picking up a boat that took him from Boulogne to Folkestone, where a car ran him to the Prince's Hotel, London, in time for an evening with Lizette Bentwitch, a close friend from Melbourne.

On 24 July, they lunched at his hotel and spent the afternoon shopping. On 25 July, Monash sat for Australian painter John Longstaff. At night he and Lizette went to the theatre to see

Naughty Wife. They went again on the 26th to see *Going Up*. It was light relief that helped him escape the hell across the Channel.[4]

Monash visited the War Office in London each day. He did press interviews, which he considered important in putting an Australian perspective—spin—on events. The British War Office had underplayed his corps' contribution. It didn't want Dominion forces to be perceived as taking the brunt of the fighting, or more bluntly, as cannon fodder. It was feared that Australian Prime Minister Hughes might feel it necessary to pull his armed forces out of the conflict if he thought they were over-exposed. Nonetheless, Monash felt compelled to fly the flag for himself and his men.

Time was swallowed up fast. He accepted an invitation to attend the opening of Australia House on the Strand on 3 August, but never made it. After just five days of comparative bliss, the War Office rang his hotel late on Sunday 28 July to give him the coded message. He could have done with a month, but at least it was a break from the constant grind, misery and din of war, and the interminable demand for decisions.

Colonel John Monash aged 48, early in 1914.

Monash (centre, in profile) inspecting troops from 4th Brigade before Gallipoli in October 1914.

Monash (seated, without head gear) close to Turkish trenches at the Front at Gallipoli in May 1915.

Monash (left) and his Chief of Staff Major J.P. McGlinn at the pyramids in Egypt before the Gallipoli invasion in April 1915.

Monash at 50 years old in October 1915 in Cairo after promotion to Major-General.

Monash (third from left) at Gallipoli waiting for direction to evacuate on 13 November 1915.

Monash (at left, in slouch hat) with King George V reviewing Monash's
3rd Division on 27 September 1916 at Salisbury Plain.

Monash, aged 52, on 25 May 1918, at his 3rd Division HQ at Gilsy in the
Villers-Bretonneux sector of France.

Harry Chauvel in August 1916.

General Sir Edmund Allenby.

Mustafa Kemal (fourth from left), the Turkish commander at Gallipoli.

Troopers in Palestine after the weather has come in, and horses were the only form of transport that could move.

A German plane brought down in the Sinai Desert.

Turkish troops manning the trenches.

Chapter 30

A-Day Approaches

Monash was picked up by car before dawn on Monday 29 July and driven to Dover, where a destroyer was waiting for him at 7 a.m. It took him to Boulogne. A car then drove him the 130 kilometres to Bertangles where he lunched with his staff and division commanders.

On 31 July Monash called for a conference with his commanders and asked for their plans. They were put to the meeting for discussion, comment and questions. Monash, as usual, dominated the conference without taking it over. He encouraged criticism on even the minutiae.

Haig dropped in to Bertangles, giving words of encouragement to all the commanders. He went out of his way to express how much confidence he had in Monash. At this conference, they worked out the deployment of the field and heavy artillery, the tanks and armoured cars, and the cavalry brigade, which Haig had repeated must be used. They also covered the use of infantry, the methods of attack and the tactics.

On 1 August, Monash summed up the meeting in memos sent to all the divisions, and they covered many of the outstanding queries. Blamey remarked later that he doubted that any commander in any major battle in history would have matched his leader for preparation.

'Elements of the meticulous, careful forethought reached every member of the AIF,' he noted, 'and gave them even greater confidence and inspiration.'[1]

Bean expressed a similar sentiment, but decades after the event: 'the range and tireless method of his (Monash's) mind were beyond any that came within the experience of the AIF,' he wrote. 'His men went into action feeling, usually with justification, that, whatever might lie ahead, at least everything was right behind them.'[2]

The Australian 1st Division was transferred from under the command of the British Second Army to join Monash's corps. It had been rushed down from Flanders early in April when Amiens was threatened during the first battle of Villers-Bretonneux. The 1st was then hurried back to help the hard-pressed British line near Hazebrouk. Now the division mustered for something big, although as the soldiers travelled south by train, they could only make guesses based on rumours. They were pleased to be joining Monash and the rest of the Australians. They had heard of the success at Hamel and were expectant about joining a far bigger campaign. These experienced soldiers were disappointed to learn as they arrived at Amiens that they would be held in reserve for whatever was about to unfold.

The movement of two Canadian divisions (about 30,000 troops and equipment) to a point south on Australia's right flank—on the other side of the Amiens–Nesle railway line—was kept as secret as possible. The reason, leaked everywhere by HQ, was that the Canadians were relieving the Australians, so they could have a long, well-earnt rest after their years of hard work at the front. There was no hint that they were joining them for a massive attack.

Yet it was impossible early in August not to make German intelligence suspicious as brigades (groups of 4000 troops) began intricate manoeuvres in preparation for the attack. The Germans decided on a raid in the area into which the Canadians were thought to be moving.

On the night of 4 August, the 4th Australian Division's 13th Brigade was spread over a 5-kilometre front. If it occupied the front-line trenches the Germans would be alerted. There was no option but to defend its area with a series of small, isolated posts.

One of these posts was on the road to Roye beyond the southernmost part of the area occupied by the Australians. The Germans raided it. A sergeant and four soldiers were captured. They were taken behind lines and interrogated. The Australians refused to disclose anything but their names and units, which was their right, if they could stand the pressure of extreme interrogation, even torture.

Monash and his staff could only hope that the captured men would hold out, or that they knew nothing of the imminent plans. It decided to leave the 13th Brigade where it was and not to displace it with Canadian troops until the last minutes before the Allied attack. Monash planned to replace this brigade of the 4th Division with one—the 1st Brigade—from the incoming reserve of 1st Division. It arrived at night on 6 August, just in time to be slotted into the order of battle of the 4th Division under General Sinclair-Maclagan.

Also arriving after dark for the 4th and 5th Divisions were eighteen tanks stuffed to the brim with rifle ammunition, Stokes mortar bombs and petrol. They rolled and squealed into a small plantation a kilometre north of Villers-Bretonneux, from where the massive attack would be launched.

The strike was set for the morning of 8 August 1918 at 4.20 a.m.

•

The day of 7 August was full of tension. While it was not quite all quiet on this section of the Western Front, there was a lull. The Germans, like the Allies, had new listening devices for tapping telephones. Monash ordered the restricted use of telephones, especially in areas closest to the enemy. This meant that commanders and staff had to walk, or hop in their cars or onto horses in order to make final inspections and send directives.

'A strange and ominous silence pervaded the scene [on the morning of 7 August],' Monash noted. 'It was only when the explosion of a stray shell would cause hundreds of heads to peer out from trenches, gunpits and underground shelters, that one became aware that the whole country was really packed thick with a teeming population carefully hidden away.'[3]

At night, Monash's artillery commander, Brigadier General Walter Coxen, made his last round of battery positions—a dangerous job. The Germans were firing shells at random into the area. Coxen reached the plantation where the tanks, covered with tarpaulins, were sitting. He and the soldiers protecting him went to ground as the last of a dozen shells whistled towards them. It fell into the centre of the tanks. They exploded. A cloud of dust and smoke billowed into the area. The Germans, unaware they had hit an important spot by chance, then turned a concentrated artillery barrage on the plantation. In twenty minutes, fifteen of the tanks and their valuable cargoes were destroyed.

Coxen rushed back to Bertangles to inform Monash that the fire was an accident. The enemy was unlikely to have had prior knowledge of the pending strike or the tanks that would be in the front line. Monash had the tanks and stores replaced.

He would go on with the attack as planned. The Germans had no idea what was coming. Ludendorff sent General Hermann von Kuhl to inspect the front of General Georg von der Marwitz's Second Army, which was Monash's first target. Von Kuhl reported back that nothing was amiss. There had been sounds of tanks moving about but Ludendorff derided this, as he often did, as 'tank panic'. Nothing to worry about. All was noisy on this part of the Western Front on the afternoon and night of 7 August. But they were not the sounds normally associated with a sudden, massive attack.

•

Also on the seventh, Monash had a message sent to all of the 166,000 Australian troops in his corps. It read:

TO THE SOLDIERS OF THE AUSTRALIAN ARMY CORPS.
For the first time in the history of this Corps, all five Australian Divisions will tomorrow engage in the largest and most important battle operation ever undertaken by the Corps. They will be

supported by an exceptionally powerful Artillery, and by Tanks and Aeroplanes on a scale never previously attempted. The full resources of our sister Dominion, the Canadian Corps, will also operate on our right, while two British Divisions will guard our left flank.

The many successful offensives which the Brigades and Battalions of this Corps have so brilliantly executed during the past four months have been but the prelude to, and the preparation for, this greatest and culminating effort.

Because of the completeness of our plans and dispositions, of the magnitude of the operations, of the number of troops employed, and of the depth to which we intend to overrun the enemy's positions, this battle will be one of the most memorable of the whole war; and there can be no doubt that, by capturing our objectives, we shall inflict blows upon the enemy which will make him stagger, and will bring the end appreciably nearer.

I entertain no sort of doubt that every Australian soldier will worthily rise to so great an occasion, and that every man, imbued with the spirit of victory, will, in spite of every difficulty that may confront him, be animated by no other resolve than grim determination to see through to a clean finish, whatever his task may be.

The work to be done tomorrow will perhaps make heavy demands upon the endurance and staying powers of many of you; but I am confident that, in spite of excitement, fatigue, and physical strain, every man will carry on to the utmost of his powers until his goal is won; for the sake of Australia, the Empire and our cause.

I earnestly wish every soldier of the Corps the best of good fortune, and a glorious and decisive victory, the story of which will reecho throughout the world, and will live for ever in the history of our home land.

JOHN MONASH,
Lieut. General
Cmdg. Australian Corps[4]

Chapter 31

The Battle Begins: 8 August 1918

Monash was not being melodramatic with his message to the corps. He firmly believed his plan would work and the breakthrough in the next few days would cause the Germans to wilt and capitulate. He had two German armies in front of him. If his tactics came off as drawn up, those armies would be down inside 48 hours and the enemy would be forced to draw off other armies to rush them to Amiens. With twelve armies in the field the German High Command would know they were facing a crushing, war-ending defeat. Yet Monash, more than anyone, was aware of other 'ifs' and imponderables that, to an extent, were out of his control. He had faith in Currie and the Canadians on his right flank who were due to wing in on day two and take over the brunt of the fighting. He had next to no faith in Butler and his British Army of tyros on the left flank. But Monash felt he had that covered. As ever, there was always element 'x' to upset the calculations, yet his training to adapt to disturbances to his scheme was developed in theory back in 1912, when he trained in Sydney for the operation of a central commander in a bunker, and in practice since the cauldron of Gallipoli, where failure was more likely than success because commanders did not comprehend what all arms at their disposal were doing, or how they could be combined. Hamel had given Monash an injection of confidence and certitude. He had timed that battle for 90 minutes and it had taken 93. Amiens was 30 times bigger, yet he had his hands on the levers of battle on a scale that suited his mind and experience.

•

At 3.30 a.m. on 8 August, Australian Gunner J.R. Armitage lay in readiness for the attack. He wrote in his diary:

'It was utterly still. Vehicles made no sound on the marshy ground . . . the silence played on our nerves a bit. As we got our guns into position you could hear drivers whispering to their horses and men muttering curses under their breath, and still the silence persisted, broken only by the whine of a stray bullet or a long range shell passing high overhead . . . we could feel that hundreds of groups of men were doing the same thing—preparing for the heaviest barrage ever launched.'[1]

At 4.00 a.m. the only noise came from Allied planes droning over the enemy as a cover for the menacing sound of those squealing tanks that kept inching forward. Monash was woken by aide Major Walter Berry. He dressed, read final reports and then walked into the Bertangles grounds. He lit a cigarette and paced the 130-metre drive of his HQ from its steps to its medieval front gates. Monash glanced at his watch. It was 4.10 a.m., ten minutes until the start. He looked up. The night sky was black except for a stray enemy artillery shell. Planes buzzed lower, as instructed, to drown out the sound of tanks beginning their crawl forward like giant armadillos. The air was thick now with the pungent waft of fuel, smoke and earlier gas attacks. In a few minutes, the five Australian divisions under his command would fight together for the first time. They would be the spearhead of a massive Allied offensive. Monash had been the key instigator of the Anzac tradition. He believed that 25 April would rank through the centuries as the true birth of the spirit of the nation; he hoped that 8 August would sit alongside it as a day of exceptional achievement.

There was more than an edge of anticipation in Monash's step as he glanced at his watch again: 4.15 a.m. The movements of his lean, hard frame were agile as he walked up the steps of the chateau. As he scanned the horizon, most of the German Army across the fields on the Somme was catching precious sleep. Enemy sentries were oblivious to what now sent a shiver up the corps commander's spine. A hundred thousand of his infantry, spread over 20 kilometres, waited for the signal to start the attack about 10 kilometres east of Amiens. Some were already crawling forward to get within 70 metres of the German line. It was about to be hit by the single biggest artillery barrage of the war.

At 4.16 a.m., Monash recounted: 'All feel to make sure their bayonets are locked, or to set their steel helmets.' Company and platoon commanders, whistles suspended near their mouths, glanced at their watches. They gave a last look over their command.

Their runners were by their sides. The officers set their compasses. They would allow them to control the infantry's direction.

'Carrying parties shoulder their burdens, and adjust the straps,' Monash imagined as he stood on the chateau entrance steps. 'Pioneers grasp their picks and shovels; engineers take up their stores of explosives and primers and fuses . . .'

At 4.17 a.m. Monash's heart beat faster. His blood pressure would be right up, as it always was at these moments of extreme tension. Less than 600 metres from him, his machine and Lewis gunners whispered for the last time to their magazine and belt-box carriers to make sure they followed up. The corps' Stokes mortar carriers slung their heavy loads. Their loaders checked for the last time to see if their haversack of cartridges were in reach.

The planes kept buzzing overhead, as the tanks clamoured forward.

Monash the battle commander was also Monash the manager as he spared a thought in his mind's eye for the 'scores of telegraph operators'. They sat by their equipment with their 'message forms and registers ready to hand, bracing themselves for the rush of signal traffic', which would begin in a few moments.

At Bertangles and in the fields behind the lines, dozens of staff officers spread their maps in readiness, to record with their coloured pencils the stream of information.

At 4.18 a.m., in pits and trenches, the last guns were run up, loaded and laid on the opening lines of fire.

At 4.19 a.m. scores of sergeants checked the range for the last time. Layers stood silently, lanyards in hand. The section officers, watches on wrists, counted the last seconds. Thirty seconds. Twenty seconds. Ten seconds.

—'FIRE.'

More than a thousand guns began Monash's beloved 'symphony': 'A great illumination lights up the Eastern horizon; and instantly the whole complex organization, extending far back to areas almost beyond earshot of the guns, begins to move forward.'[2]

Out in the field, gunner Armitage recalled: 'All hell broke loose and we heard nothing more. The world was enveloped in sound and flame, and our ears just couldn't cope. The ground shook.'[3]

Lieutenant Colonel Arthur Wilson of the 7th Field Ambulance, who controlled more than four hundred men, 29 vehicles and 17 horsed ambulances, noted in his diary: 'At 4.20 a.m., zero hour, the barrage opened with a terrific crash. Fortunately the retaliatory bombardment was non-existent.'

The attack had been a complete surprise to the Germans. Reflecting the concerns of his vital part of the operation, Wilson added: 'the one thing of which we had the greatest fear, i.e. an intensive Gas [mainly Mustard Gas] bombardment as the men formed up on the "jumping off" tape, did not eventuate.'[4]

Major Berry said to Monash: 'Sir, this is a most wonderful day for you.'

Monash turned to him, put his hand on his shoulder and replied: 'No, Berry. It is a wonderful day for Australia, and history will bear this out.'

Monash entered his office. Chief of Staff Blamey was there, smoking a cigar, his feet up on the desk.

'I have nothing to do,' Blamey said, 'so we can wait while they count thousands of prisoners.'[5]

Monash watched at the window, where he considered the harmony from Hades that he had created. He was thrilled to appreciate that 'every man, every unit, every vehicle and every tank' advanced as the early summer dawn began to break. The enraptured commander was perhaps carried away with creative and theatrical analogies when he noted that the deafening artillery blast 'surely surpasses in dynamic splendour any other manifestation of collective human effort'.[6]

Not for the German Army, rudely awoken. It was Armageddon. The barrage rained down on them. Those who collected their senses, dazed by the air-splitting sounds of exploding shells, scrambled for their helmets and weapons. They could make out the menacing sight of those brutal tanks rolling at them. Within minutes sight was lost, except for flashes. A cloak of dust, smoke and spume blinded the stunned soldiers. The German Army did what any force would do under the same fierce attack: it retreated. Many soldiers left their guns, big and small. Some—the foolhardy and the frozen—braced themselves and returned fire. But in the main part, the Germans were overrun.

Every tentacle of this mighty AIF octopus was coordinating well in the first hour.

Lieutenant Colonel Wilson noted at 5.20 a.m., one hour into the battle:

All the cars and wagons [ambulances] moved forward to their stations . . . as arranged and on time, although some considerable difficulty was experienced in getting the horses past the heavy guns and 18 pounders. A very thick fog made it impossible to see more than 20 or 30 yards ahead . . . things were apparently going well as droves of German prisoners were coming back along the main road. They were equipped with stretchers, and were carrying out wounded [both Australian and German].[7]

The Australian Corps had already penetrated the enemy to the designated imaginary 'green line'—the first stage. It moved the attacking divisions more than 3 kilometres. The return artillery died steadily, as if the enemy was running out of shells. It wasn't. The artillery was being captured, just as Monash had demanded it should be in the first phase of the operation. The harm done to the attacking forces was minimised.

The enemy's garrisons were mostly destroyed or captured. The Australians kept coming, swooping into the second and third phases in a 'walkover'. The 2nd and 3rd Divisions, who had spearheaded the assault, came to a halt, their job done.

The conflict had been going 150 minutes.

Monash kept Haig and Rawlinson at Fourth Army HQ updated.

At 7.00 a.m. he telegraphed: 'Gailly Village and Accroche Wood captured. Enemy artillery has ceased along my whole front. Flanks Corps [British and Canadians] apparently doing well.'[8]

Chapter 32

Tanks for the Mist

The Battle of Amiens had begun in mist, which turned into thick fog. This helped the attack forces, but hindered for a time the planes that Monash had requested for intelligence work at the front. Still, the phone and telegraph were used, as were the ever-reliable pigeons. By 8 a.m. the fog veil had lifted to reveal a stunning view of the Somme Valley. The midsummer sun filtered through the haze over the steep wooded slopes and folds of the northern riverside that Monash feared would give him trouble, because he had been refused control of the assault on it. Less forbidding, since it was already under Australian control, were the flatter grass and wheat spurs on the southern approach. At first view they were colourful and even serene. On the long, flat top of the finger east of the 'Long Gully' from Lamont to Cerisy, and across the summit of Villers-Bretonneux plateau, were scattered parties of Australian Infantry. Some were still digging, others were looking out from their newly dug trenches. More still strolled or stood in groups. Some smoked. To the untrained eye they may have appeared nonchalant. But these hardened Australian troops from the 2nd and 3rd Divisions, in whom Monash had unbounded faith, were relaxing. They had finished their fighting for the moment at the 3500-yard (3-kilometre) green line first objective. Soldiers from 4th and 5th Divisions 'leapfrogged' them as planned in pursuit of the scattered enemy. Mobile artillery was more active as it was pushed forward. Pioneers and engineers were clearing and repairing roads.

Tanks in their hundreds dotted the landscape. Only a few had been immobilised. Some sizzled in meltdowns from direct artillery hits, and smoke spiralled from them. But overwhelmingly they were operational, staying more or less in line with advancing troops. Thanks to Monash's risks in using them at night—a tactic only ever employed once before, at Hamel, scepticism about their use in combat had evaporated, along with the enemy's confidence in facing them. The Australian troops, ahead of any other, had grown to love these cumbersome yet brutal machines-in-arms. They would be a fixture in most wars for the next century at least.

With visibility now good, planes dotted the horizon skies and seemed to be dive-bombing close to the ground. In fact, they were swooping down to 150 metres so observers within could scribble notes or mark maps to record how the Australian and German front lines were changing by the quarter hour. They would then head back to fields near Bertangles, where the maps and notes were wrapped in weighted, multicoloured streamers and dropped. Cyclists seemed in constant motion, bumping across fields to collect the intelligence, which was whisked back to a staff office at the chateau.

This Monash innovation meant that messages, as hoped, were reaching him and his staff from the front line in just ten minutes.

•

By 8.30 a.m. Monash was able to tell Haig and Rawlinson that the green line—the first phase objective—was nearly confirmed as captured along the whole corps front. Major conquests in Australian hands included Accroche Wood, the villages of Gailly, Warfusée and Lamotte, and the entire Cerisy Valley. Thousands of German soldiers—heads down in shock or fatigue—were marching or straggling back behind the Australian lines to be locked in huge 'cages'. The first spoils of this battle, artillery guns—some with huge bores that had pulverised Amiens for months—were being hauled away.

Maestro Monash was pleased with the mellifluous sounds coming from his military orchestra. Performers not involved in the actual fighting were also blending harmoniously. The field ambulance units had already evacuated the wounded from the 2nd and 3rd Divisions. They turned their attention to soldiers of the 4th and 5th as they began engaging the enemy in the so-called 'open warfare' stage.

Lieutenant Colonel Wilson noted that the engineers were working efficiently at mending shell-damaged roads. 'It was soon possible to bring the large [ambulance] cars through to the advanced dressing stations being set up behind the successfully advancing 5th Division.'[1]

The 'red' and 'blue lines' were now the next targets. The aimed-for 8 kilometres of fresh territory was almost in Australian hands across its entire front, except for the extreme left, north of the river at Chipilly Spur.

Monash's fears and expectations had materialised. The English troops—composed of inexperienced youths and middle-aged men of the 58th Division III Corps—had fought bravely in attempts to dislodge the Germans from their fortified positions on the ridge. But it may have been a case of 'lions led by donkeys'. Poor leadership and organisation had seen the English troops beaten back, leaving Australia's left flank vulnerable to German artillery barrages.

On the southern side of the river the Australians forged forward. At 10.55 a.m. Monash could report that Cerisy, opposite the difficult Chipilly, had been captured with 300 prisoners rounded up. A quarter of an hour later the advancing troops had taken Morcourt, about a kilometre south-east of Cerisy. The Somme opposite Morcourt flowed in a horseshoe around the troublesome Chipilly Spur. To demonstrate the clean sweep south of the Somme, Monash could add the town of Bayonvillers, positioned about 4 kilometres south-west of Morcourt.

'We are nearing our second objective [the red line] and have reached it in places,' Monash telegraphed. Haig was pleased to learn that the Cavalry Brigade, that he was so keen for Monash to push into action, had passed the red line. The whole corps operation was now moving on to the final objective—the blue line.[2]

Just after noon Major General Hobbs' 5th Division took the railway-line town of Harbonnières another kilometre further south-east of Bayonvillers. It had reached the blue line, the operation's southernmost objective.

At 1.15 p.m. Monash had enormous pride and delight in telling Haig and Rawlinson: 'Australian flag hoisted over Harbonnières at midday today. Should be glad if Chief [Haig] would cable this to our Governor-General on behalf of Australian Corps.'[3]

There was enormous work to do yet. But so far the attack had been as successful as anything Monash envisaged. He had achieved much at Hamel. But this moment during the battle was the finest of Monash's military career, and perhaps his life. Whatever happened now, no one could take away his achievement of battle honours on a grand scale leading the AIF on its first-ever unified corps operation.

•

At 2.05 p.m. Monash made the 'body-count' report, telling Rawlinson that casualties were 'under 600'. There were more than four thousand prisoners with 'many more coming in'. Soon after, he could reinforce the extent of the rout by cabling his superiors that the 5th Division had captured the 51 German Corps HQ at Framerville on the final phase red line.

The 8 p.m. final communiqué to Rawlinson and Haig noted that more than six thousand prisoners had been taken. The haul was 100 guns, including the dangerous heavy and railway type, a train, and 'hundreds of vehicles and transport'. Then came the less palatable news about Allied dead. Total casualties for the whole corps were about 1100. Given that the number engaged in the assault on day one would have exceeded 150,000, this was an attrition rate of less than 1 per cent. Previously such a big assault would expect to see casualties twenty or thirty times that figure. It was a number that any general could live with. Monash, naturally ebullient, would sleep well enough on the night of 8 August 1918. His espoused policy of supporting and preserving troops with coordinated backup of tanks, airpower and artillery had worked in favour of the soldiers.

Overall, the attack had been too successful for Rawlinson and his staff to digest at Fourth Army HQ. Instead of ordering Monash to push his corps due east, the thrust was to be made south-east. The Canadians would take up the cudgel on its front. The Australians would swing their thrust to the right and protect the Canadian left flank along the Amiens–Nesle railway (the southern Australian boundary). General Currie's troops would advance between the railway and the Amiens–Roye road, heading for Lihons. The Australians were supposed to pivot to their left on the Somme to Méricourt.

Rawlinson's ultimate objective (as specified originally by Monash) for both corps was to take the important railway centre of Roye, south of Lihons. Failing that, it was hoped that the threat to capture it would force the German Army to retreat from the great bulge of territory it had eaten into during the big offensive in April and May a few months earlier.

At the least, this would stop the Germans using trains from Roye to feed its operations in this salient.

The speed of victory on 8 August was not fully understood at British High Command HQ. Monash, at the front, had a very good concept of the success and by instinct and experience, would have preferred to push on east to the big bend in the Somme, where the Germans held the towns of Bray, Péronne and Brie. Reports from the front were clear. If he ordered a further drive into the night of the eighth and into the next day, the area around that important, almost 90-degree bend in the river would be overrun by the Australians.

Monash was well aware that the territory at the river bend

had been fought over in 1915 and 1916. Then the French and Germans had sat tight and belted each other with artillery, converting the area into a wasteland. It was seared with trenches and wire entanglements in its easternmost part on the German front. But between the bend and that devastated area there was another 11 kilometres of unharmed country.

Monash was keen to know how much he was crushing the enemy. It was vital to a possible follow-up plan to drive right through the German defences and force a mass capitulation.

Chapter 33

Carter's Wild Ride

Monash had aerial intelligence, which suggested the German Reserve Army sitting behind the one he had just smashed, was in disarray. But he needed more solid evidence if he were to put a strong case for pushing due east and not letting up the pressure on the enemy. He had the Tank Corps' 17th Armoured Car Battalion at his disposal, which included two companies, each with eight cars. The vehicles could reach speeds of 32 kilometres forward or in reverse, and were three or four times faster than the tanks. Each had one forward and one rear Hotchkiss gun. They were armour-plated and protected from all but a direct artillery hit. Before midday on 8 August, Monash ordered Lieutenant Colonel E.J. Carter to use the cars to scour the roads beyond the final objective reached by Hobbs's 5th Division. The vehicles, prone to breakdown on rough surfaces, took 'moderately good' roads. Monash was relying on aerial photographs of the enemy's back country and roads within a few kilometres of the Germans' new front line.

The subsidiary roads in the zone had been all but obliterated by shell-craters. Even the well-built main Roman route from Villers-Bretonneux to St Quentin had been cut by trenches on both sides of 'no-man's-land'. Monash donned his engineer's hat, figuratively, and directed pioneers to clear the way for the cars as far as possible. After that it was up to Carter and his small contingent. He and a staff officer, 'scarcely recognizable and covered in grease and grime', reported back to Monash's corps HQ a few minutes before midnight.

The extent of the rout and mayhem caused by the AIF was exemplified by the wild ride of Carter's contingent. The squad drove through no-man's-land between the two opposing fronts. They were blocked first by trees that had been shot down across the road. Carter, his men and pioneers, chopped up the trees. He enlisted the aid of a tank, which acted like an elephant to drag the logs off the road. The armoured vehicles drove on for the enemy line, but didn't catch up with the advancing 2nd and 3rd Divisions—the first attacking Australians—until they were almost at the first objective red line.

The soldiers rested, waiting for the relieving 4th and 5th Divisions, but Carter and his marauders stormed forward, encountering 'quite a few Huns'. They were 'dealt with'.

The next Australian artillery barrage caused Carter and his men to wait in their vehicles with the motors running. When the shells fell away to a light shower, he signalled the cars forward through the second objective, the red line, then on to the final destination blue line. They had come the 8 kilometres well ahead of the infantry and cavalry. Carter sent several cars south to Framerville, a German stronghold. They found all the enemy transport horses and many lorries drawn up in the main road ready to flee.

'The head of the column tried to bolt in one direction,' Carter said in his report to Monash, 'and other vehicles in another. There was complete confusion.'

'Our men killed the lot [using 3000 rounds of ammunition] and left them there,' he noted bluntly. 'Four staff officers on horseback [were] shot also.'

After that mini-massacre, the cars ran on to the east of Harbonnières, on the south-east road to Vauvillers. They met six German steam wagons en route. Carter ordered his cars to fire into the wagons' boilers, disabling them and causing an 'impassable' block on the road. The armoured cars left the main road, and rushed on to Vauvillers, where they 'had a lot of good shooting', killing several German soldiers on the run from these fast-moving mini-tanks.

Carter led his contingent back onto the main road. He then dispatched six cars to Foucaucourt where they encountered a heavy German gun in a wood, and met the stiffest resistance to their rampage behind German lines.

'This gun blew the wheels off one car,' Carter reported, 'and hit three others.'

The three remaining cars beat a fast retreat. But the raiders motored on. Next, Carter sent two cars to the town of Proyart, where many German troops were billeted in local houses. It was mealtime and the soldiers were not expecting an attack. The fighting, as far as they knew, was going on a few kilometres west.

The two cars bumped their way into the gardens and shot through the windows at the seated Germans. Carter claimed that 'quite a lot of the enemy' were killed.

Another contingent of four cars were sent towards Chuignolles, now deep in German-held territory east of the battle. They blasted soldiers in the town, and careered through it to trenches.

'We engaged them,' Carter wrote succinctly. 'Had quite a battle there. Extent of damage not known, but considerable.'

Carter regrouped the twelve vehicles that were still running and brought them back up to the main road, still well in advance of the last objective blue line where the troops would consolidate that night. He found everything quiet. There was no artillery fire.

Not satisfied with the chaos he had caused, Carter led his cavalier convoy 200 metres beyond La Flaque, where they took scores of prisoners. They were detailed to tow back his car, which had taken one shell or bullet too many and was disabled.

It was 10.30 a.m.; Carter and his crew had then been careering around the countryside causing havoc for about three hours. Apart from the objective of disrupting the enemy, the lieutenant's goal was also to gather intelligence.[1]

•

Monash was delighted with Carter's firsthand assessment behind the lines, which had been confirmed by the air reconnaissance. There were no barbed wire entanglements to speak of. The trenches were old and overgrown, indicating that the defences were limited at best.

Carter and his men saw 'no trace of any organized system of defence of any kind and no troops'.

The only Germans they encountered were on the run in the opposite direction.

This confirmed to Monash that his masterplan had worked better than he or anyone expected. He wanted to push on east if Haig and Rawlinson would allow it. But not for the first time in the war, he was restrained. He may have been the thinking commander—preferring to make decisions in his HQ, where he controlled all the intelligence, rather than wandering around the front line risking his neck in displays of bravado—yet when it came to an instinct for forcing victory, he had a more ruthless streak than any of his peers or superiors. Except perhaps for Foch, who was not anywhere near the field of battle and who was at this stage unaware of the amazing outcome of 8 August.

The orders from Rawlinson for his force to ease up and park itself south-east stood. Monash had to resist the need to quench his thirst for territorial acquisition, and more importantly to smash through and finish the war. Carter's marauding behind the lines confirmed the Germans were ripe for capitulation. If Monash had been allowed to have his way, Ludendorff could not have had time, or even the inclination, to draw off other divisions from along the Front to bolster his armies at Amiens. He and all other key German commanders admitted that such a continued push would have forced an immediate Allied victory. It was not a case of the 'donkeys' in the British High Command making stupid decisions. The 8 August crash-through had been so swift and sweeping that perhaps only Monash on the Allied side, armed with intelligence from the air and Carter, could see the chance to end it in a matter of three or four days. (The shocked German

High Command then, and on reflection, knew of the devastating holocaust that had befallen its armies.)

Instead of being allowed to deliver a final blow, a frustrated Monash wrote new plans and directed the 1st Australian Division, led by Major General Glasgow, to assist the Canadians along the railway.

The success of the Australian advance the day before created a problem. The last two of the 1st Division's brigades arrived later than expected from the north. When instructed to march on from Amiens railway station to the front, they found it much further than anticipated. The troops arrived late on the morning of 9 August, and missed the move out by the Canadians at 11 a.m.

This logistical problem was covered by the 5th Division ordering its right line brigade—the 15th, led by the dashing Major General Pompey Elliott—that was patrolling the railway itself, to fill the breach before the troops from the 1st Division arrived. Elliott's men found stiff opposition, but hung on until the foot-weary 1st Division turned up. Then Monash ordered the swing right—south-east—of the 1st and 2nd Divisions. They sliced through the captured Framerville and ended up on 9 August at the foot of Lihons Hill. Resistance had been at times strong, but sporadic along a moving front of 6 kilometres.

The Germans had been able to regroup along a ridge at Lihons Hill. They used field and machine guns to attack the Australians, who had to dig in. The tanks were the main targets for the defending Germans. They knocked out many of them.

At night the Australians made contact with the advancing Canadians on the railway. The depth of planning had led to a huge 'Dominion' breakthrough on day one of the battle.

Chapter 34

Chipilly Spur; Germany's Black Days

On 9 August Monash had most concern about his left flank over the river. The night before, the English 58th Division couldn't budge the Germans on Chipilly. As planned, Sinclair-Maclagan had formed a defensive flank for the Australian 4th Division, yet the Germans had hit several tanks across the river. Artillery duels continued. Monash repeated his requests to Rawlinson to take command of this trouble spot. Butler objected, but then suddenly he was removed. The official line was that he was taking prearranged sick leave, unlikely at this critical time. It pleased Monash. The languid, very tall General Godley, Monash's former Chief at Gallipoli, replaced the limited, rigid Butler.

Godley was not expecting Monash's request. He demurred,

saying the sector was under his control. Monash argued hard, knowing that the 'elegant' Godley, who lacked 'technical ability', would have the grace to listen to him. Monash summed up by saying he had to attack the spur.

'The Boche have been firing on my left flank for more than 30 hours!' he told Godley. 'I've already ordered the American 131st Regiment into position at one end of the spur, ready to attack. My 13th Brigade is on the move there from the other end.'[1]

The Englishman knew from his experience at Gallipoli that Monash would not make such a strong case unless the matter was vital. Godley relented, giving Monash access to the spur. He now had 'limited jurisdiction' over the north bank of the Somme.

'This was merely getting in the thin end of the wedge,' Monash wrote. He found himself 'where I had so strongly desired to be from the first, namely, astride of the Somme Valley'.[2]

The best available brigade was the 13th. Before the 8 August attack began, it had stayed south of the railway line to deceive the Germans about the arrival of the Canadian Corps. It was now ordered to take Chipilly. But since Monash's urgent requests, Godley had appraised the situation and decided to take action before the Australians could march there. He had directed the experienced 131st American Regiment to attempt to take it. The Americans began their task at about 4.30 p.m. Two hours later, after heavy fighting, they controlled nearly the entire ridge.

At this time, the 13th Brigade arrived and sent a battalion across the river at Cerisy.

They joined the Americans, Monash noted with satisfaction, and 'helped to clear up the whole situation. This made my left flank more secure, and enabled Sinclair-Maclagan to withdraw the defensive flank which he had deployed along the river from Cerisy to Morcourt.'[3]

That night of 9 August, Monash took over the 131st American Regiment from the British III Corps and attached it to his 4th Division. Sinclair-Maclagan was put in charge of the newly captured front. This extended several kilometres north of the river to the Corbie–Bray road.

Monash's organised mind was well satisfied at the end of 9 August with the Australians' relentless advance.

His 1st, 2nd and 4th Divisions ran south to north in the line of the new front.

•

By contrast, General Ludendorff was distressed to the point where his staff wondered if he would have a nervous breakdown. That would come later in the autumn when he would receive psychiatric counselling. Now he could only attempt to absorb and counter the horrific events of the past 48 hours in which 28,000 Germans died and more than 70,000 were injured. He wrote in his memoirs: 'August 8th was the black day of the German Army in the history of the war. This was the worst experience I had to go through . . .'[4]

Ludendorff would never have dreamed that a general with a Prussian/German background born in the same year would be his key opponent and nemesis in war. Given Ludendorff's support for Adolf Hitler in a 1923 coup d'état, and the General's fascist links and paranoias about Jewish conspiracy theories, he would have been driven to his psychiatrist's couch earlier if he ever learnt that Monash was Jewish.

In his memoirs, Ludendorff described with some feeling how the Australians and Canadians attacked in thick fog 'that had been rendered still thicker by artificial means' (Monash's smoke-screen) with 'strong squadrons of tanks, but for the rest with no great superiority. The [German] Divisions in line allowed themselves to be completely overwhelmed.'

To add to the confusion he mentioned how 'tanks' had run through divisional HQ, which may have been a deliberate mis-representation on the HQ staff's behalf. In fact, they had been terrorised by Carter's armoured *cars*, which would not have sounded so frightening.

'The cars wrought dire confusion in the rear of the German front lines,' Heinz Guderian wrote. He would, a generation later, command Hitler's Panzer Divisions in their slicing through Europe using a direct copy of Monash's battle plan and methods. 'They [the armoured cars] inflicted heavy losses on columns and reserves, and held them in the neighbourhood of the two villages for several hours without suffering any losses . . . For six hours the area had stood open to British breakthrough; there had been hardly any German defenders in the way.'

The British High Command, unaware of the swift destruction of the German front-line army, and the dislocation of a second in reserve, had left the enemy completely vulnerable and defeatable.

'British [Australian] aircraft successfully attacked and pinned down the German reserves,' Guderian noted. 'British tanks were at hand in considerable numbers, and no German resistance to speak of had been encountered . . . all this to no avail. The British did nothing . . .'[5]

He was unaware that Monash, the architect of the entire plan, had envisaged continuing but had been thwarted. The lack of action had allowed the Germans to regroup.

Ludendorff recalled:

The exhausted Divisions that had been relieved a few days earlier and were lying in the region south-west of Péronne (near that Somme's big bend) were immediately alarmed and set in motion by the commander-in-chief of the Second Army. At the same time he brought forward towards the breach all available troops. The Rupprecht Army Group dispatched reserves thither by train. The 18th Army threw its own reserves directly into the battle from the south-east.[6]

The desperate Ludendorff ordered the German Ninth Army, 'itself in danger', to help out. Such was the surprise of Monash's 'big bang' that it took days before troops could reach the troubled area.

'It was a very gloomy situation,' the General noted. 'Six or seven Divisions that were quite fairly to be described as effective had been completely battered . . . The situation was uncommonly serious.'[7]

Ludendorff realised that if the Australians and the Canadians continued to attack 'with even comparative vigour' the Germans would not be able to resist west of the Somme. 'The wastage of the Second Army had been very great. Heavy toll had also been taken of the reserve which had been thrown in . . . Owing to the deficit created, our losses had reached such proportions that the [German] Supreme Command [essentially the over-worked Ludendorff himself] was faced with the need to disband a series of Divisions, in order to furnish drafts . . .'[8]

The picture of Germany's reduced capacity to resist confirmed Monash's instinct to push east. It wasn't to be. Yet the physical and psychological impact would remain and influence future peace negotiations, which were dictated for the Germans by Ludendorff and von Hindenburg.

The 'deeply confounded' General saw the writing on the wall for the Germans in the entire conflict when he concluded: '8 August made things clear for both [opposing] Army Commands.'

In the 'peace' settlement negotiations going on behind the battle scenes, the Allies had the upper hand. The Australians advanced the predicted 8 kilometres, took seven villages, 8000 prisoners, 173 guns and a great deal of extra booty. The Canadians moved forward 9.5 kilometres, secured twelve villages and took 5000 prisoners. In all, the British Fourth Army had pushed forward with seven divisions and three in support, against six German front-line divisions. The French on the right had taken a further 3500 prisoners. It was the biggest breakthrough for the Allies in the war so far, and created a massive bulge in the front line.

Monash pushed his troops on to support the Canadians with diminishing results over the next few days. But the damage was done. Germany had been heaved backwards, and was reeling from a technical knockout. It would recover and fight on, but now there was no hope of the German Army being other than on the defensive.

Ludendorff was realistic amid the gloom. A key determinate about the result of Amiens from his point of view occurred first when he was told that single Australian soldiers had captured 'whole bodies of men'. That spelt a dip in morale to Ludendorff, who wasn't fully aware of the impact of Monash's tanks advancing through the mist from less than 100 metres. Worse still was learning that 'retiring troops [Germans leaving the Front] meeting a fresh division going bravely into action, had shouted out things like "Blackleg!" and "you're prolonging the war".'[9]

This meant to him that morale was so damaged by the defeat that there was no real hope of a major recovery.

'We cannot win this war anymore,' Ludendorff told a colleague, 'but we must not lose it. We must defend.'[10]

General Friedrich von Lossberg said it was 'the worst defeat that an army suffered in the war'.[11]

On 9 August, Ludendorff had the tough task of informing the Kaiser that 'we have suffered a severe defeat'.

It was the first time Wilhelm II had heard these words. On other setbacks, he had been told about 'gallant withdrawals' and 'unfortunate stalemates'. Even for someone often out of touch with reality, his top commander's comments would have set him in a deep pessimistic malaise. His immediate reaction, however, was to say: 'I see that we must draw up the balance sheet; we are on the brink of solvency [meaning insolvency was in sight]. The war must be ended ... See you at Spa [Germany, for a meeting of the Imperial Council that would seek peace terms with the Allies].'[12]

Ludendorff was now faced with two stark options. He could retreat and re-fit, or stand and fight. He declared that the 'Grand Offensive' was no longer possible. The Germans now had one option: a 'Grand Defensive'.

He was not prepared to admit defeat for the German Empire, but he was considering a loss for himself. Quitting was on his mind.

'Leadership now assumed the character of an irresponsible game of chance,' Ludendorff, the technocrat who lacked imagination, wrote, 'a thing I have always considered fatal. The fate of the German people was for me too high a stake. The war had to be ended.'[13]

The fighting would go on. Monash was now a heavyweight boxer who, in the eleventh of twelve rounds had put his opponent on the canvas with a combination of telling punches. It was not the knockout he had planned, but it was the biggest, most important victory of the entire war and would destine its end.

Chapter 35

Haig's Emotional Response

Fighting continued through 10 August, intensely in some areas, as the Allies advanced 16 kilometres east. The smooth running of Monash's grand plan removed Amiens, the last bastion before Paris—120 kilometres south—from any danger of capture. German resistance was greater as Ludendorff shored up defences after the irreparable damage of the previous two days. Monash was disappointed. The main aim of his Amiens battle plan was to push hard east and immediately into the second phase with a knockout blow on a reserve German Army that would force the enemy to capitulate completely and end the war.

Many German commanders believed that they had been let off the hook by the Allied failure to hit hard further east to

Péronne. Heinz Guderian believed that 'the Allies had their boot on the throat of the entire German force, and took it off'.[1]

By 11 August, the Allied leaders appreciated Monash's success and what it could mean for the future. In the early morning, when Monash was preparing plans for further advance, Winston Churchill, British Minister of Munitions, called in to congratulate him and discuss the 'state of play'. Churchill was particularly interested in Monash's views about German morale. At 11 a.m. Haig was driven to Bertangles to formally thank Monash for the work done. He brought his Chief of the General Staff, Sir Henry Lawrence. General Byng of the British Third Army arrived while Haig and General Lawrence were there. Haig thought it opportune for him to discuss operations with Byng and Lawrence. Monash made as if to leave them in a room near his office, but the others insisted he stay for the entire conference. Monash was pleased that he was 'frequently asked' for his opinions.

He had been so immersed in his command that he didn't yet fully comprehend the ramifications of his breakthrough in such a decisive and sweeping victory. The Allied leaders were relieved at last to have a commander with the courage to plan victories, particularly without massive troop losses on their side.

In modern parlance, Monash was a 'winner'. Everyone wanted to make contact.

At noon, Rawlinson phoned to tell him that Marshall Foch himself was also coming to Bertangles—at 3 p.m. Fresh orders about tactical policy would be given. Monash told Rawlinson that Haig was meeting the five Australian divisional commanders at 2.30 p.m. in Villers-Bretonneux. Rawlinson then changed plans and arranged for Foch to be at an army conference in the fields just west of the village.

In this heady, spontaneous atmosphere of felicitations, Monash realised that his battle planning would be interrupted for the rest of the day when he was informed that Sir Henry Wilson, Chief of the Imperial General Staff, was also in France and wished to call on him at Bertangles. Wilson, normally someone a general would have to drop everything for, was told that he could find Monash in the village between 2.30 and 3.30 p.m. Wilson would have to join the line of VIP wellwishers.

Monash was driven in the Rolls to a shady spot under trees in a field on the outskirts of the village, which was a hive of activity. Australian and Canadian railway specialists were re-laying the track in time for the first train since 7 August to come through from Amiens. A large, wired-in prisoners' cage was in view across the main road. Small groups of Germans were being herded in to join the 3000 inmates already there.

'An immense stream of traffic was pouring up the road towards the front,' Monash noted. 'Guns, troops, strings of horses and mules, hundreds of motor lorries, ambulance wagons, and the usually motley traffic of war.'[2]

At 2.30 p.m. Haig met Monash's divisional commanders— Major Generals Hobbs, Sinclair-Maclagan, Rosenthal, Gellibrand and Glasgow. Haig made a complimentary speech, in which he became emotional.

'You do not know what the Australians and Canadians have done for the British Empire in these days,' he said. Haig tried to go on, but could not. He began to cry. The Australian commanders, unused to such displays from the stiff upper lip British Army leadership (and its own), were embarrassed. They moved away.[3] Yet the moment had its impact. Haig was strong and ruthless. Such a display of his feelings was unprecedented and telling. In the three days since the major breakthrough, he was beginning to realise that the British Empire would not be lost when he was in command of its armed forces. Until recently, he had hoped and prayed a lot more and had no way of knowing if he could prevail. Haig had taken all the criticism on his prominent chin and had been stoic enough to push it all aside as he continued to prosecute the conflict. Despite the portrayals of him as a 'butcher', a 'donkey' and even a 'mass murderer', he was a human of piety, strength of character and sensitivity, at least to the preservation of all he considered good, godly and democratic in English life. He was affected by the continual and growing negative commentary in the press, and the knowledge that the country's prime minister was fiercely against him. Haig had been fortified by knowing that he had the support of the King, who behind the scenes had more influence and power than his first minister. Now there had been a dramatic, sudden, unforeseen crushing of the enemy army. The Germans had been overwhelmed physically; he had been overwhelmed emotionally. It was now a strong possibility that he would not go down in history as one of the great losers. Haig's instinct was to believe the amazing turn of events was God's will.

On 8 August he wrote to his wife:

Our attack . . . this morning seems to have taken the enemy completely by surprise . . . I hear. Two of our armoured motor cars being sent on to round up German Corps Headquarters! Who would have believed this possible even two months ago? How much easier it is to attack, than to stand and await an enemy's attack! As you well know, I feel that I am only the instrument of that Divine Power who watches over each of us, so all the Honours must be His.[4]

His thinking was in direct contrast to the atheist, Monash, who had worked towards this victorious moment for so long and with such precision. But whoever was the benefactor, the happily stunned Haig was most grateful.

•

At this moment on 11 August Rawlinson arrived with Montgomery-Massingberd. Then Henry Lawrence, Wilson, Currie, Godley and commanders from the cavalry, tank and Royal Air Force turned up.

At 3 p.m. Rawlinson, surrounded by huge maps, began the army conference as planned. He didn't get very far before more cars appeared carrying Foch, the French Prime Minister Clemenceau, and his finance minister Louis-Lucien Klotz.

'Villers-Bretonneux, only three days before reeking with gas and unapproachable, and now delivered from its bondage,' Monash wrote, 'was the lodestone which had attracted the individual members of this remarkable assemblage.'[5]

Rawlinson rolled up his maps. There was no chance of meetings now as the VIPs praised Monash and Currie in heartfelt speeches. The relief in the congratulations was palpable. Uncertainty and hope had been replaced by a true sense that now the enemy would be repulsed.

Chapter 36

George V Makes a Point

Monash's war planning was again interrupted the next day, 12 August, when he prepared for the arrival of King George V at Bertangles. It was an appropriate moment for the King to invest him with a knighthood, bestowed months earlier. Photographers and film cameras were there to catch the ceremony, and both the King and Monash were happy with that. It was important to give credit for morale purposes for all members of the forces. The King, too, was keen to make a point. Early in the war Haig had been indifferent about his 'Dominion' commander. After the King told him of Monash, he had taken a different attitude and quickly realised what an asset the Australian was. Haig could take credit for supporting him in the minor Hamel Battle and in the big one at Amiens where Monash had put 30 years of experience in theory and practice into action. Now Monash had a record second to none in terms of planning and winning battles, large and small. The King had foreseen his worth in 1916 when he chatted with Monash for two and a half hours while inspecting Australia's 3rd Division on Salisbury Plains. Two years on, George V was making a public acknowledgement of his own good judgement.

Monash arranged a guard of honour of 600 men at Bertangles. They lined the driveway under tall chestnut trees. Monash also made sure that an impressive line-up of war trophies was placed in the chateau's grounds—a quadrangle of lawns and shrubs, flanked on three sides by copper beech trees and more chestnuts.

The booty included several hundred guns, howitzers, heavy machine guns, light machine guns, anti-tank guns, field searchlights, transport vehicles, range finders and hundreds of other minor trophies. Monash included 'a representative selection of a dozen enemy vehicles, both horse-drawn and motor-drawn, with teams of horses and harness complete, just as captured'.

Monash's troop formation was made up of a hundred men from each of the Australian divisions and another hundred from the Royal Garrison Artillery. They lined both sides of the drive from outside the front gates, with their heraldic figures and coats of arms, to the steps of the piazza in the middle of the 100-metre long chateau facade.

When the King's car came in view in brilliant sunshine along the kilometre-long tree-lined avenue leading up to the chateau gates, Monash called his men to attention. He, Blamey and the Australian Corps Chief Administrative Officer Brigadier General Carruthers greeted the King, who was accompanied by two aides.

The King took the royal salute from the guard, inspected it with Monash, and then walked with him along the drive. The King inspected the troops, stopping for small talk with several of the men. They then walked up the steps from the piazza to the reception room. Inside, Monash presented the King to the chateau's owner, the Marquis de Clermont-Tonnerre, 'a very old man with a long white beard'.

Monash then introduced his five divisional commanders with whom the King chatted. After ten minutes, they moved down to the piazza for the investiture. A sword, a small table and a foot-stool were arranged on a carpet on steps in the piazza. With about one hundred of Monash's staff looking on, his name was called. He stepped up and stood to attention in front of the King.

'Kneel,' the King said.

Monash went down on his right knee.

The King then began to knight him by tapping him on the right shoulder. Monash began to rise before the King had swung the sword onto his left shoulder, but stayed down when he saw the King's movement. The investiture completed with the King saying: 'Arise, Sir John.'

He handed Monash the Insignia of a Knight Commander of the Bath.

The King smiled, pumped his hand and made a little speech 'commending [Monash's] work and that of the Australian troops'.[1]

Onlookers applauded. The King walked with Monash around the chateau grounds inspecting the battle trophies.

The whole ceremony had been going just 30 minutes before the King's car pulled up at the steps and he left. Monash called for three cheers from the troops lining the drive. They didn't respond with much voice, especially those at the other end of the drive. Monash tried again, but the dispersed guard responded sporadically as before. It was a minor hiccup in an otherwise glittering occasion, captured for posterity on film.

•

Monash's entry in his small diary for 12 August 1918, which he would list later as one of the three or four greatest days of his life, reflected its hectic mix of war and ceremony:

Indoors forenoon.

10 brigade captures Proyant.

Prepare for King's visit being made in front of chateau.

About 50 field guns, many trench mortars, machine guns and other trophies.

Attend Army conference at Villers Bretonneux.

12.30 Divisional Commanders Attend.

Return to Corps 2.25 p.m.

The King due 2.30 arrives at about 3.00 p.m. Inspects guard walks to chateau steps Am decorated with Star and Order of KCB. O'Keefe DMS Army KCMG. Later watches Boche transport and field ambulance being driven past and then departs.

Successful attack by 13 bge N of Somme Capture 183 prisoners.[2]

The King noted in his diary on the same day:

Proceeding to Bertangles was received [by] General Monash, GOC Australian Corps & his Generals & representatives from all the Australian divisions who are now fighting in this battle. I gave General Monash & General O'Keeff [*sic*] the KCB & knighted them. They showed me some of the many Guns and machine guns & horses & carts & ambulances which they have just captured from the Germans, they got over 300 horses.[3]

Later, Monash was also awarded Knight Commander of St Michael and St George. He had his much sought-after battle-field honours. But there was no thought of striding off to become a desk-bound, paper-shuffling general. The war had not yet been won. He was right in the middle of further attack plans. The well-wishers, and even the King's visit, would have been a distraction, no matter how much the visits were appreciated. Nobody was thinking that the war would end before 1919. But Monash was keen to drive home the advantage, *now.*

•

After Amiens, Hughes could see the need for a strong politician as the top corps administrator—General Officer Commanding (GOC)—who had everyone's respect in London. The war was reaching a critical stage and he wanted to be in a position to make sure he could get his way. If the number of Australian casualties became unacceptable to the electorate, Hughes would be desperate to start pulling out the AIF. It was one thing to order it, and another to have it carried through in communication and directives from the British High Command in London to the Western Front.

Hughes now told his Cabinet that Birdwood should be replaced as GOC but not by Monash, unless he wanted it, and everyone knew he would not. Hughes was saying Monash could have his choice. If he wished to stay corps commander, he could.

It seemed that Australian Defence Minister Pearce would have to move to London to take up the GOC job. Out of courtesy to the much-respected Birdwood, Hughes, on 12 August, offered him the GOC full-time, which meant he would have to stop running the British Fifth Army. No one expected him to accept, but he did. Birdwood enjoyed Australian troops and officers more than his own British soldiers. He sensed, too, that the AIF was going to continue at the forefront of the conflict. It would be more exciting, even rewarding. Some thought the offer a slight to Monash, but he could not be a politician *and* command the corps, especially in the current heated battles. Besides, Birdwood would not take up the full-time job until 30 November. The war was too preoccupying for such an important change at that moment.

Murdoch tried to stir the issue in an article in the Melbourne *Herald* that made the future juggling seem like a downgrade for Monash. But it had little impact. Too many eyes were now on the military struggle to worry about the shuffling of administrative chairs a long way from the front.

Bean, in contrast to Murdoch, now developed doubts about his own judgement, especially as he was not supported by White, who remained steadfast about his backing of Monash. Bean continued to intrigue with Murdoch but with far less fervour. Thirty-eight years later, he would write about the Bean/Murdoch 'high-intentioned but ill-judged intervention. That it resulted in no harm whatever was probably due to the magnanimity of both White and Monash.'[4]

Chapter 37

Keeping the Pressure On

Monash kept up his fitness by walking the Australian corps' entire 14.5-kilometre front from north of the Somme to the Amiens railway line in the south. He decided it was too much for him to rotate and rest his troops. Instead of having his front shortened, as he had in the past, Monash asked Rawlinson for, and received, another British division, which had been in reserve. Two extra Canadian divisions were temporarily parked under his command, along with an American regiment. In the fluidity of war, Monash was now the acknowledged supreme battlefield commander of the Allies and all non-Australian chiefs were happy to let him have their soldiers, and they were thrilled to be with the most penetrating force on the Front. Monash now controlled 208,000 soldiers, which was more an army than a corps.

In a letter home, he spoke of the taxing time he was having, running the expanded corps and preparing battle plans. His weight was now down to just under 71 kilograms, one less than he was a month earlier and a drop of 6 kilograms from a year ago. The intensity of Monash's work and his increased responsibilities were taking their toll.

'Along with his men,' Blamey wrote of his boss, 'he suffered severely from the strain of these last months. He became very thin, the skin hung loosely on his face. His characteristic attitude was one of deep thought.'[1]

However, Monash was still walking as much as possible and using his dumbbells to keep his body toned, in an effort to counter being more and more desk-bound as he worked longer and longer hours.

By mid-August 1918, not only was he the most respected general in the field, his battle strategies and tactics were now a blueprint for the British Army. He explained them to Haig and the Third Army's General Byng as they planned another attack on the 21st. The long delay from the shattering events of 8, 9, 10 August was caused by Ludendorff scrabbling together all his available reserves, drawn from all over the Western Front, to stop the push by the Australians and Canadians, and on their flanks the British and French. Byng had to bring in supplies of troops, transport and munitions, which delayed the next push. But when Byng's army did attack, it did well and facilitated a move up by the III Corps, which had made next to no progress since 8 August, much to Monash's disappointment.

•

Kaiser Wilhelm II continued to be given optimistic opinions from Ludendorff, despite the general retreat. There was always talk of renewed 'big offensives' and 'telling counterattacks'. But Wilhelm II, in denial, continued to be troubled, as if he was receiving more honest reports. His military and civil nurses did not mention the war but engaged him on the 'important' issues of arts and sciences; 'when the emperor took up the scheme . . . the otherwise dreary hours passed in a flash, and were a perpetual refreshment . . . The problems with tanks and German fears of them, of lowering morale and the prospects of possible revolution in a disturbed Germany, were flushed away, temporarily.'[2]

The Kaiser, however, was not alone in being diverted from reality and cold facts. Hindenburg had no real idea of the location of German Army Corps and so could be less alarmist in his conversations with the 'Supreme Warlord' (Wilhelm II). But it was tending to be counterproductive to German interests. The Kaiser was directing his relatives—the Spanish King and the Netherlands Queen—to seek 'mediation' with the Allies instead of using experienced diplomats to negotiate a peace settlement. Ludendorff and Hindenburg were recommending a 'more suitable' time such as 'after the next German success'. This prevarication would mean thousands more lives on both sides would be lost as the war dragged on and the Germans limped backwards.[3]

'Ludendorff's explanation was that "perfect candor would have led to a catastrophe!" If I had told them the truth, they would have completely lost their heads.'[4]

•

Foch was not quite aware of Monash's desire to push on to Péronne straight after Amiens. If it had been his army rather than Rawlinson's, he would have ordered it, but the Allies had lost the initiative created by the aggressive Australians supported by the Canadians. The French Third Army continued to push north until 16 August. On the 17th, Mangin's Tenth French Army attacked towards Soissons. A few days later, Byng's Third struck towards Bapaume to be joined a short time after by Horne's First British Army on the left. There was a lot of movement but not any real hints of a further massive smash-through. Monash's shock troops, parked south-east at Rawlinson's instigation, were cooling their heels when to a man they were itching to fight on and finish what they, and the Canadians, had started.

Further on, the French Army's right flank (or south), General Pershing, now commanding the recently formed US First Army, was planning his own big offensive. He had the 19 divisions, equivalent to 38 British divisions. But they did not yet have tanks, artillery or aircraft. Pershing couldn't use all of the divisions immediately. Five were parked with the British, including Monash's corps. Pershing moved to retrieve three of them, which made Haig furious. Battles that were expected to finish the war (following the definitive Amiens victory and counterattack) were being fought in the British zone to capitalise on the gains of 8 and 9 August. This battleground, just west of Amiens, was the hottest area of the Western Front. If the Allies could push on here they would win or end the entire war by forcing the Germans to the peace table. Haig complained that Pershing wanted to weaken the Allies in the Amiens zone to give himself a battle record and honours as an American commander in a less important zone, which was an accurate assessment. But Pershing was going to take any advantage he could wherever his nation could operate, regardless of the overall scheme and flow of events, and even if it slowed the Allied onslaught. However, he was forced to fight in battle areas assigned to him and his American troops.

Furthermore, Pershing would not be deterred from his objective to pull all his force together. He demanded that two further US divisions fighting with the French Sixth Army be returned to him. The Americans had a plan to take the St Mihiel salient, which poked out from north-east of Verdun running to Pont-à-Mousson. Foch offered him six French divisions, but once the St Mihiel salient was 'dissolved', he wanted to split Pershing's army; half of it to fight in the Argonne Forest and half in Champagne. Pershing refused to agree, but committed his intact army to the so-called Meuse-Argonne Offensive.

•

Just as the Americans were aiming to enter the fray on a big scale for the first time, Monash was formulating an attempt to take off again on the line east that he had wanted in the first place. The direction and force applied, if successful, would eventually have the Germans on the run, rather than simply in retreat. Monash's aim would be the most damaging to the enemy. Not only was he intent on protecting Amiens, the most important city short of taking Paris itself, his major aim was to shove the Germans right back to the Somme and beyond it. The enemy had held strongholds on the river for most of the war and they afforded the best defensive positions and bases for their attacks on the front. If pushed back and east of the river, Monash and all the commanders on both sides knew the Germans would be reversing as fast as they could. It was crucial that they did not hold forts on the Somme once the winter set in. If they were still there in November, they would be impossible to remove for at least the entire winter of 1918–1919 and probably the summer of 1919.

•

Monash took time on 21 August to hold a prolonged battle conference for the British III Corps' 32nd Division and the Australian 1st Division, who were both expected to engage in the next operation, known as the Battle of Chuignes and Bray. It would be twice the size of Hamel and more than just clearing territory for the Fourth Army, again spearheaded by the hardened Australian warrior force. Monash wanted no major blocks to his attempted assault on those big enemy forts on the Somme.

Both divisions were unfamiliar with Monash's special style, strategies and tactics. He had to explain his approach and preference for tanks, full artillery and plane support. He now had two fine examples of small and large battles on which to base his lectures—Hamel and Amiens.

•

On 22 August, the British 47th Division at last advanced past Albert and Méaulte.

The left flank of the Australian 3rd Division north of the Somme had moved up to bring Monash's corps square on to the river. It was positioned nicely on the forward slopes of the high plateau overlooking Bray and La Neuville, which were now targets for acquisition. The 3rd Division's 3rd Pioneer Battalion was busy rebuilding bridges over the Somme south of Bray, and creating advanced posts on the north bank of the river.

While the engineers were doing their necessary work to prepare for Monash's corps to take control, the 3rd Division's extreme left flank—9th Brigade—was having a tight battle in its push towards Bray. The British III Corps' 47th Division had faltered, which made the 9th Brigade's left flank vulnerable.

The 9th Brigade found refuge in a chalk pit and stood firm. They held the territory gained during the day, but Monash did not ask his soldiers to attempt to take Bray. He ordered them to wait until he had replanned the next moves, given the stiff German resistance, counterattacks and the blocking of the British 47th Division. In the fluid, fast-moving situation, Monash was taking the initiative at every chance. He called up the British III Corps' 32nd Division. Then he considered this part of the Somme Valley, which consisted of smaller, broad, wooded valleys running north and south for up to 8 kilometres. Clustered in them were several villages such as Proyart, which Lieutenant Colonel Carter and his armoured vehicles had terrorised on 8 August, along with Chuignolles, Herleville and Chuignes.

On 23 August, Monash ordered two brigades of Glasgow's 1st Division to attack along the Somme in a three-phase operation. In parallel, the 32nd Division was asked to capture the village of Herleville, and 3rd Division's 9th Brigade was to take Bray.

Monash's intelligence was that the woods were heavily defended by German machine gunners. He now called up the mobile artillery and tanks that in the space of six weeks had had an enormous impact on the war. Australian spies had managed to secure Ludendorff's plan of defence, which suited Monash.

John Monash with Australian
Prime Minister Billy Hughes
just before the 4 July 1918
Battle of Hamel on the
Western Front, France.

France's Premier, M. Georges Clemenceau (first on left), visited the battlefield
three days after Australia had won the 4 July 1918 Battle of Hamel and congratulated
AIF Corps Commander Lieutenant General Monash (third from left).

Monash on 29 July 1918 at Querrieu, France, handing out decorations for courage at the Battle of Hamel to members of the 4th Infantry Brigade.

Monash on 13 July 1918 at Camon, France, addressing his 2nd Division.

AIF Corps Commander John Monash (third from left, facing camera) on 13 July 1918 at Camon, France, after Hamel. He presented the Victoria Cross to Second Lieutenant W. Ruthven of 2nd Division.

Monash (seated) in the grounds of his Corps HQ, Bertangles Chateau, just north of Amiens, France, on 22 July 1918, with his senior staff officers.

Monash (seated) with aides, 22 July 1918. Left to right (behind him): Captain A.M. Moss, ADC, Major W.W. Berry, camp commandant, and Captain P.W. Simonson, ADC.

King George V arrives at Bertangles on 12 August 1918 for the investiture of Monash with the KCB (Knight Commander Order of the Bath) and is greeted by a guard of honour.

Harry Chauvel (left) with
'Galloping Jack' Royston,
El Arish, January 1917.

Romani, looking north.

Some Light Horsemen taking in the sights.

Watering the horses.

The Light Horse advancing on Beersheba.

The railway between Maan and Amman, with a block house today.

Damaged Turkish tracks after an Australian attack on the railway line.

The hill at Beersheba from which Chauvel launched his attack.

The German General had outposts and hidden machine-gun nests as the first line of defence. But in contrast to earlier tactics, he had his soldiers form the main line of resistance forward rather than in the rear. It didn't prevent Monash's corps making a powerful thrust, which had a demoralising impact on the enemy.

The battle began at 4.45 a.m. with an artillery barrage, followed by a swift, hard attack by Monash's hybrid force. The tanks moved in line with the soldiers, who were ordered to fix bayonets in anticipation of meeting the bulk of soldiers early in the battle.

The tanks found that many of the German machine gunners fought with courage. Some even stood their ground, firing until flattened. This proved an obstacle to the tank's 'juggernaut menace'. The infantry was vital here. The most notable instance occurred when the Australian 16th and 13th Battalions, with the 16th Lancashire Fusiliers, were ordered to advance across a kilometre of open ground just west of Vermandovillers and to remove Germans from the area. It was crisscrossed with German trenches (known as the Courtine Trench). The 16th moved into position but the fusiliers failed to link up. It was important that the Australians moved forward. Lieutenant Lawrence McCarthy, commanding D Company, decided to act without the fusiliers. He led a platoon straight at the trenches, bombing them as they went. They were held up by two machine guns nestled on an earth block, which were being fired into the trench held by the 16th.

McCarthy called for Sergeant F.J. Robbins. They edged in front of the block and dropped into a trench. Seconds later, McCarthy shot a sentry, then set his sights on the machine gunners who were causing his 16th Battalion distress. He ran forward, shot them, and then moved on.

He was now on a rollercoaster killing spree. McCarthy almost bumped into a German officer giving orders to about 40 of his men. He shot the officer. His men panicked and ran for a trench. Without a pause, McCarthy and Robbins attacked the trench with grenades.

Within minutes, 40 Germans, their hands held high or behind their heads, filed out of the trench in surrender.

In about seventeen minutes, McCarthy, supported by Robbins, had killed twenty Germans, captured fifty, and seized all five of the troublesome machine guns that were blocking the 16th's advance.

The effort earnt McCarthy a VC, and rivalled the performances of Albert Jacka and 'Mad' Harry Murray—the most highly decorated soldier of the war.

•

Once this German defiance was overcome, the Australian soldiers, using their bayonets freely, were able to advance without fear of being mowed down by hidden assailants.

There was much close combat, which gave the Australians more than an edge. They revelled in using the bayonet. Ever since Monash had taken over 4th Brigade, he had drilled his men in its use. It had proved an integral part of the Australian armoury on Gallipoli and the Western Front. In the Battle of Chuignes and Bray it was wielded to great advantage.

'The slaughter of the enemy in the tangled valleys was considerable,' Monash said with less than delicate understatement, 'for our Infantry are always vigorous bayonet fighters.'[5]

Apart from the usual booty of guns, Monash noted that the

3100 prisoners taken came from ten different regiments, which indicated Ludendorff's disorganised scramble to bolster the front in this area. The Germans were just as fierce fighters as the Allies. The 1st Division, suffering most with 1000 casualties, could attest to that. But the Germans were at a disadvantage without unified divisions and strong leadership. Monash read such signs as indicators that the Allies had to strike hard, often and without delay.

The British 32nd Division, inspired by Monash's order to use tanks, full artillery and air support, was successful too. Together the British and Australian forces seized 2.4 kilometres of country in a line from Herleville to the west of the town of Cappy. The Germans had been shoved back into barren, uninhabitable territory between the British/Australian line and the Somme, which had been laid waste by previous encounters.

Monash's unique, detailed strategies and tactics succeeded for the third battle in succession in 50 days. He had cleared a path to the powerful German strongholds on the Somme, which he wanted to obliterate before the winter set in.

Chapter 38

Pedantic Lawyer

Monash was fascinated with one acquisition—a huge 15-inch (36-centimetre) naval gun that had been pounding Amiens for a long time, a replica of the 'Kaiser's Gun' that had sprayed Paris. The 1st Division's 3rd Battalion reached the monster first, after clearing Arcy Wood with a bayonet charge. Its carriage, platform and concrete foundations weighed more than 500 tonnes. Its barrel, at just under 22 metres, was longer than a cricket pitch. Monash called it 'the largest single trophy of the war'. It was a fair claim when taking into account the thousands of deaths it had caused in the vital city and its surrounds, not to mention the destruction of buildings and monuments. This thumper had a range of 40 kilometres and fired projectiles weighing a tonne.[1]

Monash's appreciation of German engineering skills came to the fore as he examined the massive weapon. He judged it was similar to the type used in 'German Dreadnoughts, and never intended by its original designers for use on land'. This is where the innovation came in. It had come from the giant German steel-maker Krupp.

'It had been installed with the elaborate completeness of German methods,' Monash, with his engineer's hardhat on and some ancestral pride, wrote with undisguised admiration. 'A double railway track, several miles long, had been built to the site, for the transport of the gun and its parts. It was electrically trained and elevated. Its ammunition was handled and loaded by mechanical means. The adjacent hillside had been tunnelled to receive the operating machinery, and the supplies of shells, cartridges and fuses.'[2]

The monster gun had first started firing on 2 June, with its maximum capacity of 28 rounds a day. Like the despondent prisoners, it would never fire in anger again. The silencing of it, in Monash's mind, was symbolic of far more than the considerable salvation of Amiens. He interrogated some of the captured German officers and found them more defeated than any others he had ever questioned. It made him contemplate for the first time that the war might not stretch into 1919 after all. His questioning in German, along with deft psychological insights, was giving him a far greater comprehension of the war's state of play than any other commander was afforded on or off the battlefield.

●

He was even more determined to pursue the enemy. Monash had been thwarted after 8, 9 and 10 August when he wanted to continue on east and drive the Germans out of the bend in the Somme. Instead, Rawlinson had been cautious. The weight of failure in the collective mind of the British High Command since 1916 had not yet been balanced by the concept of success. Rawlinson couldn't further countenance that the Germans were vulnerable and perhaps broken. Unlike Monash, he did not have an overall idea of the enemy's current vulnerability. Nor had he ever personally interrogated German officers in their own language, as Monash had gone out of his way to do since 1916. Rawlinson had no real sense of the mentality of the enemy or how to take advantage of it. Instead he had ordered the Fourth Army to push south-east. Haig was even further divorced from the real continuing developments on the Front, and he supported Rawlinson, saying that his Fourth Army should ease up after its successes. Haig felt he was being considerate to Monash and the Australians by not asking them to strike more. The 1st AIF was only one of several corps in Rawlinson's force, and the frustrated Monash was expected to conform to the overall directives.

There was no immediate need, Haig and Rawlinson reckoned, to push the Germans from the Somme near Péronne, the old turreted, ramparted and moated city at the foot of Mont St Quentin. But this was backward thinking, based on the alleged invulnerability of those strongly fortified German strongholds. Attacks on them by the Allies had had mixed success and this created the negative, even defeatist, mindset of the High Command.

On the surface, Monash's position seemed to have been swapped with that of his superiors. In the past, Monash had been appalled by Haig's desire to push on in adverse, ill-planned conditions. Passchendaele was the prime example in Monash's experience. But there had been many, just as ill-conceived, plans through 1916 involving the AIF, the other Dominion forces, the British and the French. Now, Monash was the bold one. Haig and Rawlinson, faced with real success for the first time in the war, were cautious, and in essence defeatist in attitude.

The timing was the difference. Monash chose the moment, based on in-depth assessments of the enemy's capacities, instead of attacking blindly as his superiors had done with disastrous consequences for tens of thousands of soldiers. It was better, he thought, to strike hard and demoralise the Germans now while they were *relatively* vulnerable. He knew that future battles would not be as decisive as Hamel or Amiens. The further German backs were pushed against the wall, the harder they would fight and defend.

Monash was relying here on his adage of 'better to have a plan than no plan at all'. There was one other factor that distinguished his thinking from that of his superiors. He had absolute, unbending faith in the fighting skills of his AIF machine. Despite it being depleted, overworked and suffering from battle fatigue, he had no equivocation in believing his soldiers were invincible. Even with the lack of tanks, artillery, machine guns and other weapons, in the end the raw courage and fighting skills of his men would be, in his mind, the key to ultimate success. He had seen them on Gallipoli defending the indefensible—12,000 Anzacs against 40,000 Turks on the high ground. He had directed them in Flanders and on the Somme, as they took everything before them, except in the morass of Passchendaele, which presented even tougher conditions than at Anzac Cove and Sari Bair.

Monash *knew* the enormous fortitude of his diggers. He was aware of a sense of daring that saw them discussing the gaining of VCs as if it were a competition. It all helped his grand plan to give the AIF a solid sense of identity independent of the British, something that Monash was fostering.

In every battalion there were men like the highly decorated Harry Murray and Albert Jacka, who, when an advance was stopped or the enemy was set to make a breakthrough, would risk life and limb to reverse the position and put the Australians back on the offensive. These deeds, tumbling on top of each other, would inspire squads of brave men to achieve extraordinary deeds against the odds.

Monash was aware they wished to deliver the coup de grâce to the Germans. They had volunteered to come 20,000 kilometres to do it. They had suffered and endured in the trenches from the head of Monash Valley, the Nek and Sari Bair, to Bullecourt, Pozières, Broodseinde, Messines and Passchendaele. They had seen their mates killed every hour in battle. Every survivor from 1915 until now had waited, fought and struggled in the hope of being in the position to be part of a decisive win.

The Australians were standing taller now that they were having an impact as a national entity. They were aware they would be spearheading the push for a knockout victory. The diggers were the most hardened of soldiers. They had experienced—in varying degrees depending on the individual—the contradictory, inhumane feelings that killing individually or en masse produces. Fear, hate, horror, seduction, pleasure and the simple, often detached and remote sense of 'scoring' a hit on the enemy, were high on the list.

Even those like Monash himself, with his secret aversion to the business of war, had developed a desensitised attitude, even an addiction, to killing.

In a private letter to Vic a year earlier he had expressed his deeper thoughts, which if known by the regulars in the British and Australian forces, would have confirmed their attitudes about militia men, even though he was so well proven in battle.

'I hate the business of war—the horror of it, the waste, the destruction, the inefficiency,' he wrote. 'My only consolation is the sense of doing my duty to my country, which has placed a grave responsibility upon me. I owe something to the men whose lives and honour are in my hands to do as I will. But once my duty is done and honourably discharged, I shall with a sigh of relief turn my back once and for all on the possibility of ever again having to go through such an awful time.'[3]

Now eighteen months on and plenty of battles later, Monash had buried himself deeper in the business that at heart he detested. So much so that he now believed it was time to let his soldiers fulfill the desires that he had much to do with creating and refining.

●

He kept urging a harder thrust due east. On 24 August, Rawlinson at last gave in and approved the move. Monash was elated, but then was disappointed the next day when Rawlinson changed his mind. His excuse was that the appearance of a new German division, the 41st, was evidence that the enemy was reinforcing, not withdrawing.

'We've already taken hundreds of them [the 41st Division] prisoner!' Monash protested, 'my Corps could drive them back to the Hindenburg Line.'

'It is a definite reinforcement, John.'

Monash demonstrated his far better comprehension of the enemy, when he said: 'The Division has strengthened their numbers. But it is a hotchpotch of uncoordinated groups and nationalities—Prussians, Bavarians, Saxons and Wurtenbergers.'

Rawlinson said nothing. His position began to crumble, as it often did in debate with his key commander.

'They are not well led,' Monash persisted, 'they could be smashed. There are more signs of running than withdrawal, when challenged.'

He went to point out that in the past *withdrawal* signified an ordered pulling back and a policy of destruction. The Battle of Chuignes and Bray had shown that the enemy did not have an organised plan for retreat. The German force in the area had an almost impassable river behind them—with crossings at three points: Brie, Eterpigny and Péronne. Once pushed over the river east to Mont St Quentin and the city of Péronne, the next fallback position after that would be the last one—the highly fortified Hindenburg Line.

Monash added that: 'You [Rawlinson] have got a Corps flushed with recent victories, while he [the enemy] has been suffering a succession of defeats and heavy losses.'[4]

Rawlinson wouldn't budge. His Fourth Army had done its job in drawing enemy reserves to its front. Rawlinson didn't have any tanks left. They had been destroyed, or broken down or given to other forces, and would take a month to replace. Monash didn't care. He had other tactics and strategies to overcome their loss. Rawlinson would not agree. It was time for another army to take up the 'burden'.

'The Fourth Army would now mark time,' he repeated, 'and await events elsewhere.'[5]

But Monash squeezed concessions out of his Chief. He could shorten his front, and let the French take over some of it. This would allow Monash to concentrate and focus his interest east. There was also a little out-clause in Fourth Army policy, which Monash carefully referred to: '*All Divisions, wherever possible, had to keep in touch with the enemy.*'

He asked Rawlinson if this still applied to his resting corps, and the Fourth Army commander acknowledged that it did. Monash's staff had taken notes at the meeting, so there could be no future legal doubt about this admission by Rawlinson.

It was all Monash needed. The lawyer in him was prepared to manipulate the directive so that he could carry on with *his* and the AIF's war. He was tired of waiting for Rawlinson to do something. The Fourth Army commander's intransigence was mainly because of the grand schemes of Haig and Foch right along the front. But they were tardy. Time now was of the essence. Rawlinson was restrained and was under orders to hold Monash and his like-minded generals back.

In Monash's mind, *staying in touch* justified making more than incursions in the area he had been denied for nearly three weeks. He didn't have tanks but he did have eight brigades of field artillery. On 27 August he ordered 'vigorous patrolling'. It was a precursor for Monash taking further calculated risks.

He first had to get the agreement of all his generals. They met in a vibrant café in Villers-Bretonneux, which was filled with patrons after the liberation of the area and the banishment of the German occupiers. A small band played on a stage in one corner and a woman sang. Monash explained that he had an agreement from Rawlinson to 'keep in touch' with the withdrawing German Army. Monash said his interpretation of this was to pursue them. The clause would allow the AIF to remove the 'Boche' from their last bastions on the Somme at Mont St Quentin and Péronne.

Monash repeated to his generals that he believed the enemy would be forced after that to run back to the Hindenburg Line. He asked them for their opinions. Rosenthal believed it was imperative to 'knock them off' the Somme before the winter of 1918–19 set in. Otherwise he feared the war would drag on until the following winter of 1919–20. Sinclair-Maclagan suggested taking this chance to go on the offensive. Otherwise he thought the AIF would be decimated and that a million more soldiers would be slaughtered. Hobbs and Glasgow agreed with this sentiment. Gellibrand pointed out that there were no tanks left for a further big push. Only 67 had not been put out of action since Amiens. Now there were none. Monash said they would fight without them. He reminded them this next pursuit at Mont St Quentin and Péronne would be an exclusively Australian operation.[6] Now he had their unanimous agreement on their 'legal' and sanctioned pursuit, Monash wrote a new blueprint.

To overcome the absence of tanks, which had helped protect the infantry in the three major battles of Hamel, Amiens and Chuignes/Bray, Monash had two innovations. The first was to let infantry commanders control mobile battery guns. They would help counter machine guns. The second was to insist that all batteries should carry 20 per cent smoke shell. The gunners didn't like this. They wanted all the destructive power they could get. But smoke shell blinded the German machine gunners.

'A few rounds judiciously placed screened the approach of our entry,' Monash reminded them, 'and many a machine gun post thereby rushed by us from the flanks or even from the rear.'

Hobbs (1st Division) and Rosenthal (2nd Division) had both been gunners. They backed Monash on this brilliant tactic. Again, his painstaking effort to protect advancing infantry was foremost in his thinking. He used technology and ideas in detailed tactics that no other corps commander would find the time or the inclination to concern himself with, let alone comprehend at the battle face.[7]

Now the infantry could move forward knowing that the Australian battery gunners would either blast or blind the machine gunners. Yet special acts of bravery were needed to push the advantage.

•

The 41st Battalion was having trouble on the Somme's banks trying to make Curlu. They were held up by machine guns hidden in Fargny Wood. Lance Corporal Bernard Gordon, emulating Jacka and McCarthy, decided to attempt a breakthrough. Working alone and showing uncommon cool, he moved forward, looking for German officers. He came across two, bailed them up and caused the capture of 61 of their men, along with the six machine guns that had been so hazardous. Gordon would also receive the VC.

The road to Curlu was now less troublesome, although the Germans continued to provide tough opposition.[8]

Chapter 39

Rogue Warlord

By the night of 27 August, the Australian Corps had pushed its line another kilometre or so east past the villages of Fontaine, Vermandovillers and Foucaucourt on the main road. The latter had to be bombarded with artillery, and was only captured after a hard fight by 5th Division, demonstrating that pockets of Germans were prepared to stay and fight. The 2nd Division also found obstacles to their progress in Tivoli Wood.

The corps' move extended north about 2.5 kilometres to the Cappy bend in the river, and included the crossing at Eclusier.

On 28 August the corps advanced more than a kilometre again, reaching the line Genermont–Berny-en-Santerre–Estrees–Frise. The next day all four divisions in the action had moved further east. The 3rd Division north of the Somme had seized

the villages of Suzanne, Vaux, Curlu, Hem and Clery. The corps'
three divisions south of the river were in line with the 3rd and
'stood upon the high ground sloping down to the Somme, with
the river in sight from opposite Clery, past Péronne and as far
south as St Christ'.[1]

The Australians set the pace of the conflict, and the Germans
were again forced into a disorganised withdrawal. Guns, ammunition and stores were left in their wake. HQs, hospitals and
dressing stations were abandoned like ghost sites, with equipment
intact and missing one factor—people to operate them. Monash
now had control of the whole of the Somme Valley from Clery
(a village on the horseshoe river bend) westward, and was having
bridges repaired. His background in construction was having an
impact second only to his growing number of military achievements. The Germans destroyed bridges to impede the Allied
pursuit; Monash rebuilt them. This gave him scope for options
and different routes to his ultimate aims. If one route was blocked
there were alternatives.

The rapidity of events was causing him to consider a plan he
had held ever since 9 August when he took control of Chipilly
Spur. He was in place north and south of the Somme. His aim
was to take control of the line of the river from the east. If
resistance was strong, his fallback plan was to make an assault
from the north. He wanted to make the Somme useless to
the enemy as a defence line, and force that final retreat to the
Hindenburg Line.

Monash wished to do it without reliance or assistance from any
other corps. It had to be 'an exclusively Australian achievement'.[2]

•

Monash's first object of desire in this plan was Mont St Quentin. It had to be taken, along with Péronne, 1.5 kilometres south. From a high point at the bend in the river, the *mont* looked harmless and did not stand out in the landscape. It reached about 110 metres at its apogee, and protected the northern way into Péronne. Possession of it meant control of approaches from all points of the compass. The hill was riddled with underground galleries and huge, well-furnished shelters. Domination of the hill—it was hardly a *mont*—also allowed command of both stretches of the river.

There were problems in tackling it. The Germans had defeated previous attempts. They sited their heavy artillery there. The *mont* was ringed with wire entanglements. Its forward slopes were flat and bare, making attacking troops easy targets.

Many of Monash's officers and soldiers studied it. Those who had been on Gallipoli were uneasy. It reminded some of Hill 60. Others shuddered at the memory of Chunuk Bair and the Nek. Not only was its disposition forbidding from an attacking point of view, but Ludendorff had put one of the German Army's finest divisions, the 2nd Prussian Guards, on the *mont* to hold it. Unlike some of their disorganised, demoralised countrymen, they would not run; they would fight. This division included the Kaiserin Augusta and Kaiser Alexander Regiments, which had fame and tradition to rival the British Grenadiers and Coldstream Guards.

Monash calculated that if he could take this hill and Péronne, then the Germans would have nowhere to run but east. Then his grand scheme to force the Germans off the Somme before the winter of 1918–19 would see fruition. It was nearly September. Early cold weather was expected in late October. In his mind, it had to be now, or never.

•

Monash called a meeting late on the afternoon of 29 August to elucidate his plan; no tanks were to be involved. Present were Hobbs (5th Division), Rosenthal (2nd Division) and Gellibrand (3rd Division), along with General Lambert of the British 32nd Division.

Monash would use the 32nd Division as a decoy and defence. His 3rd, 5th and 2nd Divisions were to engage in a three-pronged attack. The 3rd would go for the high ground north-east of Clery, about 4 kilometres west of Mont St Quentin. The 3rd's ultimate objective of Bouchavesnes village on the Bapaume Road was 2 kilometres north of the *mont*.

The 5th had to strike over the river at Péronne, which was situated about 5 kilometres down the river south-east of Clery. It aimed to cross the Somme Canal and marshland and take the high ground south of Péronne. The ultimate goal was the wooded spur east of Péronne.

Rosenthal's 2nd had 'mission impossible'. It was to cross the river and take Mont St Quentin head on.

This battle on several fronts was far too big and important to be called 'vigorous patrolling'. It was an attempt to take two key strategic points with a complex plan involving parts of four divisions. It would be different from anything Monash had attempted; less of a set-piece project and more fluid in operation. A crude comparison was the moveable battle on Gallipoli at Sari Bair. But he had not been in charge there. In addition, he had strong mobile artillery backup this time. There was the considerable advantage also of leading troops, no matter how fatigued, who had a recent history of winning.

Monash's concern was not the certain fickleness of the conflict. He only worried about communications. As long as his left division knew what his right was doing, and he could direct all of them, then he was ready. Perhaps his finest skills were his speed of decision-making and adaptability. They had been tested many times in the heat of battles and skirmishes. When Monash had his forensically designed blueprint plans to begin with, he was confident of being able to change direction and tactics. Commanding four different divisions that all had different objectives did not faze him. His facility to make lightning moves, no matter what the apparent obstacles, had been honed over more than four decades since he began tackling puzzles and mathematical problems as a child. This exceptional capacity was about to receive its biggest test.

Before he could begin, Monash had to show Rawlinson his plan. Would the army commander throw up his hands and say it was too big an assignment in view of Haig's current policy about the Fourth Army marking time? Or was it just too big a risk? No one had been able to dislodge these two fortified positions before.

Rawlinson came to visit him and Blamey on the afternoon before the battle was set to commence. Maps were laid for Rawlinson and Montgomery to peruse. There was much puffing of smoke and some diffident coughing. Rawlinson asked a lot of questions and was sceptical.

'And so you think you're going to take Mont St Quentin with three battalions!' Rawlinson remarked. 'What presumption! However, I don't think I ought to stop you! So go ahead and try!—and I wish you luck!'[3]

Monash was unconcerned that Rawlinson didn't believe he

could do it. The Chief of the Fourth Army was letting him have a go. Unlike Monash's superiors—Haig and Rawlinson in particular—he had yet to fail when he had total command. Rawlinson's decision to defy Haig's directives and let Monash loose was almost as if he was inviting him to take a fall and join the ranks of every member of the British High Command.

Chapter 40

McNicoll's Moment

Monash's first flexibility test came on the first day, 30 August. The bridges he had intended the 2nd and 5th Divisions to cross were either under attack or destroyed. That meant their direct assaults—the 2nd on Mont St Quentin and the 5th, in effect, on Péronne—were impossible. Monash then applied Plan B, the assault from the north. Both these divisions were sent to cross the Somme on the top of the horseshoe bend. The revised aim was to move through Clery and behind the 3rd Division front, which would bring them to Mont St Quentin from the north. He ordered the British 32nd Division to start a clamour on the river for 7 kilometres as if it was attempting to cross. This not-so-faint feint—another Monash illusion—distracted the Germans on the *mont*.

But the 32nd found they had to make a lot of noise. The 5th Brigade of Rosenthal's 2nd Division was now down to just 1320 men, not much above battalion size. It had a long, hard trek through the night. First the diggers were blocked at one bridge because the 3rd Division had not yet taken Clery on the river, let alone the Bouchavesnes Spur, a rugged 2 kilometres north-east. Rosenthal pushed the 5th Brigade 3 kilometres further west on the top of the horseshoe bend to a crossing that Monash had had repaired at Feuilleres.

The 33rd Battalion of Gellibrand's 3rd Division moved east from Clery with the objective of taking Bois Madame Wood, 1 kilometre south of Bouchavesnes. They were not quite prepared for the garrison of Germans and hundreds of machine guns. An hour into the attack on 30 August, the 33rd was held up by incessant heavy fire from the south-east edge of the wood. Its leader Lieutenant Colonel L.J. Morshead was beginning to think the mission to take the wood was impossible without another 500 men to back them up, when he was distracted by one of his soldiers—Private George Cartwright—who stood up in the heavy fire. Cartwright, his rifle at his shoulder, ran forward firing. He killed three Germans in a machine-gun crew at the post that was pinning down the 33rd. In the pandemonium he kept advancing and hurled a grenade at the post. It exploded on target. Cartwright kept coming. He jumped into the post, took control of the machine gun and aimed it at the eight Germans still alive. They surrendered.

All this had been done in full view of the rest of the battalion. Morshead and every Australian got to his feet and cheered Cartwright. It was as if they were watching a footballer making a brilliant, baulking run. Seconds later, they jumped down again. Inspired, the battalion kept attacking.

The intrepid private's bold move and the lift it gave the rest of the force was the type of act that Monash had gambled on in his ambitious plan, made without his previous reliance on tanks. It was outside the rules, and would be regarded by British and enemy officers as 'undisciplined'. Technically this was true. Cartwright had broken ranks, and he had run, but not away. If such crazed and heroic actions gained ground and won encounters that led to battle victories, Monash was happy to let it go on; he did not have to encourage it. The troops were responding with a belief in a team performance punctuated by individual efforts. In a 30-year experience in the militia before the war, Monash had taken squads of young part-time soldiers on countless bivouacs and military exercises. He understood the sporting mentality that drove and inspired them. Now that psychological insight was having telling ramifications for the biggest, most brutal military conflict in history.

•

While the 33rd's advance to clear the wood (and so help destroy the German protection north of Mont St Quentin) looked promising, a lot depended on McNicoll and his 38th Battalion (of the 3rd Division), now down to less than 400 able soldiers, a third its full strength. They had been fighting for 70 hours when they reached the outskirts of Clery.

At 9 p.m. on 30 August Gellibrand ordered the long-suffering McNicoll to attack Clery and so take the spur to its north the next morning, beginning at 3 a.m. McNicoll was disgruntled at this shock directive from a man for whom he had little time. He told Gellibrand his men were fatigued, and in need of rest. Gellibrand was not sympathetic, but nor was he bullying. Monash had told him to avoid confronting McNicoll. Instead, Gellibrand said that the 'old man' had ordered that Clery had to be taken *before* Rosenthal's attack on the *mont*. It was vital to corps plans. That was enough for McNicoll.

He would do anything Monash wanted.

•

Next morning Rosenthal's 5th Brigade was stalled on the bridge at Feuilleres. Artillery fire from Clery was preventing them from reaching the north bank. Gellibrand ordered McNicoll to get rid of the problem.

It was then 11 a.m. on 31 August, six hours later than Monash planned. Events were unfolding slowly. McNicoll, demonstrating his longevity and reliability as a fighting commander, took 50 men into Clery. After a brief fight they captured 59 Germans, and then fought off a counterattack. In the process, the artillery fire was silenced. Rosenthal's brigade could go over the bridge at Feuilleres. It battled to control the region east of the crossing at Omiecourt that had been smashed before. The AIF's well-oiled engineering machine repaired the bridge. Now there was an easy access route to the north of the horseshoe.

•

The delays caused Monash to postpone the assault on Mont St Quentin till 5 a.m. the next morning on 1 September. He saw the advantage of bringing up artillery to Clery and strategic points on the south bank of the river overlooking the prospective target of the *mont*.

The extra time also allowed some rest for the diggers. Rosenthal decided to keep 330 men of the 18th Battalion—all that was left of it—in reserve. The brigade was left with just 890 men—less than a battalion in size—for the attack. One bizarre tactic was that the men would charge the *mont* yelling, to make it seem as if it was a normal-sized brigade of 4000 men attacking.

There was no softening up by the artillery. Monash wanted a complete surprise, beginning the attack with Rosenthal's 5th Brigade (of 2nd Division) on the *mont* at 5 a.m. and followed by the 14th Brigade (of Hobbs's 5th Division) on Péronne, set for 6 a.m.

Chapter 41

Assault on Mont St Quentin

The tired troops were issued with an extra shot of rum just before attack time—5 a.m. On an overcast morning 5th Brigade made its rush like demented banshees along three lines. One 'battalion' went left and hit the ruined village of Feuillaucourt. Another went straight for the *mont*. The third went right, hoping to move on the inside of the village of St Denis. The diggers used rifles and grenades, and were backed by Lewis guns. Each section alternately gave its neighbour covering fire. They overwhelmed brickworks harbouring seven machine guns and a small sugar refinery. The Australians continued up the slopes.

The 5th Brigade's centre battalion passed through the ruins of the town of Mont St Quentin by 7 a.m. It was pushed back by the defenders, and had to take refuge in an old line of trenches. The right battalion also had a tough battle, encountering heavy machine-gun fire from another ruined sugar refinery. Both these battalions had trouble for the next hour in close fighting where flashing bayonets dominated. At 8 a.m. the 5th pushed the Australian flag into the dirt more than halfway up the *mont*.

But it was premature.

Monash hurried in the 6th Brigade and then the 7th to assist.

•

It became a long make-or-break day of further fierce fighting. There were several individual acts of inspiration, similar to that by Cartwright, just north of the *mont* that lifted the entire 2nd Division and made Monash's objectives look possible. Sergeant Albert Lowerson led a company through the right flank Mont St Quentin village, taking out German positions in the town. They came to an abrupt halt on the edge of town. There, in a huge crater, was a stronghold of Germans manning a dozen machine guns. Lowerson went into action. He spread his soldiers around the crater. On his command, he led the charge. The company took the guns and captured 30 prisoners.

Further around and down the *mont,* a company's advance was blocked by barbed wire. Private Robert Mactier was sent forward to investigate. Armed with a revolver and grenades he dashed to the wire in front of his fellow soldiers. He hurled a grenade that seemed to make a direct hit on a machine-gun nest in a trench. Without hesitation, Mactier climbed over the wire, dashed to the trench and shot the stunned gun crew. He tossed the gun out to cheers from his onlooking mates. His adrenalin pumping,

Mactier then dashed to two other trenches, and repeated his acts. Now on fierce autopilot, Mactier headed for a fourth German gun crew. But its members had seen the mayhem he had created. They had just enough seconds to aim their weapons at him and fire. Mactier was hit by a dozen bullets and fell dead metres short of his objective. He had lost this digger version of Russian roulette.

No one knew what motivated this laconic digger to do what he did. No one recalled him talking about other similar exploits. But his performance had not been in vain. The rest of his company found another level of courage and took the position. His self-sacrificial effort enhanced the burgeoning sense of invincibility of his company, battalion, brigade and the AIF overall.

•

The corps' belief that they would find a way to victory was having a knock-on effect. Further up the *mont*, Lieutenant Edgar Towner, of the 2nd Machine Gun Battalion, attached to the infantry, showed ingenuity and guts in equal measure when he single-handedly captured a German gun. He then used his experience to turn the weapon on other enemy positions exposed to him. This inflicted a score of casualties. In the process he captured 25 prisoners and called for his battalion to advance up the *mont*. Towner, in a prime position, gave support to the assaulting infantry.

•

These three instances of heroics among scores of similar deeds earnt Lowerson, Mactier and Towner the VC. Their efforts and tactical skills energised the 2nd Division, when Rosenthal, like all the commanders, was concerned about the fitness of his men for such demands.

By late afternoon, thousands of corpses littered the slopes and marshy flats. In the early evening brigadiers began reporting in that Mont St Quentin was Australia's. This time the flag was thumped in right on top of the hill.

Monash's instincts about his men and his confidence in them were justified. But if the 5th Division couldn't take Péronne, his grand plan for a wholly Australian battle victory in the toughest conditions might end in futility.

•

The night before the *mont* was taken, Monash pushed the 5th Division's 14th Brigade into the action, ordering them to take Péronne. But it was easier said than done. The brigade had to march up the south side of the river to the repaired bridge at Omiecourt and then down the north bank. It took them ten hours, until late evening, to hike the 11 kilometres. Monash was not happy. He told Hobbs that they should have moved faster. Hobbs objected. His men were struggling before the march even began.

'I was compelled to harden my heart,' Monash said, 'and to insist that it was imperative to recognize a great opportunity and to seize it unflinchingly.'[1]

Monash could almost smell a double victory. He was pushing harder than ever. His preoccupation, obsession and raison d'etre during the war was to win it. In these moments, as at Messines, his compassion and pity temporarily went out his HQ dugout window. He was squeezing the last smidgen of effort from his fatigued diggers. In this respect, he was like every other outstanding commander in history. But Monash, with command of a modern army and all its technical accoutrements, had far more raw fighting power at his disposal than any commanders before this war. Add to this his use of engineers to rebuild bridges, viaducts, culverts, railways and roads, and his force had an unprecedented adaptability, especially in battles of relentless attack and pursuit. He had built a formidable machine that could not be stopped from coming at the enemy.

Yet still there was the human element. The soldiers were cogs in Monash's machine, but not robots. Victory against such a mighty foe, even when it may have been buckling, still needed almost a superhuman effort. His soldiers had to be pushed to topple the German giant. There was no room for mercy for the enemy, or his own men.

Bean, realising the futility of continuing to attempt to oust Monash, studied him with surprising, if belated, objectivity. 'In this decisive fighting,' he reflected (much later) in his official history of the war, 'he was right to work his troops to the extreme limit of their endurance.' Bean had seen enough conflict since 1915 to appreciate and comprehend that mental and physical strength counted as much as brute force in critical moments.

'At such times victory often goes to the troops that hold out the longest, withstanding strains, toil or exhaustion in perhaps unbelievable degree for an unbelievable time.'[2]

'Casualties no longer matter,' Monash said. He had to resign himself to the fact that his soldiers were fighting the kind of battle that he had tried to minimise, even avoid, more than any other commander of either side. Now that they were in the middle of the thrust, stab and parry of close combat there was no other attitude for a leader to take. Anything short of ruthlessness against the crack Prussian Guards and specially selected volunteers would lead to defeat. Monash was compelled to keep the pressure on more than at any point in the war.

Chapter 42

Péronne

The Germans had turned Péronne into a fort. A moat and strong ramparts where 100 machine guns had been posted surrounded the ancient town. It had been a fortified town since the Roman invasion and the massive ramparts were built in the ninth century. It was besieged and heavily damaged in 1870 during the Franco-Prussian War. The Germans invaded Péronne in 1914. It became to them what Amiens was to the British. The town was pushed and pulled by opposing forces from then on. In August 1916 the Germans held it and prevented the Allies getting closer than Biaches, 1.5 kilometres west of the Somme. In March 1917 the Allies regained it, but the Germans destroyed much of the town before falling back to the Hindenburg Line. In the March 1918 offensive, they regained Péronne and had to rebuild the results of their own destruction. But they did it with a will. Péronne was the last major stronghold before the Hindenburg Line.

The German High Command called for volunteers to defend the town. These would include the most willing, capable fighters in the still-strong remnants of the German Army. The Péronne garrison commander handpicked those who put their hand up from many different regiments. The men knew they would be making a last stand against the Australians, who had developed a brutal reputation in the line opposite them for being relentless and uncompromising. The selections were told to expect tank attacks. Those that didn't blink about these two foes coming at them received the nod.

Another obstacle for the Australians was barbed wire. It ran all over the river's marshy flats from Clery south-east across to the *mont* and Péronne. The trick was finding the way through it. In 1917 both the Germans and French had cut or blasted paths in their efforts to occupy the area. The terrain itself created another barrier to the Australian force. Isolated sugar refineries and brickworks afforded the only cover. But they were a dangerous mirage.

All of them were manned as forward posts. They would not be easy to negotiate.

•

Monash called for a supreme effort by Hobbs's 14th Brigade against the volunteers at Péronne. It responded. The 54th Battalion had to take the ground between the town and the river. While its Lewis gunners engaged the Germans, infantry rushed forward, ripped out pickets and scrambled under the wire.

Many of them reached open territory but became easy prey for the gunners at the ramparts. The situation demanded desperate action. Two corporals—Alex Buckley and Arthur Hall—rose to the occasion. Slithering beyond the wire, they crept up on two separate machine-gun posts. They rushed and surprised their targets, capturing 30 German volunteers and eight machine guns. This opened the way for the battalion to cross the swamp and waterway. They reached the centre of the town, where Buckley was killed attempting a repeat of his stalking of a post.

Meanwhile the 14th Brigade's 53rd Battalion had to clear Anvil Wood in the approach to Péronne. The Germans turned their weapons on the wood. A 77-millimetre field gun did the most damage to the Australians. Private William Currey saw some of his mates killed. He snapped, and attempted to break the impasse by charging the field gun, which could not be man-oeuvred quickly enough to stop him. He killed the crew and took control of the big weapon. In a controlled rage, he then rushed a machine-gun post and broke it up. After these heroics, he was unstoppable. He volunteered to his commander to enter the wood and retrieve a company before the Australians began firing artillery. Currey succeeded.

He, Hall and Buckley were awarded VCs. Their efforts were again typical of those Monash had come to rely on to lift all those who witnessed them, while at the same time destroying German morale.

•

These uncommon acts and their resultant stimuli to the battered battalions seemed to give the 5th Division the fortress town by the evening of 1 September, but a powerful German counter-attack didn't allow the diggers to seal it. The German volunteers, like their counterparts on the *mont*, would not capitulate unless every man sensed their position was hopeless.

The close, intense, continuous fighting, which Monash had always tried to spare his men, had taken its toll in casualties and morale. A few cracks began to appear. The 59th Battalion, which seemed to have done the job at Péronne, was out of the line, resting. Most of the exhausted men were sleeping when roused to go back into action after an enemy counterattack. A handful of the men rebelled and refused to go. It was only when reminded of the consequences of refusing to fight—court martial—that they went back into the fray. Almost out on their feet, many of the men were fighting on memory, and struggling.

The pressure from the commanders continued. Monash urged them to push for a win. This was passed down to the battalion commanders, who called on their men for one last supreme effort. Midmorning on 2 September Péronne, a town that had been battled over by other armies in other wars for centuries, was under Australian control.

•

The two main objectives of taking Mont St Quentin and Péronne had been achieved. But there was still some heavy mopping up to do. On 2 September most Germans were on the retreat to the Hindenburg Line. Yet some fell back to the twin villages of Allaines and Haut-Allaines on the Canal du Nord. It lay 2 kilometres south of Bouchavesnes, and 2 kilometres north-east of Mont St Quentin—too close for comfort for Monash. He asked

Gellibrand and his 3rd Division to obliterate the threats. He gave the assignment to the 43rd Battalion. It had to clear a triangle of ground between the 2nd Division advancing north-east and a British division that Monash had brought in to move east.

'Mopping up' was a euphemism for what ensued. The Germans, aware that they could not now retreat, made a last stand in a network of trenches in the target triangle. They engaged with heavy machine-gun fire. The 43rd found itself bogged down. This time another corporal—Lawrence Weathers—decided to attempt to break through. He ran at two trenches hurling grenades. The German commander was killed. Weathers hurried back for more grenades, calling for mates to help him. Three stepped forward to go with him back into the heavy fire. They had a quick conference. The plan was simple. One of them—Lance Corporal H.H. Thompson—would keep the enemy well down in the trenches by firing a Lewis gun, which would be cover for Weathers. He dashed to a trench, jumped on a parapet and hurled grenades into it. The stunned enemy capitulated at what they saw as madness that they could not defend against. One hundred and eighty of them filed out of the trenches as prisoners.

Weathers' performance earnt him a VC.

It ended all resistance in the battles for Mont St Quentin and Péronne.

•

Easier mopping up over the whole area took another few hours. Three thousand prisoners were taken, mainly from the crack Prussian regiments. Many more of them were killed. Australian casualties amounted to just over 3000. About 600 died in some of the toughest, bloodiest fighting of the war. The stakes were high and Ludendorff's force had defended accordingly.

On the afternoon of 2 September, Monash contacted Rawlinson. He already had an inkling from Montgomery that the Australian Corps was going to be successful. But he was still excited when told by Monash: 'We are on top of Mont St Quentin.'

'I don't believe it!' Rawlinson responded.

'Come and see,' Monash offered.

'You have altered the course of the war!'[1]

To be more accurate, the Fourth Army Chief could have added 'much earlier than anticipated'. But still this comment, reflecting the High Command's surprise, was not exaggerated. The Germans, who had fought much harder than in any of Monash's three recent major victories, were retreating to the Hindenburg Line. Now Foch, Haig and all the Allied Army commanders realised that Monash had been right in his instinct and judgement. The Germans were at breaking point. They had been pushed there by daring, brilliantly planned tactics and courageous soldiering.

Rawlinson took up the offer and arrived at Péronne AIF HQ at dawn on 3 September.

'Where's General Monash?' he asked staff.

'At the station,' one replied, 'he has been there all night.'

Rawlinson and his entourage drove to the Péronne station. They found Monash, helmet on and ankle deep in mud, directing his engineers and pioneers to reconstruct the train station. He was in his other element, and for a time, transported back to work in Australia that began in 1884 on Melbourne's Princes Bridge spanning the Yarra River. To support his battle corps, Monash wanted the Péronne railway up and running towards the Hindenburg Line, 24 kilometres east. The station and a great lattice bridge had been smashed by the Germans. They had to be fixed, no matter how long it took. Trains were vital to transport troops, weapons, other heavy equipment, food and water supplies. Roads and bridges had to be built from scratch or reconstructed if Monash was to have his big guns come across the river.

The enemy in the overall conflict still had factors keeping it strong militarily. Its submarine campaign may have fallen short of aims, but it was still potent. The Allied blockade of all goods heading for Germany, from motor fuel to food, had been tough, but the Germans were hardy and resilient. They had survived it so far.

Rawlinson had a firsthand taste of Monash's relentless drive to defeat the enemy.

'By this bold and successful action,' Rawlinson wrote to other British generals, in reference to taking Mont St Quentin and Péronne, 'the heart was knocked out of the Boche.' He gave high praise to Monash's tactics and strategies. 'It broke the [natural, well-engineered] Somme line of defence . . . defended by troops second to none in the German Army.'[2]

Chapter 43

Monash and Ludendorff Feel the Strain

The battles of Mont St Quentin and Péronne distinguished Monash further as a battle commander. Even Charles Bean recognised them as the only important battles by Australians on the Western Front in which quick, free manoeuvre played 'a decisive part. It furnished a complete answer to the comment that Monash was merely a composer of set pieces.'[1]

No one is on the record as ever saying Monash was such a limited 'musician', but it was Bean's begrudging way of giving him a backhanded compliment, again decades after the event.

English writer A.K. Smithers, steeped in traditional battle concepts and reflecting the prevailing British attitude to war, showed more integrity in his appraisal. He reckoned Mont

St Quentin and Péronne were the 'true measure of the greatness of John Monash as a General . . . it meant throwing to the winds all those articles of faith about "advancing under the greatest possible protection" and not exposing the soft bodies of men to the lead and steel of defenders . . . Monash faced this knowledge [that the battle would be costly in casualties] and accepted the inevitable with the fortitude of Ulysses Grant.'[2]

In other words, Monash could stand the comparison of the best generals of the last two centuries, when the situation reverted to old-fashioned battle conditions. On one level, such comment would have pleased him, given his penchant for military history, and the American Civil War in particular. He even suggested that the capture of the *mont* was a bit like the surprise tactics employed by one of his heroes, Stonewall Jackson. But the Battle of Mont St Quentin and Péronne had been a necessity at a key turning point in the war. It produced an anomaly in his style, which was years ahead of every other battle commander on both sides.

That change, and the increased number of casualties, was adding to the strain on him, which was exacerbated by the many sleepless days and nights, and the need for never-ending decision-making. Every Monash directive would mean death and injury for Australians or the enemy. As the battles and casualties mounted, no matter how rational and ingenious Monash was, there was nowhere to escape from the insanity of war.

•

Within 24 hours the heavy artillery and other weaponry was being put on a train to pursue the Germans. Thwarted from the earlier chance at Amiens to finish the war, he now saw a second opportunity, this time a complete victory on the Hindenburg Line, and much earlier than anticipated by anyone. If he could do it quickly, he might just save his men a rotten winter, or even another year of combat.

It put him under extreme pressure to meet a tight deadline.

•

Monash was a keen amateur student of medicine, with a special interest in psychiatry and psychology. He had used the latter to measurable success with his study of the diggers. There were also a few flops. He did not read his men well in May 1915 on Gallipoli when he urged a ceasefire so that both sides could look after their fallen. He did not anticipate, or like, the fraternisation with the Turks in those poignant, few precious hours. He underestimated his diggers in early propaganda about the Germans, who were painted as inhuman brutes. Some of the diggers had seen enough of their opposite numbers to know that they themselves on occasions were no less brutal than the 'evil Huns'. Monash dropped this approach.

However, he had usually got his messaging right. He cleverly emphasised very early in the war that his charges 'fight for Australia' and their mates first, the British Empire second. This had been novel in 1915. The empire had always been the first call by governors and politicians, but after Gallipoli, Monash switched the written and spoken motivation for fighting. He had picked his 'audience' very well and was the only senior Australian commander pushing the nationalistic line. It worked, culminating with his grand message three years later to all troops before Amiens.

In the weeks since then he had picked up a new sense within his force. The combined divisions were a moving state within a state; a small mobile country in itself. Once again shrewdly, he called on his officers and diggers to 'fight for the AIF'. It was one big warrior army/family. Some of the men had been together since late 1914 and had spent more time together than they had with schoolmates at secondary school. Most had been together three years, living and fighting closely and depending on each other in life and death. Monash had been the first commander to allow soldiers to be next to their closest mates when they prepared to go into battle, or in the vernacular, 'go over the top'. This thinking, unerringly accurate, was that they would do just that bit more supporting, and be supported by, those best friends.

Monash's library at Iona in Melbourne had been replete with books, mostly in German, on the new 'science' of psychiatric analysis since 1901 when the German doctor Alois Alzheimer identified the first case of what later became known as Alzheimer's disease. Monash had been fascinated by Sigmund Freud, from when he first published (also in 1901) his *Psychopathology of Everyday Life*. Since then he had consumed everything written by Freud and others in the field.

As Monash ploughed on after the Germans, Ludendorff's severe mental issues became noticeable after the shock of the collapse of his two armies at Amiens. He had deteriorated ever since. He had expected to break through the Allies, take Amiens, march on to Paris and score an overall victory in the war. The reversal had been too much of a jolt. Having exhausted every medical approach to 'cure' his depression, he consulted an old friend, a Dr Hochheimer, a retired military physician and Freudian who had been practising psychiatry in Berlin. He met

317

Ludendorff in early September. Hochheimer reported to his wife his concern that Ludendorff thought little about his *soul*. 'He had only worked, worried, body and mind tensed, with no relaxation, no fun, and hastily eaten meals. He had not breathed correctly; he had not laughed; he had seen nothing of nature and art, heard nothing of the rustle of the forest and the ripple of brooks . . . and therefore had all the more hurt his force of energy and creative power, and thus himself . . .'[3]

Ludendorff, to the doctor's surprise, agreed and asked for help. He began, literally, sniffing the roses, sleeping more and drinking less alcohol. He learnt to calm down; he had massages. He even, at Hochheimer's direction, began singing 'German folk songs as soon as he woke up'. He did not scramble for intelligence, or battle reports. Ludendorff became cheerful and good humoured.

But the gentle edifice of therapy came tumbling down on 12 September when thirteen divisions of Pershing's army supported by four French colonial divisions—a total of 650,000 men—smashed the St Mihiel salient using guns, planes and tanks. They easily overwhelmed the two German divisions and took 15,000 prisoners. It was an American hammer smashing a walnut. It may not have had the shock or impact of Amiens, nevertheless it stunned Ludendorff, even though he had evacuated the salient before the Americans hit.

Chapter 44

Hughes' Attempted Assertion

In the second week of September 1918 on the Western Front, Monash had distracting problems that were nearly as pressing as his battle plans to win the war. Since all the five divisions had begun to fight as one corps under his command there had been a shift in the motive for fighting on the Western Front. The success of the AIF in five weeks since 8 August had meant that a powerful bond had developed between all its divisions. When the divisions had been used to fill gaps and plug holes for the British armies, they had cried out to be identified as *Australians*. Now they were together, they wanted to be viewed as the *Australian Corps*. Monash, as ever, articulated and set the mood with his preaching to the troops. He was no longer appealing to their patriotism.

He was beating a drum for the powerful, lean fighting machine he had developed. It was a subtle change in propaganda. The AIF had gained a reputation as a formidable entity and, more importantly, the soldiers themselves now believed they were unbeatable. In the psychology, motivation and philosophy of any competition, let alone war, this was the most powerful force of all. Monash continued using sporting analogies, to which he knew, from decades of experience, the diggers responded.

Part of this switch in emphasis was motivated by the lack of recognition the AIF was receiving in the press, which was the fault of the British High Command. News reports given to journalists for consumption worldwide never mentioned other than *British* successes. (This has been perpetuated in the great majority of books, films and documentaries produced in the last hundred years.) Few were aware that the battles of Amiens, Chuignes, Bray, Mont St Quentin, Péronne and even, by comparison, modest Hamel, were led, and largely won by, Australians. It peeved Monash, his staff commanders and soldiers. Their mail and press cuttings from Australia reflected the ignorance of AIF achievements. Monash lobbied hard for more recognition, using as his line that the Australians were sporting and competitive by nature. They liked to see their winning scores on the board. He could have added that the 'scores'—battle victories—could be recorded with a little more flourish; a fraction more sense of occasion. He thought Bean's writings about Péronne were bland. Perhaps the historian's effort was all a consequence of battle fatigue. This was his fourth year on the job. Maybe it was a case of *Bean there, reported that.*

Monash yearned for someone like English writer Ashmead-Bartlett to inject life into the newspaper reports. It was all part of his effort to boost the Australians' sense that they were in a powerful 'team' that could beat any other force. Feature stories that included a sense of drama would build that feeling of invincibility.

Monash and others were doing what they could to circulate the stories of heroics and victories in internal bulletins and here and there in the Australian press. Names such as Murray, Jacka, McCarthy, Gordon, Cartwright, Lowerson, Mactier, Towner, Weathers, Currey, Hall and Buckley were already legendary. Many acts deserving of them were being reported as the AIF continued on its winning way.

Monash's expectation was that once the diggers received clippings from home, and read about their exploits and 'importance' in battles, it would help motivate them further. It was the same with reports of heroism, which were to be seen the same way a 'best on ground' story about a football match would be read. The only difference was that on the Somme, awards for heroism were for best on *battle*ground.

●

Monash was now using his prestige within the British Army as its most successful corps commander. He told Rawlinson and others in the British High Command that he did not accept their argument that it was better not to publicise Australian successes since German propaganda was saying that the British were climbing to victory over Australian and Canadian corpses. Nor did he buy the High Command argument that political opposition to the war in the Dominions would use any publicity about their successes as evidence that the troops were being used as cannon fodder in the toughest fighting zones.

For once, Monash, Hughes, Murdoch and Bean were as one in their drive to obtain the due owed to the AIF for its victories. Each had his own motive. The journalists wanted their by-lines on big Australian victory stories. Hughes wished to strut the world stage with influence. The AIF had taken more than its fair share of the burden of the conflict. Hughes and his government wanted the prestige to flow from that, enabling him to have a say at the expected peace settlement that would follow the end of the war.

Hughes showed perspicacity about how important recognition of Australia's contribution to the war effort might be to its future security. He knew that the British ruling elite from the King down appreciated the AIF's efforts. But after recent trips to the United States he was aware of the ignorance about them in Washington DC. He couldn't find anyone who realised that Australians and Americans had fought together, under an Australian commander. Hughes, the pragmatist's pragmatist among politicians, saw the United States, like England, as insurance for survival as a 4-million strong independent nation of Europeans at the bottom of Asia. Americans, Hughes appreciated, were strong on loyalty and 'paying dues'. He believed that the United States had to understand that Australia had fought hard and made huge sacrifices for the Allies' cause. Publicity was one way, perhaps the main way, for this to be communicated to the powers in Washington.

Hughes and Murdoch arranged for three press parties to be taken to the Australian front from 12 September. A journalist for the London *Weekly Despatch*, Arthur O'Connor, described Monash as 'somewhat rugged with alert yet kindly eyes'. He spoke 'quietly, deliberately, unhesitatingly'. He was 'a strong man', and summed him up as 'intellectual, original, democratic, ruthless'.[1]

Monash had charisma in an era when it was not a hackneyed, meaningless description associated with film stars or script-driven, semi-literate political candidates.

By opening up to the press he did much to redress the problem of Australia's record being absorbed under the heading *British Victories*. But it also created another situation of conflict for him and Hughes. Monash's public prestige would now lift even further after his profile rose to where it should have been, just when Hughes was under increasing pressure at home from some quarters to reduce the AIF size and effort in the, hoped-for, final stages of the war.

The diggers had done more than enough and the status was theirs, the argument went. Time to bring the boys home.

Hughes had been based in London since June and monitoring the politics behind the war, especially the conflict between Prime Minister Lloyd George, and Haig and his High Command. Lloyd George had been continuing to withhold British manpower from Haig in the hope of limiting his capacity for mass offensives. They led to huge casualties, which caused even the anaesthetised British public, through the press, to protest. Apart from offending Lloyd George's sensibilities, high body counts threatened his chances of re-election. He was gambling on the Americans taking over the war early in 1919. This would spare thousands of British troops, his election hopes and his chance for history to see him in a favourable light.

Hughes now fell into a similar feud over numbers at the front, with his commander-in-chief, Monash; the Australian prime minister knew their stoush was also about electability and his place in the history books. He had been told by someone very senior in the British High Command that the war could stretch into 1920. Hughes didn't see how the AIF could go on at such frenetic pace and end up with any of its divisions intact.

The prime minister had long been urging that he have power of veto over how, when and where the AIF was used. During the big battles from 8 August on, Haig had ignored him, and the Australian prime minister had been forced to remain quiet. But in the lull after the Battle of Mont St Quentin and Péronne, Hughes arrived at the front making his demands again. Instead of going through Haig, who was blocking him with lack of responses and 'too busy to talk' signals, Hughes turned up with the first contingent of journalists on 12 September. His trusty supporters, Murdoch and Bean, were in tow and ready with notebooks in hand. Once more, they had both been urging the prime minister to confront Monash.

He accommodated them and the other writers and journalists at Amiens, not at his hut HQ at Belloy-en-Santerre. This way they would not interfere with his planning for the Hindenburg Line offensive. Unlike Hamel, the proposed attack this time would be kept secret, even from the prime minister.

At lunch, Hughes took the time to chat with Monash. Blamey characterised the meeting as a confrontation between an 'Alsatian [Monash] and a Bantam Cock [Hughes]'.[2]

The prime minister had been cautious with Monash on the battlefront just before Hamel in early July. The general's stature since then had grown exponentially. But this time Hughes believed there wouldn't be a battle for some time. (The plans were kept from everyone but the High Command and top commanders.) The apparent lull between conflicts was the moment for the 'Bantam Cock' to strike. Hughes told Monash that the AIF must cease all fighting by early in October, less than three weeks away.

This was not quite the blow to Monash that the 'pogrom' (as he referred to it in one letter to Vic) inflicted, courtesy of Bean and Murdoch, in June and July. But he could do without the interference. He had come to the conclusion for different reasons than Hughes that the AIF couldn't go on longer than early October anyway. It would be a relief if he could get them out by then. He felt near breaking point himself and was well aware that his fighting infantry felt the same way. The Australians had been used, willingly, as shock troops. They were always at the pointy end of action—the arrowhead in thrust after thrust. There was a limit, no matter how he rotated his troops. He and they were fast approaching it. The near mutiny of a handful of the 59th Battalion was one of a few similar incidents among men that had been straining to join the hotspots after the Australian Corps took shape in May 1918. Now there was a growing feeling within the ranks that they had done far more than their fair share. Monash was watching this. But he was determined not to let go or stop. Not yet. Not until he considered he had done his job. Monash had told others, Bean and Murdoch among them, that he wanted control of the corps to prove himself as a commander. But he was well beyond that, even if he didn't recognise it himself. Commentators and journalists were beginning to acknowledge him as the Allies' best battlefield commander.

When Hughes sprang his surprise 'order', Monash remained composed. He tried to explain to Hughes that he too wanted them out of the line by early October, but in war, it would be irresponsible to withdraw men on an appointed day so far ahead. What if they were in the middle of action? How would other corps react seeing the Australians marching off? Also once winter set in, it could be difficult to withdraw his troops. They were an integral part of the fighting force needed to win the war. Taking them out without regard to the conditions at the time would be tantamount to handing the German defence a huge advantage.

Hughes would have none of it. He warned Monash that the corps *had* to be out of the line by that date. Monash's job depended on it. Instead of acceding to the demands, Monash kept his powder dry. He would have thought again of his prize-winning essay in 1912, when he made clear his view *that politicians must not interfere in how commanders conduct war.* He felt alienated from the prime minister, who was using his rightful power as a democratically elected national leader. Monash, the commander of the AIF, would attempt to defy the elected leader, by using his own influence within the British military structure, as he had contemplated doing when Hughes was about to remove him from his command just before Hamel. Monash could not, *would not*, walk away from his position now; not when the aim he had programmed himself for—winning the war—might be only weeks away.

Hughes told Murdoch after the meeting he thought 'the General' had something up his sleeve. Would he dare to cable Pearce and other members of the Cabinet and protest with his exceptional powers of persuasion, he wondered. Monash's prestige at that instant was so high that Hughes thought he, as prime minister, might well be overruled.[3] In effect, he feared a long-distance coup. But Monash was subtler than that. The lawyer, ever present in him, noted a loophole in the prime minister's order, if he needed it. Hughes had not specified which day 'early in October' that troops had to be pulled out.

Haig agreed that the Australians should be away from the front line by the same time. So despite his caution, Monash remained more or less in accord with Hughes. The difference was that the prime minister might well call it quits for good and disband the volunteer corps. Monash believed the war could stumble on through the 1918–19 winter (although he was working hard to make the enemy fall apart before then). To think otherwise would cause complacency, which he thought irresponsible. Hughes' dictum had bought him time. He would worry about its consequences later. The situation was so fluid and unpredictable, it was best not to worry too far ahead.

Chapter 45

The Politics of Interference

Hughes told Murdoch: 'He [Monash] sees only one thing. He wants to fight on. He wants to be there at the finish.'[1]

The prime minister was being critical, though many would see it as praise, and would be more damning of a commander who wished to drop out before his mission was accomplished.

Murdoch urged Hughes to take action to show Monash who was boss. Why not direct Birdwood, who was head of the AIF's administration, to order Monash to send 800 original Anzacs to Australia, *immediately*, for two months' leave? It was a clever ploy. This way the prime minister didn't have to face Monash or any of his generals, or anyone in the British High Command. Hughes followed the suggestion. Then he accompanied Bean and

King George V knights Monash on
12 August 1918.

Monash, aged 52, approaching the
peak of his military powers in
May 1918, just after being made
Australian Corps Commander.

Monash with Prime Minister Billy Hughes on 14 September 1918.

Journalist Keith Murdoch and Prime Minister Billy Hughes on the Western Front in September 1918.

Monash (seated) with the Prince of Wales (later King Edward VIII) at a London function in October 1918.

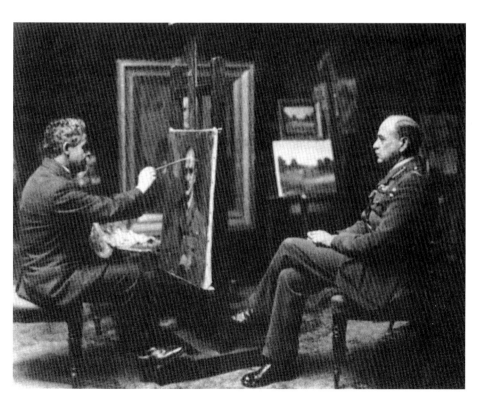

Monash being painted by James Quinn in 1919.

Monash leading the Australian troops in a London victory march on 19 July 1919 in front of Buckingham Palace.

Monash with medals and sword on 25 April 1927. He led 30,000 diggers in an Anzac Day march reviewed by the Duke of York (the future King George VI).

A wrecked tank near Gaza. They rarely worked effectively in the desert. Horses could go 80 kilometres in a day and were more reliable in the heat and terrain.

The 3rd Light Horse on the move near the Sea of Galilee, September 1918.

The Light Horse in the Jordan Valley. Chauvel considered the four-day foray against the Turks there in May 1918 a 'failure'. Allenby thought otherwise, declaring 'failure be damned'. He believed the venture had shaken the enemy, and set up the British army and Anzac Light Horse for a final drive towards Damascus.

The Daughters of Jacob Bridge over the Jordan, being repaired by Chauvel's engineers.

The Light Horse on the move in Jerusalem.

The 1st Light Horse in dune country, Belah, January 1918.

Colonel Ryrie at the head of the 2nd Light Horse at Esdud, January 1918. Ryrie, a Member of Federal Parliament, annoyed Chauvel by breaking from the war to attend a London Empire Parliamentary Conference.

Lieutenant General Sir Harry Chauvel. He believed the Battle of Romani, in which he led the troopers from the front, in early August 1916, was the most important battle of the Desert War. It stopped the Turks' advance on Egypt and was their first reversal. After Romani they were on a long retreat to Turkey until 30 October 1918.

Murdoch to Bray, where the likely chosen ones were and told them of his decision. The two journalists then rushed to report the story to pre-empt any move by Monash to cable the Cabinet back in Australia to stop it.

Hughes' action in undermining his chief military commander with his troops was a desperate show of strength, something always dreaded in army circles. Monash's earlier action just before Hamel, of telling Hughes he would not go if fired as corps commander, had forewarned the prime minister and his co-conspirators that they had better think through any attempts to weaken his command. They were now getting some retribution by stepping into Monash's military state, geographically outside Australia and under British control, but bound to Australian governmental rules.

Hughes caused even further disruption, by telling the troops he would make sure they all saw out the winter of 1918–19 in good weather and conditions in Italy and France. This vote-garnering exercise was as thoughtless as it was counterproductive. Assuming the AIF was still in the conflict, it could never promise three months' sunny vacation.[2]

Monash was furious and worried. He agreed with the idea, and the principle behind relieving the Anzacs, but not the timing. Most of the men would come from Glasgow's 1st and Sinclair-Maclagan's 4th Division only days before they were preparing to go into action in the first battle for the Hindenburg Line.

Monash didn't think the soldiers chosen would be happy to leave at such short notice. Birdwood, who had to do Hughes' bidding, didn't agree. He did his usual pressing of the flesh with the soldiers concerned and found the prospective furlough-makers 'happy . . . with smiles on their faces'.[3]

Yet all Monash's commanders agreed with him. How would the privileged 800 be selected from 6000 eligible Anzacs? Pompey Elliott was bitter that his brigade would be broken up and rendered inoperable for 1919.

'If Mr. Hughes had been in the pay of the Germans,' he commented, 'he could not have dealt us a more paralyzing stroke.'[4]

Monash protested to Hughes. Murdoch, on the prime minister's behalf, had delight in telling the general he had better comply with the rest for the 800 or else Hughes would take further action, presumably to fire him. Monash consulted his commanders. With more battle plans being drawn up, the suggestion was that Monash should comply, but slowly and with only about half the 800 men Hughes had ordered out of the war. That way 1st and 4th Division could go into the next battle, almost intact. Two hundred or so soldiers from each would drop their numbers by about 7 per cent. It was just manageable for one more battle.

Monash, however, was well aware that this sort of threat to his force was intolerable for future encounters. He could not call back any of the exhausted 2nd, 3rd or 5th Divisions from their well-earnt rest. They had only been a week away from the bruising Mont St Quentin and Péronne battles.

Monash approached Haig about how to handle the attrition. The commander-in-chief was sympathetic. Prime Minister Lloyd George was giving him similar grief by holding back men for the front.

Haig invited Monash to join him on a horse ride for a discussion. Monash told him of Hughes' political games.

'Don't worry John,' Haig said. 'If Hughes makes it intolerable with his withdrawals I'll give you another Corps.'

'I appreciate that, Douglas,' Monash replied, 'but I only wish to command the diggers.'

'I understand that. Birdy [Birdwood] feels the same way about them.' He paused and asked, 'How do you propose we resolve it?'

'You could give me Americans.'

'You know they don't know how to fight trench warfare. What we've seen so far [from the Americans] has not been encouraging.'

'They can be trained. They handled themselves very well and courageously at Hamel and Amiens.'

'How many would you want?'

'50,000.'

'Done.'5

Just two months earlier he had been officially denied absorbing even *one* American soldier under his command. Now his influence was such that his request was granted without question or argument. He would control two divisions of Pershing's troops. Monash was thrilled. The additional men from another country increased his independence and confirmed his power over his own military state. The force was now international and confirmed the British High Command's faith in him. Even if Hughes was able to fire him, Haig would ensure he had a fighting corps for these late thrusts at the enemy. Monash was most likely now to have a chance to achieve his messianic, driving goal to be there at the death of the war, and see final victory.

•

That problem solved, Monash was ready for the final assault less than a fortnight after he had won the battles for Mont St Quentin and Péronne. Rawlinson, Montgomery and the other

Fourth Army Corps commanders (Butler, now over his health problems, and General Walter Braithwaite, who had served under Ian Hamilton) met him at AIF HQ at Belloy-en-Santerre, close to the Somme, which had been occupied by the Germans.

'There, quite informally, over a cup of afternoon tea,' Monash recorded, 'the great series of operations took birth which so directly helped to finish the war.'[6]

Despite his run-in with Hughes and the perennial plotters working against him, he was at the peak of his military powers. Rawlinson was giving him everything he wanted to continue to lead the fight. Blamey recalled the days less than a year earlier when the AIF would have to beg for equipment. Tanks were then out of the question. Big artillery was not forthcoming. Machine guns were begrudgingly handed over. Now it was a case of, 'The equipment should be with you in a few days', or 'Another Division? I'll see what can be arranged.'

Haig, Rawlinson and Montgomery were only too willing to give assistance. They knew Monash had the skills and determination, and the right, willing force. Until August, these British commanders were men destined for the 'forgotten' or 'detested' file in history. Now, with victory a distinct possibility, their reputations were being salvaged. Haig was no longer 'the butcher of the Somme'. For the moment, Rawlinson was no longer being referred to as one of the 'donkeys leading lions'—the front-line soldiers— a moniker that arose after the disastrous charge at the Somme in 1916. If Monash and the other forces he was taking with him could drive on, then the three of them might just emerge with winners' epithets, which would be for life. Winning this conflict, allegedly the war to end all wars, would not just be talked about at the Officers' Club. It would be recorded for posterity.

All three were fox hunters in the British tradition. They loved to ride to the hounds. Now they could do it on the battlefield. The hounds were Monash and his soldiers, and the foxes were the Germans.

In September, the scent was strong.

•

Monash surveyed the country where the chase would continue. For 14 kilometres east, the country was beautiful, composed of woods and valleys, with deserted villages here and there; good fox territory, although they were nowhere to be seen. Beyond this was another area similar to the one on the Somme, which had just been won. It was 10 kilometres long and became more and more devastated the closer it came to the Hindenburg Line. This was the result of trench warfare by the British Fifth Army from September 1917 until the great German offensive of 21 March 1918.

Reconnaissance in this belt showed unusual signs of life, not of the former French inhabitants, but of the Germans burning villages, stores and ammunition as they retreated. Those unforgiving foxes had teeth. Their destination—the Hindenburg Line (the Siegfried Line to the Germans)—was an 80-kilometre-long, 7.2-kilometre-wide system of trenches and fortifications. Perhaps only the Germans, with their industrious capacity for unaesthetic but efficient construction, could have conceived of and created it. They had built it over three months until the early spring of 1917. It was a solid barrier that could be manned by a minimum of soldiers so that a maximum number could go forward and attack the Allies.

It had formed an impregnable wall to British and French assaults.

Chapter 46

Tank Illusion

On 16 September Monash brought his Division Commanders Glasgow (1st) and Sinclair-Maclagan (4th) to a meeting along with Courage (tanks), Chamier (air force), Fraser (heavy artillery), and the four generals on his own staff. Glasgow and Sinclair-Maclagan were fresh and had been resting, while Rosenthal, Gellibrand and Hobbs had exhausted themselves and their men winning at the *mont* and Péronne.

Monash had requested that the Australian Corps would have a shortened front of 6.5 kilometres, and this was acceded to. That was just feasible for the limited number of Australians, around 6900 soldiers and officers, left available for this new thrust, once Hughes' requested Anzacs (450 in the end, not 800) had been subtracted. The British III Corps would be on their left;

the British IX Corps and First French Army would be on the right. The entire attacking line would run for 27 kilometres. Its aim would be to smash the Hindenburg Line, but not in one hit. It was too vast. The 7.2-kilometre-thick fortifications were composed of four barriers or targets, which would have to be taken in separate attacks.

The first was the Hindenburg Outpost Line (also called the Hargicourt Line). Second was the Hindenburg Main Line, consisting of a long canal and tunnel system. The third target was the Le Catelet Line. The final enemy defence was the Beaurevoir Line.

Monash received a huge boost when an innocent-looking lorry was captured on another front. It contained vital maps and documents concerning the whole Hindenburg system. His appetite for the minutia was whetted and then satisfied when he sat down to peruse the many detailed maps, and descriptions of every tactical feature of the defences. The position of every gun emplacement, searchlight, machine-gun pit, observation post, telephone exchange, command station and mortar was well marked.

Monash spent many days hovering over the maps, which showed the topographical and tactical features of the ground, while the documents laid out action plans for every garrison unit.

They formed a fine starting point for the scheming on how to take target number one: the Hargicourt Line. The French and the British Armies would make a synchronised attack with Monash's force.

His main worry was the lack of tanks. He had missed them at Mont St Quentin and Péronne, and after his experiences from Hamel on, would be uncomfortable without them again. He requested several hundred, but the tanks being repaired and those coming off English production lines would not be there in time.

Monash was appalled when told that only *eight* would be ready for his use on 18 September. Yet he was determined to have his tanks, even if he produced them by using one of his conjuring tricks. He ordered the manufacture of dummy tanks to make up the shortfall. That directive resulted in raids on dumps and stores as pioneers and engineers competed to produce some odd-looking monsters. Each dummy was hauled forward just before dawn on attack day.

When the sun came up the enemy would see a frightening line of tanks on the horizon.

This extra Monash illusion played a big part in the outcome when the 1st and 4th Divisions (each on a frontage of one brigade), fortified with a shot of rum, attacked in heavy rain after an artillery bombardment. The enemy this time did not include any Prussian Guardsmen. They mainly surrendered or ran, with some opposition coming at the hamlet of Le Verguier. Monash's old brigade, the 4th, was given the demanding task of taking it. Three battalions—the 13th, 15th and 16th—combined in an assault. The 13th's Sergeant Maurice Buckley (alias Gerald Sexton) led the way in the dawn attack as the fog and smoke cleared.

Perhaps he had read about his namesake Alex Buckley at Péronne, or maybe he had an extra shot of rum. Whatever the reason, his actions were extraordinary. Sexton rushed a field gun and a mortar on the bank straight ahead. Firing his Lewis gun from the hip, he blasted the field-gun crew, and then turned his attention to the mortar crew. Sexton urged his section to follow him. Impatient to take out the mortar and its crew, he sprinted 100 metres under heavy machine-gun fire and achieved his objective, without help. Sexton then returned to the bank and fired into four entrances to dugouts. Thirty prisoners emerged.

It was then he realised he had flushed out the HQ of the German 58th Infantry Regiment.

Sexton could have been forgiven for taking a rest behind the lines, but in keeping with his fierce dedication, continued on with the 13th Battalion, leading attacks—with assistance now—on five other machine-gun posts.

He deservedly would also receive a VC, despite them now being much tougher to attain, such was the fury and intestinal fortitude being shown by so many in the final push by the AIF east of Péronne.

Acts of outrageous daring now were coming faster, as if the men sensed they really were approaching some sort of climax. It was being hastened by all sorts of rumours, some of them conflicting, about going on leave to an exotic place, or home.

They were also reading about Australian victories in newspapers being circulated among the troops. Monash had been right. The soldiers had been inspired by the stories they had heard, or read, in bulletins. But reading them in clippings from the major city papers, or just the local town journal, had more influence. They presented more credibility than word of mouth or official army propaganda.

One of many soldiers impressed by what he was reading was Private James Wood of the 48th Battalion (positioned on the right or southern side of the Australian front at Le Verguier). Leading a four-man patrol, he stumbled on a strong entrenchment of Germans on a ridge *behind* the 12th Brigade. If the enemy advanced or the 12th fell back, the entire battalion could be wiped out. Wood asked one of his patrol team to dash for assistance. When the runner didn't come back with help after half an hour, Woods consulted with his two mates. They could see activity at the enemy position. They were preparing for something, maybe an advance from the rear. If Wood didn't act now, he reckoned the Germans might make their move on the 12th Brigade.

The three intrepid soldiers hit the two trenches as the Germans were donning their kit in preparation for a march and attack, as Wood had guessed. The Australians killed one of the enemy; 30 others fled leaving six machine guns. Wood and his mates settled in the trenches.

It took the Germans only minutes to realise that just three men had jumped them. The enemy decided to counterattack. Wood and co. could have stayed in the trenches and fired out with their rifles, but they would soon be overwhelmed by the opposition. Wood decided they had to defend with grenades and hope that the runner had obtained help in time to save them. He crawled onto a trench parapet and hurled grenade after grenade as the other two men handed them up to him. The blasts created such disorganisation that the 30 Germans could not reach the trenches. When they regrouped, they found themselves surrounded by Australian reinforcements. The runner had done his job, just in time to save Wood and the others.

The position was secured. Le Verguier belonged to the Australians. Private Wood would soon be reading about his own exploits and citations.

●

By 10 a.m. on 18 September Monash had control of the old British front line of 21 March. It had taken three days short of half a year to restore the status quo.

The day's objective, the Hargicourt Line, was still 1700 metres away. Both divisions pushed on now with an expectation that there would be fierce opposition from the trench system that had defied the Fifth Army for years. Glasgow's 1st Division encountered some resistance, which led to tragedy and more heroics. Many men would be considered unlucky after fighting from Gallipoli through Flanders and on the Somme for four years only to be cut down at the final hurdle. One high-profile instance was the popular captain Wally Hallahan, a machine gunner of the 11th Battalion. Forty-eight hours before he was to be married to an English woman while on leave in London, he was called back to fight in the battle for Hargicourt. The veteran Anzac and his future bride were planning to return to Australia on home leave.

Hallahan would never be married or make it back. He was killed during the battle on the outskirts of the town.

Despite the Australian onslaught and the confidence that they would prevail against fierce opposition, the weakened troops still needed inspiration to meet their objectives. A mate of Hallahan's in the 11th Battalion, Captain E.W. Tulloch, provided it. Tulloch refused to be bogged down by two machine guns at the entrance to the town. He selected two fighters and rushed the Germans. They killed fifteen of the enemy, captured as many and knocked out the guns. This would have earnt the captain a VC before the battles of Mont St Quentin and Péronne. Instead he was awarded the Military Cross (MC) and a promotion to lieutenant colonel.

By dark on 18 September this kind of endeavour ensured that Glasgow's men had overwhelmed the Hindenburg Outpost garrison.

•

Sinclair-Maclagan's soldiers of the 4th Division had a tougher assignment. They were advancing in full view of the Germans and on more difficult terrain. They were exhausted 450 metres short of the objective. Monash conferred with Sinclair-Maclagan. They decided the troops should be rested, while the artillery was brought up for a drenching of the enemy before a final assault.

The 4th Division attacked at 11 p.m. and encountered a determined enemy. Not long after midnight, Sinclair-Maclagan's men speared the Australian flag into the ground to signal another quick, decisive victory, this time in the Battle of Hargicourt.

The numbers were satisfying to Monash. Thanks to Hughes' subterfuge, he had gone into the battle with what he perceived as the bare minimum of men. The 1st Division's strength was 2854 infantry. They suffered 490 casualties, but killed four times that number, while capturing 1700 Germans. The 4th Division (3048 soldiers) had 532 casualties. It killed more than 2000 and captured 2543. After the anomalous brutal hand-to-hand encounters of Mont St Quentin and Péronne, Monash was relieved to produce figures more in keeping with his doctrine of using the machines to do damage and of protecting his foot soldiers.

'There is no record in this war,' Monash noted, 'of any previous success on such a scale, won with so little loss.'[1]

The British Corps left and right had not been quite as quick, or successful. The IX Corps on the Australians' right would take another day to reach their target. But the III Corps on the left had no hope of bringing their line up level with the Australians by 19 September.

Chapter 47

Compassion at the Front

Just when Monash was pleased with the first victory in the multi-staged attack on the Hindenburg defences, he was confronted by another problem with rebellious troops, this time because they *wanted* to fight, not avoid it.

It began with one of the most inanely timed orders from the British High Command in the entire war. It had decided to reduce the number of battalions in each brigade from four to three. Monash was happy with the theory this move seemed to support: that more weapons could compensate for fewer soldiers. He thought an extra 30 Lewis guns in a battalion would be adequate. But the order came just before the climatic battles in the war. Command wanted the AIF to disband eight battalions.

Monash had to sit down with his divisional commanders and work out who would go. It was a painful process. When informed by their officers, only one of the eight battalions said it would comply with the order. Seven went on strike. They ignored all directives from the AIF, generals, staff and commanders. Then they sacked their officers, installed their own and demanded that Monash negotiate with them.

It was, in effect, a mutiny, but perhaps the strangest in the annals of war. Some of their members—the Anzacs—had been happy to take up Hughes' recent offer to go on leave to Australia, or Italy and France. But that was a different proposition from being broken up and informed they were no longer needed. The psychology of being told they could not fight with their mates, and the corps itself, before completing the job they had come to Europe to do, was bad enough. But it was too much to take when coupled with the added blow that they had been selected, while three other battalions in each brigade had not. It was an insult to their pride. It shattered the very sense of the lives these diggers had experienced over four years.

Monash's building of such a 'winning' entity, which was now generating publicity commensurate with its progress on the battlefield, along with reports of amazing individual exploits, had been *too* successful. Nobody wanted to be dropped from the successful 'team'.

The High Command had never really understood the mentality of the Australian soldier. Monash did. He secretly sympathised with the men and was touched by their courage. He went against all protocol and army rules and met with the mutineers' representatives from the 37th Battalion, who spoke for all the rebels.

Monash had a dilemma. He understood their grievances and was furious with the timing of the disbanding order. On the one hand, he couldn't *officially* allow these battalions to survive. It defied everything he had preached about obeying orders. On the other hand, if the order was enforced and the mutineers resisted, the situation could be dangerous. Not only that; all the other battalions, who hated one of them being dissolved like this, might go on strike too. This was happening just when Monash was drawing up his grand plan for what could be the AIF's biggest battle of the war.

He first tried to appeal to their commonsense.

'I have done a thing unprecedented in military annals in holding an informal conference such as this,' Monash told them, 'but I realize that the AIF is different from any other army in the world.'[1]

There would be no charges or arrests if they went quietly, he informed them. Did they want their battalions to go out of existence with a bad reputation, especially after the wonderful, professional way they had built their names?

Monash didn't talk about 'breaking up' or 'disbandment'. He used softer language, emphasising 'dispersal' and an 'honourable end'. But the new rebel leaders were stubborn. The meeting ended with no resolution.

The mutinous action had immediate ramifications for events on the front line.

The day after the conference, the British III Corps had still not managed to fight its way to level with the line the Australians had secured. Butler, back as the III Corps leader, asked for help. Could Monash spare a battalion to take over 450 metres of the front allotted to III Corps? Monash agreed. The 1st Battalion of

1st Division was asked to oblige, just as they were leaving the line for a break after doing their job with brutal professionalism. Already aware of the stalemate at the conference between the rebels and Monash the day before, the 1st Battalion's diggers protested at this sudden order. They had been called on to fill the gaps and do the work that the English troops had failed to do many times before. This was a demand too far.

A total of 119 men refused the order to move to the unoccupied front. This was the second crack in the AIF edifice in 24 hours, and the third since the night of 1 September at Péronne.

The rest of the 1st Battalion obeyed orders and took up the slack on the 450-metre front as requested. The 1st Division commander, Glasgow, a strict disciplinarian, went into a rage. He had the men charged with 'mutiny', which carried the death penalty. Glasgow disagreed with Monash's handling of the rebellion the day before. Glasgow thought a stand had to be taken before mutinous acts became endemic. Monash had to mollify his divisional general, but he also realised he couldn't let this situation hang in the air, as he had done with the rebels at the conference.

Monash suggested the 1st Battalion men's charge should be changed to 'desertion'. The result was still ugly, with the men facing up to ten years' imprisonment in the notorious Dartmoor Prison in England. And it was a tragic possibility, given the incredible work these soldiers had done, many of them for up to four years since Gallipoli. But it avoided the horrific prospect of 118 diggers (one charge was dismissed) being executed by firing squad, as Glasgow had urged, although it was not Australian policy. Monash refused to contemplate that or where such action would have headed. But Glasgow was insistent, demanding 'as their commanding officer' that 'every single mutineer' be executed.

'As your commanding officer,' Monash replied, 'I order you to put them on charges of desertion.' Then, eyeballing Glasgow, he added, 'Otherwise you will be countermanding a directive from a superior officer.' He paused and said: 'And you seem to be well aware of the penalty for doing that.'[2]

Glasgow was incensed but cornered by Monash's barristerial logic. The 118 new rebels were to be kept under 'close arrest', which meant that they were confined to camp. The corps commander had to confirm the sentences. The paperwork for that sat on Monash's desk and was ignored. He wrote that he had no intention of seeing the men incarcerated and wanted their sentences dropped. But it was too early to do so. Had he used his power then to veto the sentences, it may have encouraged others wavering in the ranks to desert. He decided to wait until a more appropriate moment to act.

With that problem suspended, Monash, playing judge, advocate, witness and negotiator, held a crisis conference over the seven 'disbanding' battalion rebels with Birdwood and the five divisional commanders. If the AIF now enforced the brigade break-up, the other battalions would strike in sympathy. This would destroy the massive assault, at least before the winter weather set in, on the Hindenburg fortifications.

The conference agreed that the last battle should be over in about two weeks (around 9 October). Could the order to break up the battalions be stalled until then? Haig and Rawlinson, as ever looking to the mood of his Chief, demurred.

'I doubt we can do this, John,' Haig said.

'Douglas, I appreciate your position and the ruling,' Monash said, 'but you know the diggers. It will be one out, all out. We just will not have the benefit of the AIF at a critical moment.'

Haig still seemed uncertain.

'I know John is right,' Birdwood said. 'We will have a terrible situation on our hands.'

'Avoidable if you decide on the technicality [of when they disbanded],' Monash added.

'Alright, John,' Haig said, 'but please, they are to be disbanded no later than October the 9th.'[3]

Once more, Monash's calm application of a legal loophole had won him the outcome he wanted.

PART 4
Syria and Chauvel's Ascendancy

Chapter 48

Chauvel's Fast Work

Word of Monash's persistent efforts and success changed the mood of Allenby's Eastern Expeditionary Force, and in particular Chauvel's predominantly Anzac Desert Mounted Column, which had mainly rested in August and September. Throughout the month news came through about the Allies winning a mighty battle at Amiens, and Monash kept his Australian counterpart abreast of the further victories at Mont St Quentin and Péronne. Chauvel cabled, then wrote, his congratulations to Monash knowing that he had been the mastermind behind the successes.

Monash had extolled the virtues of tanks to Chauvel and how he planned to use them at every opportunity. Chauvel in turn told him the futility of having them in a desert war. He still depended on the horse and camel, primarily, which he acknowledged might never again be used on such a scale in a major war.

Monash assured him it was only a matter of time before the war was over on the Western Front. He was adamant that it would not go beyond 1918. Chauvel was uncertain although he bowed to Monash's brilliance and certitude. The state of affairs in the 'main game' had wide ramifications for the sideshow in the Middle East. Allenby sniffed overall victory wafting from the Western Front. It was time to drive home the sword, literally, on the Eastern Front. But first, Allenby told Chauvel, there was time for a little mischief and deception, to which they were amenable after the amazing 'win' at Beersheba.

It began with a commotion at Fast's Hotel in Jerusalem early in September. Officers, American journalists and an assortment of other patrons were informed that they had to vacate the building that morning. The word came from the manager, Monsieur Caesar, who had received official yet confidential instructions from a high place. Guests had to be cleared out. He was a legend after a long time as the head waiter at the Continental Hotel, Cairo. His word was not God's but it was Caesar's, and that was good enough for most in the Holy City. Those who objected were assisted in packing their belongings and helped out into the street. Sentry boxes were placed at the front door of this former German house. It had been taken over in December 1917 by the British Canteens Board and mainly used by officers over the past ten months. Now, notices headed 'GHQ' were pinned on every bedroom door. Something big seemed to be happening. Stories spread that Commander-in-Chief Allenby and his vast staff would be based there soon. Rumours filtered into the bazaar that Fast's would be his advanced headquarters for a mighty push east from the Jordan Valley. This was it. The Holy City buzzed with the news.

Before noon, the enemy heard the story and believed it. Just like the British foot soldiers' feint at Gaza when Beersheba was taken by the Anzac Light Horse, Chauvel and Allenby were up to their old tricks. They were creating a vast and elaborate illusion that would have done Houdini proud. Even Monash, the finest trickster on the Western Front, who had been a teenage illusionist with cards, could not have bettered this sophisticated fraud.

The detail of how Chauvel would wave his magic wand was left to him and his staff. It needed the coolest of characters, and the front of a world-class poker player to pull off this giant 'con'. The Australian had always played his cards close. He was a quiet disciplinarian, who had the utmost respect of the officers under him. Here his underlying strength as a man and general was to be tested in conditions only surpassed by the strictures of battle itself. The secrecy required on so many levels reflected the trust every officer and commander had in Chauvel. He was not a leader by bluster. But bluff was a strong suit, the conundrum being that bluff only worked because beneath it lay a substantial plan. If Chauvel wished to fool the enemy with a ruse, then his troopers would go along with it. His every move since the dark days of mid-May 1915, when huddled 'cheek by jowl' with Monash in the valley of death at Gallipoli, had been in the interests of the men under him. Chauvel had pulled out of the fray at Courtney's Post on Gallipoli when staying in the fight would have seen his troops decimated. Like Monash, he maintained a care for the men under him in the bigger war theatres.

The charade in Jerusalem was cover for a serious punch further west, first with the XX and XXI Infantry Corps. When a hole in the enemy defences on the Plain of Sharon near the coast was created, Chauvel and a large slice of his force would crash through it, ride hard to the north-east and tackle the enemy in their HQ and communications centres at Nazareth and El Afule.

It was bold, daring and plausible, *if* the enemy was taken by surprise. Chauvel and his commanders gave no written orders. In secret at night, the troopers were moved west to the Mediterranean coast. They were not allowed to sightsee, which left them with few options for filling time other than playing cards. Some of them sneaked down to the coast for a swim at dawn. During the day they had to be out of sight or still. Horses were kept hobbled as they drank. All cooking was done using smoke-free cubes. Mules and camels, with their groans and rumbling, were kept well clear of the 8-kilometre inland strip from Jaffa to Ludd where the Light Horse hid. Jaffa, which they could see from their camps in the orange, lemon, almond and olive groves, was out of bounds. Waiting in the heat was boring, even if it were preferable to sitting around in the oven of the Jordan Valley.

•

Just before the scheduled attack of 19 September, Allenby arrived at the mess tent of divisional HQ to meet Chauvel and his commanders and brigadiers for a pep talk.

'I came here Gentlemen,' he said, with his characteristic certitude, 'to wish you good luck, and to tell you that I consider you are on the eve of a great victory. Practically everything depends on the secrecy, rapidity and accuracy of the cavalry movement.'[1]

•

The same morning, a devout Muslim Indian sergeant went AWOL from British General Barrow's Cavalry Division and reached the Turkish stronghold at Nablus, 55 kilometres from Jaffa. He had been tormented by the thought of his brother Muslims being defeated on a massive scale and decided to defect and tell all. He was taken to a Turkish officer saying he wished to defect and inform him of a massive plan of deception. His breathless divulgences brought a sceptical response at first from the experienced Turkish officer, who knew of the feint at Gaza and other British tricks. But when the Indian had laid out what he knew, the officer believed the defector was telling the truth. The astute Mustafa Kemal, who had been appointed the head of the Seventh Army by the Turkish Sultan himself, was alerted.

He believed the story and sent a rushed message to General von Sanders, 60 kilometres north of Nablus at his HQ in Nazareth.

•

The Indian sergeant's disappearance and assumed defection was reported to Barrow, who passed on the bad news to his commander, Chauvel. With Allenby's terse comment about the need for 'secrecy' still ringing in his ears, the Australian considered the possible crisis but decided not to change anything in the schedule. Too many wheels of the attack were in motion. He would have to pray that the defector would not be believed.

•

Von Sanders dismissed the defector's report out of hand. He did not have the benefit of seeing the sincere Indian in front of him with all the detail in his head. On paper, the claims seemed fantastic and far too elaborate to be true. The scheme ran contrary to every military intelligence report the German commander had read in the past week.

Von Sanders opined: 'It is just another British deception.'[2]

Chapter 49

The Big Con

Part of the grand Allenby plan was to take risks on the Jordan by leaving it denuded of fit troops. Major General Chaytor was to stay in the valley with his sick and jaded Anzac Division (made up of three Australian and one New Zealand brigade), which had been there the longest and had been the most debilitated by malaria. Its numbers were swollen to keep up the impression that Allenby was putting everything into a drive east. Next to the Anzacs now camped two battalions of British West Indians, two Jewish battalions and the 20th Indian Infantry Brigade. To the enemy from a few kilometres away, and even to spies close by, this was a build-up in keeping, at least in numbers, with the rumours. Much play was made of them arriving in daylight when the amount of dust kicked up was an indicator of thousands of soldiers being marched into the area. Dirt and dust sprays 20 metres wide and high were generated by mules dragging wagons and tree branches. Anzac patrols, which were customary precursors to large-scale attacks, were stepped up, alerting the Turks to a projected move east. Makeshift pontoon bridges were strung across the Jordan. Had the Turks stepped on them they would have realised they could not have supported traffic. But they looked real to a casual observer. There was a flurry of horse-feed purchasing, giving the appearance to locals that a big movement of cavalry was coming. Some would pass such suspicions onto the Turks. False wireless messages were sent from the old Desert Mounted Column HQ.

Fifteen thousand dummy horses made of canvas were eased into the valley and along the lines during the night. In the morning they looked realistic from a distance. Any observer concentrating on these equine marvels for any length of time would have been impressed, then suspicious of how still they were. Chauvel also put it about that there would be a race meeting at a track in a small village near Jaffa on 19 September to mark the end of the long, hot summer and change of seasons. It was advertised as 'The Great Horse Show'. Hundreds of horses were said to be committed to the event of eight races. Programs were printed. The publicity in effect designated the Jaffa area as a 'play' or 'dead' sector. The movement of horses would be seen as connected to the event. Another horse-racing program distraction was set up at Jericho, which was to further fool the Turks that the bulk of the troopers were still a long way from the Mediterranean coast. The local populations were expected to turn out to see the parade before the races at Jaffa and Jericho. Jaffa was a bluff; Jericho went ahead, with Anzacs on leave and locals, bribed to attend, forming a crowd of a few thousand. The spectacular warhorse Bill the

Bastard, at 100 to 1, won the main race on the program from a stellar field, including three Arab racing stallions.

Back in the Jordan Valley, the West Indian and Jewish troops were marched around, again creating the sense of a considerable force kicking up further walls of dust.

•

Away to the east near the Hejaz, T.E. Lawrence was playing his part in the ruse concerning the decoy Light Horse invasion. He gathered a mounted force of Arabs, supported by British armoured cars and a French mountain battery at Kasr el Asrak, 80 kilometres east of the big Turkish/German base at Amman. This contingent was set for raids on the railway north, east and west of Deraa, the vital rail junction. These incursions were timed to distract the Turks and make them believe that the Arab attacks were part of the push east from the Jordan Valley. Lawrence even went to the trouble of using his agents to filter into the Arab farming area around Amman where they used gold to buy up the entire local barley feed for horses. Without spelling it out, the agents let slip that the feed would be needed for an imminent massive British Cavalry push in their direction.

•

The air force helped in this scam. The six British squadrons of the Royal Air Force, and the No. 1 Squadron, Australian Flying Corps (AFC), carried on their superiority in the skies that had become apparent earlier in the year. When the summer began there were more than a hundred German planes in any week buzzing above. Some spied, others bombed and strafed. By the end of the summer they were down to under twenty. The dominance of the Australian Flying Corps in this 1918 shift of power above the battlefields was acknowledged when 25-year-old Captain Ross Smith, the former Gallipoli machine gunner turned pilot, was given the only big 'bomber', a Handley Page, to be used on the Middle East Front. It was bestowed on him in part for his devastating performances in the air against the odds. A classic encounter in the hot summer came when he and another Allied pilot flew into the midst of seven enemy planes, and took them all on. They engaged in the most stunning dogfight of the Middle East war, shooting down four planes. The other three, seeing their companions spiral into the sand and hills, departed the scene.

In the eight-week build-up to the mid-September secret mission, the AFC destroyed fifteen enemy aircraft that entered war zone airspace. Another 27 were forced to ground. The German pilots and spotters in the planes were unable to complete their job. There was no photograph reconnaissance that would have picked up the positional changes in a substantial part of the British force. With so many enemy planes being brought down or beaten off, the troops on the ground were also better protected than at any time in the desert war. That dominance allowed the AFC to carry out more reconnaissance and attacks with bombs and machine guns on ground targets.

It all added up to cover the big clandestine movement of men, animals and machines from one front to another. Soon everything was in place on the Mediterranean coast for the anticipated shock attack on the enemy.

Chapter 50

The Light Horse Column Breaks Out

As soon as night fell on the day before the attack on 19 September, the lazy countryside east of Jaffa, bathed in late summer heat, became a seething mass of movement under strongly moonlit skies. The artillery, cars, men, horses, camels and mules brought up to the front in the last few hours jammed every thoroughfare going north. Silence was imposed, although the groaning of wagons, purr of lorries, crunch of boots, the odd groan of the camels or whinny of the horses could not be avoided. Despite the Indian defector, it seemed the secrecy had worked to fool von Sanders and Kemal. The latter was the only Turkish commander who had not experienced defeat. He had an image of invincibility after his mighty leadership on Gallipoli. Kemal was no great strategist or tactician. He was more than that. He had inspired his troops to defend Turkey and they had succeeded. His late appointment (in March 1918) had been welcomed by the Turkish troops.

Chauvel passed on the intelligence to his senior officers that Kemal had been put in command of the Seventh Army. Without spreading it through the ranks, he quietly informed his senior officers of Kemal's appointment, just to add an alertness and dedication to winning. Chauvel was not aware of the friction between Kemal and von Sanders, the German head of his country's military mission in Turkey for five years.

Von Sanders often overruled the Turks. He did not agree to Kemal's demands to amalgamate the three Turkish armies in Palestine and Syria. Kemal thought his disparate force was undernourished, listless and ripe for demoralisation and defeat. By coordinating the three armies, he believed he could focus them on winning. Yet the fact that a Turk put up such a radical development meant it was going to be rejected.

•

The moonlight was helpful for the Flying Corps. Smith went up in his Handley Page bomber with three lieutenants. At 1 a.m. on 19 September, the plane unloaded bombs on the rail junction at El Afule, which was to be the target for Chauvel's Light Horse during the day. Now it was softened up and shaken. With the moonlight still good, the ebullient Smith decided to fly back to base and reload. This time he dumped an even bigger weight of bombs on the German aerodrome at Jenin. This would have the dual impact of grounding the enemy pilots and stopping their support for the ground troops.

At 4 a.m., the moon set. Chetwode's XX Corps and General Edward Bulfin's XXI troops made their last-minute adjustments to weapons and gear. They were to attack on a 13-kilometre front between the railway and the coast to confront an enemy less than 2 kilometres away. A smash-through would open the gap for the cavalry.

By 4.30 a.m. the first fingers of dawn crept over the Judean hills. The big gun symphony began with 300 artillery pieces blasting off in a fifteen-minute bombardment. The second most important day (after Beersheba) in the battle for the Middle East was underway, involving 540 guns, 12,000 horsemen with either sabres or bayonets, and 57,000 soldiers carrying rifles.

•

The infantry of the XX and XXI Army Corps stomped off on time. The cavalry and Light Horse waited. They were travelling light. Most took rations for two days, which in itself was an indicator: this mission was more than a raid but expected to be less than a protracted battle, *if* the intelligence Chauvel had received was accurate. Many horsemen discarded groundsheets and greatcoats; although some retained them knowing that it would be freezing in the heights at night. Most blankets, tents, horse rugs and any 'surplus' kit was left behind.

•

When and if it penetrated the Turkish trenches, the cavalry would pour through the breach led by Barrow's 4th Division and Scottish Major General Henry Macandrew's 5th Division consisting of yeomanry and Indian Regiments armed with lances. The 4th would thrust north towards von Sanders' HQ. The 5th would cut through a pass towards Samaria and then Nablus, 70 kilometres north of Jerusalem and 80 kilometres in from the coast.

They would be followed by Light Horse from the Australian Mounted Division, including a brigade of Australian and New Zealand companies, a remnant of the Imperial Camel Corps, and a Scottish Horse machine-gun squadron.

•

Chauvel had to wait for the result of the first few hours knowing that engagement would begin within the first hour of daylight. At 7.30 a.m. he strolled from his tent at Sarona to a pool in a nearby valley and had a relaxing morning swim. He had left nothing to chance as far as was possible in a project full of imponderables. The force was to ride 80 kilometres in a day to a key Turkish communications centre and rail junction at El Afule.

Just after he arrived back at his tent, he learnt that the British Infantry had broken through the Turks' Eighth Army in four hours, leaving a massive breach in its trench defences on the Plain of Sharon. It was the chance for the contingent of cavalry, then the Light Horse, to ride through and swing north-east, with Chauvel following in a 50-vehicle convoy. His corps was under instructions to avoid the fight on Sharon and to move at speed to make sure that the Turkish Seventh Army at Nablus to the east was well south of them by the afternoon.

This was a moment the Light Horse revelled in. Their advantage of mobility was marked, and the sleeping enemy would be unaware for hours that a mighty cavalry force was striding north of them and heading for a vital centre.

•

The intelligence that Allenby relied on was accurate. Barrow and Macandrew encountered no opposition through the narrow passes that led south of El Afule. But von Sanders' force had been alerted. At dusk, a captured Turkish officer informed Barrow that an infantry brigade heavily armed with machine guns was marching 12 kilometres south from El Afule to block them at the 23-kilometre, shallow, stony pass at Mus Mus.

It was now dark. Barrow and his Australian Chief of Staff Colonel W.J. Foster galloped forward of their long column, moving two abreast, to urge the leading brigade to speed up its movement through the dangerous, tight pass. It moved up from an elevated ridge, which rose from 100 metres above sea level to 400 metres.

Troopers were sometimes forced to walk single file. One slip would see a horse tumbling into an abyss. Here and there, the troopers took some of the load off their horses and carried it themselves to make sure the mount could be eased through.

The aim was to be well clear of Mus Mus before the enemy arrived. At dawn the entire 4th Division was almost through and moving onto the Esdraelon Plain at Megiddo, the Armageddon of ancient times. This was the site that St John predicted in the Book of Revelation would host the last great battle on earth. For the moment, the plain was a more prosaic Bedouin grazing area. A century earlier, it had been a non-combative, wheat-growing district. The 4th Division reaching it coincided with the

5th Division moving closer to the coast, hitting the plain of Abe Shushe, 25 kilometres south of Haifa.

The vanguard of the 4th Cavalry was just onto the plain when it ran into the lead battalion of the Turkish force sent to intercept it. The enemy began deploying its column and machine guns. The British leader of the Indian 2nd Lancers bringing up the rear (of the 4th) made a decision to charge. Before either side could think, the attack was on; the Indians wielding their lances, crashed through the unsettled Turkish lines, wheeled around and attacked again, using their frightening weapons to devastating effect.

In a few minutes they had killed 46 soldiers and taken 476 prisoners. The first engagement of the big attack had been a resounding victory.

During the battle, von Sanders was still asleep at the predominantly Arab town of Nazareth, 30 kilometres away to the north-east. He knew about the British Army's smashing through of his Eighth Army and its retreat. But he believed there was a buffer of his own infantry and cavalry that would block any significant further advance.

He expected possible setbacks, but not so fast.

Chapter 51

Von Sanders Slips the Net

Chauvel and his convoy reached Megiddo early on 20 September and made it his HQ. He used wireless communication and contact with the air force to keep in touch with the various Light Horse forces on the move. When the morning fog lifted, he could see Nazareth in the distance. Chauvel was religious and the thought of capturing the town in which Jesus Christ spent most of his life inspired him. So did the prospect of taking von Sanders, the most senior German military figure in the Middle East. But there were no gloating or even expectant remarks in his letters written at the time. These experiences touched his deep beliefs, although he kept his thoughts private. Chauvel did not see himself as a latter-day crusader. Yet he was conscious of the importance of victory and what it would mean to his Light Horse, especially those who had been on Gallipoli and had experienced the dark days. Thoughts such as those spurred on every commander and trooper.

Nothing but a complete rout of the enemy would do.

•

The British 13th Cavalry Brigade's Brigadier General P.J.V. Kelly led his men towards Nazareth, but took his time. He stopped at each village en route and scoured it for Turks, picking up the odd surprised soldier and adding him to a growing group of prisoners. At dawn on 20 September, he reached the outskirts of the city. Nazareth nestled in a hollow plateau between two 500-metre-high hills at the southern point of the Lebanon mountain range. Kelly's men and horses were exhausted after riding for twenty hours over 80 kilometres without rest from Arsuf on the coast north of Jaffa. His decision to divert to search in the small towns en route drained the energy of his force and affected his own decision-making as he entered the city.

•

Von Sanders, wearing pajamas and armed with a torch, rushed from his headquarters when told by a breathless officer that 'the British Cavalry' had entered the town. He yelled for his driver to retrieve his Mercedes. The chauffeur, woken by his commander's bellowing, obeyed. Then the German commander-in-chief scurried back to his rooms to dress and grab some vital papers, which he stuffed into a satchel. They drove off, the chauffeur with strict orders to put his foot down. The exits were blocked, except for the road north to Tiberius.

•

Kelly erred in not blocking off every road out of Nazareth. He built his prisoner numbers up to 1200 and searched the buildings until they found von Sanders' HQ. There the 13th Brigade collected important papers that the German commander had not had time to collect in his haste to depart. Plenty of booty in the form of cars—a fleet of Mercedes among them—and a big cache of arms were gathered. Reluctant members of von Sanders' staff led the captors to an abundant stock of champagne and sweet wine.

The 5th Cavalry Division's Macandrew arrived a few hours later and was disappointed to hear that von Sanders had managed to flee. Yet he accepted Kelly's excuse that his squadrons were depleted and exhausted after the arduous day. Macandrew commandeered a Mercedes and was driven south to report to Chauvel.

•

Chauvel had El Afule in his safekeeping. He was aware Nazareth had been taken and he wished to know about von Sanders. There had not been any word either way. Had he been taken? Perhaps he had been killed; maybe he had escaped. Chauvel wanted this biggest of fish netted and was concerned that no news was bad news. That aside, he was feeling confident. The two target towns had been taken with the lightest of losses. The infantry, still some distance away, was progressing without serious opposition.

He could safely report back to Allenby that he had achieved his mission. It had taken 30 hours.

Without waiting for further directives, Chauvel ordered Barrow to move at once on Beiran, 24 kilometres east of Megiddo. With two of the enemy's three armies in disarray, Chauvel knew he needed to strike on. He called a midday conference at El Afule and arrived at 11 a.m. Impatient for news of von Sanders, he decided to drive on to Nazareth. Coming his way was a large Mercedes. Chauvel was excited. Was someone bringing him the trophy of von Sanders? Much to the Australian's chagrin, only Macandrew alighted from the vehicle and Chauvel was furious to learn that von Sanders had escaped. The British commander gave his quick report. Chauvel quizzed Macandrew and established that Kelly had been tardy in his approach to Nazareth. His biggest mistake was not to have his squadrons surround the city. Chauvel had been used to his Australian and New Zealander commanders barging into places such as Beersheba and Es Salt, sometimes too recklessly. They would never have dallied in villages wasting energy and time. Nor would any of them have failed to surround a town and secure every exit. He didn't vent his displeasure at Macandrew, but he would report to Allenby the detail of this 'failure'. He predicted the Chief would be aggrieved. Capturing Liman von Sanders would have been the individual prisoner coup of the Middle East war.

There was little doubt that Kelly would lose his command.[1]

•

Failing to capture the German commander had no impact on the immediate progress of the war. By the evening of 20 September the British Infantry divisions were marching towards the retreating Turkish armies, which were being pushed east. The British Air Force and the Australian Flying Corps were bombing and strafing them, making life uncomfortable even if there was no major conflict. Chauvel's self-imposed directive now was to cut off the Turks and round them up. He controlled the communications and his squadrons were eager in pursuit. The Turks, without leadership, fatigued and underfed, were providing little resistance.

Chauvel was more confident than ever before in the war. On the evening of 20 September he took time to correspond with Sybil.

'I have had a glorious time,' he said. 'We have done a regular Jeb Stuart ride . . . I am writing from a hill close to Lejjun [Megiddo] overlooking the plain of Armageddon [now Esdraelon] which is still strewn with Turkish dead "harpooned" by my Indian Cavalry early this morning.'[2]

From his tent opening he could see Nazareth, Mt Tabor, El Afule, Zerim (Jezreel), Mt Gilboa and Jenin. He told his wife of Macandrew's success at Nazareth, without mentioning the escape of von Sanders, which would not have passed the censor. Chauvel also reported that it was the first time in the war the cavalry had managed to gallop through a gap in the enemy lines.

'I am feeling very pleased with myself,' he said, 'no time to write more, darling.'[3]

For someone so circumspect, his mood was a clear indication that the war had swung his way.

Chapter 52

Operation Jenin

Former trooper and Gallipoli veteran Ross Smith, in his dual role of bomber pilot and reconnaissance reporter, informed Chauvel that a 10,000-strong enemy infantry force was marching towards the town of Jenin, 15 kilometres south-west of Megiddo. The advance guard of the Australian Mounted Division had just reached him after coming 90 kilometres in 22 hours, which had meant no sleep for two days and nights. After watering, feeding and a brief rest, Chauvel ordered Brigadier Wilson and his 3rd Light Horse Brigade to ride to Jenin to intercept the Turkish force. This brigade and the 4th were almost over-keen in their exuberance. They and the New Zealanders had taken the mounted lead in the Sinai and Palestine. They were not impressed with following either the Indian Lancers or the British Cavalry on this, the most massive and definitive attack of the Middle East war. Chauvel had held them back, calculating that the toughest fights might occur in protracted battles after the first day. He had been proven astute in holding strong, fresh reserves for the coup de grâce, as seen at Beersheba and Romani. The same strategy on a far broader scale was in play in these Megiddo battles.

An added factor was the desire of the brigades to use their swords for the first time. Wilson unleashed his 9th and 10th Regiments for the ride to Jenin. The Notts Battery clattered its way with them, while the 8th Regiment remained behind as a reserve and to protect Megiddo.

Arthur Olden, who had been active at Es Salt in the last important Light Horse mission of late April–early May, was temporarily in command of 10th Regiment. It had been given the honour of leading the advance at a steady 16 kilometre an hour pace, with the 9th Regiment bounding along as a flank-guard. After covering about 5 kilometres of fairly even, cultivated ground, with 'only crab holes and countless stinging hornets to mar its perfection as "real cavalry country"', it had to step up its pace to make Jenin by dusk.[1]

They encountered a small Turkish outpost halfway to Jenin at Tannuk. It was dealt with by the 9th, which soon caught up with the 10th as it reached Jenin just before sundown.

An enemy force of more than a thousand soldiers was encamped in olive groves to Jenin's north-east. Lieutenant P.W.K. Doig, with a troop on the right flank of the vanguard, was assigned to attack. Swords were drawn. Doig led the charge straight into the camp of Turks. After a few of the shocked enemy had been wounded, the rest surrendered. The footsore soldiers, looking gaunt and weak, were in no shape to fight, especially after realising they were being assaulted by Australian cavalry. Doig organised the taking of the entire force, which included 300 Germans, and 400 horses and mules. The enemy prisoners were marched to the rear and handed over to a troop of the 9th Regiment. Doig then assisted the advance on Jenin by picketing the heights on the right flank.

•

Wilson did not stop for this swift action. He moved his main body forward, swept around Jenin and closed the roads leading out north and east. The 10th then moved into the town from the north as darkness settled. Seeing the columns galloping in, with the troopers' swords drawn, the Turks surrendered. But German snipers and machine gunners in some of the houses made clear their intention to fight. The Australians moved fast and efficiently, pinpointing their attackers. They moved in their machine gunners from Captain G.H. Bryant's squadron. A firefight ensued. The defending Germans decided to try to escape but were cornered by the machine gunners and they too surrendered.

The Australians reflected that although they had rushed to reach Jenin before sunset, the fact that they had entered the town in semi-darkness, which soon faded to black, had worked in their favour. The enemy's impression was that a large force was approaching, especially with the horses thundering in, the troopers wielding swords and the quick deployment of machine gunners.

In reality, Wilson had just 280 troopers. They captured 3000 Turks and Germans, 90 per cent of whom were armed. The attacking force moved so briskly in rounding up this big batch of prisoners and herding them together in the town, that they had no time to assess the imbalance of the forces.

The collapse of Jenin's defenders was the signal for 'countless hordes of Bedouin' that appeared from everywhere to commence looting the stores of food, clothing and equipment. The narrow streets were soon blocked. All transport was brought to a standstill.

'Men, women and children,' Olden wrote, '[were] all the time screaming "Arab! Arab!" as if that was the pass-word with the "Inglese" to permit them to rob and pillage.'[2]

The Australian force did not have the numbers to stop the mayhem. Not even firing rifles and pistols over the heads of the rioting Bedouin could prevent the frenzy. The troopers were hamstrung by the orders to keep the peace with the Arabs at all times. The regiments were not about to enforce anything. A guard was placed over a Turkish hospital in the main street, which was overflowing with sick and wounded enemy soldiers, along with two brave German nurses. Troopers tried to put out a fire of ammunition and bombs at the train station 2 kilometres south of the town. They gave up, allowing the bullets to fire off and cause the exploding munitions to light up the night sky.

•

Wilson was confident that the Turks were unlikely to make a stand. He placed the 10th Regiment on the Nablus road. R.R.W. Patterson, a 23-year-old Victorian grazier with the machine-gun squadron, was sent with two guns and 23 troopers to support it. The moon had disappeared, leaving the area in pitch black apart from the occasional flicker from the ammunition dump fire. Patterson moved out on the road well ahead of the regiment. The small contingent of troopers had been on the road only a few minutes when 21-year-old West Australian

T.B. George dismounted and put his ear to the metallic road. He signalled for his good mate Patterson to do the same. They could hear the muted tread of feet coming their way. Within two minutes the crunch of the marchers was audible on a road that narrowed between hills.

Patterson was in two minds. The oncoming force sounded considerable, perhaps a few thousand enemy soldiers. He could turn and go back to the 10th and alert them. Or he could stop and fight.

'Let's try to bluff 'em,' George whispered, 'get 'em to surrender.'

Patterson thought it might be too late to retreat anyway. He spread his men on both sides of the road in elevated positions seconds before the 3000-strong force of Turks and Germans wheeled close. Patterson called for his gunners to fire over the heads of the enemy. The head of the column halted in fear and confusion. They could not scramble easily up the hills. They could fall back or charge forward. Patterson yelled for a ceasefire: 'You are outnumbered! I call upon you to surrender!'

There was a silence among the enemy commanders, then an urgent conversation. A woman called out in English. She suggested they meet on the road. Patterson wished to know who she was. The woman replied she was a German nurse travelling at the front of the column with the commanding officers. She said that she spoke for them.[3] Patterson summoned his considerable courage and walked onto the road, meeting her halfway between the forces.

Keeping a stern manner, he informed her of his 'superior' force. He demanded that her side should give up and avoid a massacre, knowing that it would be his tiny contingent, outnumbered 130 to 1, that would be slaughtered if a firefight ensued. The nurse passed on his conditions to the enemy commanders. They conferred and decided to surrender. Patterson ordered them to lay down their arms and to march on to Jenin.

This was the most audacious bluff of the war. It indicated that the enemy was so demoralised and hungry that they had little interest now in making a stand.

Chapter 53

Turks Falling

None of the 60 Australian Light Horsemen left in Jenin that night had any sleep. They spent a nerve-racking time minding close to 6000 enemy troops, including many high-ranking Turkish officers and 300 Germans. All through this ordeal, the ammunition and bombs at the train station fire continued to explode. It intermittently lit up the black, moonless sky and made the Australians' hazardous guard activity a fraction easier. Yet the sporadic illumination worked against them too. The Turks realised they had been duped. Disgust turned to anger as they were rounded up in the town's only sizeable square. Four machine guns were trained on them. On three occasions, groups looked as though they might try to escape. Each time, the troopers mounted and waded among them, swords at the ready. It managed to quell any mass attempt to break out.

The weary guards were pleased to see the dawn. Wilson did a count of his prisoners and the booty, including five artillery guns, twelve machine guns, two planes, and a wagon loaded with 250,000 pounds' worth of gold and silver coins. First light also attracted the local Arabs. They swarmed in along all tracks to Jenin with their women, donkeys, mules and carts, loaded them up with everything they could grasp and departed. The Australians were unhappy at the Arab men letting their women bear the burden of every kind of weighty 'trophy' while they drove the animals off into the morning heat. But the troopers had long ago stopped trying to force the men to carry things. They had to accept this custom so alien to their own culture where the men did the heavy lifting.

•

An hour after dawn on 21 September, the 8th Light Horse took the massive haul of prisoners to an ancient prison at Megiddo. Dysentery had taken its toll in recent weeks. Malnutrition and dehydration were further weakening the enemy soldiers. They begged for water, which the troopers could not spare. Soon their ranks were swollen by other prisoners taken by George Onslow's 5th Brigade on the west side of the Samaria ranges.

Only half of the Turkish Seventh and Eighth Armies were left. They struggled on a north-east track across mountains to Besain, which lay 25 kilometres from Jenin and just 8 kilometres from the Jordan. Their fate as a force to be reckoned with was sealed by the relentless air force. The No. 1 Australian Squadron did the reconnaissance and spotted the long column of enemy transport and soldiers following the tracks along the valleys. They used wireless radio to let the various British aerodromes know of the targets. Within minutes British pilots were aloft carrying full loads of bombs for the hapless retreating enemy.

Inside an hour, they located the main Turkish force plodding along. It had just entered a gorge when six British and Australian bombers flew low towards them. The planes dropped their bombs and strafed the cars, lorries, horse-transports and troops as they swooped. There was an immediate logjam as the planes turned and made repeat runs over their quarry, who could not surrender even if they wished to. The air force was pitiless. As soon as they ran out of bombs and ammunition they hurried back to their bases to refuel and reload. With hardly any break, a new wave of planes dived at the enemy convoy. There was nowhere to hide or take cover, except under the transport, which was targeted and destroyed.

Many of the pilots, showing a lust for killing and a desire to finish the opposition once and for all, made up to four separate attacks during the morning massacre. Even those enemy infantry-men who made dashes through side tracks and gorges were hunted by the 'sky demons'. Some Turkish soldiers were still unfamiliar with planes and believed they were sent by Allah as retribution for past transgressions. Many of those who did escape the air attacks and scrambled their way towards Besain were confronted by Barrow's yeomanry and Indian Lancers, whose weaponry was the dread of all those who faced them.

•

Among those on the run from the Australians was Seventh Army leader Mustafa Kemal. The wheel of fortune had come full turn, as it was apt to do in war. The Australian mounted riflemen had been under siege on Gallipoli from Kemal and his Turks, and had been lucky to escape. Chauvel and thousands of troopers had been among them. They had been beaten and humiliated. Losing was not part of the Australian and New Zealand psyche. But the no-win finish on the peninsula had forced acceptance of failure. Now, close to the Jordan, Kemal and his Turks were feeling the pressure of defeat, hounded on the ground by the Light Horse. They were being harassed from the air by pilots such as Ross Smith, P.J. McGinness, and Wilmore Hudson Fysh, all Gallipoli veterans who had swapped horses for Bristols.

Kemal had been one of the first to leave Jenin when he knew the Light Horse was bearing down on the Seventh Army base. He was better off alive and leading than dead or captured. Kemal was aware that complete defeat was imminent, but while there was not wholesale surrender, it was his duty to do what he did best: command.

At the Jordan, he steadied the rump of his rattled army. The British Cavalry and Light Horse were closing. The Turkish and German soldiers wanted to cross the river and keep running. At the fourteenth-century Bridge of Jacob's Daughters Kemal waited until most of the remnants of his army were over it. While other commanders urged him to make the dash over the muddy waters, Kemal, cool as ever, realised that if the three-arched, grey bridge was blown, it would slow their pursuers enough for his troops to make Damascus. If the bridge was left, there would be a danger that the remainder of his army would be caught and cornered on the stony path to the Syrian capital.

Kemal could see the British 11th Cavalry Brigade in the distance coming at the double from one direction, and closer still the 10th Light Horse from another. The commander began running. He called German demolition crews to set the charges, and for the machine gunners and Turkish soldiers left stranded to halt the Light Horse. He was barely over to the east bank when the first arch collapsed. He was up the slope when the second went, and out of sight when the 500-year-old monument collapsed.

•

After a bloody fight, involving French colonial Spahis who had arrived in support of the Light Horse and British, the Australians sent out two flanking squadrons to look for a place shallow enough to cross the river. It was evening. Darkness was coming fast.

It took an hour before a local directed them to a shallow-enough spot. The Light Horse began the tricky manoeuvre. The water was freezing, the current strong. The leading horses and men were halfway across when German machine gunners opened up. A few were hit; four men were swept away. But it was not the Nek. They kept coming. The gunners saw they could not stop the advance and ran.

It was dark when the Australians reassembled on the east bank. They had to dry themselves and their mounts and settle them down. Many of the horses were unhinged by the crossing. They would not drink or feed. There could be no mounted attack on the rearguard of German and Turks on the east bank the next morning. The 10th Light Horsemen would have to wait.

•

Chauvel and his corps still had work to do west and east of his base at Megiddo. He sent a small force to take the port of Haifa, which the air force had led him to believe had been evacuated by the enemy. But the force was met by a strong artillery and machine-gun defence. Macandrew was sent to clean up. He too met stiff resistance. He ordered the Indian Lancers and the cavalry to charge, and they broke through. Haifa and nearby Acre were secured.

Chauvel turned his attention east again to the battles on the Jordan. In the early morning of 22 September, Chaytor's New Zealanders took Jisr ed Damiye from the Turkish Fourth Army. A Jewish battalion cleared the West Bank. Most of the enemy Fourth had crept away in the night east of the river, aware that the British force was squeezing them from the north coming down from Besain, and from the south (Chaytor's international force—Australians, New Zealanders, Jews and West Indians) coming up from Jericho. The north–south pressure was on a front of 25 kilometres and closing. The only enemy option was to pull back east to Amman.

The Turkish Fourth Army headed towards Amman and the Hejaz Railway, even though it was aware that Lawrence and the Arabs had cut them off from the main junction at Deraa. The Turkish commanders now had to hope the railway could be rebuilt and their force could join up with the 4000 soldiers in the town and 6000 more at Maan. This was the vague plan, now wishful and turning wistful. Enemy communications had broken down everywhere. The chance for consolidation and any form of solid defence was slipping away.

Chapter 54

Smith Chips In

Chauvel held the plain from Haifa on the Mediterranean coast to Besain a few kilometres from the Jordan. The Seventh and Eighth Turkish Armies had been broken and there was little impediment to an advance on Damascus. Yet there would still be resistance elsewhere. The rumps of the Seventh and Eighth and the retreating Fourth Army, which was on the run, would provide it, especially if they were able to link up. Chauvel's 20,000 horses employed on the mission had enjoyed some rest and plenty of water in the preceding day or two and the local Arab threshing floors supplemented the horse-feed. There were no major problems with transport. Most of the men were still fit and well. The air force ruled the skies. Casualty figures were not complete, but Chauvel was relieved to learn he had lost no more than 60 troopers in the past 72 hours of hectic engagements on a wide front and over a large territory. This was a low figure for such a sweeping action by several prongs of the Light Horse and cavalry, which had already resulted in the dislocation of two enemy armies. A combination of a brilliant strategy and tactics, and the weakened condition of the impoverished enemy were responsible for, if not a walkover, then a gallop-over.

Chauvel was in high spirits when Allenby arrived at Megiddo on the morning of 22 September.

'How many prisoners have you taken?' was one of the Chief's first questions.

'15,000,' Chauvel replied.

'No bloody good to me!' Allenby replied with a laugh, 'I want 30,000 from you before you've done!'

At that moment, the Chief was well pleased with the outcome of these battles.

His next question was: 'What about Damascus?'

Chauvel was all in favour of taking it and was confident it could be done. Yet Allenby gave no orders concerning the main prize. A move on that city would depend on the fluid developments in the next few days.[1]

That final coup was very much up to Chauvel's judgement, and the Chief's order when it was imminent. The first steps were to direct Hodgson to seize Semakh and Tiberias on the Sea of Galilee and then take the important nearby bridges of the Yarmuk River.

•

Lawrence, who had conferred with Allenby just before Chauvel, flew back to his base south of Umm Tayeh on the morning of

22 September in the observer's seat of an AFC Bristol. It was accompanied by two other planes, one flown by Ross Smith. The airmen, fresh from their 'kills' in the gorges approaching Besain, were eager to engage German planes in the Deraa area, which was now the last frontier of the Middle East war. The three planes and Lawrence were greeted by thousands of Arabs, who cheered and waved weapons near the makeshift landing strip.

It was 10 a.m. and the airmen were just in time to join Hubert Young and Alec Kirkbride for a breakfast of porridge or fried sausages. The discussion over the meal was all about the blistering success of the cavalry and infantry in the western plains and hills; how the Jordan was almost in British hands; and how the Turks were descending on Amman and pushing out from there.

All the men were excited. The enemy was in chaos and on the run. The war was reaching a climax. They were interrupted by a report that German aircraft were in the area. Smith and another Australian pilot, Lieutenant E.S. Headlam, put down their food and stood up.

'Our Australians,' Lawrence wrote in *Revolt in the Desert*, 'scrambled wildly to the yet-hot machines and started them in a moment. Ross Smith with his observer [Lieutenant E.A. Mustard] leapt into one and climbed like a cat up the sky.'

The enemy craft were two Pfalz scouts and one DFW two-seater. The enemy turned tail for home as soon as they spotted the two Bristols.

'Ross Smith fastened on the big one and after five minutes of sharp machine-gun rattles, the German dived towards the railway line. As it flashed behind the low ridge, there broke out a pennon of smoke and from its falling place a soft dark cloud. An "Ah" came from the Arabs about us.'

The plane crashed at Mafrak, killing the lone German on board. The Australians then set it alight, making sure it would not enter the fray again. Five minutes later, Smith and Headlam landed their planes.

'Ross Smith . . . jumped gaily out of his machine swearing that the Arab Front was the place [now that the German Air Force was defeated near the coast]. Our sausages were still hot; we ate them and drank tea.'

Smith told Lawrence he wished he could stay in the area with an enemy plane coming along every half hour but after breakfast he had to fly west to pick up his big Handley Page bomber. He would then bring back a load of petrol, food and spares for the Arab front, which was where the action would be from now on.[2]

Just as he finished eating, at 10.30 a.m., his remark about German planes coming every half hour proved prescient. Three more Pfalz scouts were reported in sight. Smith and Mustard once more dashed for their plane. Retrieving the Handley Page would have to wait. They soared aloft again and pursued the German machines, which were forced to ground. Two landed near the railway and ran along the ground to Turkish forts, which they hoped would provide some protection. The Australians chased the third to the well-defended Deraa. Smith and Mustard turned around and went looking for the two Pfaz scout planes. The Australians strafed them from close range, pumping 50 rounds into each.

Smith and Mustard flew back to their base on the coast. Observing their departure, the Germans attempted some retribution for the morning's attacks. In the afternoon another DFW two-seater flew low and bombed Lawrence's camp. Lieutenants Peters and J.H. Traill took off to engage it. They flew close. Traill pumped his Lewis gun at the lumbering enemy machine. It faltered and began to smoke. The Germans made an emergency landing near the aerodrome. Fulfilling air combat etiquette, which was uncompromising and brutal, Peters dipped low and made a run over the stricken plane seconds after it came to a halt. The German pilot and observer were attempting to escape the plane before its fire spread. Traill let go gunfire, killing the two enemy airmen.

•

Smith returned later in the day with the Handley Page. The Arabs lining the airstrip welcomed it in with even more enthusiasm than the Bristols, cheering and firing their weapons. Much to Lawrence's joy, the next morning another AFC Bristol dropped sixteen bombs on the Deraa aerodrome. This attack set a hangar on fire, obliterated two DFWs and disabled two others. After this softening up, Smith was airborne in the Handley Page, heading for Deraa. He throttled back as much as he dared, dipped to 1000 feet and swung in low over the aerodrome and the station, depositing nearly a tonne of bombs with accuracy and to devastating effect.

Every enemy plane and all the stores at Deraa were destroyed.

This attack decommissioned Deraa as a junction of importance for the rest of the war and ended the activities of the German Air Force based there.[3]

Chapter 55

Grant and the 11th's Charge at the Sea of Galilee

Commander William Grant of 4th Brigade was sent to Semakh, a small village of mud huts 1.5 kilometres from where the Jordan entered the Sea of Galilee (Lake Tiberias), to take on the German/Turkish defence there. Planes had seen troops evacuating by motor launch on the lake. Grant took his machine guns, part of the 12th Regiment and the 11th. The latter had been on reserve at Beersheba and had watched its brother regiments gain legendary status for the most daring charge of the war. The 11th's troopers were motivated to make their own reputation as they trotted along by moonlight in the early hours of 25 September. They arrived just before dawn and were met by heavy machine-gun and rifle fire from the enemy force. No one knew its strength or the nature of the terrain they would have to cross in the dark. Grant had two choices. He could wait until he had more support, which would mean he had to take the town in daylight. This would mean high casualties. The alternative was to charge now in the Beersheba manner. Grant decided on the latter. This would be regarded as either brave or foolhardy after the event. He lined up the machine guns on the left and sent forward an order to Colonel John Parsons, who bellowed: 'Form line and charge the guns!'

The 11th Regiment troopers drew their swords for the first time in anger. Aboriginal trooper Frank Fisher, the great-grandfather of Olympic sprinter Cathy Freeman, was one of the forward scouts. Parsons was leading the main body of troopers. A squadron commander, Major James Costello, was close behind. His squadron would be first out, followed by a second led by 55-year-old Major J. Loynes, a fearsome Boer War veteran. A minute after the order, they galloped straight towards the flashes from the guns. At first this attack seemed easier than Beersheba as they overran machine-gun nests. But fire from the railway station and other stone buildings 1.5 kilometres away disabused the attackers of any thoughts of a fast walkover.

As the chargers drew closer, several horses went down in the rough terrain's potholes. Others were hit by the fire that intensified as the defenders—Germans and Turks—realised the force of the charge. The wall of bullets caused the troopers to split. Loynes swung to the left at the village. Costello moved right of the troublesome station, from which the gun flashes were coming. Most defenders were in the buildings. Some were concealed in rail trucks and carriages.

This was the most dangerous time for the troopers, their most vulnerable moment. They could be picked off by snipers and machine gunners shooting from windows down into the streets. Several troopers and their mounts were felled. Loynes swept around the town. He commanded his squadron to dismount and head for the station. He picked out a drain and a stone fence running along it, and ordered his squadron to dash for the position, just 20 metres from the station.

A firefight ensued for an hour. No one could gain the advantage until Grant's machine gunners moved in close and focused on the windows being used for enemy fire. They soon hit their targets. The flashes from the buildings diminished. The German members of the defence in all positions could see they were losing the fight, despite outnumbering their opponents two to one. They began passing round liberal amounts of rum. This fortified their spirits. Then they threw hand grenades, not with great accuracy, but still enough to cause the troopers trouble.

It took the mature, headstrong Loynes to lead a charge at the main station and break the impasse. His men battered down the door. They rushed in wielding bayonets and swords and pursued the enemy in the darkness into every room. The Germans scrambled up the stairs. They were stalked 'from floor to floor and room to room' until everyone was killed or captured.

Outside, the surviving enemy soldiers made a run for the railway line east. The chasing troopers brought them down with machine-gun fire. About 30 Germans rushed for the lake. They scrambled onto a motor launch pursued by the gunners. The launch took off, but not before the gunners by the lake let loose, hitting the boat. It caught fire. Only one enemy soldier survived. He could be seen swimming for the shore and dashing off.[1]

This fight was one of the bloodiest since Chauvel's cavalry took off six days earlier. Fourteen Australians were killed. So were 61 horses, with another 27 wounded. The enemy had 98 killed. Another 365 prisoners were taken, 150 of them German.

The increased number of Germans at Semakh indicated a forward defence for von Sanders, who had been at Tiberias, another 7.5 kilometres north and on the east of the lake. But after his embarrassing experience at Nazareth, the enemy commander-in-chief had long since fled the area. The Australians were getting too close.

Chapter 56

Allenby's Uncertain Directive

By the same day, 25 September, Chaytor's Anzacs had shoved the Fourth Army east beyond Amman, captured the city and snared the enemy force's rearguard, taking 2500 Turkish, German and Austrian prisoners. Chauvel directed them to hold their gains, then to attack the Turkish force of an estimated 6000 soldiers coming up the Hejaz Railway from the garrison at Maan, 190 kilometres south. The enemy had fought off the Arabs from there for months. Now, cut off from supplies, they were compelled to come north in the hope of joining other Turks from the Fourth Army. Yet the weakened force was in no shape for a prolonged battle. Their main concern was the marauding Arabs who they knew would massacre them without regard for the conventions if given a chance.

•

Young visited Lawrence's tent in a camp at Nuwayma at midnight on 25 September and suggested that the Arabs should be taken out of the war and retired to the Druse Mountains. They had done their bit, he said. They could wait until the British took Damascus.

Lawrence would have none of it. He wanted the Arabs to be seen to take Damascus. It was what he had entered the fray for in the first place. A lot was at stake now, not the least being Lawrence's own integrity. He had promised the Arabs Damascus. He wanted to deliver it, no matter how cosmetic the act.

Young had played along with Lawrence's whims and aims, knowing of his strong relationship with Allenby. In the military advisor's mind, the main objective was for the British to take Damascus. Yet he understood Lawrence's sensitivities and position, and did not press the issue. The Arabs would move on to Damascus at the same time as Chauvel's front-line cavalry and Light Horse force, and there all the issues about control and ownership would culminate.

The next day, Young and Lawrence met with four Arab tribes, including the tall, straight-backed, 52-year-old Sheikh Auda Abu Tayi, leader of the Howeitat. Auda was a brutal man who in essence was a psychopath. Some fitting this description did not look the part, but Auda did. His beard and moustache were trimmed in his tribe's style and shaven under the jaw. His dark hair, streaked with grey, aquiline nose and ungenerous eyes gave him a mature, eagle-like appearance that made many nervous, and he played on it with his bullying mien. His rages were legendary. Those who crossed him were said never to survive. He had taken his blows and was wounded thirteen times in fights. There were apocryphal stories about him tearing out victims' hearts and eating them. Tribesmen who fought alongside him swore by his ferocity. He boasted of having killed 75 Arabs in close combat. No one challenged the number for fear of being number 76. (No one had kept count of how many Turks he slaughtered.)[1]

He was also quite the ladies' man. He married 28 times.

Lawrence had plotted to get Auda on side because of his influence with all Arabs. He was vital to any successful move on the Turks and on this occasion was the most supportive of the move to blow up bridges, and take forts, prisoners and weaponry, including big guns. During the subsequent action, Turkish resistance disintegrated in every direction.

•

As the Arab regulars and non-regulars swarmed north on 26 September, Chauvel motored to Jenin for a conference with Allenby. The Chief asked about the Desert Mounted Column's state of play. Chauvel told him that two of his divisions were hovering at Nazareth and Tiberias. The third, led by Barrow, was crossing the Jordan as he spoke. Chauvel had given him orders to take Deraa, and link up with Prince Feisal's Arabs, who would come under his control with the final step in mind: a drive up the stony old pilgrim's road to Damascus. This was the longer route into the prized city. The aim was for Chauvel, coming by a shorter route north, to be there with the rest of his corps at the same time as Barrow.

Chauvel intended his corps to travel light. The transport, including lorries, would be left behind to speed movement. When rations ran out, the troopers would live off the land. His only reservation was how the Arabs would cooperate. He had been let down by the Beni Sakhr in the second attempt to take Amman. With this in mind he had given Barrow specific orders that he and his 4th Cavalry Division would take charge of them.

Allenby approved the plan.

Chauvel wished to be clear on how he was to handle the 300,000 population of Damascus. Allenby had not informed his Mounted Corps leader, the most important field commander in the war, about the secret Sykes-Picot Agreement. All Chauvel had heard were rumours about it. They had not concerned him until now, when he was about to take the capital. It was not his role as a soldier to immerse himself in politics.

'What should I do about the administration of the city?' he asked.

'You know what we did in Jerusalem,' Allenby replied. 'Do exactly the same. Send for the Turkish Vali [the civil governor] and tell him to carry on, giving him what extra police he requires.'

Chauvel had taken plenty of towns in the last two years. But he knew there was more at stake. He probed further.

'What about these Arabs? There is a rumour that they are to have the administration of Syria.'

'Yes, I believe so,' Allenby said, evasively, 'but that must wait until I come.'

Behind the scenes Allenby was struggling to get clear the political message from London. The carve-up of the Middle East planned in the Sykes-Picot Agreement had originally, in 1916, seen the French getting control of Syria. But the British War Council looked at the cost of its support in money, gold, arms and specialists put in to supporting the Arabs and argued with the French that they (the British), by rights, should 'receive' Syria after the war. The council bargained also that the Arabs wanted the British to be their backer. Both points were valid, but the French insisted that a deal was a deal. They wanted the initial arrangement to stay as it was. Allenby had been trying to juggle administration of the Middle East war and the politics. Hence his vagueness over what should be done once the British, primarily now the Light Horse, took Damascus.

As an afterthought, the Chief told Chauvel: 'If Feisal gives you any trouble, you are to deal with him through Lawrence, who will be your liaison officer [with the Arabs].'[2]

Chauvel thought these orders were sketchy and very un-Allenby-like. He was to go off with the misty hope of meeting up with Lawrence before entering Damascus. If he did not, Chauvel would have no guidance on how to deal with the Arabs in what he was certain would be a shambolic, even chaotic, situation. This offended his ordered military sensibilities.

•

On 27 September the squeeze on the enemy was apparent. Smith dropped Lawrence a note telling him that Chauvel's advance cavalry led by Barrow was just 25 kilometres away at Ramtha. An estimated 8000 Turks in two parties were now converging between the British and the Arabs around Deraa. These were mainly enemy troops from the defeated Seventh and Eighth Armies that had been pushed east from Besain to Lake Tiberias.

Despite being fatigued and on edge, Lawrence savoured the moment. It was what he had longed for. He collected another two Arab leaders—Nasir and Nuri—and their tribes, giving him a force of tens of thousands. Then he sanctioned the pursuit and massacre of retreating Turkish soldiers.

Chapter 57

Night of the Anzacs and Turks

A major problem developed in the south near Maan when a 6000-strong Turkish force left their garrison. They had run out of supplies, food and water and were forced to make an attempt to join up with their other armies floundering in the north.

Early on 28 September, this rogue force was reported by a British Bristol pilot to have reached Ziza, a few kilometres south of Amman. He flew low to observe the Turks hurrying to dig trenches. They were being hounded by a swarm of an estimated 10,000 Arabs on horseback and on foot. They prowled wide of the Turks, not prepared to take on the rifles and machine guns, but content for the moment to encircle and harass with yelling and firing their rifles into the air.

The pilot dropped a note into the camp for the Turkish commander, warning him that Chaytor's Anzac force controlled the region and all its water and food. There was no point in putting up a fight. Their plight was useless. If he did not surrender, the note concluded, his camp would be bombed in the night. The message was clear. After such destruction, chaos would rule. Then the Arabs would move in.

There was no response from the Turks. The pilot informed Brigadier Colonel Donald Cameron of Anzac's 5th Regiment and prepared to join a bomber force to attack the Turks in their camp that evening. Cameron had further intelligence that the Turks were so weak they could not fight. He sent two squadrons of Queenslanders to explore the enemy situation and to see if there was any chance to negotiate a surrender. The easy approach by the troopers gave clues. There were many enemy soldier stragglers in the region. They had broken from the ranks in a desperate search for food and water. The troopers gave a couple of stragglers sustenance in exchange for finding them the enemy commander, Ali Bey Wahaby. A meeting was arranged with Cameron.

At the rendezvous, the Turk commander said he was prepared to surrender. But on looking around at the few hundred Australian troopers on horseback he was not ready to capitulate and give up arms to such a small force. He feared that once he did, the Arabs would then massacre his men. He would only give in to a British contingent big enough to defend his unarmed men against the Arabs. Cameron assured Wahaby that this would be arranged. In the meantime, his two squadrons would stay with the Turks. Wahaby still would not lay down arms. Cameron was forced to agree that they could keep them, while they were technically under Anzac control. He was anxious now to prevent the air raid.

Cameron sent a telegraph message to Chaytor asking for urgent reinforcements and to make sure the aerial bombing was not carried out. The air force could not be reached. Cameron improvised by sending a dozen of his troopers into the camp to lay out ground signals for the air force to make sure no bombs were dropped. But there was no guarantee that the signals would be understood or even noticed. The prevention of the raid was no certainty, Wahaby was informed. He just shrugged. Reflecting the general attitude of many of the Muslims regarding the likely outcome of the war, he said: 'It is the will of God.'[1]

The Australians, less convinced of divine intervention, did all they could to prevent an attack from the skies. Chaytor was kept informed. He realised the gravity of the situation, especially with such a massive haul of prisoners, whose lives were now in his hands. He ordered Brigadier General Ryrie to round up as many of his troopers as possible, then motored to meet Wahaby himself before they arrived. The enemy commander tried to convince Chaytor to stay away while the Turks fought the Arabs. The Anzac leader would not have been tempted by this option, no matter what his sentiments, but he did understand the Turks' predicament. Chaytor had a division to run. He left the area, telling Cameron to pass on his order to Ryrie to sort out the problem.

•

Ryrie was informed his mission was urgent. He left packhorses behind and led his support squad at the double, arriving just before dark. He found the Turks in the trenches fending off the Arabs, with the Australian troopers grouped to one side awaiting orders.

To the relief of all, Cameron had received a message that the air force had called off the bombing raid. That left Ryrie with some difficult negotiations to be had with the Arabs and Turks. He first met two Arab sheikhs. They urged him to wipe out the Turks, saying they would fight with the Australians. Ryrie was wary. His experience over three years in the desert campaign was that the Arabs were more inclined to loot than fight.

He then consulted Wahaby and his Turkish commanders. They again tried to convince him to let them destroy the Arab force. But like Chaytor, he would not countenance such a solution, as tempting as it may have been. The Turks pointed out that the darkness would cause the Arabs to close in. Would he stand by and let the Turkish force be attacked, possibly wiped out?

Ryrie believed the Turks were his prisoners, and therefore his responsibility. He would not like a repeat of Lawrence's experience in the north where Turks were massacred. The Australian weighed his options and decided that the Turks could keep their arms. His troopers would join the Turks in their camp and stand-by in support if needed.

•

Ryrie, accompanied by six armed troopers, had a second meeting with the two sheikhs. The articulate, no-nonsense brigade commander remained on his horse, saying he wished to be brief and was too busy to dismount.

Ryrie eyeballed the sheikhs and, using an interpreter, said he wished to make it very clear that the Turks were his prisoners. He was obligated to protect them. His men would be in the camp with them. If the Arabs invaded during the night, Ryrie said he would hold the sheikhs responsible.

The sheikhs asked indignantly what would happen if the Turks attacked *their* men. Ryrie, who at 53 still appeared ready to go fifteen rounds in a boxing ring, said: 'I am in charge [of them] and that will not happen. I repeat that if any of your men invade, you, as their leaders, will be held responsible.' He paused, glared and added: 'In that case, you will be arrested and executed.'

With that chilling remark hanging in the air, he bid them good evening and galloped off.[2]

•

As night fell on 28 September the Australian troopers south of Amman filed into the Turkish camp in one of the most extraordinary moments of the war. They were outnumbered about ten to one and felt vulnerable. But the Turks, grateful that the Australians were not leaving them to the Arabs at night, welcomed them. These two fierce foes, who had fought each other for three and a half years since Anzac Day 1915, sat down together at camp fires. They exchanged food. The Australians handed out cigarettes. After a short time, there was laughter and attempts to communicate. The Turks managed to express their admiration for their long-time enemy, and the Australians reciprocated.

Those Turks in the trenches exchanged machine-gun fire with the Arabs during the night, but there was no attempt by the Arabs to close in. Ryrie's blunt warning had been heeded.

Dawn broke. Tensions eased. The Australians stayed in the camp and had breakfast with the Turks. Then the New Zealand Brigade arrived at 8 a.m., swelling the number of Anzacs to the point where Wahaby felt comfortable about giving up all his weaponry. The Arabs stayed clear as the 6000 surrendered Turks were marched out of the camp and on to Amman.

Chapter 58

Monash's Biggest Assault

While Chauvel and his force had a week of war-determining success at the end of September in the Middle East, Monash took the time during a lull for his army to draw up plans to breach the German defences with his entire force, including the 118 rebels charged with desertion, if necessary. He was as fed up and fatigued by the endless battles as any of his front-line diggers. But he kept up the inexorable drive, knowing that within a week he would call 'time' on his entire military machine. His final plans for the five divisions under his command were adopted, except for the Beaurevoir Line, the last German stronghold that had to be taken. Monash had it marked down for taking on day one. Rawlinson suggested that he should wait to see the result of the prior stages—the taking of the canal and tunnel system that made up the Hindenburg Main Line, and the Le Catelet Line.

The documents captured earlier from the Germans showed that the canal would be the toughest to take without a huge number of casualties. Whereas both British and French forces on his flanks were prepared to attack it directly, Monash would not. He had been disturbed deeply by sending his gallant soldiers into terrible fighting at St Quentin and Péronne without their usual protection. Then he had no choice. This time he did. There was an alternative to the direct attacks that would see fewer losses, and he took it. Monash decided to drive over the tunnel to the north. After that, the troops would storm the section of the canal on his part of the front, from behind and in front.

The concept was to envelope it, then strangle the German defence.

•

For the first time in the war, all the Allied armies on the Western Front prepared to advance together and attack and pursue the enemy with just short intermissions.

Previous operations such as the Somme in 1916, the Chemin des Dames, with Arras-Vimy, in April 1917, and the Third Battle of Ypres from July to November 1917 had been carried out in isolated sectors on the Front. The Germans in all three instances had been able to respond by bringing large forces and reserves to combat and parry them. Their defeat at Amiens had been so devastating that drawing off other enemy forces to stop a complete war-ending victory had proved over the following six weeks impossible to do adequately. The enemy edifice had begun to crumble even before this final combined Allied swoop east.

There would be four great blows. On 26 September the American First Army and the French Fourth Army would open the campaign between the Meuse and Reims, 150 kilometres north-east of Paris. On 27 September the British Fourth Army would strike in the Cambrai sector 150 kilometres north of Paris. On the same day the British Fourth, spearheaded by Monash's force including 50,000 Americans, and supported by the French First Army, would have the most ambitious aim of crunching right through to the Hindenburg Line, in the region of the St Quentin Canal due east of Amiens. On 28 September the British Second Army and the Belgium Army, supported by the French Sixth Army, planned to attack in Flanders.

In all, thirteen armies (including a late American inclusion) were set to attack on one long fighting front of 220 kilometres.

•

Monash was confident that his corps, the biggest of this offensive, would succeed from its launch on 27 September. But before any attack could be made he attempted to educate the Americans—the 27th and 30th Divisions commanded by Major General G.W. Read as a corps—to his methods and tactics. Read was happy, at Rawlinson's polite request, to act as 'an interested spectator' while Monash commanded his men. The American was sensible. His 50,000 troops given over to Monash were inexperienced. They had not, like the Australians, learnt from all their mistakes, and wins, on the battlefield over four years.

Monash organised what he called an 'Australian mission' under Sinclair-Maclagan, which had the task of teaching the Americans. Chosen from the resting 1st and 4th Divisions, 217 officers were to instruct their American cousins. They lacked training in all areas of warfare, from discipline, 'quick initiative and capacity to anticipate the next action', to understanding of weapons and explosives. That old chestnut that had agonised Monash from his early days in the militia—communicating clear orders—was a problem. The Americans underrated the need for a good system of supply of food and water to the troops. They didn't seem to understand how to attack and then protect themselves from unnecessary losses. None had been to mopping-up school. They had never even heard the term.

Monash became concerned at his final conference with his own generals and the American generals and their staff. He explained the 'set-piece' plans.

'It was to be a straightforward trench to trench attack,' he noted, 'from a perfectly straight "jumping off" line to a perfectly straight objective line, under a dense Artillery and Machine-Gun barrage, and with the assistance of a large contingent of Tanks.'[1]

It was a yawn for his commanders and staff, who had heard much of it before at Messines, Broodseinde, Hamel and the first stage of the Amiens on 8 August. But it left the Americans frowning. They asked so many questions that Monash was forced to give a three-hour lecture, complete with chalk, blackboard and diagrams. At the end of it, he believed the US generals knew and understood what was happening. The problem was, could they pass it all on down the chain of command to 50,000 neophytes?

Big sections of the two American divisions attacked on 27 September with the task of taking the section of the line that the British III Corps had still not managed to reach. They had fallen 900 metres short, causing a dangerous situation on

Monash's left (north). It had to be taken before the Australians and the rest of the Americans entered the battle on 29 September.

Monash's battle plan was the best he had ever prepared. It drew on all his experience of attacking since the difficult days on Gallipoli.

Everything began well, but then went awry. The Americans swept over and past trenches, not realising that many Germans, warned of the coming attack by the artillery barrage, had ducked into shellproof dugouts. The Americans did not do the usual 'mopping up' after streaming through and over trenches; they did not allow for the Germans bobbing up out of the trenches behind them. The concept hammered to the generals did not seem to have filtered down the chain of command. The result was many unnecessary casualties. To make matters worse, Monash lost contact with the divisions. Not even his planes could find them. The Americans did not use their flares to alert the air force of their locations.

The problem flowed on into the second day when Monash wanted to move his artillery up to allow further barrage cover for the troops. This wasn't possible if the Americans were fighting or lying wounded in areas that could not be pinpointed.

Monash wanted a day's delay to get the mopping up done, but Rawlinson refused. The other armies were attacking their sections of the canal. He didn't want Monash's corps behind and unable to pressure the Germans in front of him. Monash then asked for more tanks. They were granted. He told Haig he was 'in a state of despair' over the situation. The American failure had offended his tidy mentality. Haig told him not to worry, but to attack the next day—29 September—as planned. This forced Monash to gamble, not knowing if his left flank was even partially cleared up. He had trouble sleeping before the 5.55 a.m. assault by 200,000 men, the biggest number he would ever command in one battle.

•

The 1000-gun artillery force hammered the target. Special fused shells that could cut through the wire emplacements were catapulted at the enemy. Mustard gas was sent out for the first and only time by the AIF. It caused the Germans to scramble to put on their masks.

The Americans moved out first, two sections of the two divisions side by side, followed by Australia's 3rd and 5th Divisions. The right attacking US division did well. It and Hobbs's 5th pushed forward nearly 2 kilometres ahead of the left division.

The star of the 5th's advance was Major Blair Wark of the 32nd Battalion (8th Brigade). At 9 a.m. it followed the American division into the battle near Bellicourt. Wark showed ingenuity by commandeering one of the few tanks in the battle and directing it to overrun two nests of troublesome machine guns. Midmorning the 32nd came across 200 Americans from the division that had gone out in advance of them. Their officers had been killed and the soldiers were wandering aimlessly. Wark, a forceful leader, encouraged the Americans to join his battalion, telling them it was safer to do so. The Australians knew where they were going. Together, they could tackle the enemy better. The Americans, eager for direction and success, fell in with Wark's men. Within minutes they were glad to have done so. Wark grabbed another tank. He believed the shock value of even one such machine was valuable. Relishing his enlarged force, he organised an attack on the village of Nauroy. It was theirs after a twenty-minute encounter.

Wark's men commandeered machine guns and artillery, and took prisoners. His expanding force was now encouraged to push on. The first target was Étricourt, a base for a dangerous battery of 77-millimetre guns. Wark selected his six best fighters, then struck out for the battery. He soon captured it and those manning the guns.

By early afternoon, Wark and his force reached the outskirts of the tiny hamlet of Joncourt. He organised a solid defence. It was challenged by a 400-strong onslaught from Germans in the town, but Wark's fighters successfully repulsed the attack.

Chapter 59

The Americans Falter

While Wark and co. forced their way to a strong attacking position, the American division on the left and Gellibrand's 3rd were not so fortunate or successful. They were caught in a powerful German counterattack. By late afternoon the situation was unclear. The right attacking force of Americans and Hobbs's 5th Division had launched itself over the (Bellicourt) tunnel, while the left had not made it.

The problem, again, had been the inexperience of the Americans, who couldn't achieve their objectives. Monash's plan had been based on what was attainable by his battle-hardened, disciplined and drilled troops. The Americans—courageous, cheerful and willing—were not up to a battle on this scale. Blamey, a bullyboy on occasions, tongue-lashed an American divisional commander. But it was well after the event. Monash was angered that the American generals had built up the capacities of their commanders well beyond reality.

Instead of lamenting the situation, he, Rawlinson, Montgomery and Sinclair-Maclagan held a hurried meeting late on the afternoon of 29 September. Monash had no compunction about throwing away his plan, which had been based on his own troops' abilities. He faced the fact that he had not allowed for the human factor. Every other scheme he had created since Hamel, when he was first in charge, had more or less followed his blueprint.

The rewrite called for AIF reserve brigades to attack north and take the town of Bony and the left (north) end of the tunnel.

Minutes after the meeting, Monash rang Gellibrand to explain elements of the revised plans. His 3rd had taken the brunt of the fighting after the American debacle. Monash told him that the British Corps to the north and south, along with the French, had done well. He thought that the British successes would reduce the amount of opposition. Some of the Americans would be withdrawn. The XIII British Corps would be 'pushed up' to take over from them, while the Australian front would be shortened to just 3600 metres.

The onus was now on Gellibrand and Hobbs's 5th Division to take complete control of the troublesome tunnel. Monash expected 5th Division to push hard from the right (south), and make its way along the 'railway ridge' to the third line of resistance—the Le Catelet Line. Gellibrand was ordered to call up as many tanks as he could in one group. Hobbs would do the same.

Gellibrand broke in: 'My real trouble is artillery action in view of the possibility that Americans were in the line [in front of 3rd Division].'

'Exactly so,' Monash replied. 'The question is whether you cannot do without artillery action. We cannot tell where the Americans are.'

Monash thought Hobbs could safely bombard the German stronghold of Bony, which the Americans were not near. He said he would leave some of the Americans in the action as long as they were doing well. When the Australians could do without them, he would order all the Americans to be withdrawn.

'Work it out,' Monash told him, 'In view of the success in other parts, things will be better tomorrow than today.'[1]

The new plan was implemented on 30 September. The German resistance was reminiscent of Mont St Quentin and Péronne. They knew it was their last stand. If this section of the mighty Hindenburg fortifications collapsed then Germany would lose the war. The defending soldiers faced capitulation or death, and many bravely chose the latter.

With fighting often hand-to-hand in the 'perfect tangle' of trenches, no one could really judge if the new plan had worked by early afternoon. Tension mounted. Just after 5 p.m. Monash upbraided Gellibrand on several points, including the fact that he had not reported tank losses, and for attacking on such a narrow front.

Gellibrand tried to explain that he only had 200 men. There was no other option but to maintain a smaller front. Monash refused to accept that the battalion had shrunk to that size. But Gellibrand knew the situation. Monash was bullying him. He was desperate not to lose the battle after the Americans had let him down.

Monash *knew* how strong his old division was. But that was the problem. He was thinking of it with battalions at something like full strength, not half destroyed. Still Monash would accept no excuses for them not performing. If they were slow or bogged down, Gellibrand had to call the bluff of his commanders. This exasperated him. He had been to the front. It had to be a slow, hard fight. Gellibrand's diaries at the time conceded that it was his job to push his men, as it was Monash's to push his divisional heads.

In the next three hours, Gellibrand found the right message, or perhaps the right battalion leaders. Cannan and McNicoll led the way in concentrated, fierce encounters. By nightfall the 3rd Division, struggling all day at the troublesome north end of the tunnel, had advanced 900 metres.

●

Monash was in contact with Hobbs too. His division was progressing. Wark began a pre-dawn assault on Joncourt and took it by midday after heavy fighting. He would later be rewarded with a VC. It took another winner, Private John Ryan, to keep the 5th's momentum going over the tunnel. Armed with bayonet and grenades, he led the repulsion of a determined German counter-attack at Bellicourt.

By late afternoon the division was clearing the tunnel like a shark in a fish school.

●

Satisfied that his second plan (it was a complete rewrite, not just a revision) was working, Monash snatched two hours' sleep before ordering a set-piece frontal attack—a replica of the start two days earlier—by 3rd Division early on the morning of 1 October.

Gellibrand protested. The problem was still on his left flank. Monash revised the intelligence coming in, agreed without hesitation and apologised. His anxiety not to lose, along with the strain of six months in charge, was beginning to show. Yet he remained in control of himself and the mission.

The flank attack proved correct and the Germans at last cracked due to the pressure from all directions. The British IX Corps on the Australians' right had done well, outflanking the enemy. By midday the tunnel, which seemed to have been defended more strongly than at any point along the long, beleaguered fortifications, was won. The reserve brigades of 3rd and 5th Divisions had taken Bony as directed. These divisions then pushed on, as Monash had originally planned, to soften up the Beaurevoir Line, the very last objective; and this aim was achieved. His shock troops had the most impact in what was shaping as the beginning of the Allies' crushing of the enemy right along the front.

However, the Allied armies were not as penetrating elsewhere, although all made progress. The French–American thrust from 26 September in the Argonne region was blunted. Pershing's approach was to cram men and guns into the battle area in the belief that the sheer weight of them would overwhelm the Germans, as he had at St Mihiel on 12 September. But this was not as effective in an area of hills, gullies and forests. The aggressive Commander Lieutenant General George S. Patton had quick success taking the town of Varennes, but stalemate soon followed. Little ground was taken while the American and French casualties mounted. Not wanting a failure on his hands, Pershing delegated command of the American First Army to his foremost field general, Hunter Liggett, who would spend more than a month reorganising his force before the next strike. Pershing mean-while activated a second army under another general, Robert Lee Bullard, at St Mihiel, a much safer area for the US hammer-on-a-walnut approach where the Germans were weaker and easier to attack.

Pershing, keen to preserve his reputation, took a step back, calling himself army group commander and commander-in-chief.

Chapter 60

Damascus:
A City Uncontrolled

Coincident to the Allied thrust in late September on the Western Front, the British forces were rapidly closing in on Damascus, which, if taken, would be similar in relative importance to Monash's success at Amiens. The aim now was to take Damascus, then Chauvel's Desert Mounted Column, with the Arab force in tow, planned to push on north through Syria with the aim of destroying the retreating Turkish armies, or pushing them over the border into Turkey.

The Arabs in Damascus, who had been waiting for this moment, stopped their subservience towards the Turks and became hostile to their former 'masters'. There was even rebellion in the ruling ranks, with Turks and Germans attacking each other over the desperate need to acquire transport out. Gunfights began over the governor's fleet of Mercedes. Von Sanders had fled days earlier, beginning the 320-kilometre journey to Aleppo in Syria's north.

His last notes on the town mentioned how the Arabs had become threatening, the city unruly:

> Armed bands of Arabs arrived there daily, which though they did nothing but arrange fantasies and fire into the air, formed an ominous element in the city . . . [It] was full of Sherif Feisal's agents who incited the population. The four-coloured flag of the Sherif was displayed from many houses. Baggage trains were tangled in the streets. More and more Turkish soldiers left their ranks and scattered through the city . . . there were fires at the station at Kadem, terminus of the Hejaz railroad, and the German depots there.'[1]

Von Sanders was trying to organise the dwindling remnants of the Seventh and Eighth Armies outside Damascus. Mustafa Kemal with the survivors of his Seventh Army had straggled into the city, but was on his way out again. First he had planned to head west to Beirut, but learnt Chauvel was moving to block the road. Now he was left only with a push north. He had decided to give up Syria and form a line of defence in front of the Turkish border, with Aleppo the last major town in the north to be defended.

On 30 September, the number of Feisal's flags poking from the city's buildings increased. Messages about Arab rule and freedom were hung from many balconies, which in the past would have received swift retribution. Now the Arabs were openly defiant. No one was pretending anymore about how they felt about the Ottomans. The worst aspect of this was the abandoned hospitals.

Thousands of wounded and sick Turks were left without medical or any other kind of help. With no sanitation and clouds of flies, many were dying in the wards and corridors.

Djemal Pasha, well-protected by a strong armoured force, had managed to make it back to Damascus. The Turkish military governor let the city's leading citizens know he was departing, this time for good. In an orderly act, he passed his temporary control to Emir Said al-Jezairi, grandson of the Sultan of Algiers. He was pro-Turk. His record in standing up to Imperial European powers was well established. In the late nineteenth century he created the nationalist movement in his country, which had been annexed by the French. He had defied them for fifteen years before being captured and sent into exile in Damascus. These credentials were the reason Djemal Pasha favoured him. The Turk would rather leave a Muslim in charge, someone who opposed the British and French, the two powers with covetous eyes on Syria. Emir Said would not be looking for a short tenure. He was ambitious, as was his brother Abdul Qadir. They had no intention of transferring his power to Feisal or one of his emissaries.

Chauvel thought Qadir a closet French supporter, despite his claims that he was 'anxious to see the British in control of Syria'. Chauvel believed that he and his brother were still drawing 'the huge subsidy granted by Louis Napoleon in 1852 to their grandfather', when he agreed to live in Turkey and stop disturbing the peace in French North Africa.[2]

•

The connections of Lawrence and key Arabs such as Feisal, Nasir and Auda had been slipping into Damascus and were plotting to take control when the chance arose. But with the turmoil, all these key figures would need to be there to sort out the conflicting interests.

After this handover of power, Djemal Pasha made his hurried departure from Damascus just as the big guns of Chauvel's approaching Australian Mounted Division became audible.

•

At 8.50 p.m. on 30 September, a Turkish troop train left Damascus, with soldiers and other passengers forming a desperate throng on the roof and hanging from the sides of carriages.

It was the last one for the night.

•

At the same time, the Australian Mounted Division was on the city's outskirts. In what had become a conventional move, Chauvel had ordered his troopers to attempt to block every road out. Hodgson's brigades were sent to bar the way north to Homs, Hama and Aleppo. Macandrew and his 5th Cavalry Division had been instructed to leave operations against the crushed Fourth Army to Barrow and to move up in support towards Damascus. Chauvel directed Macandrew to detach a brigade to cut off a rogue Turkish force, after an Australian pilot had spotted it marching north from Kiswe towards Damascus. The 14th Brigade of Indians and Yeomanry were selected. It galloped into the Turks with lance and sword, destroying the main part of the force. The commander and staff of the Turkish 3rd Cavalry Division was among the big haul of prisoners and it was a fitting end. This outfit had not once in the entire campaign taken on Chauvel's Light Horse. Before Beersheba, they stayed clear of them. After it, the Turkish Cavalry was never seen until this humiliating capture.

•

Chauvel further asked Hodgson to cut the road west to Beirut, which ran through the tight, vulnerable track of the formidable Barada Gorge with its massive overhanging rocks and steep cliffs, green, yellow and brown by day, black and forbidding at night. Any force attempting to escape, no matter how well equipped, would be no match for the Light Horse, who would make clear their capacities as riflemen. They would dominate a brutally unfair fight. Wilson's 3rd and George Onslow's 5th Light Horse Brigades positioned themselves in vantage points on the cliff tops overlooking the V-shaped, narrow gorge. It wound between near vertical mountains of the Anti-Lebanon range's eastern buttress. The waters flowing from the mountains, which were snow-capped until June, formed the flowing Barada River, which crisscrossed the narrow path. The road and rail route to Beirut via the Lebanons was carved along its banks.

The brigades were engaged from midafternoon with a column of about 4000 enemy soldiers, including hard-fighting German machine gunners, who were attempting to escape Damascus by heading west. The Germans operated from the top of trucks and trains. They were defiant but no match along the gorge for the Australians, who held the heights. The Light Horse machine gunners raked the pass causing mayhem and confusion. The trapped Turkish/German force could not move forward. Their vehicles could not turn back, especially with the line of trucks, vehicles and horses behind them in the slim pass. They could not take refuge either side of the road. There was no way of challenging the Australian snipers and machine gunners by clambering up the cliffs and becoming even easier targets.

The enemy was forced to turn back to Damascus, but was caught in the passage of death. There was nowhere to hide from the incessant rain of bullets from above. The ease of the slaughter took many minds back to 19 May 1915, when 10,000 Turks attacked Monash Valley on Gallipoli without artillery support and were picked off as if, as one digger put it, at a 'wallaby hunt'.

The Light Horsemen fired until their weaponry was too hot to handle. By nightfall the column in the gorge was still.

'All night long continuous fire was maintained,' Olden of the 10th Light Horse wrote of what appeared to be overkill, 'sweeping the head of the Gorge . . . making it practically impossible for any living thing to escape.'

No enemy troops entered the gorge in the night. He recorded that about 700 of those trapped became casualties. There were also hundreds of animals killed, including camels, horses, mules, donkeys, sheep and dogs.

'Truly,' Olden concluded, 'the net was fast closing on the doomed city!'[3]

Chapter 61

First In; Best Placed

Chauvel gave orders to Hodgson to begin the city's encirclement at first light on the morning of 1 October. Hodgson
chose Wilson's 3rd for this mission. Allenby, playing along with
Lawrence's scheme, sent crisp orders to Chauvel, who passed
them on to all his commanders: 'No troops are to enter Damascus
unless absolutely forced to do so.'

Brigadiers were directed to arrange posts on all the roads to
make sure this was adhered to.

This would ensure that the Arabs, led by Feisal, would be seen
to be first into the city. Allenby and Lawrence hoped it would
be a case of first in, best dressed, but not quite in the black and
white way some Arabs did. It was widely thought among leading
Syrians that whoever entered Damascus first would have the best

chance of ruling Syria. This belief had spread when, in June, British diplomat Mark Sykes released a document, virtually a clarification of the 1916 British/French Sykes-Picot Agreement, which was meant to carve up the Middle East for the British and French. This new document went to seven leading Syrian exiles in Cairo, who were making claims in anticipation of taking over once the Turks were forced out. In short, this group felt they would be entitled to any territory they 'conquered' from Turkey in the war. This so-called 'Declaration of Seven' had no binding clauses in law, but in the build-up to the Turks' defeat and banishment from Syria, its effect was electric. The thought reached fever pitch in the minds of acquisitive Syrians, who saw all sorts of riches, wealth and power emanating from their presence in Damascus, enabling them to make claims at the right moment.

Allenby had not been consulted on the extra Sykes declaration and viewed it as unauthorised. None of the key leaders of the revolt had been party to it. Allenby's aims on behalf of his government were more limiting for the Arabs and more subtle. He wanted to make it seem as if the Arabs had taken Damascus. This would lessen French rights to the country, which was his government's wish. It would also increase Britain's chance of major influence.

Lawrence's thoughts were in accord with Allenby's over the French. But he fervently hoped that being first in would enable the Arabs to take control of Syria as a 'Brown Dominion', as he called it. In other words, Syria would be like Canada or Australia in terms of British influence. They were both former colonies. Lawrence's creation would enable the country to bypass a colonial era and move straight to stage two as a Dominion. He hoped the strong link forged by him with the Arabs would also mean that the French would not get a look in, regardless of the Sykes-Picot Agreement, which had handed them Syria. It added up to the British planning to doublecross the French.

•

The 3rd and 5th Brigades spent the freezing night of 30 September in the hills above the Barada Gorge. Those not engaged in superfluous firing on the beleaguered and silenced enemy force were kept awake by the one-sided battle and fireworks of exploding ammunition dumps, which the enemy had set to destroy as they departed.

Wilson noted the instruction to keep out of the city. He sent out scouts to reconnoitre all exits and a way across to the north. They rode out from the conquered Barada Gorge and found the track crossing south-west to the ancient caravan route to the Jordan, Judea and Egypt. They also discovered the path south: the old pilgrim's road to Mecca via Deraa. But they could not find a track around the city to the north.

Wilson felt he had no option but to go through Damascus itself.

There was a considerable enemy garrison in the town, and intelligence reports spoke of the Arabs' 'excitement', which could mean anything in terms of responses to foreign troops. No one knew how the Arabs would react. Were they still under Turkish/German control? Would they be forced to defend the city against invading horsemen? This job required the best of the best.

With that in mind, Wilson turned to the hardened, brilliant 10th Light Horse Regiment, which had experienced so much against the Turks all the way from the Nek. It would be the brigade's advanced guard. He took second-in-command of the 10th Regiment, Arthur Olden, to see Chauvel.

'My scouts could not find the road north out of Damascus,' Olden told Chauvel, 'we'd have to go through the city to find it.'

'It is your mission to seal the city,' Chauvel replied, 'which means all routes in and out.'

After a brief silence, Olden remarked: 'Then we'll have to go through the city to find the northern exit. We'd have to take control of Damascus.'

'I don't want anyone like von Sanders ever slipping our net again.'

'I understand General, thank you.'

Olden realised that Chauvel was consenting to him taking Damascus, if possible.

•

Just before 5 a.m. Olden, ordered the A, B and C Squadrons—400 horsemen (half the force that took Beersheba)—to saddle up. It was still dark. Most of them had not slept much with the noise coming from every direction around their bivouac near the gorge. Yet still these troopers were ready. Olden sensed that this could be *the* moment of his career, if not his life. The Ballarat-born son of a Swedish mining agent had given up his dental practice to join the Western Australian Mounted Infantry in January 1913. He had enlisted in the AIF in October 1914 and embarked for Egypt in February 1915 as lieutenant with C Squadron, 10th Light Horse Regiment. He landed at Gallipoli on 20 May and was wounded twice, in May and July. Olden had a survivor's guilt complex for being spared in battle when so many of his close mates and associates had made the ultimate sacrifice. He had missed the carnage at the Nek on Gallipoli when his fellow troopers were butchered. This fact above all others drove him on and on in the Middle East conflict. An element of revenge propelled him. It nagged deep in his subconscious.

Olden, promoted to captain then major early in 1916, was detached to other units for most of the Sinai Campaign, but his mind was never far from the 10th. His record and the respect he had throughout the Light Horse allowed him to be placed back with the West Australian Regiment for the attack on Beersheba on 31 October 1917. Olden assumed temporary command when the regiment's two senior officers were wounded in the failed incursion across the Jordan from 30 April to 4 May 1918. Fate seemed to be pushing him to greater challenges and dangers. But he felt a lesser sense of self-preservation than most. Every battle was a bonus. An instance was his direction—as second-in-command—of a dismounted bayonet-charge by the 8th Light Horse against a sizeable Turkish stronghold guarding Es Salt. He was never in two minds about what should be done. This decisiveness influenced his men. Yet there was nothing reckless about Olden's tactics and style. He planned well and measured caution against daring. Consequently, his troopers attacked with confidence.

•

Eight days earlier, on 22 September, the 10th—with (now temporary Lieutenant Colonel) Olden up front and commanding—led the Australian Mounted Division in the encirclement of the Turkish armies in Sharon and Samaria. He captured Jenin with a brilliant charge by just one squadron. In a 48-hour operation he took 8107 prisoners and five field guns. This earnt him the Distinguished Service Order (DSO).

It was no surprise that Wilson went to him for the lunge at Damascus, even though he knew Olden and his men would be fatigued after the all-night massacre of the Turks. They would ride on adrenalin. None wanted to miss the moment and they saw their assignment as a great honour. It could be the culmination of the regiment's long journey that began in Cairo early in 1915, and was sidetracked to the hell of Gallipoli before it returned to Egypt, refreshed and reconstituted by early 1916. From there, the regiment had ridden through the Sinai, then Palestine and now Syria. The troopers had experienced many hardships, which were compensated by regular 'wins' along the way until this final, major 'event'.

Olden and his troopers thought of war in terms of sport, although not quite the 'point-to-point' that Lawrence accused them of sarcastically after the war (in a different context). Their contests were less like steeple-chasing and more like football grand finals, or even boxing contests. The only difference was that in their 'matches' not just injuries were expected. Death was part of the competition.

This regiment, and all those which had been at Gallipoli, had a terrible start. Only a complete victory, where the enemy had been obliterated, would salve some of the pain suffered and memories of mates killed. Winning, to the Anzacs, had been part of their character and make-up when they joined as callow youths. Now after three and a half years for the longest-serving of them, it was nearly everything. They had put up with privations that would have surprised even the hardiest before they began the journey. Now the act of seeing the fight right through to the last round was their motivation to carry on.

•

This regiment of 400 men and 400 horses, including Bill the Bastard as a packhorse, was perhaps the prime example of a grand cavalry squad. They believed they had no peer in this war or any other. The troopers behaved and performed as if it was beyond debate, yet rarely with boast or bluster. Instead there was a clinical, laconic, almost languid professionalism about their work when they went on patrol or on an assignment.

Lawrence, always the analyst, observed them in the air, on horses and on the ground, in action and at play over two years. He noted:

> These Australians, shouldering me in unceremonious horseplay had put off half civilization with their civil clothes [presumably he would have appreciated them more in Arab garb]. They were dominant to-night, too sure of themselves to be careful: and yet:— as they lazily swaggered those quick bodies, all curves with never a straight line, but with old and disillusioned eyes: and yet:—I felt them thin-tempered, hollow, instinctive; always going to do great things; with the disquieting suppleness of blades half-drawn from the scabbard. Disquieting: not dreadful.[1]

Even these hardened troopers were excited at that prospect of the next day, 1 October. The oasis between the mountains and the desert, set in bleak surrounds on two rivers, was now the key city in the Middle East war.

Olden and his 400 were on the ride of their lives. They intended to conquer Damascus.

Chapter 62

Olden and the 10th Conquer Damascus

The 10th Regiment's three squadrons began their advance descending from the steep hills to the Barada River where they watered their horses. They then crossed the river and headed for the Dumar station where a train had drawn up. The horsemen of the lead squadron drew their swords and charged round a bend in the road. About 800 Turks were crowded close, hoping to get on the train. They were called on to surrender, which they, and all on board, did. The Australians looted the train, finding four chests of gold and silver coins, which were commandeered. There were also boxes of cigars. They were German and of a good enough quality to entice many of the troopers to light up. They rode off puffing, pleased with the fruits of the diversion early on the mission.

A troop was left to guard the prisoners. The column moved on but the troopers, shrouded in cigar smoke, en route to Damascus were blocked on the road at the head of the gorge by the carnage created in the night by the two Australian brigades. Human and animal remains and broken transport littered the way for about 1.5 kilometres. The troopers cursed, chomped on their cigars, dismounted and began the unappealling task of clearing a path, under occasional fire from hidden snipers in the gorge. They carried wounded enemy soldiers to the riverbank where they would be picked up by ambulances. The dead were put on one side of the road. They made an eerie sight as the first hint of dawn slid over the gorge. Wounded animals were shot. They were dragged clear, leaving enough space for the column to move on.

Seeing that this experience had annoyed, delayed and sobered his men, Olden called for the warhorse Bill the Bastard, hero of Romani, to be moved to the front of the column. He would gallop at the head, riderless and with stirrups reversed. Olden asked that the word be passed along the long column: 'Bill the Bastard today is symbolic of all our fallen cobbers from the Nek and elsewhere. They are gone to God, but they are with us today!'

The troopers responded by applauding and cheering the mighty stallion as it was led to the front. The initiative had restored the 10th Regiment's spirit. They rode on and at the next turn could see the tips of Damascus's minarets, now sparkling in the day's first light. They began the direct ride to the city and its spread of green gardens, made even more colourful by flowering fruit. The cool orchards included jasmine, whose aroma along with the whiff of the citrus flowers was sharp and pleasant in the crisp autumn air along the 30-kilometre, half-hour ride to the city.

On the left was the gorge. On the right was the river and the railway separated from the road by a high stone wall. On the other side of the river, 500 metres along, were military barracks. The horsemen could see a big body of troops, estimated at 12,000, in the parade ground. Some gathered with rifles by the wall. Others disappeared into the building. These were Mustafa Kemal's troops. They looked bedraggled and disorganised. Had he been there they may have rallied to take on this modest invading force. Yet this was not Gallipoli. The commander had slipped away on the road to Homs, just avoiding the roadblocks set up by the Australians.

The troopers drew swords at the sight of lifted Turkish rifles. But they were not fired on. Olden ordered them to keep their column formation. Riding to the front, he lifted their rating to a gallop, which brought up a shroud of dust, and created a rumble like rolling thunder that was heard in the city. It drew crowds into the streets that had been alive during the night. The Light Horse eased back a fraction. There was no target, no opposition. But the momentum of the initial move kept them thrusting forward, almost as if they were inviting an enemy to emerge. None did. Damascus was in turmoil, not from military confrontation, but because of expectation mingled with fear.

The troopers reined in their mounts and placed swords back in scabbards as they neared the city centre. Hundreds of exuberant Arabs in different types of garb approached. The Australians were seen as the long-expected and awaited 'British' troops, who were liberating them, and who would make sure, they hoped, that the Turks would never come back. Some in the crowd revealed the identity of their allegiances. There was the rugged Druse from the Hauran Mountains; uniformed gendarmerie; European-suited Syrians (including a section of the 60,000 Christians living in the city of 300,000); Jews, Greeks, Armenians and even some Turkish civilians. They were excited. Rifles were fired into the air. The Australians, unaware at first that this was not hostile fire, reached for their revolvers.

The column followed the road onto a bridge that crossed the Barada River near the Victoria Hotel. They had to force a passage through the throng as it surged close. The Australians were in no mood to acknowledge men and women thrusting themselves at them, trying to touch them and their horses. The troopers were alert and grim; they had expected a fight rather than a festival. They had not expected the enemy to have fled.

They made a path through the crowded streets to the town hall (*serail*). Its steps were busy with officials and well-dressed locals. It was not yet 6.30 a.m. but there was more activity than was usual at midmorning. Olden halted his column. An interpreter was called for. A Greek stepped forward.

'Where is the Governor?' Olden asked.

'He waits for you in the hall,' the Greek replied.

Olden and three lieutenants dismounted and drew revolvers.

They were led up a marble staircase to the Governor's salubrious antechamber. The little party walked in and holstered their revolvers as they were in the presence of various officials and important locals in their robes. It appeared to be a solemn, important moment. Emir Said, loving the pomp, was sitting at a high-backed, gold inlaid chair in front of a conference table. He was wearing a suit and tarboosh. He looked dignified and quite pleased with himself in his rule of Syria and its capital, which had been his for less than a day.

Officials approached Olden. They stood in the centre of the

room. They asked Emir Said to come forward. The Australians realised they were in the middle of something rehearsed and ceremonial. In the minds of Emir Said and his brother Abdul Qadir, this official handover would legitimise their power in the city and the 'nation', no matter how it was to be constituted postwar. If the 'British' accepted Emir Said's position, and then protected it, he would truly be in charge.

Emir Said reached to shake hands with Olden. Speaking in Arabic, which was translated, he said: 'In the name of the city of Damascus, I welcome the first of the British Army.'

The Australian was handed a document which began: 'You are the first British Officer to enter Damascus, in the bravest manner known of the Saxon race . . .'

He preferred that the paper said 'Australian' rather than 'British' officer, and he was bemused by the reference to 'Saxon race', which to him was uncomfortably close to a description of at least part of the enemy. But he was in no mood for editing such niceties. Nor did he have the time.

Olden informed Emir Said that the city was surrounded by Chauvel's troopers, which was no bluff. Resistance, the Australian said, was futile.

'Does the city surrender?' Olden asked.

'Yes. There will be no further opposition in the city.'

'What then, is all the firing in the streets?'

'It is the civil population welcoming you.'

'Who are all the uniformed men in arms?'

'They are gendarmerie. What are they to do?'

'They may retain their arms for the present, prevent looting by the Arabs, and otherwise maintain order.' Olden paused as Emir Said digested the information and nodded. Then Olden added: 'As for the shooting in the streets, issue orders that it must cease immediately, as it may be misunderstood. You will be held responsible for this.'

'You need not fear,' Emir Said replied. 'I will answer for it—that the city will be quiet. We have expected the English here and have prepared for them.'[1]

Olden demanded that he write out his surrender.[2] The Governor was being most agreeable, deferring to the new military ruler. By doing so he thought he was keeping his job. He then began a speech in Arabic. The other Arabs present applauded often. Olden put his hands up and asked him to save it for Commander-in-Chief Allenby, who was expected later. This surprised the assemblage. Emir Said pointed to a table of food and drink. Olden declined the offer. He had to hurry on to the Aleppo Road north in pursuit of the enemy, a thought which would have galled the new governor much more than the rejection of refreshment, given that the Turks had commissioned him.

Olden asked for a guide. Emir Said turned to Zeki Bey, an Armenian, who obliged this request. The Australians bade their farewells and hurried out of the building. Undaunted by such exalted historic company, Olden and his men bustled down the steps to their waiting column of troopers, who had not dismounted. A huge crowd now squeezed around the *serail* to witness the event and get close to the new rulers. A huge cheer went up when Olden and co. emerged.

Olden mounted his horse, turned to his men, waved the surrender paper and said: 'Troopers! You and I are now in the line of some of the great names of history. This surrender of Damascus and Syria brackets us with Egypt's Ramesses II, Greece's Alexander and France's Napoleon!'

The troopers raised their slouch hats and emu plumes high and cheered.

'The march now assumed the aspect of a triumphal procession,' Olden noted later in his diary, 'the dense masses of people rapidly becoming hysterical in the manifestations of joy.'

As dawn began to settle on Damascus at 6.45 a.m. on 1 October, the populace viewed the horsemen as their saviours and emancipators. 'They clung to the horses' necks, they kissed our men's stirrups; they showered confetti and rose water over them; they shouted, laughed, cried, sang and clapped hands.'[3]

Rugs, silks, flowers, perfumes, fruit and other 'delicacies' were thrown from windows to the troopers. Arab women high in building windows lifted their dark veils and shouted: *'Meit allo wesahla! Meit allo wesahla!* (A hundred welcomes).' The call was taken up like a Mexican wave and carried along the column in one continuous chant. Olden and his men were mystified as to why they had been greeted with such fervour. They were unaware of the build-up and preparation for the moment when 'liberators' and 'conquerors' (the 'English') would arrive. The Australians' grand galloping entrance, with swords drawn or pistols in hand, had confirmed their status. There had been rumours that the Germans were planning to burn the city on departure. The explosion of ammunition dumps at the station seemed to support this fear. But the arrival of the horsemen had alleviated any possibility of such an act. Hence the Arabs' greeting, which had a sense of relief as much as joy.

The Armenian guide was either revelling in the crowd adulation at the head of the 'parade', or he was following Emir Said's instructions to delay the Australians. Whatever the motive, he led the troopers on a merry dance around the city, and took them every way *but* the route they wished to go. Olden became irritated. He asked if anyone in the crowd could show them the shortest route to the north-east road out of the city. Another Greek man stepped forward and helped. The man mounted a horse and joined the head of the column.

Seconds later a British pilot, who had been released from prison, rushed up and joined the ride on a pony he had 'borrowed' from an onlooker. (The pilot would later fight with the troopers.)

The new Greek guide directed them, single file, through the narrow, winding streets of the bazaars, where there was a second wave of welcome and appreciation. Storekeepers pushed close, offering fruit, sweets, cigars and cigarettes.

'They neither asked—nor would they accept—any payment,' Olden wrote, adding dryly that this was something 'miraculous in the east'.

By a little after 7 a.m. the amused and bemused 'conquerors' of Damascus trotted out along the road north to Homs and Aleppo. They were glad to have left the city, which they found suffocating and squalid, with a stench that they had breathed in other cities such as Jerusalem. It suited the troopers to ride freely along poplar-lined avenues with sweeter smelling orchards either side.

Having accepted the city's surrender, they were part of the sizeable Light Horse and cavalry force that would now lock it down and pursue the enemy north.

Chapter 63

Deception at the Reception

Two hours after Olden and the 10th Light Horse had made their triumphant sweep through Damascus, Lawrence and the Arab leaders drove into the city on the heels of the advanced protection guard of the British 5th Cavalry Division. It was 9 a.m. The streets were still crowded but not as they had been when the Australians galloped in and out. The car and its occupants seemed nothing more than curios. A photograph of Lawrence in the front seat shows people looking on, but without enthusiasm. Excitement in the streets was not as it had been earlier. (It would reach the heights again later in the morning when Lawrence, Nasir, Nuri, Auda and other Arab leaders toured the city.) The main event in the mass's collective thoughts had occurred at 6.30 a.m. when the first of the 'British'—Olden and his 10th Light Horse—had taken the surrender and sanctioned Emir Said.

Lawrence arrived at the town hall and hurried up the crowded steps to the antechamber where he found Nasir and Nuri in confrontation with Emir Said and his brother Abdul Qadir ('my old enemy', Lawrence wrote).

The brothers were claiming they had formed the government, along with 'Shukri el Ayubi, of Saladin's house'.

Lawrence was stunned. This was not the way he intended it to happen. In June 1917 he had anointed Ali Riza al Rikabi as the governor-to-be. This had been confirmed and understood by the Arabs in the fifteen months since. Shukri was supposed to be his deputy. But where was Rikabi? No one could find him. Lawrence quizzed Shukri about the usurping of power by the Algerian brothers Said and Qadir.

Lawrence claimed that Shukri told him that the Algerians had stood by the Turks until they ran from the city. Then they stormed the committee set up in Feisal's name and took over. They, not the absent Rikabi, had greeted the all-conquering Olden and his troopers.

Lawrence was furious and 'dumb with amazement'.

In despair, he and the others kept asking, 'Where is Rikabi?'

•

Rikabi had in fact left Damascus in search of Chauvel. He wished to submit his services to the real power, which he knew lay with the British. He found Barrow and passed on all his ideas for the planned transfer of governorship from the Turks to him. He proved a disappointment to Lawrence and of little consequence to Chauvel. The plans were next to useless. Events had moved too fast.

•

Chauvel, his chief-of-staff Godwin and an aide-de-camp rode over on horseback from Kaukab in the morning to see Barrow, whose division was in reserve. He also wished to see Lawrence, who should have been with Barrow.

'I met Barrow at 7.30 a.m. a few miles south of the city,' Chauvel wrote. 'He told me that Lawrence, who had been his guest for the last three days, had slipped off early that morning without saying anything to him.

'I was anxious to get the civil administration of Damascus arranged for without delay. Here was my only political adviser gone off without any instructions and without, so far as I know, knowing what those instructions would be.'

He told Barrow to bivouac outside Damascus and directed his aide-de-camp to select a spot for his own camp in the same area. He then borrowed a staff car and drove with Godwin to the city, arriving at about 9.30 a.m.

'I found Lawrence in his white and gold Arab costume on the town hall steps,' Chauvel recalled, 'surrounded by a large crowd. With him was another magnificent person whom he introduced as Shukri Pasha.'

The General wished to know why Lawrence had left Barrow without seeing him or leaving instructions. Lawrence's 'excuse' was that he *thought* Chauvel would like him to come in (to Damascus) at once, assess the situation and then make a report to him. Lawrence informed the General that Shukri was the new governor.

'Shukri was quite obviously an Arab,' Chauvel observed. He asked to see the Turkish Vali at once, as instructed by Allenby.

'The Vali fled the City yesterday with Djemal Pasha,' Lawrence lied. 'Shukri has been elected Military Governor by a majority of the citizens.'[1]

This was not true either. Emir Said was officially the governor. There had been no election. Lawrence himself had 'appointed' Shukri as the stand-in since Rikabi had disappeared. But Chauvel had no way of knowing of the deception.

Lawrence also told Chauvel that Shukri was 'a lineal descendant of Saladin' as an additional reason for accepting him as governor, which was another fiction. (Shukri took Chauvel to lunch a few days later and 'vehemently denied' Lawrence's fanciful comment.)

'Saladin was a Kurd and a man of no [distinguished] family,' Shukri told Chauvel. 'I am descended from the Prophet [Mohammad].'[2]

'I took Lawrence's word for it [Shukri's election],' Chauvel said, 'and agreed to Shukri's appointment, arranging for Lawrence to be liaison between us and telling him to let me know as soon as possible what police would be required.'[3]

Lawrence did not think any aid would be needed. It would be better, he added, to keep troops out of the city.

Chauvel then departed.

Chapter 64

Lawrence's Cry for Help

Chauvel drove off from Damascus after his tense meeting with Lawrence in search of Hodgson to learn the situation with the Australian Mounted Division. He came across war historian Henry Gullett, who filled him in on the force's status. Chauvel then went to his own HQ and sent a message by plane to Allenby, informing him of his approval of Shukri's appointment. Next, he 'became immersed in the usual problems for a Corps Commander of supply, collection of prisoners, orders for the morrow, etc.'.

In the middle of this, the 'bronzed and bearded' Captain Young, wearing Arab headdress and a British uniform, turned up from Damascus. Chauvel had sent for him. Young was senior supply officer with the Hejaz forces. Before they got down to business, he asked him for an update on Damascus.

Young informed him that Shukri had not been elected by a majority of citizens, but 'only by a comparatively small faction, i.e. the Hejaz supporters'.

Chauvel realised he had erred in appointing Shukri governor and was annoyed at Lawrence's blatant deception. It meant that 'by installing him, I had virtually admitted the rule of King Hussein over Syria'. This was not going to thrill the large minority of Christians. Nor did it excite the city-living Syrians—who had little time and some contempt for their desert-dwelling cousins—who had followed Lawrence, Nuri, Nasir and Auda into the city. They were mounted and armed with rifles, swords, daggers and revolvers. Their horses were weighed down with ammunition. There were also Joyce's 300 mounted khaki-clad regulars of the Hejaz Camel Corps, the only troops who had accompanied Feisal, who was yet to make an appearance, all the way from southern Arabia. The rest were from the country north of Deraa. In the northern advance, tribe after tribe had been enticed into 'service' by gold and the prospect of looting.

'The better class of inhabitants,' Chauvel noted, 'was appalled at the idea [of King Hussein ruling the city].'

The consequences seemed to be already being played out in the streets.

'There is chaos in the city,' Young informed Chauvel, 'the bazaars are closed. Looting is going on.'

The Hejaz supporters were trying to downplay the British role in driving out the Turks. They were telling the populace the Arabs had done it.

'That was quite evidently why I had been asked [by Lawrence] to keep my men out of the city,' Chauvel realised, 'and why I had not been asked for any police.' This was even though Lawrence and Shukri knew that 'I had a whole regiment of Australians standing by for the purpose [of policing] in the grounds of the Turkish barracks. The Hejaz people were trying to cope with the situation with their newly formed gendarmerie.'

Young advised 'a show of British force as soon as possible'. He also suggested Chauvel should not take over the British Consulate, which was being prepared for him.

'By doing so,' Chauvel noted, 'I would define the British as well-meaning allies—not the conquerors of Damascus.'

Young thought it would be better if he took possession of 'Djemal Pasha's house, which was the best one in the place'. Lawrence was reserving it for Feisal.[1]

This heralded a big power play. Chauvel would display a representation of the force that had swept the Turks up from the Sinai, Palestine and Syria in the last two years. It would be a cold reminder to any rebels, rioters, potential coup leaders and assorted thugs that there was military muscle ready to act against them. Furthermore, he was not about to let a 'nuisance' (as Chauvel viewed Lawrence) of a major deceive him, or usurp his role, whatever his purpose.

Chauvel felt he could not undo the Shukri appointment because he had already told Allenby of it.

'But I could put up a show of British force and take possession of Djemal's house,' he said. 'I could also police the place if necessary.'[2]

•

Lawrence busied himself in the evening of that first very long day with the administration of the city. He heard reports of disturbances that had closed the bazaars but did not think they were a major problem. Early on 2 October he was woken to the news that Abdul Qadir was rebelling with support from the Druses, who were looting shops owned by Christians. The rioting of the previous evening that Young had reported had been stepped up. The problem had been compounded in the night by desert Bedouins swarming in, lured by the vision of a good loot in Damascus. Many had already made off at dawn with their camels and mules laden with army stores and merchandise.

•

Lawrence got in touch with Chauvel and called for help. The General sent a second Light Horse regiment to the barracks in the town as a precaution. Its troopers intended to take on a policing role. The gendarmerie had proved inadequate.

Chapter 65

Parade of Force

Chauvel ordered Lawrence to meet him at his camp outside the city and told him of his plan to parade his force. Lawrence protested against this, telling him it was unnecessary. The General was adamant. Lawrence asked him if he would salute the black, white and green Hejaz flag hanging from the town hall balcony as he rode past.

'I declined,' Chauvel noted, 'I was by no means sure that it had any right to be there.'

This was the moment of frustration where the Australians irritated Lawrence the most and precipitated his 'after the fact' uncomplimentary remarks in *Seven Pillars of Wisdom*:

The sporting Australians saw the campaign as a point-to-point [a steeple-chase], with Damascus as the post; where the best horse would past first. We [Lawrence and the Arabs] saw it as a serious military operation, in which any unordered priority [of how Damascus was entered, for instance] would be a meaningless or discreditable distinction. We were all under Allenby and Damascus was the fruit of his genius.[1]

This was a thoughtless slight. Chauvel and his key generals of course saw it as a 'serious military operation'.

The clash between Allenby's two key 'players' was also the result of him not letting his left hand know what his right was doing. His vague directive to Chauvel about taking Damascus and Lawrence's role in the scheme (as the liaison officer with the Arabs) left Chauvel in the dark, which was part of Allenby's game. Lawrence did not seem to understand or care that the final push into Damascus was Chauvel's plan, which Allenby had approved. Nor did he not seem to comprehend or care that Allenby had instructed Chauvel to set up an administration in Damascus similar to that in Jerusalem. It had to have a Turkish civil governor and Chauvel was obligated to provide whatever extra police the governor required.

Lawrence tried in his writing to present Chauvel as a lightweight martinet overly concerned with protocol and ceremony. This was an attempt to strengthen his case for claiming that the Arabs took Damascus first. Chauvel became his bête noir, and he had to colour him in this way.

Chauvel did not know the details of Sykes-Picot, although as he expressed to Allenby he had heard rumours about some agreement for an Arab takeover of Syria. Lawrence now knew it in detail.

These two very different characters had developed a contempt for each other over the course of the war. Chauvel was old enough to be Lawrence's father. He knew his history but was a typical general, whose life had been in the military. Chauvel's experience on Gallipoli and in three years of battles meant he had few peers as a successful senior commander in World War I. Lawrence was well below him in rank and had one experience of running a small battle. Chauvel understood better than most the impact of guerilla and terror tactics. He had seen them close up in the Boer War. But he much preferred the challenge of a set-piece battle. Almost all Lawrence's experience was of guerilla warfare. Each saw taking Damascus as the culmination of years of work: the main goal in the Middle East war. They were both fighting for British victory but from different perspectives. Allenby's distance from the front caused them to fill the vacuum of leadership in Damascus. They each saw the other man as threatening what they believed was the best conclusion to the campaign.

•

The British War Cabinet, pulling Allenby's strings, did wish to make it appear as if the Arabs had won Damascus from the Turks. It would be useful in their power play and rivalry with the French. The propaganda behind the scenes was clear. Henry Gullett experienced it first hand. He wrote to Chauvel soon after he had taken Damascus.

> On the question of the Arabs v Australians and the entry to Damascus we are, I fear, butting against policy laid down from London. Apparently the Arabs were to have entered first but did not fancy the job until the Light-Horse made the way safe for them.

Like the other correspondents I was advised of the policy and asked by GHQ to say anything I could in favour of the Arabs. I disregarded the request and made repeated efforts to disclose that the Australians were first into the town. But the Censor each time took steps to prevent it.

The same policy was adopted in regard to British and Indian troops, as exemplified at Deraa. The Arab was glorified all the way by GHQ. A passing reference I made to the fine work done by the little band of British officers, who directed the Arab operations, was cut out.

I enclose an article I wrote . . . giving in some detail the story of the 3rd Brigade's entry. I headed it 'First into Damascus'. The Censor altered this to 'Entry into Damascus'. And in the text where I wrote 'the first troops into the city were the Light Horsemen from Western Australia'—the Censor altered the sentence to read 'first British troops'.[2]

The problem was that Chauvel, if not given a political directive, would act according to his military priorities, which were to defeat the Turks, and protect the Syrians in the city and his own men. This put him at odds with the secretive Lawrence, who seemed to Chauvel to be running interference with his war operations.

•

Lawrence, desperate to make it appear that the Arabs were in charge, made a last demand of Chauvel: he wanted to know if he objected to a small detachment of the Sherifian gendarmerie riding in front of the column to 'clear the way'. This was part

Lawrentian petulance, part cheek and part attempted one-up-manship. Chauvel reacted generously. He agreed.

'This seemed a quite reasonable request,' he felt, 'as police in any large city would do the same thing.

'When these people arrived at the rendezvous,' he recalled, 'about every second man was carrying a huge Hejaz flag, which he was waving about in a most unmilitary manner. Some of my staff wanted me to despoil them of these but I decided to let it alone. It could not detract from the object I had in view.'

Chauvel thought 'it showed a sense of humour on the part of Lawrence, which was worthy of recognition!'

Chauvel led the 'show of strength' on horseback at noon, with a squadron of the 2nd Light Horse Regiment acting as bodyguard.

'It [the military column] was representative of every unit in the Corps,' Chauvel said, 'including artillery and armoured cars, with the three divisional commanders and their staffs riding also in the show.'[3]

The parade featured British Yeomen and gunners, New Zealand Light Horse, Indian Lancers and a detachment of French Cavalry (which would have infuriated Lawrence) from Onslow's brigade.

The effect was 'electric'. The bazaars were opened. The city went about its normal business. The impact was what Chauvel wanted. He laughed good-naturedly at Lawrence's attempt to upstage him, believing that the Arabs and their flags made his own point stronger. The long, sombre and fearsome column of artillery wagons, machine guns, armoured vehicles and tough, slouch-hatted troopers on their walers spoke for itself. This line-up of grey hardware contrasted with the bright, 'carnival' impression of the Arabs at the front.

Everyone in Damascus was now fully aware of where the real power lay. To drive home the point, symbolically at least, Chauvel took over Djemal's house as Young had advised and allotted the British Consulate to one of his divisional commanders.

All this upset Lawrence even more. The clash between the most outstanding battle commander of the Middle East war and the brilliant 'guerilla' leader and adviser of the Arabs and British had peaked.

•

Chauvel was now in overall charge of the city and he had many issues to deal with. Not the least was the terrible state of Damascus's large Turkish military hospital. It had been neglected since before the Turkish leaders made their escape from Damascus. The Arabs were certainly not going to do the wounded and sick former occupiers any favours.

'It was cleaned up,' Chauvel said. 'The dead were buried by the fatigue parties of Turkish prisoners.'

They were supervised by his corps' medical staff. Australian doctors directed Turkish medicos and orderlies before the hospital was handed over to the Arab administration. Lawrence wished all hospitals turned over to the new regime. Chauvel refused. He kept the European ones, knowing he would need them for his corps. (The new rulers failed to reach any suitable standard with the Turkish hospital; Chauvel took it over a second time after just four days.)[4]

By the night of 2 October, electric light had been restored. The city was calmer.

Chapter 66

The Firing of Lawrence

Allenby was preoccupied with the behind-the-scenes politics of the Middle East carve-up, now that it was apparent that the British and the French would soon take control of the region. He sent a message to Chauvel late in the afternoon of 2 October that said he would be making a quick visit to Damascus the next day at 1 p.m. Allenby would be there no longer than an hour, and then he would be off again. Early on 3 October, Lawrence let Chauvel know that Feisal would arrive in the afternoon by special train from Deraa.[1]

'He [Feisal] wished to have a triumphal entry,' Chauvel noted, 'galloping in like an Arab Conqueror of old at the head of about 300 horsemen.'

The idea did not appeal to him, given, Chauvel mused, that

Feisal had 'very little to do with' the taking of the city. But he didn't think it would do any harm.

Midmorning on 3 October, Chauvel took time to visit the tomb of his hero, Saladin, at the Umayyad Mosque, the oldest place of worship in the Muslim world. It was the most important religious structure in Syria, which ranked architecturally and in its decorative splendour with Jerusalem's Dome of the Rock. Chauvel removed his footwear in deference to the sanctity of the building, which was second only to the holy mosques of Mecca and Medina. He paused in front of its elaborate facade, before making his way behind the building to the small archeological garden that lay along the north wall. He darted past a few columns dating back to the original Roman Temple of Jupiter and entered the Mausoleum of Saladin, a small white building topped by a rust-red dome. The famed adversary of the Western Crusaders died in Damascus in 1193 and the original tomb was erected on the site in that year.

Chauvel related to Saladin's well-documented personal austerity, which the visitor felt was reflected in the mausoleum. He found inside it two cenotaphs. On the right and holding Saladin's body was a walnut tomb, decorated with motifs typical of the twelfth century. On the right was a more expensive modern marble tomb donated by the German Kaiser (Wilhelm II) in 1898. Chauvel paid his respects to someone who had captured his imagination long ago, and would take time to reflect on the amazing link he now had with a legend from history.

After the visit, Chauvel and Godwin drove to Kaukab, just outside Damascus, to greet Allenby. Chauvel wanted to know if the Chief thought he had done the right thing in appointing Shukri.

'Yes, Harry, you did,' Allenby replied, 'under the circumstances as they were. But there are complications with the French [who objected to being double-crossed]. I want to see Feisal at once.'

'He won't be in [Damascus] until 3 p.m.,' Chauvel said, 'he wants to make a "triumphant" entry.'

'I can't wait until 3 p.m., Harry. I must get back as far as Tiberias tonight. You must send a car for him and request him to come in and see me at once. He can go out again for his triumphal entry.'

Chauvel dispatched his aide-de-camp and Hubert Young, who was officially an officer of the Hejaz mission, in his 'best Rolls-Royce' to retrieve Feisal. Then they lunched with Allenby at the Hotel Victoria.

'He [Feisal] managed to dodge my emissaries somehow,' Chauvel said. In fact, he refused the ride in, 'and arrived at the Hotel Victoria on horseback at a handy gallop followed by forty to fifty Bedouin horsemen. As a triumphal entry, it fell a little flat. It was an hour before the populace expected him.'

A conference was held. Present were most of the main players in the entire Middle East conflict for the Allied side. At the table were Allenby, Chauvel, Godwin, Feisal, Nuri Said, Nasir, Joyce, Lawrence, Colonel Frank Stirling, Young and Lieutenant Colonel K. Cornwallis, of Cairo's Arab Bureau. Perhaps only two people, Auda and another British officer from the Arab Bureau, Bertie Clayton, were missing from the diverse and unlikely team that changed history in the region.

Lawrence acted as interpreter. Allenby, in his usual crisp style cut to the salient issues, directing his comments to Feisal. Chauvel took his own notes, as he always did at such meetings.

'France is to be the protecting power over Syria,' Allenby said. Before Feisal could react through Lawrence, Allenby went on: 'You, as your father's representative, are to have administration over Syria—less Palestine and the Lebanon—under French guidance and financial backing.'

Feisal did not like what he was hearing. Allenby ploughed on: 'The Arab sphere [of influence] would include the hinterland of Syria only. You will have nothing to do with the Lebanon, which stretches from the northern boundary of the Palestine [about Tyre] to the head of the Gulf of Alexandretta.'

Feisal began talking in Arabic to Lawrence as Allenby concluded: 'You are to have a French Liaison Officer at once, who will work, for now, with Major Lawrence, who will give you every assistance.'

Feisal could now get a word in. He objected.

'I know nothing of France in this matter,' he claimed, which was a touch disingenuous. Lawrence had sugar-coated his articulation of how events would unfold politically once Damascus was taken. He had made obstacles to Feisal's rule appear surmountable. Nevertheless, the hard facts were a shock to Feisal. He would not have expected the underlying 'truths' of Sykes-Picot, namely French Imperial control, and no Lebanon, to be thrust at him without equivocation.

'I am prepared to have British assistance,' the stunned 'Prince of the Hejaz' said. 'I understood from the Adviser [Lawrence and/or Young] whom you sent me that we were to have the whole of Syria including the Lebanon but excluding Palestine.'

Allenby listened as Lawrence translated.

'A country without a port is no good to me!' Feisal added, 'I reject any French Liaison Officer and will not recognise French guidance in any way.'

Allenby turned to Lawrence and asked: 'But did you not tell him that the French were to have the Protectorate over Syria?'

'No, sir,' Lawrence said, also disingenuously, 'I know nothing about it.'

'But you knew definitely that he, Feisal, was to have nothing to do with the Lebanon?'

'No sir, I did not.'

There was further discussion around the points made, some of it heated. Then Allenby addressed Feisal again and now was most pointed in his message, which was an unambiguous order: 'I am Commander-in-Chief, and you, for the moment, are a lieutenant-general under my command. You will have to obey orders. You must accept the situation until the whole matter is settled at the conclusion of the war.'

Feisal digested the blunt words in the translation. He was unsettled.

'Do you accept this [decision]?' Allenby asked.

Feisal indicated that he did. He got up, shook hands with Allenby perfunctorily and left with his entourage.

Lawrence remained. 'I will not work with a French Liaison Officer,' he said. Before the Chief could comment he added, 'I am due for leave. I'd better take it now and go back to England.'

Lawrence was stunned and humiliated. All the subterfuge, plans, schemes, deceptions, hopes and dreams, seemed, in one blinding moment, to have evaporated. The game, all along, *was* to install the French as controller of Syria. It was the moment Lawrence dreaded. The duping of his beloved Bedouin was a reality and had been exposed.

Allenby did not like being defied over his instruction to work with the French.

'Yes!' he said to Lawrence. 'I think you had [better go back to England]!'

Lawrence left the room without shaking hands or acknowledging anyone else.

There was a nervous silence in the room. Chauvel, not given to filling such vacuums, said to Allenby: 'I think you were a little hard on him.'

Chauvel did not record in his notes if he gave reasons for defending Lawrence, whom he did not care for then, or later. But he would have recognised his hard work on behalf of the Arabs, and the British cause, as Allenby did.

The Chief responded:

'Very well, send him down to my headquarters and tell him I will write to Clive Wigram [King George V's equerry and right-hand man] asking him to arrange an audience with the King. I will also give him a letter to the Foreign Office so he can explain the Arab point of view.'[2]

With that, Allenby left by car for Tiberias.

•

Chauvel visited Lawrence in his hotel room and 'thanked me outright', Lawrence said, 'for my help in his difficulties'. This generosity made him feel 'mean'.

'I have come to feel that the trouble between us,' he added, 'was a delusion of the ragged nerves which were gangling me to distraction these days. Certainly Chauvel won the last round.'[3]

As a last gesture of goodwill, Chauvel gave Lawrence one of his Rolls-Royces for the long drive back to HQ Cairo.

On 4 October, Lawrence of Arabia was on his way, never to return to Syria.

Chapter 67

Montbrehain: Last Push of Monash's Diggers

On the Western Front early in October, a weary but cheered Monash congratulated all the divisional commanders on their successive victories in reaching the Beaurevoir Line. He reserved special praise for his old 3rd Division and Gellibrand, with whom he had argued several times during the battle. Rawlinson visited Monash and told him his job was brilliantly done. He should go on leave. Monash was grateful and in need of rest. Tremors in his right hand that had begun less than two months earlier had returned with a vengeance. He could hide them by putting his hand in his pocket. It was a warning.

He managed to carry on. He would not leave the conflict before it was over for his mighty army.

He wrote to a friend on that day: 'At times, when I feel very tired, I am tempted to hope that it will be the last serious work I shall ever do in my life.'[1]

He decided to stay in charge for another two days and depart on 5 October. In the meantime, he sent the 3rd and 5th Divisions out of the line to join their comrades in the 1st and 4th. The 2nd Division, which had been resting for a month, now was ordered in for a last push on 3 October.

The night before, the Germans let go the biggest gas bombardment of the conflict. But it didn't stop Rosenthal and his men. The 2nd Division's 5th and 7th Brigades, making a spine-chilling noise after an artillery barrage, surged out over a 5400-metre front with a full-on attack on the Beaurevoir Line. The enemy would normally repulse such a thinly dispersed force, but they were shell-shocked. The Australians were on them before they organised their defences. Their engagement was still tough, but by midday the last German line collapsed.

Rosenthal, daring as ever, thought he could go on as far as the heights that looked down from the German side on the fortifications. But the ten hours of brutal fighting was enough. He settled for a strong footing on Beaurevoir Spur.

Rawlinson was thrilled by the result. Monash wanted 2nd Division out of the line now that the Hindenburg fortifications had been smashed. But his Chief had two last demands. The Americans were meant to relieve 2nd Division, but they needed 24 hours to get organised and into the new front line. Could Monash ask Rosenthal to stay put for just one more day— 4 October? And while his division was there, could it advance the line further east? Rawlinson was responding to Haig's obsession with using the cavalry, which could ride in and exploit what the infantry, tanks and artillery had softened up for them. Monash's men needed to secure a bit more of the area to make it easier for the men on horseback.

Haig was looking ahead to days at the Officers' Club when he could reminisce about charges in the grand tradition in *his* war to match the reverie of those wallowing in *their* wars of the previous century. Monash had regarded the cavalry as superfluous. When Haig wanted them in a battle, Monash had obliged, but they had been pushed to the rear in any attack plans. Now that the main conflict was all but over, the cavalry was going in as window dressing to please the commander-in-chief and a few mates.

The Haig/Rawlinson demand was unreasonable, given the effort put in already. Monash and Rosenthal conferred. It could be done with fresh troops. All divisions in the AIF had been pushed beyond any limits they imagined they could endure. But Monash had fed them on victory. When battalions were flagging, he urged his commanders on. They in turn were able to squeeze that little extra out of men who had gone beyond expected, acceptable limits. The spur always was 'the win'; the aim of flying the Australian flag in a position once held by the enemy was enough. The fact that they had never failed to do it since being a unified corps lifted them at critical moments. That unsaid, but assumed, sense of being unbeatable, which Monash had promoted and his diggers had sustained and believed, was at work for the very last time in the Great War.

With whiffs of mutiny in the air in recent days, it would have been a different story if Monash's AIF had a mixed record of victory and defeat. But with a string of momentous victories behind them, beating the formidable opposition was the motivation.

'I selected as a suitable objective the village of Montbrehain,' Monash wrote. 'It stood on a plateau that dominated any further advances.'[2]

It was a few kilometres east of the Hindenburg Line. The village itself featured steep streets and blind corners. Its elevation and natural internal defences—rises and tight alleys—promised some tough house-to-house fighting.

Rosenthal drew up his 6th Brigade, which like the 5th and 7th Brigades had not seen action for a month. They had some tank support, but the battle for Montbrehain was a tough project.

The 6th Brigade began its attack at 6.05 a.m. on 5 October. Again, the adventurism of one man—this time Lieutenant George Ingram—lifted the entire force. He led a thrust against a German strong point on the ridge, capturing nine machine guns and 42 prisoners. But it was just an appetiser for the main achievement, when he led a rush on a quarry defended by 42 machine guns and a hundred of the enemy. Apparently not sated, Ingram left his men to clear up the area while he went into Montbrehain in search of a sniper.

Ingram had heard that a sniper, or snipers, had picked off about twenty unsuspecting men from the British 139th Brigade when they had advanced on the ruins, thwarting their takeover of the town. The Australian deliberately went alone. He wanted the element of surprise to be in his favour.

Ingram stalked his way into the town's narrow streets round sharp, blind corners, waiting for fire that was aimed in the direction of his brigade. One location began to betray itself. The shots were not coming from an elevated position, which was where the unlucky British forces had been looking.

After an hour of stealthy movement among the ruins, Ingram spotted the source. A machine gun was aimed out of a house's cellar ventilator. Ingram crawled from the side of the cellar while shots were was coming from it. When within a metre, he stood up and fired his revolver into the ventilator, killing the sniper. Hearing other shocked German voices in the cellar, he dashed round to the back of the house, booted down the back door and bailed up 30 of the enemy. Ingram then waited coolly until his men entered the town.

His bravery was rewarded with the last VC for an Australian in the war.

One other soldier at Montbrehain who unaccountably missed out on a VC was Lieutenant N.F. Wilkinson of the 6th Machine Gun Company. He was attached to the 2nd Division's 2nd Pioneer Battalion. They had been pinned down at the southern entrance to the village by heavy machine-gun fire. Wilkinson, knowing everything there was to know about machine guns, was surprised by the intensity of the defence. Instead of blindly rushing in, he selected a soldier to accompany him on a quick reconnoitre. They took a roundabout route to a railway cutting. They eased along it, keeping their heads down. The fire became louder as they reached an embankment. For a moment Wilkinson was stunned. He could see, from a side-on position, an estimated one hundred Germans with their machine guns pointing in the direction of his battalion. Wilkinson sent his companion back to his men with the order to bring up two gun teams.

He had a nervous wait. The gunners he had ordered were waylaid fighting two German machine-gun crews that had positioned themselves along the cutting, minutes after the runner passed through the area on his way back to the battalion.

The Australians arrived after 25 minutes, set up and began firing from the side-on position. This caused mayhem among the German gunners, who did not have time to re-position their weapons. The result was 30 Germans dead and 50 more wounded. The other twenty or so scattered.

One of the captured Germans said that if they had known the Australians were their opponents, they would not have attempted to defend Montbrehain. It was one of scores of such comments recorded by the end of this frantic period of annihilation for the Germans. They thought that the Australian style of fighting was epitomised by one rogue soldier, either for reasons of bravado, courage, showmanship, competition or just plain insanity after so long in combat, catching the Germans by surprise. Man for man, the enemy was just as courageous as the Australians. This element of apparent craziness, or near suicidal intent, simply defied the tenets of rigid German discipline. Yet these reckless acts caused a change in the outcome of many encounters. If the Germans had the upper hand, it would often be lost after a gutsy initiative from left field. Added up, these moments of inspiration in search of glory or an end, turned a battle, and cumulatively, finished the war.

Montbrehain was the last in an amazing string of battles beginning at Hamel on 4 July and ending three months later. As always, when the Americans arrived to take over they found the Australian flag fluttering from a pole over the skeleton of the town's post office. It was the symbol that kept the AIF going far beyond the limits of endurance in war.

•

There was always a cost. At Montbrehain it was a price too high for indulging Haig's whim. The 2nd Division suffered

430 casualties, despite performing to the highest standard seen in the entire war.

•

Monash ordered the 2nd Division out of the front line, leaving no Australians in the war. Their job was done. Over the past six months, they had taken 29,144 prisoners, and liberated 116 towns and villages over 660 square kilometres. No one knows precisely how many enemy soldiers were killed, but 60,000 would be a conservative figure. In the same period, Australia lost 5500 soldiers and had 24,000 casualties. They had taken on 39 enemy divisions and beaten every one of them, from the crack Prussian Guards who fought to the last, to cobbled-together forces that ran when attacked.

Long before the great German offensive of 21 March, the enemy knew where the strength in the Allied armies lay. They were careful not to attack where Dominion forces were in the front line. After 8 August, captured German commanders were admitting that the combination of tanks and Australians coming through the dawn mist was overwhelming.

Monash pointed out that the period of the last thrust from 8 August to 5 October was the least 'costly' period for the AIF, despite it providing the shock troops and being the spearhead of the campaign. The key reason was that although his plans provided victories, he created them whenever possible with machine and weapons protection for the infantry, without lessening its role. It was his greatest conjuring trick. His strategies delineated the Australians from the rest of the Allies. It marked a change in the way war was conducted from a nineteenth-century mentality, where men were viewed as cannon fodder. Monash's detailed command of the equipment, the weaponry, and all the technological accoutrements of war, put his thinking perhaps a half-century ahead of his contemporaries.

The difference was that he could put theory into practice, and he did it to devastating effect.

●

Prince Max von Baden, the Kaiser's cousin, was made chancellor of the German Empire, which was the wrong new captain for the sinking ship of state. General Ulrich Baron von Marshall, the Kaiser's new chief of the Military Cabinet, called him an arrogant ignoramus, incapable of any work at all and hampered by being heir to a federal throne. Four days into the chancellorship he asked for an immediate armistice on land, water and in the air. It was the beginning of the end of the war. Fighting would go on, but the enemy had no line of defence left in France. It would have to retreat at an increased pace.

With this news, a spent Monash later in the day departed for London and saw a congratulatory General Birdwood and Cyril Brudenell White en route. Arriving early on 6 October, he told Major General Thomas Dodds at AIF London to provide him with a car. He was to keep people—press, politicians, friends, relatives, anyone—away. Even Prime Minister Hughes was not to disturb him.

Monash, exhausted and relieved, just wanted a quiet day or two to himself and his constant companion in the United Kingdom, Lizette. He didn't feel like ever returning to the front. At that moment he believed the continual run of battles was over for him and his men.

•

His morale lifted when he learnt that the most compelling reason for going to war—the defeat of the German military dictatorship—seemed to be coming to fruition, with the Allied democracies on top in both the main theatres of war in Europe and the Middle East. The German Empire was torn and on the brink of defeat. Unrest in Germany was widespread. There was talk and rumour of revolution by the masses, as there had been in Russia less than a year earlier. Rear Admiral Paul von Hintze, one of Germany's most respected diplomats, attempted to bring about an establishment-backed 'revolution from above' by persuading the Kaiser to sign a document that made official the removal of the relatively impotent Chancellor von Hertling. Wilhelm II put his scrawl on the front page in the hope that he would save his throne. A parliamentary government would be formed to satisfy the Reichstag, the German Legislative Assembly, by including Social Democrats.

For the past two years while at war, Ludendorff had been the nation's unofficial ruler, with Hindenburg the genial public face of the military and Wilhelm II the increasingly ceremonial monarch acting as a rubber stamp for Ludendorff's directives. Ludendorff and Hindenburg would be under the new chancellor's control. These two were relieved that the pressure of the coming defeat would be on the new government and Reichstag.

Early in October, Ludendorff learnt of the attack on and penetration of the Hindenburg Line, and the ever-pressing movement of the Allies, which ran on a front from Ghent in northern Belgium right down to St Mihiel, 200 kilometres east of Paris. He called an urgent meeting of senior staff officers of the German High Command and told them the war could not be won and that 'unavoidable and final defeat was close at hand'.

It was a shock. The officers had never been given the full story of defeats, and had been kept busy creating new defensive lines. Bulgaria had given in, Ludendorff added, and Austria-Hungary and Turkey were 'at the end of their strength'. The German Army, he said bitterly, 'had been poisoned by communist-socialist anarchy. As a consequence, the troops could no longer be relied on.' Germany now had to prevent a revolution by negotiating an armistice based on US President Wilson's fourteen-point peace plan, which had been put to the Germans several weeks ago.

There was confusion. No one had actually read the plan; not even Ludendorff.

Chapter 68

Glory Days

Monash showed a remarkable resilience of mind and body by 'recovering' from four years in the Front's killing fields in a very short time. He went on his day in the country with Lizette with that nervous twitch in his hand, but it was soon less noticeable, although he was mentally flat for 72 hours. On returning to London and going to a West End theatre production on 8 October he was ready, although not that willing, to see Hughes at the Prince's Hotel the next day.

Hughes listened and even took notes. He was better disposed towards Monash than before. It was beginning to dawn on the prime minister that Australian troops had been dominant on the remaining two biggest fronts of the war. As the government provider of these all-conquering diggers and troopers, he realised he was going to have some influence at peace talks when the war finally finished. Monash impressed upon Hughes the mighty impact of the diggers in the final push and told him to be confident that the AIF had done more than any army to end the conflict and defeat the Germans.

The general made it clear to an astonished Hughes that the war would be over within a month or two. This ran contrary to all intelligence and newspaper reports. But even if Hughes was not enamoured personally with Monash, he knew his reputation as the greatest general of the war. He had enormous credibility, and Hughes believed his every word.[1]

•

Monash was never carried away with the sudden limelight. The fortune he had in staying alive and the brutal experiences he had been through wouldn't allow it. He was well centred in his own personality and character and did not need continual affirmation of his greatness. He was happy to go unrecognised, and revelled in the anonymity of wearing civilian clothes.

Monash's nephew and bodyguard Eric Simonson recalled an incident at the theatre in October. He was in uniform; Monash was in civvies. At the interval Simonson was engaged in conversation with a Light Horse officer, who had just arrived from Egypt, when Monash joined them. The officer was in full flow explaining an action during the Middle East campaign.

'Oh, yes,' Monash said, recalling the battle discussed, thanks to Chauvel apprising him of the detail, 'that was when Chauvel moved a brigade round the right flank.' The Light Horse officer was surprised, but carried on. A few minutes later, Monash broke in again with a pertinent comment. The officer was confused.

'Were you in Egypt with us?' he asked.

'No,' Monash replied.

'I do know you from somewhere,' the officer said, with a puzzled look, 'weren't you the quartermaster at . . .'

'No.'

The conversation about the Light Horse continued and centred on its very recent success at Damascus. Monash made a penetrating remark about the 10th Regiment under Olden, not the Arabs, taking the city. This showed an insider knowledge of the campaign that could only have come from Chauvel or his chief-of-staff.

'Look, I do know you,' the frustrated officer said. 'Who are you?'

'Monash,' was the quiet reply, just as the warning bell announced the interval was over.

The shocked officer, on instinct, stepped back to give a hurried salute. He was close to a wall and crashed into it. Monash and Simonson left the officer standing to attention, his feathered AIF hat askew.[2]

Monash was also kept level-headed by the nagging knowledge that there might still be a job to be done on the front. The war was not quite over, even though the honours began to pour in as if it were. The French gave him the Croix de Guerre with Palm; the Belgians made him a Grand Officer of the Order of the Crown and awarded him their Croix de Guerre. The Americans, more modestly, offered the Distinguished Service Medal.

Monash was conscious of explaining Australia's success, and was ready for more conflict, if ordered to return to the front. But the hand tremors, though diminishing, were a private reminder that he was really one of the many tens of thousands of Australian casualties.

•

A week after Monash's meeting with Hughes, Blamey—at the Front with the five divisions—reported that Rawlinson had asked how long before the AIF would be ready to go into battle again. Two months, he replied. Two days later, on 20 October, Rawlinson rang to say that the AIF would be needed in *one week.*

Hughes had demanded the diggers be out of the war in the first week of October, but he was now being overridden by the British High Command, which still believed the war would drag on.

Blamey and Hobbs were alarmed. They wrote to Monash, asking him to prevent it. Hughes had told the men they would be on leave from early October. That had yet to be granted. If they were forced back into action with at least two divisions unfit (1st and 4th), there could be problems.

Monash was now speaking for himself as much as his men. He and they had had enough. His judgement was that a good break was needed—two months and more if possible—from early October. But the British High Command wanted to throw its spearhead and most accomplished corps back into the fighting. Monash wrote to Hughes asking him to intervene. They met and decided to see Sir Henry Wilson, Chief of the British General Staff and Lloyd George's principal military adviser, independently.

Hughes told Wilson the AIF had done enough, but Wilson was frosty. He was unhappy that Hughes had promised the AIF it would be out of the action for the winter. Monash later told Wilson that Hughes had instructed him not to allow his corps to fight anymore. Monash put his case that it needed at least a few months to recuperate. He was gambling that if he could stall the High Command, the war would be finished before the Australians were called on again.

Wilson promised to refer the matter to Cabinet, but it wasn't done with much force. Rawlinson still demanded that the Australians prepare for more combat.

•

On 27 October 1918, the day the diggers in France were supposed to resume at the front, Monash and Birdwood went to see Haig at High Command HQ. The commander-in-chief wouldn't budge. Monash explained the poor condition of his 1st and 4th Divisions. Haig conceded they could be spared unless matters became urgent. The other three divisions, which were fit, would have to go.

Monash, in his awkward position of serving two masters, the British High Command and his prime minister, was never more conflicted. In the end his duty was to his men, who were bound to the British Fourth Army. After three weeks off he felt far better and ready, if needs be, for battle command once more. He wrote to Hughes to explain that he had tried to prevent the AIF being used again. He was surprised to learn that the prime minister had been persuaded by someone in the British Cabinet, probably fellow-Welshman Lloyd George, that the Australians' presence on the battlefront was important to the final victory, if only to put further pressure on the German Army and Government to finally capitulate. Having read Monash's account of the corps' efforts, Hughes saw the value in flying the flag to the very end of hostilities and then on to peace negotiations, in which he wanted a say.

(For instance, what would happen to former German possessions in the Pacific?)

Monash used his report to Hughes as the basis for his account for Pearce and the Cabinet in Australia.

He wrote of the decisive part his corps played in the Allied 1918 campaign, splitting it into five stages. First, there was the arrest of the 21 March German offensive. Second, there was the turning of that enemy campaign into a defensive one.

'Next followed the great, initial and irredeemable defeat of 8 August,' he said. 'According to the enemy's own admissions, it was the beginning of the end.'

Fourth was the stopping of Germany's respite on the Somme, which may have allowed it to recover for another year of war. And fifth was the overthrow of the 'great defensive system'—the Hindenburg fortifications. It was Germany's 'last bulwark' to safeguard its hold on French soil, 'a hold that would have enabled him to bargain terms'.

Monash was adamant that whatever contrary claims were made, Germany's suing for peace in earnest from 5 October was caused by its defeat on the battlefield. It followed so closely after his force had smashed the Hindenburg defences that Monash believed it was a 'final, determining cause' of the capitulation.

Hindenburg and Ludendorff had been seeking an armistice in late September, but it had been half-hearted and not sustained. Both were deluding themselves that their army could recover. They were unwilling to face the consequences of defeat. Monash believed that the corps played an important part, sometimes a predominant part, in each stage of operations that led to Germany's overthrow.

'There was no better testimony for such a conclusion,' he wrote, 'than the admissions of Ludendorff himself.'

Monash also asserted that the AIF's performance was better than 'any similar body of troops on the Western Front'.[3]

On 1 November, the Australian Corps was ordered to the front once more. Since they had last been in the line, the fighting and pursuit had gone on. The German retreat had seen it give up Lens, Armentières and the Aubers Ridge without a struggle. This enabled the British Second and Fifth Armies to occupy Lille and the industrial centres adjacent to it. Germany's tactic was to delay the inevitable by destroying bridges, ripping up railways and bombing every important road intersection. The pursuing British and American troops were exhausted as the armistice negotiations continued, with the Germans filibustering.

Chapter 69

Kemal's Last Stands

Just as the fall of the Hindenberg Line did not result in a swift end to the war on the Western Front, the fall of Damascus did not mark the end of the armed conflict in the Middle East. It would not be over while Mustafa Kemal still had the will to fight. He retreated to a top suite at the grand Baron's Hotel in Aleppo, 350 kilometres north of Damascus, and managed to cobble together a force of two divisions from the remnants of the Fourth and Seventh Armies.

The Ottomans, who had built Aleppo as a trading city, had always felt more comfortable in this northern Syrian town, which was connected more to Turkey to the north and Iraq to the east than to Damascus. Aleppo is set on a large, featureless plain where the valley of the Quweiq River entered it. Kemal believed he could make a more effective stand in this ancient place than in

Damascus. If he could not, he was closer to home if he was forced to retreat.

Allenby kept the pressure on in pursuit, urging Chauvel to mop up the remains of the Turkish resistance. His corps was depleted by illness, mainly malaria picked up in and around Damascus. But he sent Macandrew and his 5th Cavalry Division north 320 kilometres to Aleppo supported by an Arab force, and with Barrow and the 4th Cavalry as backup at Homs.

Macandrew's advance cavalry arrived 5 kilometres south of Aleppo on 23 October. He was encouraged by the sight of traders and locals coming in and out of the city unhindered. It did not appear to be a town under siege. He sent a demand for surrender into the Turkish fort. It was passed to Kemal. His response, which was more of a non-response, was: 'The Commander of the Turkish Garrison does not find it necessary to reply to your note.'

Macandrew directed his 15th Cavalry Brigade, which had also been weakened by illnesses such as malaria and influenza, and his squadron of armoured cars, to advance on the city. They were beaten back. The Arabs under Nuri then attacked the defensive Turkish trenches south of the city on 25 October. The enemy held their entrenched positions once more. But that night, 1500 Bedouin went around them to the east and broke into Aleppo. Kemal, for the third time, left a city in haste, bringing his garrison and two divisions with him north.

The next day Macandrew rode in to Aleppo to a positive reception—after having received a similar welcome earlier at Homs, on their way to Aleppo—where 70,000 citizens greeted him and his conquering cavalry warmly.

A hot fight ensued in the north of Aleppo. Kemal, just as he did at Gallipoli, oversaw his soldiers' defence, ordering them to stand and fight. Only at night did he withdraw. Macandrew held Aleppo and was content with that for the moment. Chauvel arrived in the city and ordered Hodgson there with his Anzac Mounted Division to aid the 5th Cavalry.

•

The Anzacs in Syria were on their way, on 27 October, for one last swipe at Kemal and his Turks. But they had not even reached Homs when they heard an armistice had been concluded with the Turks at Mudros on 30 October.

The war in Syria was over. (But not quite elsewhere. Britain captured Mosul, Iraq's northernmost province, fifteen days *after* Britain and Turkey signed the Mudros Armistice ending hostilities. This bold act secured the oil territory the British wanted so much and drew protests from the Turks that grew louder at the Lausanne Peace Conference four years later.)

•

The last push from north of the orange groves at Haifa from 19 September to 30 October 1918—a space of 42 days—had been an overwhelming success for Chauvel and his Desert Mounted Column. They had taken about 80,000 prisoners while covering up to 800 kilometres. In so doing they had suffered only 649 casualties (compared with 5666 overall by the Eastern Expeditionary Force). He would sleep well. No commander of such a big force of men and horses could dream of better. If wars had to be fought, the performance of his multipronged, speedy and highly flexible corps in conjunction with a strong infantry and backed up by a spirited air force, was what any general would regard as perfection.

Chauvel could not bask even modestly in his glory just yet. He had many chores to attend to—the main one being repatriation. There was a logjam of shipping around the world as capitulation by Germany on 11 November led to a huge problem in returning soldiers to their various homelands across all oceans. That was the biggest headache administration-wise.

A second worry was occupation. No 'peace treaty' ever left an occupied nation happy. There was always disgruntlement and issues for the occupier. A large force had to sit on the Rhine in Germany to make sure it honoured the Armistice. There was continuing trouble on the Afghanistan border with north-west India. Civil war in Russia would see Anzacs volunteer to fight with the White Russians against Lenin's Bolsheviks.

Supervision of troops was needed in several spots in the Middle East. British interests in Palestine, Iraq and Egypt had to be supported and policed. The worst trouble spot in the region appeared to be in northern Syria on the border with Turkey.

Allenby needed Chauvel's cool management. He kept him based in northern Syria to handle the situation there. The Turks were still sabre-rattling north of Aleppo. They were feigning little knowledge of the Armistice's detail. Mustafa Kemal had somehow mustered about 6000 soldiers, who would be loyal to him to the end, as long as he stuck with them. They were fatigued and bruised but still under arms. There was also the withdrawing Sixth Army, which had been fighting the British in Iraq. It had another 10,000 armed men. A further 16,000 fighters in the Second Army, who had not divested themselves of weaponry either, hovered in the north-west at Cilicia. About 32,000 hostile soldiers were therefore defending Turkish borders, as opposed to just 2500 of Chauvel's horsemen at Aleppo. The Turks were supposed to be on the other side of the border but they were still all in Syria. If Kemal and the other generals decided to confuse 'peace' with taking back a 'piece' of northern Syria—especially as the Ottoman Empire had lost so much, so suddenly—Chauvel would have real trouble.

The Turks were playing dangerous games. They spoke of the British armies as 'gendarmerie' who they wished to leave in Syria. Kemal was less subtle. He told one of Chauvel's aides-de-camp that he had no intention of following the directives set out in the Armistice.

Chauvel had never been so proactive in directing demands to his Chief. He suggested two choices to Allenby in handling this. His first was military. He would need infantry support for his Light Horse to move against Kemal. This was a tricky option, making Chauvel the aggressor when a ceasefire had been agreed to by both sides. But there were ways and means. He could move on the Turks and say they had threatened his men and had not complied with the Armistice.

The other choice was diplomatic/political. Allenby should have Kemal removed and replaced with someone more amenable to the agreement. The Chief moved fast. He sent a cable to the British representative in Constantinople. Soon afterwards, Kemal was fired and out of the war, a direct result of Chauvel's demands. (It was a turning point for Turkey; Kemal would now fight to take political control of his nation.)

Then trouble began in the towns to Aleppo's north. The Turks were whipping up anti-British sentiment, making life tough for the patrolling troopers. The situation was serious. Chauvel responded by moving his HQ to Aleppo and calling up Barrow and his 4th Cavalry Division to the city. A British Infantry division was also pushed north, but bad weather had destroyed roads and bridges, delaying their arrival.

The disturbances increased in the towns between the Turkish border and Aleppo. Chauvel moved to occupy them, learning that the main culprit was the Sixth Army under the troublesome General Ali Ihsan. He was breaking every clause in the Armistice declarations.

Allenby was fed up. He organised meetings in the Turkish capital and took a French battleship there, accompanied by British General Archibald Wavell. Allenby, nicknamed 'The Bull', was in good form. He told the foreign minister and key figures in the Turkish military administration that they were flouting the Armistice agreements outrageously. They were to dump Ali Ihsan forthwith as Commander of the Second Army or he would make other moves to ensure it was done. Allenby did not specify what they would be, but his red face, words, decisive manner and size had an impact.

'I met the [Turkish] Minister of Foreign Affairs and the Minister for War,' Allenby wrote. 'I gravely told them why I had come, and refusing to hear any arguments, I left them with the text of my demands in English and Turkish. They were taken quite aback; and I do not think they will forget it while they live.'

The Turkish Second Army General Ali Ihsan was recalled before Allenby had even returned to his battleship.[1] He was the second victim of Chauvel's demands.

PART 5
Post-Armistice

Chapter 70

The Best Man in France, and England

On 10 November, Monash began moving to HQ at Le Cateau, France, while Glasgow and Sinclair-Maclagan and their divisions were on their way to the front, with the other three soon to follow after the corps had rested along the banks of the Somme between Amiens and Abbeville.

•

Wilhelm II refused to step away and it was left to Chancellor Prince Max von Baden to announce arbitrarily that the Kaiser and his son the Crown Prince had abdicated. The government was handed over to the leader of the Social Democrats, Friedrich

Ebert. Wilhelm II refused to accept what he called a coup d'état, but no one reacted or cared. The issue was to dissolve the monarchy. Hindenburg was left with the unpalatable mission of putting the Kaiser on his special silver train, which would take him to Holland and exile. Wilhelm II was the last Kaiser. With cousin Nicky assassinated, King George V was the only one of the trio of cousins and grandchildren of Queen Victoria left as monarch. He was the least vocal or powerful of the three, yet the shrewdest and the best judge of character. George V had stayed with Haig, who had the respect of the key British and French commanders despite continued press and public disapproval. The King had also supported Monash on his rise to becoming the most effective general and battle commander at the most critical period of the war. George V was relieved that he had played a part in the overall Allied victory, and in keeping the British monarchy afloat.

●

Monash felt a surge of satisfaction as he drove on 11 November towards his new chateau, which had been the base for General Georg von der Marwitz, the Second Germany Army Commander. Monash's corps had been pitted against them for several months. But Monash's feelings became numbed as his Rolls, with the Aussie flag at full mast, sped the 200 kilometres from Eu to Le Cateau. The journey took him over the entire length of his battlefields from Villers-Bretonneux. If he felt like a conquering hero, he never expressed it. He was more saddened than anything as he passed 'the formidable and forbidding desert of eighty odd miles devastated by war'.[1]

The spacious chateau was set in country with hedgerows and woods like those of rural England. It was untouched by the holocaust of the previous four years. The departing Germans had stolen the paintings and used its many grand mirrors and windows for target practice, leaving the place 'cold and cheerless'.

•

On the afternoon of 11 November 1918, German diplomats climbed aboard a train in the forest of Compiègne to meet Marshall Foch and Allied representatives. The Armistice was signed and officially ended World War I.

•

Monash had just settled into the ghostly palace when the order arrived for cessation of hostilities. After the intensity of the AIF operations until 5 October, it was an anticlimax, but a welcome one.

Monash would never again have to command in war.

•

There was a new kind of mopping up to complete. Soon after the real Armistice on 11 November, Monash was summoned to see Hughes in London on 18 November. There was no way to keep the Bantam Cock at bay now. Without a war to fight, the politicians could step in and take charge again.

Monash had no idea of the backbiting going on over preparations for transporting the troops home. He had assumed that the AIF's administration—the General Officer Commanding (GOC)—would handle it. But Hughes had other ideas. He wanted total control. This could be achieved by putting demobilisation and repatriation under political *not* military management.

Monash let it be known that he would like to take over GOC of the AIF, if and when Birdwood stepped down. But he didn't really care. It would be nothing like being a fighting commander. As usual, Murdoch and Bean were pushing for White. Bean idolised him, though with a little less passion than before. Murdoch still saw him as someone he could manipulate, and that was important because the big stories now would be in 'getting the boys back home'. But Hughes, as was his habit, remained a contrary kind of bird. He had never been convinced about White's capacities.

Bean alleged in his diary that Hughes had reservations about Monash because he was a 'Jew' and 'showy'. This kind of observation was nowhere expressed in the prime minister's own writing—or anyone else's. Hughes had become a Monash supporter, to a certain point. There was no doubting his status. The British in high places were referring to him with great deference as 'the best man in France'. Monash now carried enormous clout. And that would be useful in achieving things in the repatriation planning. Hughes both admired and feared him. He would like to see Monash do the job and stay out of Australia for as long as possible, just in case he had any latent political ambitions. Hughes' political antennae were sensitive. If Monash, the popular, mighty warlord came home during the euphoric immediate postwar period, he and others might have ideas about becoming prime minister of Australia. A couple of hundred thousand war veteran votes and their families spread all over the nation would be the general's for a start, not to forget the newspaper support for him.

The top job would be his if he wanted it, and Hughes would not be able to prevent it.

Monash had no idea of the prime minister's thinking and was surprised to be offered Director-General of Repatriation and Demobilisation. It pleased him. He didn't fancy sitting on the Rhine with nothing to do in a cold winter. Birdwood loved his job; he would stay where he was for the moment. That left White as the bridesmaid again. He was keen to stay and assist Monash, but Monash wanted his own staff. He had great respect for White, yet he had become used to harmony, and the two had never quite clicked. Monash recommended to White that he go home and run the army. After the initial shock, White was not unhappy about the idea.

There would be nothing for him to do under Birdwood now, given that Monash had once more been given the number one job in determining the fate of the AIF.

Chapter 71

Back to Gallipoli

The Light Horse experience in the Middle East came full circle early in December 1918 when a group of Anzacs was attached to the 28th British Division and sent to Constantinople and Gallipoli. The men from the 7th Light Horse Regiment and the New Zealand Canterbury Mounted Rifles had almost all served on Gallipoli. Despite their weariness, all Anzac units had fought for this honour.

The Anzac contingent included Bill the Bastard, who had become a legend after his exploits at the Battle of Romani. Now he was being sent back to Gallipoli once more for pack work with several other horses.[1]

The troopers' party embarked from Kantara on 27 November and arrived at Chanak on 5 December. The Mediterranean crossing was rough. Many of the fatigued and physically vulnerable men contracted influenza. They were billeted in a rat-infested hospital between Maidros and Kilid Bahr. The weather remained bad during their six-week stay. Some Anzacs died. Their fate, it seemed, was always to end their days on Gallipoli.

A few of the more fortunate troopers visited Constantinople and found it crammed with refugees and soldiers from the defeated armies. They were Russians fleeing the civil war, Armenians searching for safety, and Turks on the run from armies in the Middle East and Europe. Tens of thousands were sleeping on the streets. There were, as ever, locals—Turks—who prospered. They were the criminals who dominated the black market and the prostitution trade, which was rampant. The Greeks, eager to trample on their ancient enemy, were prominent. Their blue and white flag was hanging from doorways and balconies. They harassed Turks into removing their fezzes.

Constantinople, with its churches, mosques, frescoes, mosaics, palaces, covered markets and fishing villages, was going through a period of decadence and mild hysteria with the changes in the months after the Armistice. The cafés were alive with dancing, boozing and drugs. The nightclubs had similar attractions, along with White Russians and others singing melancholic songs. Young female refugees offered their bodies for the price of a meal. In the atmosphere pervading the city, they rarely went hungry.

The troopers' main mission was to find graves of fellow Anzacs along the Gallipoli peninsula, and to bury the remains of diggers. They were also engaged in collecting artifacts, 'trophies' and memorabilia for the Australian national memorial collection (later the Australian War Memorial).

It was an emotional moment for the men who had served on this barren finger of land, and provided a memory that would stay with them forever. They wandered down to the already legendary Anzac Cove, then up into the hills, jagged ridges and ravines, searching for the remains of diggers, who lay where they had been felled on the Nek, Dead Man's Ridge and all the other chillingly but aptly named trenches in or closer to the Turks' former strongholds. Often they would find the remains of comrades who had managed to invade the Turkish positions before being cut down.

The returning troopers were not forensic scientists. Putting dog tags, bones and the shredded remains of fatigues into bags was not a pleasant job. But it meant so much to every one of them. It was a duty that no one would shirk. On the contrary, they did it willingly, caringly, knowing that, in the spirit of the Anzacs, it would be done for them if they were dead. This was part of the glue between comrades living or departed that was already an Anzac tradition. No matter how long their fallen mates had been left to the winds, rain, snow, heat, flies and maggots, the kinship was the same. For some, who had crept away in late 1915 leaving the fallen where they could not reach them or in the makeshift graves at Anzac Cove, this return to the scene of battle was important therapy. The latter-day diagnosis of 'survivors' guilt'—the terrible 'black dog' of depression that stayed with troopers who lived when their mates did not—was partly salved for some by this burial and retrieval operation.

On the nights the Anzacs crept away from the cove in December 1915, some stopped and wept at the gravesides of their friends. They spoke to the wooden crosses, swearing they would come back. They were angry that they had to leave. They sailed away with sad feelings that they were leaving their fellow diggers on foreign soil under the control of the enemy. This would make many tough men break down, years, decades, even a lifetime later.

The words 'they shall never grow old . . . we will remember them', were never more poignant than for those who survived Gallipoli. Others, not able to slay the black dog, would return to Australia and become drunks, drug addicts and social misfits.

•

The peninsula was now undefended. The Turkish Army was almost completely demobilised in the area. The locals were friendlier than the distracted soldiers in Constantinople, which was remarkable given the invasion of 1915. Some of the unemployed, ill-fed former Turkish soldiers, who wandered the villages, were enlisted to help the Anzacs in their grim yet important work.

The stay was a deeply touching and intriguing interlude for the horsemen. Everyone regarded the visit as a pilgrimage to a sacred place.

Chapter 72

Repatriation

Refreshed with the new challenge of getting the diggers back to Australia, Monash summoned his senior commanders and officers to Le Cateau. He announced that Hobbs would take over as corps commander. No Australian divisions would be going to Germany as part of the occupying force. Instead, he would be steering them home, but it would be a massive and complex operation that would take time, perhaps up to a year. Monash was already bubbling with plans for helping every soldier prepare for his new civilian life.

An item on Monash's agenda concerned the 118 soldiers from 1st Brigade that had 'deserted'. Monash and Hobbs thought it would be a good idea if Glasgow, as their divisional head, pardoned them. Glasgow, still smarting from being overridden by Monash over the issue, refused. Monash was no longer corps commander. He could not force Glasgow to pardon the men.

After the meeting Monash took Hobbs aside for a chat about the alleged 'deserters'.

'It would be a fine first act as Commander,' Monash told him, 'if you pardoned them. I don't want any Australians spending Christmas on Dartmoor [Prison].'

'But Glasgow won't agree,' Hobbs said.

'He'll be ropable. But don't concern yourself. You are corps commander. All divisional commanders take orders from you now.'

Fortified, Hobbs's first directive as head of the peacetime Australian war machine was a humane one. The soldiers were pardoned.[1]

•

Corps staff arranged a banquet to farewell Monash. On the way back to London with his aide and nephew Paul Simonson, he saw the sights in Brussels and squeezed in a trip to Waterloo to go over the battleground he knew so well but had never seen. On returning to London, he had a memorable time at the Australian and New Zealand Luncheon Club and was pleased to see Sir Ian Hamilton, for whom he never lost a kinship. Hamilton congratulated him warmly, and reminded him again of that hellish day two years before the war in Lilydale, outside Melbourne. With Hamilton observing, Monash had sent the soldiers under his command in 4th Battalion on a tough exercise in 40-degree heat. All survived, but Monash was criticised for going through with the war games under the hot conditions. When challenged by a reporter from the *Age* Monash commented: 'I'm training them for war, not a pic-nic.'

Hamilton was more than impressed. He, with good humour, would forever claim, accurately, to have picked him as general material long before anyone else.

Churchill, Hughes, Birdwood and Hamilton all spoke at the Luncheon Club. Hughes and Birdwood referred in their speeches to Monash, *just*. But remarks by Hamilton and Churchill were dipped in praise, saying that he had proved to be the most out-standing battle commander at the most important time. The mention of his name would have been enough to make him feel good. But the fact that every time it was mentioned there was spontaneous applause was even more gratifying. He was now well aware that he was very much flavour of the month. Monash was happy for the recognition for him and those that had fought under him. But he was not a twenty-year-old pop or film star. He was 53 and had had a life without fame. Now that it touched him, there would be no life changes or swollen ego. Monash simply enjoyed the moment. He accepted that the way he was being feted in England would not last. It made it easier to enjoy.

Hughes was not so thrilled on such occasions. The prime minister had sensed Monash's palpable strength in his own force-field at Hamel in July and again in September when he had tried to undermine Monash. Yet he didn't expect the former corps commander to be the focus of attention *away* from the battle-field and in a civilian atmosphere dominated by top British politicians and businessmen. No one wanted the prime minister's autograph on a menu, but the conga line of people wanting to press Monash's flesh curled out the door. This occasion would have impressed on Hughes the importance of this figure, who he would claim to have appointed. The prime minister had never experienced such respect and admiration—which bordered on hero worship—for anyone, let alone himself. The London-born Welshman and the first minister of the Crown in Australia was downgraded in Monash's presence. He might as well have been the rock-breaker and swagman of his youth for all it was worth at such gatherings in the presence of this quasi-rogue warlord.

Hughes regarded Monash as driven and ambitious. Could the momentum of his war effort and his influence in England propel him into politics in Australia? Could he be a political threat? Hughes was planning a federal election in 1919. He would make sure Monash wasn't there for it.

Monash noticed Hughes' reaction and sensed an enmity. Their rapprochement, which had seen him secure the repatriation post, was short-lived. The negative feelings between them would grow. Yet in those heady days, Monash had few enemies. The British elite of the military, society, academia, the press, business and Jewish community embraced him. The royals, particularly, continued to be enamoured with him.

On 12 December 1918 Monash attended the British Empire Boxing Tournament and was supporting the Australian contestants when he received an invitation from the King's second son, Prince Albert (the future King George VI, who was just two days short of his 23rd birthday) to join the royal box. Present also was the Marquis of Milford Haven (formerly Prince Louis of Battenberg).

'Prince Albert is a real jolly boy,' Monash recalled, 'full of fun.'

Monash was surprised when asked to spend the rest of the evening with him, but he should not have been. So far, apart from being a royal, the military had been the Prince's life. He had served in the navy for four years until 1917, and was now in the air arm of the navy and in the next year was heading for the air force. Albert, like his father, appreciated men like Monash, who had saved them from fates unknown. He had plenty of questions, and Monash went away far more impressed with him than the moody, self-absorbed Prince of Wales, who had often seemed disgruntled when under Monash's command in Egypt in 1916.

'It's a pity that Albert was not the first born,' Monash wrote to his wife. 'Despite his hesitancy of speech, he is the one with character, humour, diplomacy, intelligence and a real back-bone.'[2]

•

The pinnacle of those early postwar celebrations for Monash came on 27 December 1918 when he attended a state banquet at Buckingham Palace given by the King and Queen for President Wilson. Monash was one of about sixty guests. He spoke to the President and King for about five minutes each, but with Queen Mary for closer to fifteen minutes. One of the subjects discussed was how her son David, later King Edward VIII, was faring on Monash's staff after he had been placed there at the King's specific request.[3] Monash was at his diplomatic best in response. He had little time for the playboy Prince.

Whoever prepared the seating arrangements at the dinner knew what they were doing. Monash couldn't have found the company more stimulating. He was placed between the author Rudyard Kipling and Lord Burnham (the *Daily Telegraph* owner). Monash and Kipling had been born in the same year. Monash even kept a scrapbook over twenty years, in which he cut and pasted Kipling poems and short story extracts from Melbourne newspapers.[4]

The author, who had won the Nobel Prize for Literature, was an imperialist, who believed anyone born beyond the English Channel was a 'lesser breed', which was not a good basis for a rapport with Monash. But the Australian had read a fair swathe of his works, enjoying his tales about British soldiers in India and Burma. He had read *Kim* and *The Jungle Book* to his daughter Bertha when she was six. Monash's familiarity with Kipling's work wouldn't have bridged the gap between them, but it helped develop a rapport. Opposite him were seated Churchill and the British-born American portrait painter John Singer Sargent. Monash found Sargent a little too serious and reserved, but they had something in common in their appreciation of the Spanish painter Velázquez. Churchill was at his anecdotal best. Even his stutter had an eloquent resonance.

Monash, tongue in cheek, ranked the occasion up there with being in the company of notorious bushranger Ned Kelly, whom he had met at Jerilderie 41 years earlier. In the unrestrained atmosphere of the victors' banquet Monash regaled his dinner companions with the story of that meeting one hot summer's day in the Australian bush in 1877.

Five days after the banquet, he was reminded of another meeting that he would also never forget—this time on Salisbury Plain just two years earlier with the King of Empire. Monash was appointed Knight Grand Cross of the Order of St Michael and St George (GCMG). The Order was the sixth most senior of the British honours system, with the pinnacle being The Most Noble Order of the Garter. The GCMG was not thrown about lightly (and it is still an exclusive 'club' today). It distinguished him from the scores of decorated British generals. In Australia only Ronald Munro-Ferguson and Deputy Prime Minister Sir Joseph Cook had been awarded such an honour. Hughes would not have recommended it, and Monash already had a better-than-average knighthood. The most likely explanation is that the King put down his name for the enhancement.

His coat of arms showed a sword enclosed in a laurel wreath that depicted his finest achievement at the Battle of Amiens, the Lion of Judah and the compasses of Solomon. When combined they embraced the symbols of his heritage: war, wisdom and engineering. He chose a prosaic Latin motto, *For War and the Arts.* Perhaps, in keeping with his university struggle in that language, he left out a negative; *For the Arts, not War* may have been more appropriate. Then again, fighting had been on his mind. It had consumed his whole being for four years.

The aftermath would continue to do so as he rolled up his civilian sleeves, dropped the military formalities and applied himself to the big challenge of repatriation. He wanted the return of 180,000 diggers to be done with dignity and promise for every one of them.

Monash felt an unfathomable sense of debt, bound up with honour, guilt and admiration, in regard to his men. He had created a fighting machine and had pushed, urged and cajoled it from Hamel and Amiens to Montbrehain. Now was the time to practise more of what he had preached to his officers, and serve it.

The diggers couldn't all be sent home at once. Monash organised each division into groups of 1000 soldiers—a number suitable for travel by train and then ship. The longest-serving diggers were to be sent home first.

Those waiting would be offered 'Extra Military Employment'. Monash had to persuade Hughes to drop the idea of establishing national workshops useful for Australian industrial development.

They would take too long to set up and it represented only a relatively small number of potential jobs on returning home. Monash overcame the prime minister's dislike for formal education and instead contacted established institutions, mainly in England but also in several other countries. They were urged to open their doors to the diggers. A variety of institutions from Oxford and Cambridge universities to farms, factories and even trade unions, invited them in. There were a few odd requests. One Tasmanian wanted to be a lion tamer. By the time a circus was found that was willing to help, he was on his way home. A Queenslander thought it would be useful to have a qualification in deep-sea diving. Only the navy had such a school in England. A few applied to join cricket teams as professionals.

There was a big rush to Yorkshire to learn about the wool manufacturing industry. But diggers were welcomed all over Europe. Some studied for exams in a special school set up at the mouth of the Somme that would prepare them to enter Australian universities, the civil service or professions.

Monash weaved his creative administrative magic to turn the corps of trained belligerents into a huge educational enterprise, in which 40,000 took part. It was hoped that the result would be to create a pool of qualified men who could slip back into civilian life with less difficulty than if they had done nothing while waiting in camps of boredom and potential trouble in France and England.

Monash and Hughes had several meetings over repatriation in the first months. Hughes' attitude towards him had deteriorated ever since the day at the Australian and New Zealand Luncheon Club. Monash came to realise that Hughes had a complex about being overshadowed by him in London, and it led to the prime minister being discourteous and treating him shabbily. Monash, in response, had trouble being polite.[5] He had the feeling that the prime minister was intent on slowing up the repatriation process.

Monash may have mentioned this to Murdoch, who now focused more positively on Monash. He was the key to weighty stories. There was nothing more important to Australians in the last months of 1918 and most of 1919 than how and when the diggers were coming home. Murdoch had an eye to the headlines with the papers at home and the pressure from the public was to speed up the diggers' return. Aware that Hughes was against this, Murdoch saw Monash as a useful conduit. After some natural initial caution, Monash began to see the newspaperman as helpful to him too.

Murdoch, in an apparent break with Hughes, began sending back dispatches that suggested the government was slowing down the return of the diggers. It put pressure on the federal Cabinet in Melbourne. Hughes, virtually an expatriate prime minister in London, was forced to tell the press that everything was being done to hasten the diggers' return. A Murdoch cable early in 1919 was stark. He wrote that the government had capitulated over the issue and called Monash the 'driving force'. He even warned that if politicians got in his way, Monash would go home.

Murdoch wrote: 'Never can there be any questions about Monash's brain. It is there, a living, searching, strong intelligence, breeding ideas, and judging them shrewdly. His motto is Action, and his energy already pulsates through the demobilisation scheme.'[6]

Encouraged by the line Murdoch was now taking, Monash responded more often to his requests for interviews, which allowed him to put his case.

'If we can concert,' Murdoch quoted him saying, 'the means and machinery to enable our men to equip themselves for their future industrial life, then we are going to render a service to our nation that cannot be measured.'[7]

Such a patriotic appeal and sentiment helped Monash fight Hughes' surreptitious filibustering.

The only signs of unrest surfaced in the 3rd Division's artillery early in January 1919 when the soldiers went on strike. Monash urged Gellibrand to go easy on his men, and he blamed the problem on officers being too strict. Monash sent a message to the gunners, urging them to be patient. The repat scheme would take effect soon. This helped, along with input from Hobbs, to smooth matters.

Chapter 73

The Light Horse Rides Again

Chauvel could not go to the United Kingdom on leave so he arranged for Sybil to visit Cairo in January 1919. They embarked with a small party of friends on a tour of the entire region in the footsteps of the Anzac Mounted Division, the Desert Column and the Desert Mounted Column. This would take them through Egypt, the Sinai, Palestine and Syria.

Near Beirut they encountered inscriptions in the cliff-face close to the mouth of the Dog River. They had been put there by Syria's conquerors from Ramesses II and Alexander the Great to Napoleon, who had recorded their victories. It was decided that the Desert Mounted Column should carve a few notches there too, just for the record. The job was entrusted to the British Royal

Engineers. To Chauvel's annoyance they changed his wording to make sure the current 'myth' about the Arab connection with the British was maintained in a 'politically correct' but factually inaccurate manner. It read: 'The British Desert Mounted Corps aided by the Arab forces of King Hussein captured Damascus, Homs and Aleppo, October 1918.'

This was useful for the British in the Sykes-Picot Agreement. The Arabs had to have been seen to conquer the cities mentioned so that they could make claims against the French in the upcoming peace conferences to settle politics, national geographic boundaries and 'ownership' in the Middle East.

Chauvel made sure that it was changed to an official inscription: 'The Desert Mounted Corps, Composed of British, Australian, New Zealand and Indian Cavalry, and the Arab forces of King Hussein, Captured Damascus, Homs and Aleppo, October 1918.'

If anything, Chauvel's correction was overly generous given that the cavalry was 70 per cent Anzac.

●

The Chauvels' grand tour included travelling north to Aleppo and east to Deraa. They met Allenby in Jerusalem, dined with acting chief administrator of Palestine, Ronald Storrs, and stayed at the Hotel Victoria in Damascus, which Chauvel found less comfortable than his last stay in Djemal Pasha's luxury house.

They arrived at Haifa on 20 March 1919 and were greeted with the news from Field Marshal Wavell that Egypt was in revolt against British rule. He had to wait where he was. The rail to Cairo had been destroyed. Chauvel took Sybil via Qantara on a guarded train.

The Light Horse, waiting patiently to be shipped home, were rearmed and re-equipped to put down the uprising. They were issued with horses, which was doubly frustrating for the men who had shot their mounts rather than obey the British Government's decision to have them commandeered for the Indian Army. Chauvel had passed on control of the Desert Mounted Column, but he felt obligated to stay, especially with his Anzacs spread around Egypt and few British troops in the area. Insurgents were tearing up railway lines and destroying communications. British residents were being attacked in the streets and their homes raided by Muslim extremists. Egyptian students were marching through Cairo carrying banners proclaiming 'Down with the British' and 'Egypt for Egyptians'.

Violence flared everywhere. Soldiers and nurses were attacked. Some were murdered. Civil servants went on strike. The outbreak spread to Egypt's lower provinces and to the Delta lands to the north. The situation was dangerous and the responsibility for any counteraction would fall to the Light Horse. The indefatigable Wilson and his 3rd Brigade were already galloping across the desert to a train that would speed them to Cairo.

•

The 11th Light Horse Regiment was rushed to the equine base at Moascar, 200 kilometres from Cairo where it was re-equipped, remounted and then dispatched to various towns. It left Moascar on 18 March for patrol duties extending to Tel el Kabir. Escorts were provided for barges moving on the canals.

A soldier of the 3rd Gurkha Regiment was murdered by Arabs while on patrol. The killers were found by the 11th's Aboriginal specialist trackers, Corporals Allen and Smith, in a village near Abu Hammad on the Cairo–Port Said railway. The village leader refused to take responsibility and became defiant. The troopers surrounded the village. Women and children were escorted out. The troopers then marched in and attacked the men in fist fights. Once satisfied they had made their point, they set fire to the houses.

After the incident, three villagers confessed to the crime. They were later court-martialled and sentenced to death. According to the 11th Light Horse historian, the Australian action resulted in no more trouble from rebels in the area. A few days later, British HQ decreed that no 'native villages' were to be burnt, without direct reference to the incident.

'Although the rebellion went off to a flying start,' he noted, 'the sight of Australian detachments galloping through town and villages soon caused the rebels to lose their nerve.'[1]

•

The grumbles from the troopers were few. They had been looking forward to going home, but the sense of comradeship that arose as regiments and squadrons reformed for battle galvanised them for the job. It was all most of them had known for the early years of their adult life.

All but two regiments of the Anzacs were back in the saddle. The troopers would have preferred organised battles. They had little time for the hide-and-seek war that terrorists and guerillas went in for. When rioters came into the open they were no match for the charging rifle- and swordsmen, hardened soldiers who had taken on everything over the last three years (or four if they had also been at Gallipoli). For them, it was hardly a challenge to put down mobs. However, in several sharp skirmishes about twenty of the troopers ended up casualties.

Some of the biggest names in the Light Horse—Wilson, Olden and Foster, officers who could convince their men to go anywhere with them—were in the saddle and leading once more. The Light Horse broke the rioters' collective will. Many of the ringleaders were rounded up and put in chain gangs to repair the railways they had blown up.

'The Australians and New Zealanders formed the greater part of the British force employed,' Gullett noted. 'Owing to their mobility, their reputation, and their decisiveness, they were the dominant factor in temporarily restoring tranquility to Egypt.'[2]

With all quiet on the Eastern Front, the troopers were billeted with good rations, before embarking at last on the long boat trip home. Chauvel too, could rest easy. He and Sybil returned to England to prepare for an Anzac parade, a Dominions march through London and a pleasant reunion with Monash and Vic. The two men had many notes to compare and many questions to ask each other despite their long correspondence.

•

Chauvel was told of Monash's problem with the British shipping controller: Australia was readying troops faster than he could supply ships. Monash treated the situation as a battle. The con- troller was the enemy, and he soon realised what German Army commanders faced when tackling the Australian.

'I have now got the Shipping Controller absolutely beaten,' he wrote in full combat language, 'have created such a pool of troops in England, and have secured such a rapid rate of delivery from France . . . that by no possibility can the Shipping Controller catch up to me.'

Monash was back on the Somme, attacking the *mont* and Péronne: 'I am not giving him any rest. Scarcely a day passes that I do not deliver an attack upon him from a new angle.'[3]

Monash loved the new position's challenge. It was just the right therapy for him in 1919, as his men launched into their own rehabilitation with study and training. The more problems that arose, the more he relished the role. While it was accurate to blame the shipping controller, he never thought the job he oversaw would blow out to create such a huge demand. Carriers were needed for several countries, including South Africa, India, the United States and Canada, as governments struggled against bureaucracy and shipping companies to sail troops home.

Monash also had to face administrative bungles. The British High Command changed its mind several times on whether it needed Australian troops to occupy Germany or not. This affected tens of thousands, and helped lead to unrest in the artillery of 3rd Division, who were given five different directives in three months concerning whether they would be needed or not. It was infuriating for him and them to be pushed and pulled as if they were still on the front line. Monash began to use his weight here and there, and more than a few British bureaucrats in the military and government felt both his wrath and the subtle use of his now intrinsic, intangible power. In the heady first year after the war, his name carried weight, and he used it.

One of many examples occurred when the British War Office attempted to veto an Anzac Day farewell march through London. The excuse was that there would be a parade of Dominion troops eight days later, on 3 May. Monash would have none of it and insisted on the Anzac Day parade. He had become father to this memorial and was not going to have his child disappear on its fourth birthday. He would make one call to Haig. If he didn't fix it, Monash would contact the King. The monarch had often told him to be in touch if he wanted *anything*. So far he had only taken him up on this offer by accepting leather vests for the 3rd Division when the King had said the lads would freeze in France in the winter without them.

He didn't have to use his ultimate contact in the British system. The War Office, on the threat of Haig being approached, capitulated. Monash reminded his troops: 'You represent the great and immortal Australian Army Corps. Every man should try and look as he ought to feel, proud of his division and the Australian Army.'[4]

Monash and Hobbs rode at the head of the 5000 diggers on the 7-kilometre march. It wound from Hyde Park next to Buckingham Palace along The Mall across Trafalgar Square, then down The Strand to Australia House, where the cheering crowd was twenty deep. Monash took the salute from the Prince of Wales, Haig and Chauvel, representing his Light Horse. Hughes, again in an inferior role, was on the saluting stand too. It was another reminder of Monash's capacity for the poignant cere-monial occasion, something which politicians aped and envied, but for which they never quite had the drilled skills. Overhead Australian pilots did some spectacular, if not overly adventurous diving and loop the loops.

Monash's fetish for precision and strong performances was satisfied by the Anzac Day event that he was determined to immortalise.

Chapter 74

Hughes Struts World Stage

Australian Prime Minister Billy Hughes attended the Paris Peace Conference of 1919 secure in the knowledge that his armed forces had done exceedingly well on the two major battlefronts of the Great War. He was a feisty, witty fellow at the best of times but the efforts of Monash and Chauvel and their respective armies had equipped him with extra confidence as he strove for his main objective: to secure Australian (and British Empire) control over the old German colonies in New Guinea and the islands, including Nauru. Australian armed forces had seized these territories in 1914 and Hughes wanted to annex them under direct Australian rule. He was now ready to 'fight' in political terms to blunt German aims, and those of other empires, such as the Japanese in the Pacific, for the foreseeable future.

A French journalist covering the Paris Conference saw Hughes as 'frail, narrow-shouldered, stooped, with the long metallic face, seamed with lines, of a Breton peasant. At first he sits doubled up like a spider and lets others talk . . . but suddenly he straightens out, darts forward his thin arms and the double trident of stretched-out fingers, and cuts through the flabbiness of the discussion with a word.'[1]

He was initially opposed by US President Woodrow Wilson, who idealistically yet naively believed the colonies of great empires were only 'territories held in trust till the day their peoples would gain independence and rule themselves'. However, Wilson was not naïve enough to believe anything other than self-interest was at play in Paris at the conference. He distrusted the old empires, who were set to carve up the ex-colonial territories of the defeated powers, notably Germany and Turkey. But, again submerged in reverie ahead of his time rather than reality, Wilson wanted to make a new and 'more just' world order. His views and aims clashed with those of Hughes. At one point in the Paris talks, he asked Hughes if he was going to oppose the wishes of the twelve hundred million people represented at the conference against the few million Australians represented by Hughes. In typical style, the prime minister retorted: 'I represent 60,000 dead; those Australian personnel who gave their lives for Australia's interests in the war.'[2]

It was a telling point for which Wilson had no answer. The American Army lost 53,402 in combat (figures that were later doubled to take into account those who died from influenza ʳing and after the war). The US population was then 92 million. ˑalia lost 53,560 from its 4 million. The numbers reflected ˑact of the two nations in the war. Most of the Australian casualties happened in the big, deciding battles of the war on two fronts. (The United States was not in the Middle East and was brought into the fighting on the Western Front after the decisive battles, primarily Amiens, were won.) Most of the American losses occurred in fringe battles or those other than the deciding conflicts, and when the almost spent Germans were retreating.

Wilson, frustrated and outperformed, called Hughes a 'pestiferous varmint', a description that the prime minister was happy to dine out on. Unlike his two grand armies, Hughes was fighting above his weight. Like them, he made impressive headway. He settled for annexation under another name; a form of colonial administration—'mandates'—which gave Australia control of New Guinea. A prime motivation for Hughes was securing Australian borders to the north, where he feared expansion of the Japanese Empire. On paper at least, Hughes came away from the conference with some 'wins' apart from the mandated territory. He helped guarantee that Germany would be held responsible for the full cost of the war and, most controversially of all, thwarted Japanese ambitions for a 'racial equality' clause in the peace treaty. He also sank, for the moment, Japanese desires in the South Pacific. Hughes also boosted the British Empire as an Imperial trading and defence bloc.

He had grand 'form' spruiking on behalf of the empire. He'd arrived in Britain in March 1916, when national morale was low. He was immediately coopted by Lloyd George, then munitions minister, and newspaper baron Lord Northcliffe (thanks to his quasi-protégé, Keith Murdoch) to go on a speaking tour with the slogan 'Wake up England!' Hughes was a most effective speaker. He exhorted Britain to obliterate Germany, turn its back on free trade, and establish a far greater economic union with all countries of the empire. It would have flattered his considerable ego that 50,000 women signed a petition in an attempt to cajole him into standing for the UK Parliament. He engendered strong support from influential businessmen and manufacturers, which led to him being offered a Cabinet post. 'The Little Digger', as he was known, was even touted as England's next prime minister.

Lloyd George would have something to say about that but there was no doubt that he had the highest regard for his little Welsh mate, even though they often broke into their native tongue in heated arguments that mystified the English.

Before the conference, armed with the reports of the success of his diggers and troopers, Hughes began attacking the terms of the Armistice devised by Wilson, especially the clause that said Germany should pay reparations only, and not an additional 'indemnity' to the victors. Hughes was more vociferous than any representative of the empire, and became Lloyd George's 'attack dog'. Before the conference, he did not let up on attacking Wilson's 'vision', laudable in theory, of establishing the League of Nations and international free trade. Instead, as ever, Hughes plugged for preferential trade policies that would block Germany's economic recovery and strengthen the empire.

The British prime minister, not without his own cunning, saw the benefit of letting loose a political leader who appealed so strongly to British emotions, instincts and prejudices, including racial ones. It saved Lloyd George from having to appear the demagogue on the eve of a general election in late 1918. He appointed Hughes chairman of the 'Indemnity Committee', which would attempt to squeeze as much as possible out of the vanquished Germans.

With Hughes' strong guidance and influence, the committee reported that Germany should pay the astronomical cost of 24 billion pounds. It was the ambit claim to outdo all others, and ignored the complaints of the pacifist British Treasury official John Maynard Keynes, who wanted to let the Germans off far more lightly. Lloyd George shrewdly used the figure in the election campaign a month before the conference to fire up the electorate. It fell for the manipulation and returned him to office in a landslide.

Despite Hughes' good intentions on behalf of Australia and the empire, his forceful approach to 'making Germany pay' helped push the Germans into an economic abyss, and seeded the conditions for fascism to arise in Europe.

Hughes' concerns with Australian security were tied to the White Australia Policy, originally conceived during Federation in 1901 to protect workers from immigrant foreigners. It was feared that Asians would take their jobs and eventually outnumber 'the few million misplaced Europeans at the bottom of Asia'. The policy was blatantly racist, as were those of most nations at the time. Hughes effectively vetoed Japan's desire to be acknowledged as an equal with the white Anglo-Saxon empires in forming the League of Nations. Japan already resented being discriminated against in immigration, investment and trade by the British Empire and the Americans. The conference snub was humiliating. It remained a simmering issue with the Japanese, especially military extremists, who saw the peace talk outcomes as useful propaganda for their aims. Japan, itself racist in the extreme, wished to be the dominant power in the region, no matter what the ethnic make-up of their proposed subject nations. Their slaughter of more than fifteen million Chinese, beginning with the seizing of Manchuria in 1931 and ending in 1945, was the strongest testimony to their beliefs at the time.

•

Hughes was prominent at the Peace Conference but he was not responsible for destroying Wilson's fourteen-point plan for his postwar new world order. The bargaining of the major powers sank the US President's idealism and the hopes of the many colonial leaders, who read into the plan a promise of self-determination. The big three—Wilson, Clemenceau and Lloyd George—had meetings in which the American was left 'bamboozled', according to a disgruntled Keynes, as Clemenceau pushed for the economic crushing of Germany. Clemenceau would have been happy to see the defeated nation dismantled. (By the time Germany was smashed again in World War II, the victors had learnt from their mistake. The Americans instituted the $14 billion Marshall Plan for Western Europe to reconstruct infrastructure, regenerate heavy industry and revive European commerce. This produced the 'German Economic Miracle'.)

Both Monash and Chauvel were more concerned with Australia's defence in the Asia Pacific region. From experience, they were keen for their country to have a strong military. Their submissions to Hughes about Australia's achievements and needs gave him significant leverage as he strutted Paris with a veto in reconstructing the world postwar.

The events of 1918 put Australia centre of the world stage for the one and only time in its short history.

•

Chauvel's report to Hughes added to the prime minister's confidence at the Paris Conference. Despite the propaganda about Lawrence in the Middle East, which grew to mythic proportions in 1919 and beyond, Hughes was well aware that Chauvel and his 30,000 horsemen, wielding bayonet, sword or rifle, had the biggest impact on the defeat of the Ottoman Empire in the Middle East war from 1914 to 1918. The Light Horse influence had been buried under the Lawrence mania, and other than a handful of antipodeans, historians and reporters gave the 'credit' for defeating the Turks to Allenby. The Desert Mounted Column, commanded by Chauvel, was 70 per cent Anzac troopers and cameleers. But if mentioned at all, they were rated below the British Army and Cavalry, which accounted for just 15 per cent, at most, of the column.

Monash realised that the diggers' efforts would be swamped in the wash-up of reporting and writing, and overlooked, with the huge number of historians from the United Kingdom, France and the United States focusing their gazes on the experiences and achievements of their own countrymen. The situation was not helped by Bean's work—he struggled to give credit where it was due because of his skewed attitude towards Monash, which diminished, by association, the diggers' impact. At one point Bean even refused Monash access to files when he wished to write a report on Amiens to mark its tenth anniversary. However, Bean could not stop the publication of Monash's book *The Australian Victories in France in 1918*. He rushed it out in 1919, and it sold well in Australia and the United Kingdom but did not have the impact he would have wished.[3]

●

Chauvel's struggle was even more challenging, though over time the troopers' global legacy has become as strong as their more widely reported digger brothers under Monash.

The Third Battle of Gaza, when the 4th Light Horse Brigade had its amazing breakthrough at Beersheba on 31 October 1917, was a key factor in the Middle East victory. But every one of the other 25 battles—fought in combination with the indefatigable British Infantry and supported by Lawrence and the Arabs—cumulatively pulverized the enemy over 30 months and ended Turkish hegemony in the Middle East.

Their input at the critical moments enabled Chauvel's horsemen to defeat the Turks, who had ruled the Middle East for 400 years. It opened the region to the West, which then extracted its lifeblood for the next century: oil. The troopers would not have been conscious of their impact beyond the battlefield. But over the decades, those who followed developments in the region they had once conquered would become aware of the consequences of their success.

As Western industry grew exponentially, especially in the second half of the twentieth century, more and more oil was needed to fuel developments. In 1944 a prominent petroleum geologist, Everette DeGolyer, reported to the US Government that he was certain the Middle East nations were sitting atop at least 25 billion barrels of oil—a third of which he believed was under Saudi Arabia. His report to the State Department commented: 'The oil in this region is the greatest single prize in all history.'

His estimate proved to be conservative. Chauvel or any trooper learning this would have reflected that a quarter of a century earlier they were responsible for the eventual exploitation by the West of this 'black gold'.

The second major outcome of victory in the Middle East was the migration of Jews into Palestine. The troopers would have been aware of their impact at the time. But no one could have predicted the creation of the state of Israel 30 years later and the developments and chaos in the Middle East that followed in the next seven decades.

A third legacy was the fulfillment of Arab nationalism in Syria, Iraq, Lebanon, Saudi Arabia and other states that would not have emerged, however chaotically and at times brutally, without the roll back of the Ottoman Empire.

For Australians, even though the digger and Light Horse efforts were never on home soil, there was significance of another kind. The war experience, beginning with the horrors and failures of eight months on Gallipoli, followed by three years of battle success in the Middle East and on the Western Front, developed the spirit of a nation. Before those dark, frenetic years from 1914 to 1919, Australia—founded in 1901—was a nation in name only. In 1914 the country was still a collection of rival states with no real sense of cohesion outside the federal government, then based in Melbourne. The values of mateship, selflessness, courage, sacrifice and ingenuity were forged and squeezed out of those packed years of conflict on the Eastern and Western Fronts. These formed the backbone and overriding mentality of a nation with democratic ideals that Monash articulated so well.

POSTSCRIPT

Chapter 75

John Monash

Monash's force had done most at the big battles—Amiens, St Quentin, Péronne and the Hindenburg Line being just a few of them—to defeat the German Army. His elevation to power and success led him to go his own way, occasionally in defiance of his superiors, and this began on Gallipoli. He felt then and learnt later that he was better equipped to command on the field and off it in modern warfare than any member of the British High Command. But he had to finesse, even at times bully, his way forward to achieve his main aim, once it was apparent that his battlefield methods proved successful.

Monash was regarded as the most outstanding battle commander of World War I. Most experts ranked him as the finest commander on the Allied side, although revisionists in recent decades in Australia and the United Kingdom, with a disregard for the facts, have tried to elevate others. Among those to recognise that Monash had no peer among the battle commanders was Sir Basil Liddell Hart, the leading English military commentator and historian of the time. He said Monash might well have replaced Haig as commander-in-chief of the British forces, had the war continued into 1919. Liddell Hart was a great believer in the advances in technology changing the face of conflict, something at which Monash excelled at understanding and utilising.

'He was in some ways an utter contrast to the traditional idea of a great military commander,' Liddell Hart commented. 'He, more than anyone, fulfilled the idea that gradually developed in the war—that the scale and nature of operations required a "big business" type of commander, a great constructive and organizing brain. His views were as large as his capacity.'[1]

Lloyd George, who had been thrashing around in 1918 for a Haig replacement, came to the same conclusion, too late to do anything about it.

'Monash would . . . have risen to the height of it [commander-in-chief],' Lloyd George wrote. 'But the greatness of his abilities were not brought to the attention of the [British War] Cabinet in any of the dispatches . . . Monash was, according to the testimony of those who knew well his genius for war and what he accomplished by it, the most resourceful General in the whole of the British Army.'[2]

These views were supported by a long list of experts for decades after the war. They included British historian A.J.P. Taylor, who portrayed Monash as 'the only General of creative originality produced in the First World War'. Sir Anthony Eden, who saw combat in the 1914–1918 war and went on to be British prime minister in the mid-1950s, said much the same thing, as did the great World War II commander, Field Marshal Bernard Law Montgomery (of Alamein), Sir Ian Hamilton and Sir Winston Churchill.[3]

Liddell Hart, who had done his homework on Monash far beyond his combat duties, further remarked that the strongest testimony to his capacity was 'the distance he went in spite of a tremendous compound handicap of prejudice'.[4] The historian was considering Monash's four alleged handicaps: birth (in a far-flung colony); race (Jewish); background (German descent); and the fact that he was from the militia, not the regular army.

Unfortunately the integrity of the written record of the Great War was badly distorted regarding Monash, largely due to Australian historian Charles Bean. He had failed to bring Monash down during the war, but then did much to denigrate him in private, and downgrade his impact in the official history. There were several confected and fabricated comments made during the war when he was trying to unseat Monash once he became commander-in-chief of the 1st AIF.

Bean's subterfuge drew out an outstanding feature of John Monash's character: his capacity to rise above the prejudice without complaint. He was the outsider who overcame enemies of many varieties and was instrumental in the decisive moments in 1918 that won the war.

Monash never forgot, and did most to commemorate, the Gallipoli experience. When the British military and historians wished to forget it, he was first to hold an Anzac Day Service—one year after 25 April 1915—in the Sinai Desert. He fostered the tradition. Monash viewed the Australian action on the Turkish peninsula as important in creating an Australian 'spirit'. It also marked a delineation to him of the sense of being Australian as opposed to 'British'.

In the 1920s, as Australia ran into a depression, those on the far left and right, inspired by revolutions in Russia, Germany and Italy, urged him to take over the country as a dictator. Everyone knew he had the power to raise an army. He was aware of his position, with about 180,000 returned diggers, all still averaging less than thirty-five years of age in the mid-1920s, and most still willing to fight under him. But Monash was no Lenin, Hitler or Mussolini. He was the opposite in every respect. Yet when a crisis did occur early in November 1923 in Melbourne, Monash demonstrated his postwar potency. The police went on strike. The Victorian Government pleaded with him to help stop the murdering and pillaging mobs in the city's streets and suburbs. Monash agreed on his terms. He called for a curfew. Within 48 hours, he raised an armed brigade made up of ex-servicemen. They soon quelled the rioters. By Monday the mobs had dispersed. The curfew was lifted. On Tuesday the Melbourne Cup was run as usual. Monash turned up with his partner Lizette Bentwitch (Vic had died in 1920).[5] The members' enclosure clapped and cheered him. This show of strength inspired ex-diggers across the nation. Yet he had no aspirations to take over the federal government, which many were demanding. In speeches, radio and newspaper comments, Monash made his views clear. He became a little exasperated. In a letter to one would-be powerbroker in Sydney he wrote:

What do you and your friends want me to do? To lead a movement to upset the Constitution, oust the jurisdiction of Parliament, and usurp the Government power? If so, I have no ambition to embark on High Treason, which any such action would amount to.

What would you say if a similar proposal were made by the Communists and Socialists to seize political power for the benefit of the proletariat and the extinction of the bourgeoisie, as they have done in Russia? Would you not call that Revolution and Treason to the Crown and Constitution?

Depend upon it, the only hope for Australia is the ballot box and an educated electorate.[6]

Monash believed, like Churchill, that democracy was the best option. He and tens of thousands of other Australians had sacrificed much in the fight against dictators and in defence of democracy. To turn around and become a dictator would have defied all that had been achieved by the Anzacs in World War I. It would have been utterly disrespectful to the 60,000 Australians who had given their lives in the conflict on the Western and Eastern Fronts and on Gallipoli.

•

Throughout the 1920s, Monash could not ignore these troublesome calls for him to be a dictator, but he got on with his busy life, despite failing health due to high blood pressure. He created, from an idea on paper to inception, Victoria's State Electricity Commission, which served to electrify the entire state and drag Victoria from a near backwater to the most productive state in the Commonwealth. Monash also served as vice-chancellor of Melbourne University, his alma mater. He scheduled his time by the minute, mainly in service to the community, education and the arts.

Yet Monash's influence still troubled those whose power

would be usurped by it. The recently elected Labor Prime Minister James Scullin saw the risks and noted the burden on Monash. He promoted him to General and asked him to attend the opening of the new city of New Delhi and take a relaxed tour of India. He was away for three months from December 1930 to March 1931. The political pressure eased while he was out of the country. Monash's health failed soon after his return, but he insisted on attending Anzac Day commemorations on his white charger, and taking his last march-past.

He died on 8 October 1931, aged 66.

Harry Chauvel spoke at Monash's funeral and outlined his achievements in various commands during the Great War, culminating with the Battle of Amiens and the advances made after it. Chauvel noted that Monash had given up a large part of his life 'to the service of his country, which he served faithfully and well to the very end. We mourn Sir John Monash as a great soldier and great citizen. His life will ever be an example of patriotism to those who follow.'

Chapter 76

Harry Chauvel

After the war the Chauvel family lived in a flat in South Yarra, Melbourne, opposite Christ Church and close to army HQ. Chauvel had no other intention than continuing his career with the army and was appointed Inspector-General of the Australian Military Forces on 10 December 1919. He was also made a member of the Council of Defence, the body that determined all defence policy submitted to the defence minister. Monash joined him early in 1920, and the two effectively ran defence for several years together. They socialised often and invited each other to private celebrations of their important victories and family events. Chauvel was to experience the unmatched preparation of his friend at meetings. Monash always came better researched than anyone else on the council. He would make his case like a barrister with a brief. More than once Chauvel returned home and spoke in admiration as much as complaint to his wife Sybil about 'Bloody Monash!' and his application to hard background work.[1]

•

Chauvel liked his routines. One was to ride in South Yarra's Domain (usually the Tan track around the Botanic Gardens) on a black gelding that was brought to him from a nearby remount depot six mornings a week. On Sundays he never missed attending church. He would later become a warden and was occasionally asked to give a sermon. Chauvel's experiences in the holy cities and fighting in a region so replete with biblical history allowed him to speak with authority and feeling. He would not exactly follow a calling, but he felt it a duty to impart his thoughts and strong beliefs. He was conscious of being spared in the war, when so many Australians had not been. Nor did he have any physical or mental scars.

His faith sustained him.

•

Chauvel's record was naturally appropriated by Edmund Allenby, whose reputation was restored. Allenby would be remembered above and beyond his rivals such as Haig and Gough in the British High Command. He could thank Chauvel, and to a lesser extent T.E. Lawrence, who would go on to world fame from the 1920s due to books and later films (notably David Lean's *Lawrence of Arabia*). Most of them contained slanted propaganda that focused on the 'romance' of Lawrence and the Arabs, and ignored the predominant force of Chauvel and his Anzac Mounted Column.

Monash did his utmost to counter the British propaganda when he spoke at a dinner the night before Chauvel returned to Australia in 1919. Monash drew on his deep comprehension of the Napoleonic Wars and reminded his audience that the Australians had a bigger, more powerful mounted army than Napoleon. He cited the Battles of Romani and Beersheba and stated that few, if any, in history had matched those instances of brilliant tactical command. He suggested that Chauvel's efforts using horsemen and cavalry were greater because of the massive odds against them in both battles. Monash made a further claim: that Beersheba was the greatest ever cavalry charge in history.

> Napoleon was an outstanding commander, but he often had ten times the number [of cavalry/troopers] Chauvel had at Beersheba . . . just ponder what the Australian troopers faced . . . banks of machine guns and artillery, thousands of entrenched armed Turks, snipers, and planes dropping bombs and strafing the advancing horsemen. Yet they fought through and took the town, which led to the major breakthrough of the Middle East War . . . Compare that again to relatively meagre arms arraigned against Napoleon . . .[2]

Chauvel would never have made such elevated comparisons in public. It would have sounded like boasting. But he was grateful to Monash. They both knew that the British and Americans were dominating the portrayal of how the wars on both fronts were won, and that the forces from the Antipodes would receive short shrift by historians. It was already apparent from the way T.E. Lawrence was being portrayed in newspapers, magazines and in stage plays, that the efforts of the Light Horse would be largely lost to history.

•

'Australia has come out of this war a nation,' Chauvel told a Sydney audience early in October 1919 to mark the first anniversary of the taking of Damascus, 'and it rests with the people of Australia to make it a great nation.' Yet that was the most optimistic comment he made. His message was that Australia should bunker down and prepare for future conflict. The emphasis should be on more training and discipline in the army, which was not what a war-weary nation wished to hear. Nor did many outside the services comprehend his thinking. Only those who had been with him on Gallipoli (and in the Middle East and on the Western Front) understood. Chauvel did not share the hope for lasting peace. He had seen too much that suggested otherwise.

The main lesson from Gallipoli and the Middle East conflict, he said, was that Australia should have an independent force, ready for anything in its region and equipped to help its allies. He was lukewarm about an Australian alliance with the United States, but after Gallipoli he saw merit in not relying on the United Kingdom alone. This was a change from his thinking after the Boer War, which Monash described as 'British Empire Maintenance'. Before Gallipoli, Chauvel was willing to go with the empire anywhere. When on Gallipoli, he went through some soul-searching. Chauvel had been brought up thinking he was British, which was natural given that 'Australia' did not exist. His upper-class British heritage ensured his establishment mentality. He was pleased, but not ecstatic, about the 1901 formation of the

Australian Commonwealth. Chauvel went with the flow. He was a career soldier, not an academic or politician. But after Gallipoli his thoughts changed. He viewed the whole expedition to Turkey of the 75,000-strong Allied Army as folly. He invited trouble expressing his opinion to his superiors, which almost cost him his job. Chauvel saw the campaign to deliver Turkey to the Russian Tsar as a massive waste of life, and an inept military and political move. He felt very much like a pawn in a chess game beyond his influence. Anzacs, he realised fully, were expendable in defence of empire.

•

Harry Chauvel retired as Australian Chief of the General Staff and Inspector-General in 1930. He had fought the good fight in the face of decreasing funds for the army during a depression. He had warned in report after report, year after year, that Australia had to be prepared for threats, not just from acquisitive European powers but from those closer to home. Chauvel was not just suggesting that the numbers in the armed forces should be increased rather than see them dwindle. He was thinking of the attempts to improve the skills and disciplines of the force after the Boer War and before World War I. He again preached the importance of an esprit de corps, and with a stronger voice than in the early 1900s. But the maintenance of this was not the will of the government. Most politicians had not served in the Great War. They were not moved by such rhetoric, as compelling as it was coming from a great old soldier.

He was not alone. Monash had been saying the same thing. He and Chauvel were wary of thinking that negotiating a mutual defence treaty with the United States solved all problems. The government believed that the country was safe under the US umbrella. They could run down the nation's armed services with impunity.

Monash had put it allegorically. The decision to cut military and defence funds was 'like deciding that we will have no more burglaries and then dismissing the police force'. Chauvel agreed. Monash had seen the Americans in action at the end of World War I. He had commanded 50,000 of them, and would not have been comfortable relying on them, or any other nation's army, for Australia's survival as a free and democratic nation. Chauvel, the long-term professional soldier, had not experienced the United States in war. It had not entered the Middle East conflict. Yet he agreed with Monash that every possible defence resource could and should be developed in Australia. They had both commanded the dominant forces in their respective theatres in the critical second half of 1918. They *knew* what was possible if there was the will to build a viable, mobile, flexible military. After Gallipoli, they were critically aware of what could happen to Australian forces if officers and soldiers were not well trained, strong and independent.

But the opposite to their expressed views had occurred. Only Chauvel's strong dedication had kept the force from collapsing altogether. He had met lethargy with vigour, and uninterest in a neglected force with enthusiasm.

He died on 4 March 1945, aged 79, satisfied that Australia would overcome the Japanese threat, which it did when World War II ended five months later.

Chapter 77

The Record: Revised and Buried

Monash's book *The Australian Victories in France in 1918* did well but was swamped by British and American versions of events for the next century. Revisionists, incapable of finding narratives with any integrity, decades after the war, struggled and failed to find other reasons for the Allied victory. Monash and his warrior force of diggers, all volunteers, were hardly mentioned when they were, in reality, the driving force in defeating the German Army, a fact acknowledged by the Germans themselves. The 1st AIF's 100-day *original* blitzkreig (July to October 1918) was the deciding factor. So much so that Adolf Hitler was convinced by General Heinz Guderian to use Monash's tactics and battle plans for the German blitzkreig that consumed much of Europe in the first half of World War II.

In the 1920s and 1930s, T.E. Lawrence's literary opus, *Seven Pillars of Wisdom*, became the accepted 'official' version of events in the Middle East war of 1915 to 1919. The brilliant, romanticised movie, *Lawrence of Arabia*, based on the book, was first seen in 1962. It distorted the facts to another level and cemented Lawrence's part-fictional account of the Eastern Front conflict.

Chauvel in 1921 wrote a short account of events in the Middle East and placed it in the Australian War Memorial archives. His analysis was completely at odds with that of Lawrence. Where Lawrence did a sterling job in organising the Arabs to hold one Turkish army on the Hejaz Railway, Chauvel and his Anzac-dominated Desert Mounted Column were the main force in defeating two Turkish armies in Palestine, Jordan and Syria. That task completed, Chauvel's force swept across to help Lawrence and the Arabs defeat the Turks that had been stationed on the railway.

The most important generals and their armies on two of the three major fronts of the Great War should be remembered and celebrated for their efforts in 1918, the only year in which Australia strode centre stage and had an impact on world history.

The way to ensure this recognition is to promote Monash and Chauvel to the five-star rank of Field Marshal. There is precedent. Birdwood was given this status in 1925; Blamey in 1950; and Prince Philip in 1954. With due respect to all three, their records, and those of all British Field Marshals of World War I, are inferior to those of Monash and Chauvel, whose elevation is long overdue.

Acknowledgements

First and foremost, I wish to thank Sue Hines, publisher at Allen & Unwin, who wanted a different, compelling narrative on the Great War. I had long held the view that the Anzac experience on Gallipoli, as important as it was in comprehending Australian history, had swamped the much more powerful impact of the 1st AIF in 1918 on the two major battle fronts that decided the 1914–1918 war's outcome. Military historians, academics and others, through first, lack of comprehension, or second, a desire to push other agendas, have failed to acknowledge the integrity of events of that time. Whenever you hear or see the trigger words 'glorifying', 'revisionist' or 'Australia was fighting above its weight,' you know the commentator falls into one of those two categories, or more often than not, both.

I believe this book's account, based on the real-time events and original sources, was necessary to put on the record so that the accomplishments of the 1st AIF are understood before we enter the second century since 1918, and before a plethora of unconvincing claims will be made in explaining the events and outcome of the war. They will feature arguments about Field Marshal Rawlinson's achievements, or even that of Field Marshal Haig, on the Western Front. The Americans will push the 'success' of General Pershing. Those three and any number of other main players in 1918 owe any impact at all to the overriding brilliance and genius of John Monash when the battles with the German army really counted.

Similarly, in the Middle East, T.E. Lawrence will gain most accolades from the British, while Field Marshal Allenby will be given much recognition. But neither man individually, or in combination, had anything like the achievements of Harry Chauvel and the Desert Mounted Column, which was 75 per cent Anzac.

Others to offer help, encouragement, advice, information and perspectives were Tim Fischer, Mike Guy, Major General Jim Barry, Leon Levin, Thos Hodgson, Jack Grossman, Colin Bennett, Michael Bennett, Rod Kemp, David Kemp and Richard Joslin.

Notes

CHAPTER 2

1 Bean was not as competent a reporter as he was a war chronicler. He did everything from Gallipoli on to hold Monash's advance back, or even destroy him. Bean hated the idea of a Jew running the Australian Army or in any senior post. He preferred an Anglo-Saxon, with his pro-British, pro-Empire vision. But it went beyond this to a more personal vendetta, which lasted several decades and infected views about Monash for the next century at the Australian War Memorial, which Bean helped create.

CHAPTER 4

1 Terraine, *Douglas Haig*, p. 53.
2 Monash War Letters, 30 September 1916, NLA MS 1884, S4.

CHAPTER 5

1 Monash, *War Letters of General Monash*, p. 161.
2 Chauvel to wife Sybil, 3 December 1916. Chauvel Papers, AWM.
3 Clay, *King, Kaiser, Tsar*, p. 337.
4 Due to Monash's influence, none of the small number of Australian army volunteers charged in 1918 with mutiny was executed. Australia, under Monash's direct influence, had a 'no execution' policy. This prompted a telling exchange between Monash and Haig. Haig noted, critically, that Australia had the worst incarceration record of all the Allied armies. Monash retorted: 'That's because we do not execute, Douglas.'
5 Monash, *War Letters of General Monash*, 15 May 1917, p. 173.

CHAPTER 8

1 Terraine, *Douglas Haig*, p. 366.

2 Ibid.

3 Bean, *Official History*, Vol. II, p. 245.

4 Terraine, *Douglas Haig*, p. 367.

5 Serle, *John Monash*, footnote, p. 283.

6 Hyatt, 'Sir Arthur Currie at Passchendaele', p. 100.

7 Currie was caught in an embezzlement scandal in 1913 relating to his real estate company and he faced bankruptcy. To pay off his debts, he diverted government funds set aside for his regiment. Late in the war when he had achieved much, rich friends paid off his debts and thus avoided probable prosecution for Currie.

CHAPTER 9

1 Hammond, *History of the 11th Light Horse Regiment*, p. 79.

CHAPTER 10

1 Terraine, *Douglas Haig*, p. 215.

CHAPTER 11

1 Asprey, *The German High Command at War*, pp. 63–5.

2 Ibid.

3 Ibid.

4 Ibid.

CHAPTER 12

1 Newcombe was a royal engineer and one of the men involved in Allenby's stepped up 'association' with Prince Feisal's force.

CHAPTER 13

1 Hogg, *The Guns 1914–1918*, pp. 134–5.

2 Edmonds, *History of the Great War, 1918*, pp. 396–7.

3 Blake, *The Private Papers of Douglas Haig, 1914–1918*, p. 296.

4 Ibid., p. 298.

5 Clemenceau, *Grandeur and Misery*, p. 39.

CHAPTER 14

1 Monash, *Australian Victories*, pp. 26–8.

2 Ibid., p. 26.

3 Ibid., p. 27.

4 Ibid., p. 27.

5 Private diary of Captain Paul Simonson, p. 145.

6 Monash, *Australian Victories*, pp. 26–8.

7 Monash War Letters, entries in 1916, 1917, 1918, NLA MS 1884, S3, S4.

CHAPTER 15
1 Monash, *Australian Victories*, p. 34.
2 Ibid.
3 The items from the Red Baron's plane are still in Monash's personal collection. The only other person believed to have a piece of the Red Baron's plane is New Zealand film director Peter Jackson.
4 Monash War Letters, NLA MS 1884, S4.

CHAPTER 16
1 Ludendorff, *My War Memories, 1914–1918*, vol. 11, pp. 609–10.

CHAPTER 18
1 Gullett, *Official History*, Vol. VII, p. 613.
2 Olden, *Westralian Cavalry in the War*, p. 229.
3 Ibid., p. 263.

CHAPTER 19
1 Hill, *Chauvel of the Light Horse,* p. 151.
2 Ibid., pp. 160–1; Perry, *Bill the Bastard*, pp. 216–21.

CHAPTER 20
1 Birdwood to Pearce, 13 May 1918, Birdwood Papers, AWM.

CHAPTER 21
1 Birdwood to Pearce, 13 May 1918, Birdwood Papers, AWM.
2 Ibid.
3 Birdwood Papers, 15 June, 25 June 1918, AWM.

CHAPTER 22
1 Monash, *Australian Victories,* p. 48.
2 Ibid., p. 44.
3 Ibid., pp. 44–50.

CHAPTER 23
1 Monash to Birdwood, 29 June 1918, Birdwood Papers, AWM.
2 Thompson, *On Lips of Living Men*, pp. 140–1.
3 Ibid.
4 Ibid.
5 Ibid.
6 Ibid.; also letters between White and Monash, Monash Papers, Box 92, AWM.
7 Monash to Birdwood, 2 July 1918, Birdwood Papers, AWM.
8 Bean, diary, D116, 14 July 1918, 3DRL606, AWM.

CHAPTER 24

1 Anecdote from Lord Wavell, Wavell Papers, Imperial War Museum, London.
2 Monash, *Australian Victories*, pp. 53–5; Bean, *Official History*, Vol. VI, 1918, p. 274.
3 Monash, *Australian Victories*, pp. 55–60.
4 Ibid.
5 Ibid.
6 It began an association between the nations that would increase substantially during 1918, and then through another six wars.
7 Monash, *Australian Victories*, p. 62.

CHAPTER 25

1 Monash, letters with White, Monash Papers, Box 92, AWM.
2 Bean diary, 14 July 1918, 116 3DRL606, AWM.
3 Murdoch, letters, 12 July 1918, Murdoch Papers, AWM.
4 Monash, *Australian Victories*, pp. 62–3.

CHAPTER 26

1 Gullett, *Official History*, p. 676.
2 Lord Kinross, *Ataturk*, p. 135.
3 Ibid., p. 137.

CHAPTER 27

1 Monash War Letters, 2 August 1918, NLA MS 1884, S4.
2 Major Warren Perry, interview, August 2003.
3 The Battle of Amiens was thereafter referred to as a 'Dominion' battle and victory.
4 Monash, *Australian Victories*, p. 73.

CHAPTER 28

1 Monash, letter to Major General Bruche, 10 October 1919, Monash War Letters, NLA MS 1884, S4.
2 Monash, letter to daughter Bertha, 2 August 1918, NLA MS 1884, S4.

CHAPTER 29

1 Monash, letter to daughter Bertha, 2 August 1918, NLA MS 1884, S4.
2 Ibid.
3 Ibid.
4 Monash, small diary, July–August 1918, NLA MS 1884, S5.

CHAPTER 30

1 Blamey, Monash Memorial lecture, *Age*, 9 October 1948.
2 Bean, *Anzac to Amiens,* [1946] 1993, p. 342.

3 Monash, *Australian Victories*, pp. 115–25.
4 Ibid.

CHAPTER 31

1 Armitage, diary, 'Battle of Amiens', AWM.
2 Monash, *Australian Victories*, pp. 115–25.
3 Armitage, diary, 'Battle of Amiens', AWM.
4 Arthur Wilson Diaries, AWM.
5 Blamey Papers, PR00332, AWM.
6 Monash, *Australian Victories*, pp. 115–25.
7 Arthur Wilson Diaries, AWM.
8 Monash, *Australian Victories*, pp. 115–25.

CHAPTER 32

1 Arthur Wilson Diaries, AWM.
2 Ibid.
3 Monash, *Australian Victories*, pp. 115–25

CHAPTER 33

1 Monash, *Australian Victories,* pp. 108, 127–9.

CHAPTER 34

1 Monash, *Australian Victories*, pp. 115–25.
2 Ibid.
3 Ibid.
4 Ludendorff, *My War Memoirs*, extracts published in *The Times,* 22 August 1919.
5 Guderian, *Achtung-Panzer!*, p. 120.
6 Asprey, *The German High Command at War*, pp. 448–51.
7 Ibid.
8 Ibid.
9 Lloyd, *Hundred Days,* p. 68.
10 Ibid.
11 Guderian, *Achtung-Panzer!*, p. 120.
12 Ibid.
13 Ludendorff, *My War Memoirs*, vol. II, pp. 680–1.

CHAPTER 35

1 Guderian, *Achtung-Panzer!*, p. 120.
2 Monash, *Australian Victories*, pp. 115–25.
3 Serle, *John Monash*, p. 350; Monash War Letters, 11 August 1918, S4.
4 Haig, *War Diaries and Letters, 1914–1918*, pp. 440–1.
5 Monash, *Australian Victories*, pp. 115–25.

CHAPTER 36

1 Monash, small diary, 12 August 1918, NLA MS 1884, S5.
2 Ibid.
3 George V's unpublished diary, 12 August 1918, Royal Archives, Windsor Castle.
4 Bean, *Two Men I Knew*, p. 173.

CHAPTER 37

1 Blamey wrote this in an obituary for Monash, which appeared in *Reveille*, 31 October 1931, p. 10, Monash Papers, AWM. Also in S16.
2 Asprey, *The German High Command at War*, p. 452.
3 Ibid., p. 453.
4 Ludwig, *Hindenburg and the Saga of the German Revolution*, p. 168.
5 Monash, *Australian Victories*, p. 58.

CHAPTER 38

1 Monash, *Australian Victories*, pp. 161–2.
2 Ibid.
3 Monash, letter to Vic, 16 March 1917, NLA MS 1884, S4.
4 Monash, *Australian Victories*, p. 168.
5 Ibid., p. 167.
6 Private diary of Captain Paul Simonson, p. 125.
7 Monash, *Australian Victories*, p. 169.
8 Ibid.; also Laffin, *Guide to Australian Battlefields on the Western Front 1916–1918*; Bean, *Anzac to Amiens*.

CHAPTER 39

1 Monash, *Australian Victories*, p. 170.
2 Ibid., p. 167.
3 Ibid., p. 181.

CHAPTER 41

1 Monash, *Australian Victories*, Chapter 11; see also NLA MS 1884, S4.
2 Bean, *Official History*, Vol. VI, pp. 487–8.

CHAPTER 42

1 Bean, *Official History*, Vol. VI, pp. 487–8.
2 Serle, *John Monash*, p. 355.

CHAPTER 43

Rawlinson to Allenby, 14 November 1918, in Essame, *The Battle for Europe, 1918*, p. 149.
Bean, *Official History*, Vol. VI, p. 873.
Asprey, *The German High Command at War*, p. 464.

CHAPTER 44
1 *Weekly Despatch,* London, 18 June 1919.
2 Blamey's response to questions after his Monash Memorial Address, 1948. Report from Dr Robert Kerr, who attended.
3 Bean, *Official History*, Vol. VI, p. 879.

CHAPTER 45
1 Pedersen, *Monash as Military Commander*, p. 278.
2 Ibid.
3 Letters between J.M. and Birdwood, September 1918, Monash Papers, AWM; September 1918, Birdwood Papers, AWM.
4 McMullin, *Pompey Elliott*, p. 488.
5 Private diary of Captain Paul Simonson, p. 126.
6 Monash, *Australian Victories*, p. 221.

CHAPTER 46
1 Monash, *Australian Victories*, p. 232.

CHAPTER 47
1 Monash's notes of the meeting with the rebels in Monash Papers, Box 89, AWM.
2 Private diary of Captain Paul Simonson, p. 78.
3 Ibid., p. 83.

CHAPTER 48
1 Hammond, *History of the 11th Light Horse*, p. 121.
2 Gullett, *Official History*, p. 676.

CHAPTER 51
1 Allenby was even more displeased, at least outwardly, than Chauvel about von Sanders' escape. Kelly was removed from his command.
2 James Ewell Brown Stuart, a cavalry commander for the Confederates in the American Civil War, led a 1200-man force around the opposition Union Army in three days in 1862. He was doing reconnaissance work for General Robert E. Lee.
3 Chauvel to Sybil, 20 September 1918.

CHAPTER 52
1 Olden, *Westralian Cavalry*, p. 263.
2 Ibid.
3 Gullett, *Official History*, p. 708.

CHAPTER 54

1 Gullett, *Official History* p. 728.
2 Hamilton, *First to Damascus*, p. 161.
3 Cutlack, *Official History*, pp. 164, 165.

CHAPTER 55

1 Gullett, *Official History*, p. 733; 11th Regiment history; 12 Regiment history, AWM; see also History of 4th LH Brigade, including 11th, 12th, 13th Regiments by Lt G.W. Nutting, R 940.41294n987h.

CHAPTER 56

1 Auda was brilliantly played in the film *Lawrence of Arabia* by Anthony Quinn.
2 Chauvel, letter to AWM, 1 January 1936, p. 5.

CHAPTER 57

1 Gullett, *Official History*, p. 725.
2 Ibid., p. 287.

CHAPTER 58

1 Monash, *Australian Victories*, pp. 246–50.

CHAPTER 59

1 Phone transcripts, box 190a, Gellibrand Papers, AWM.

CHAPTER 60

1 Von Sanders, *Five Years in Turkey*, p. 296.
2 Chauvel Papers, report on *Seven Pillars of Wisdom*, AWM, p. 4.
3 Olden, *Westralian Cavalry*, p. 279.

CHAPTER 61

1 Lawrence, *Seven Pillars of Wisdom*, p. 638. Lawrence implied he was watching them in an upbeat mood (on 30 September) before their mission to be first into Damascus early the next morning. But they were not at Keswe, where he said they were, but at least 10 kilometres away. His 'always going to do great things' remark was ambiguous in tone, although, given their record, had to be interpreted as praise. His comments were in *Seven Pillars of Wisdom* and put together, not from raw notes before the events of Damascus, but after. The Australians angered him and upset his plans. He had no idea on 30 September 1918 that they were going into the city before him and the Bedouins. When they did, he had to do some fictionalising of his narrative about the taking of Damascus, which he admitted to his biographer, Robert Graves, was false.

CHAPTER 62

1 Olden, *Westralian Cavalry*, p. 283.
2 Discovered in research for 2014 ABC TV documentary *Great War Horses*, in which the author features.
3 Quote from Olden in his diary, *Westralian Cavalry*, p. 284.

CHAPTER 63

1 Lawrence, *Seven Pillars of Wisdom*, p. 642.
2 Chauvel, letter to AWM, 1 January 1936, Chauvel Papers, AWM.
3 Ibid.

CHAPTER 64

1 Chauvel, letter to AWM, 1 January 1936, pp. 7, 8, Chauvel Papers, AWM.
2 Richard Chauvel, Harry's grandson, said his grandfather's view of Lawrence was that he was rarely there when he was wanted and a nuisance when he was.

CHAPTER 65

1 Lawrence, *Seven Pillars of Wisdom*, p. 643.
2 Chauvel, letter to AWM, 1 January 1936, pp. 7, 8, Chauvel Papers, AWM.
3 Ibid.
4 Chauvel Papers, AWM, p. 8.

CHAPTER 66

1 In the film *Lawrence of Arabia* Allenby is seen to be in Damascus for several days, organising everything and staying in a salubrious house, which was meant to be that of the Governor. All records show he was in the city for no more than an hour for lunch and the meeting with Prince Feisal and Lawrence.
2 Chauvel, notes, pp. 9–11, Chauvel Papers, AWM.
3 Lawrence, *Seven Pillars of Wisdom*, p. 653.

CHAPTER 67

1 Monash, letter to Dr J. Springthorpe, 2 October 1918, NLA MS 1884, S4.
2 Monash, *Australian Victories*, pp. 278–81.

CHAPTER 68

1 Monash, diary entries throughout October 1918, small diary, NLA MS 1884, S5.
2 Thompson, *On Lips of Living Men*, pp. 139–40; Monash, letters to Vic, 3 November 1918, NLA MS 1884, S4.
3 Monash, *Australian Victories*, pp. 286–7. Much the same material went into Monash's script for White, his letter to Pearce and his book. See Pearce, 5 November 1918, Monash Papers, AWM.

CHAPTER 69

1 *London Gazette*, 8 August 1919; Allenby Papers, British Museum letter, 5 February 1919.

CHAPTER 70

1 Monash, letter to Vic, 19 November 1918, NLA MS 1884, S4.

CHAPTER 71

1 Bill the Bastard did not return to Egypt but was given to Turkish farmers. His tombstone and grave are located in the north-east corner of the Commonwealth War Graves Cemetery, Gallipoli. The tombstone says 'Bill, Australian Light Horse 1914–1924 . . . A waler and one of the best'. The reference to 1914 was when Bill first joined the army as a trial horse in Sydney at about five years of age. He did not have a certificate but his birth year was most likely to have been 1909.

CHAPTER 72

1 Monash, notes on transition of command of AIF, NLA MS 1884, S4, S14.
2 Monash, letter to Vic, 13 December 1918, NLA MS 1884, S1.
3 Posted items, NLA MS 1884, S13, S14.
4 Monash, letter to Vic, 13 December 1918, S1.
5 Monash, letter to friend (Beadsmore), 20 September 1920, S1.
6 Murdoch, Melbourne *Herald*, 28 February 1919.
7 Ibid.

CHAPTER 73

1 Hammond, *History of the 11th Light Horse*, pp. 67–78.
2 Gullett, *Official History*, p. 788.
3 Monash, to Murdoch, 15 April 1919, S4.
4 Item in *Evening News* (London), 26 April 1919, Monash Papers, AWM.

CHAPTER 74

1 http://primeministers.naa.gov.au/primeministers/hughes
2 Ibid.
3 Monash, *Australian Victories*.

CHAPTER 75

1 Liddell Hart, *Through the Fog of War*, p. 149; also his Monash obituary in *Daily Telegraph* (UK), October 1931.
2 Lloyd George, *War Memoirs*, Vol. 6, London, Odhams Press, 1938, pp. 3368, 3382, 3424.

3 Taylor, *The First World War*, p. 232: Sir Ian Hamilton and Sir Winston Churchill, speeches at the Australia and New Zealand Luncheon Club, 11 December 1918.

4 Liddell Hart, *Through the Fog of War*, p. 149.

5 Monash's wife, Hannah Victoria, had died of cancer early in 1920. Later Monash invited Lizzie Bentwitch to join him from England. They were partners for the next eleven years until Monash's death in 1931.

6 Monash, letter to Major General Harold Grimwade, 23 December 1930, NLA MS 1884, S1.

CHAPTER 76

1 Interview with Chauvel's grandson, Richard Chauvel, September 2008.

2 Monash, speech, NLA MS 1884, S14.

Select Bibliography

General Sir John Monash and the AIF
PRIMARY SOURCES
1: National Library of Australia, Canberra
Monash Papers, MS 1884
1: General correspondence, 1879–1931
2: Correspondence with particular individuals, 1860–1931
3: Correspondence, special categories, 1918–1920
4: Correspondence, WWI, 1915–1920
5: Diaries and notebooks, 1879–1931
6: School and university
7: Engineering, 1886–1932
8: Military, 1908–16
9: Arbitration and Royal Commissions, 1896–1929
10: Subject files, A to Z and souvenir albums
11: Manuscripts, 1881–1928
12: Scientific matters, 1914–1930
13: Travels, 1907–1931
14: Press cuttings, pamphlets and other printed items, 1894–1929
15: Photographs and glass slides
16: Death and memorials
Additions in 1983; 1994
2: National Library of Australia, Canberra
Hughes, W.M., Papers
Murdoch, Sir Keith, Papers
Novar, Viscount (Sir Ronald Munro Ferguson) Papers, 1914–1918
3: Australian War Memorial
C.E.W. Bean diaries and notebooks (entries on Monash throughout WWI)

Birdwood, Field Marshal, Lord, Collection 1914–19
Blamey, Field Marshal Sir Thomas, Papers 1914–18
Cox, General Sir H.V., and Diaries, 1915–1917
Elliott, Major-General H.E., Papers
Gellibrand, Major General Sir John, Papers
Godley, General Sir A.J., Correspondence, 1914–17
Pearce, Sir George, Papers, relating to War of 1914–1918
White, General Sir C.B. Brudenell, Papers
4: Mitchell Library, Sydney
Rosenthal, Major General Sir Charles, diary, 1914–18
5: Imperial War Museum, London
Allanson, Colonel C.J.L., Papers
Birdwood, Field Marshal Lord, Papers
5: Liddell Hart Centre for Military Archives, London
Hamilton, Ian, Papers
Liddell, Hart, Captain Sir H.B., Papers
North J., Papers
Wavell, Lord, Papers
6: Royal Archives, Windsor Castle
King George V's Diary, 1916–1918

BOOKS

50 Famous Australians, Colorgravure Publications, Sydney, 1950
Asprey, Robert B., *The German High Command at War*, William Morrow & Co., New York, 1991
Bean, C.E.W, *Anzac to Amiens,* Penguin Books, Ringwood, Vic., 1993
—*Official History of Australia in the War of 1914–18*, Vol. II: *The Story of ANZAC from 4 May, 1915, to the evacuation of the Gallipoli Peninsula,* Angus & Robertson, Sydney, 1987
—*Official History of Australia in the War of 1914–18*, Vol. VI: *The Australian Imperial Force in France during the Allied Offensive, 1918,* Angus & Robertson, Sydney, 1942
—*Two Men I Knew: William Bridges and Brudenell White, founders of the A.I.F.,* Sydney, Angus & Robertson, 1957
Blake, Robert, *The Private Papers of Douglas Haig, 1914–1918*, Hutchinson, London, 1952
Cameron, James, *1914*, Cassell, London, 1959
Carlyon, Les, *Gallipoli*, Pan Macmillan, Sydney, 2001
Clay, Catrine, *King, Kaiser, Tsar*, Walker & Company, New York, 2006
Clemenceau, Georges, *Grandeur and Misery*, Literary Licensing, New York, 1930
Coulthart, Ross, *Charles Bean*, HarperCollins Publishers, Sydney, 2014
Cutlack, F.M. (ed.), *War Letters of General Monash,* Angus & Robertson, Sydney, 1935

Doyle, Sir Arthur Conan, *The British Campaign in Europe, 1914–1918*, Geoffrey Bles, London, 1928

Edmonds, James, *History of the Great War, 1918*, vol. 1, Naval & Military Press, London, 1933

Edwards, Cecil, *John Monash*, State Electricity Commission of Victoria, 1970

Essame, Hubert, *The Battle for Europe, 1918*, London, Batsford, 1971

Evans, Martin Marix, *1918: The year of victories*, Arcturus Publishing, UK, 1920

Fischer, Tim, *Maestro John Monash*, Monash University Publishing, Melbourne, 2014

Guderian, Heinz, *Achtung-Panzer!*, Cassell, London, 1999

—*Panzer Leader*, Da Capo Press, New York, 2002

Haig, Douglas, *War Diaries and Letters, 1914–1918*, Gary Sheffield and John Bourne (eds), UK, Weidenfeld & Nicolson, 2005

Hamilton, Jill, *From Gallipoli to Gaza*, Simon & Schuster, Sydney, 2003

Hogg, Ian, *The Guns, 1914–1918*, Pocket Books, New York, 1971

Holt, Major and Mrs, *Battlefield: Ypres Salient*, Leo Cooper, London, 2000

Horner, David, *Blamey*, Allen & Unwin, Sydney, 1998

Hughes, Aneurin, *Billy Hughes*, John Wiley & Sons, Sydney, 2005

James, Robert Rhodes, *Gallipoli*, Pan Books, London, 1974

Jones, Ian, *Ned Kelly: A short life*, Lothian Books, Port Melbourne, 1996

Joynt, W.D., *Saving the Channel Ports*, Wren Publishing, London, 1975

Kingston, Beverley, *The Oxford History of Australia, 1860–1890*, Oxford University Press, Oxford, 2001

Kitchen, Martin, *The German Offensives of 1918*, Tempus, Stroud, 2001

Laffin, John, *Guide to Australian Battlefields on the Western Front 1916–1918*, Kenthurst, NSW, Kangaroo Press and AWM, 1992

Liddell Hart, Basil, *Through the Fog of War*, London, Faber & Faber, 1938

Lindsay, Patrick, *The Spirit of the Digger, Then and Now*, Macmillan, Sydney, 2003

Lloyd, Nick, *Hundred Days*, Viking, London, 2013

Lloyd George, David, *War Memoirs*, Vol. 6, London, Odhams Press, 1938

Ludwig, Emil, *Hindenburg and the Saga of the German Revolution*, London, William Heinemann, 1935

Macdougall, A.K., *War Letters of General Monash*, Duffy & Snellgrove, Sydney, 2002

Macintyre, Stuart, *The Oxford History of Australia, Volume 4, 1901–1942*, Oxford University Press, Oxford, 2001

McMullin, Ross, *Pompey Elliott*, Scribe, Melbourne, 2002

Magnus, Philip, *Kitchener: Portrait of an imperialist*, John Murray, London, 1958

Middlebrook, Martin, *The Kaiser's Battle*, Book Club Associates, London, 1978

Mitchell, James, *A Deepening Roar: Scotch College, Melbourne 1851–2001*, Allen & Unwin, Sydney, 2001

Monash, John, *The Australian Victories in France in 1918* [Hutchinson & Co., London, 1920], Black Inc., Melbourne, 2015

—*War Letters of General Monash*, Black Inc., Melbourne, 2015

Morehead, Alan, *Gallipoli,* Macmillan, South Melbourne, 1975

Nicholson, G. Harvey, *First Hundred Years of Scotch College Melbourne, 1851–1951,* Brown, Prior, Anderson, Melbourne, 1952

Palazzo, Albert, *Defenders of Australia: The Third Australian Division, 1916–1991,* Australian Military History Publications, Loftus, NSW, 2002

Pedersen P.A., *Monash as Military Commander,* Melbourne University Press, Melbourne, 1985

Perry, Roland, *Monash: The outsider who won a war,* Random House Australia, Sydney, 2004

Priestley, J.B., *Margin Released,* William Heinemann, London, 1962

Reed, Paul, *Walking the Salient,* Battleground Europe series, Leo Cooper, Barnsley, South Yorkshire, 2001

Rees, Peter, *Bearing Witness,* Allen & Unwin, Sydney, 2015

Rose, Kenneth, *King George V,* Phoenix Press, London, 1983

Rule, Edgar John, *Jacka's Mob: A narrative of the Great War,* Military Melbourne, Melbourne [1933] 1999

Serle, Geoffrey, *John Monash,* Melbourne University Press, Melbourne, 1982

Simonson, Paul, private diary, held by the Simonson family

Smithers, A.J., *Sir John Monash,* Leo Cooper, Barnsley, South Yorkshire, 1973

Taylor, A.J.P., *The First World War,* London, Hamish Hamilton, 1963

Taylor, Phil and Cupper, Pam, *Gallipoli, a battlefield guide,* Kangaroo Press, Kenthurst, NSW, 1989

Terraine, John, *Douglas Haig: The educated soldier,* London, Hutchinson, 1963

Thompson, John, *On Lips of Living Men,* Lansdowne Press, Melbourne, 1962

Warner, Denis and Peggy, *The Tide at Sunrise,* Angus & Robertson, Sydney, 1975

Williams, John F., *German Anzacs and the First World War,* UNSW Press, Sydney, 2003

Zwar, Desmond, *The Soul of a School,* Macmillan, Melbourne, 1982

ARTICLES AND PAMPHLETS

Brasch, Rabbi Dr R., 'Sir John Monash', *Royal Australian Historical Society,* vol. 45, part 4, 1959

Çelik, Kenan and Koç, Ceyhan, *The Gallipoli Campaign International Perspectives 85 Years On,* Canakkale, Turkey, 2002

Croll, R.H., *I Recall, Collections and Recollections,* Robertson & Mullens Ltd, Melbourne

Dumble, Sandra, 'Edmund Augustus Samson, Teacher' (Scotch College), paper, Scotch College Archive, Melbourne, 2003

Forestry Ministry Office of National Parks and Wild Life, 'Gallipoli Peninsula, Historical National Park', 2001

Holgate, Alan and Taplin, Geoff, *The Contribution of Sir John Monash to 20th Century Engineering,* Monash University Engineering Dept, Melbourne, 1982

Hyatt, A.M.J., 'Sir Arthur Currie at Passchendaele', *Stand-To,* vol. 10, no. 1, Jan–Feb 1965

McQueen, Humphrey, 'Gallipoli's Shadows', *Age*, 26 April 2003

Mathews, Race, *David Bennett: A memoir*, Australian Fabian Society, Pamphlet no. 44, 1985

Meredith, Helen, 'Coming of Age', *Weekend Australian*, 7–8 August 1983

Monasch, B.L., 'The Life, Labours, Joys and Sorrows of B.L. Monasch', *Jewish Historical Society Magazine*, 1986

Northwood, Vernon R., 'Monash', *SEC Magazine*, December 1950

Perry, Major E.W.O., 'The Military Life of General Sir John Monash', *The Victorian Historical Magazine*, 109th issue, Vol. XXVIII, No. 1, Dec 1957

—'General Sir John Monash: Scholar, Engineer and Soldier', *Jewish Historical Society Magazine*, Vol. IV, Part VI, 1957

—'Monash: The Biographer's Dilemma', *The Australian Quarterly*, March 1961

—'The Police Strike in Melbourne 1923', address to the Royal Historical Society of Victoria, 28 October 1969

—'Major General Sir Charles Rosenthal—Soldier, Architect and Musician', *The Victorian Historical Magazine*, vol. 40, no. 3, August 1969

Steele, Major Alan B., *The Western Front: A general outline*, The Arrow Printery Pty Ltd, Melbourne, 1930

General Sir Harry Chauvel and the Light Horse; Major T.E. Lawrence

PRIMARY SOURCES

1: National Archives of Australia, Canberra

Bringing Them Home Project: Participation, Aborigine, Australian. June 2004

WWI and Boer War biographical files

2: Australian War Memorial, Canberra

—brochure, George Lambert, Gallipoli & Palestine Landscapes

—Letter to the Director, AWM, Canberra, 1 January 1936, concerning T.E. Lawrence's book, *Seven Pillars of Wisdom*, PR00535003

The Chauvel Papers:

—2DRL/0793: Papers relating to Palestine Campaign

—MSS1406: Annotated typescript autobiography of H.C.'s military career

—PR00535: Collection of papers relating to H.C.—diaries, letters, photographs, reports and album

Sir Henry George Chauvel Albums:

—PR00535003: Album—Egypt, Gallipoli, Sinai, 1914–1917

—PR00535004: Albums—Palestine, Syria, England, 1917–1919

The Australian Light Horse Association:

—R 357.10994H17a

Brigades:

—3rd: History, Wilson 940.41294W749n; also, narrative of operations, 27 October 1917 to 4 March 1919, 224 MSS27

—4th: Nutting, G.W., R940.412994N987h

—5th: Wynn, N.I., 'Behind the Lines', R940.400994W988

Regiments:
—1st: The Boys in Green, R 357.10994B789
—2nd: Bourne, G.H., R940.41294B775h
—3rd: Smith, Neil C., R940.41294S655t
—4th: Smith, Neil C., Men of Beersheba, 940.41294 5655m
—5th: Wilson, L.C.H., R940.41294W749h
—6th: Berrie, George, Under Furred Hat, R 94041294B533u
—7th: Richardson, R940.41294R516s
—8th: Simpson, Cameron, Maygar's Boys (see Bibliography)
—9th: Darling T.H., With the Lighthorse in the Great War, R 940.41294D221
—11th: Hammond, Ernst, History of the 11th LHR, R 94041294H225h
Spur magazines: October 1999
—p. 6, Boer War, first casualty of Australians
—p. 11, 500,000 horses lost in SA
—p. 13, Kitchener
—p. 14, Chauvel at Coronation
—p. 17, Chauvel and Boer War statue unveiled
—p. 20, Breaker Morant
—p. 22, Idriess on Suez . . . Battle of Romani
—p. 25, Chaytor
—p. 33, Bert Canning's brief diaries
3: UK:
Bodleian Library, Oxford Reserve Manuscript Collection
British Library Additional Manuscripts Collection: various T.E. Lawrence correspondence, war diaries and pocket diaries
Imperial War Museum London: Knightley and Simpson Papers
King's College, University of London, Basil Liddell Hart Centre for Military Archives
Public Record Office Kew: Foreign and War Office files; Arab Bureau Files; Intelligence files

BOOKS
Asher, Michael, *Lawrence: The uncrowned king of Arabia*, Penguin, UK, 1999
Barr, James, *Setting the Desert on Fire: T.E. Lawrence and Britain's secret war in Arabia, 1916–18*, Bloomsbury, London, 2006
Bean, C.E.W., *Anzac to Amiens*, Penguin, Ringwood, Vic., 1993
Brown, Malcolm, *T.E. Lawrence*, New York University Press, New York, 2003
Bruce, Anthony, *The Last Crusade: The Palestine Campaign in the First World War*, John Murray, London 2002
Brugger, Suzanne, *The Australians in Egypt 1914–1919*, Melbourne University Press, Melbourne, 1980
Carlyon, Les, *Gallipoli*, Macmillan, Sydney, 2001
—*The Great War*, Macmillan, Sydney, 2006

Churchill, Winston, *Great Contemporaries: A gallery of pen portraits*, Mandarin, London, 1990

Coulthard-Clark, Chris (ed.), *The Diggers: Makers of the Australian military tradition*, Melbourne University Press, Melbourne, 1993

Cox, John, *The Miraculous 'Lives' of a Man Called Jack*, Lime Leaf Publications, Melbourne, 2002

Crombie, Kelvin, *Anzacs, Empires and Israel's Restoration, 1798–1948*, Vocational Education and Training Publications, Osborne Park, WA, 1998

Cutlack, F.M., *Official History of Australia in the War of 1914–18*, Vol. VIII: *The Australian Flying Corps in the western and eastern theatres of war, 1914–18*, University of Queensland Press, St Lucia, Queensland, 1984

Fisk, Robert, *The Great War for Civilisation: The conquest of the Middle East*, Harper Perennial, London, 2006

Frindall, W.H., *The Wisden Book of Test Cricket, 1877–1984*, Guild Publishing, London, 1985

Garner, Brian, *Allenby of Arabia*, Coward-McCann, Inc., New York, 1966

Graves, Robert, *Lawrence and the Arabs*, Jonathon Cape, London, 1927

Gullett, H.S., *Official History of Australia in the War of 1914–1918*, Volume VII: *The Australian Imperial Force in Sinai and Palestine*, University of Queensland Press in association with the AWM, St Lucia, 1984

Gullett, H.S. and Barrett, Chas (eds), *Australia in Palestine*, Angus & Robertson, Sydney, 1919

Hamilton, Jill, *From Gallipoli to Gaza: The desert poets of World War One*, Simon & Schuster, Sydney, 2003

——*First to Damascus: The great ride and Lawrence of Arabia*, Kangaroo Press, Sydney, 2002

——*Gods, Guns and Israel: Britain, the First World War and the Jews in the Holy City*, Sutton Publishing, UK, 2004

Hammond, Ernest W., *History of the 11th Light Horse Regiment, Fourth Light Horse Brigade, Australian Imperial Forces, Great War 1914–1919*, William Brooks & Co., Brisbane, 1942

Hill, A.J., *Chauvel of the Light Horse*, Melbourne University Press, Melbourne, 1978

Horsfield, Jenny, *Rainbow*, Ginninderra Press, Canberra, 2007

Idriess, Ion L., *The Desert Column*, Angus & Robertson, London, 1932

James, Lawrence, *The Golden Warrior: The life and legend of Lawrence of Arabia*, Abacus, UK, 2000

Jones, Ian, *The Australian Light Horse*, Time-Life Books, Australia, 1987

Kartinyeri, Doreen, *Ngarrindjeri Anzacs*, South Australian Museum, South Australia, 1996

Lord Kinross, *Ataturk: A biography of Mustafa Kemal, father of modern Turkey*, New York, Quil/Morrow, 1992

Lawrence, T.E., *Seven Pillars of Wisdom*, Jonathan Cape, London, 1935; Dell, USA, 1962

—*The Mint*, Jonathan Cape, London, 1955

—*Revolt in the Desert*, Jonathan Cape, London, 1937

Macmillan, Margaret, *Paris 1919*, Random House, New York, 2002

Mitchell, Evelyn, *Chauvel Country*, Macmillan, Australia, 1983

Nutting, Anthony, *Lawrence of Arabia*, New American Library, US, 1962

Olden, A.C.N, *Westralian Cavalry in the War: The story of the 10th Light Horse Regiment, A.I.F., in the Great War, 1914–1918*, Alexander McCubbin, Melbourne, 1921

Overy, Richard, *Atlas of 20th Century History*, Collins, US, 2006

Parsonson, Ian M., *Vets at War: A history of the Australian Veterinary Corps 1909– 1946*, The Australian Army History Collection, Australian Military History Publications, Loftus, NSW, 2005

Paterson, A.B., *Happy Dispatches*, Lansdowne Press, Sydney, 1980

—*Selected Verse of A.B. Paterson*, Angus & Robertson, Sydney, 1921

Pedersen, P.A., *Monash as Military Commander*, Melbourne University Press, Melbourne, 1992

Perham, Frank, *The Kimberley Flying Column*, Boer War Reminiscences, Timara, NZ, 1958

Perry, Roland, *Monash: The outsider who won a war*, Random House, Sydney, 2004

—*The Australian Light Horse*, Hachette, Sydney, 2009

—*Bill the Bastard*, Allen & Unwin, Sydney, 2012

Roberts, Paul, *The End of Oil*, Bloomsbury, London, 2004

Roderick, Colin, *Banjo Paterson: Poet by accident*, Allen & Unwin, Sydney, 1993

Sanders, Liman von, *Five Years in Turkey*, The Navy & Military Press, UK, 1927

Sheffield Gary and Bourne, John (eds), *Douglas Haig: War diaries and letters 1914– 1918*, Weidenfeld & Nicolson, London, 2005

Simpson, Cameron, *Maygar's Boys: A biographical history of the 8th Light Horse Regiment AIF 1914–19*, Just Soldiers, Military Research & Publications, Canberra, 1998

Starr, Joan, *From the Saddlebags of War*, The Australian Light Horse Association, Brisbane, 2000

Thomas, Lowell, *With Lawrence in Arabia*, Popular Library, New York, 1961

Tuchman, Barbara W., *The Proud Tower: A portrait of the world before the war, 1890– 1914*, Bantam Books, New York, 1967

Wallach, Janet, *Desert Queen*, Weidenfeld & Nicolson, London, 1996

Wavell, Lord, *Allenby: Soldier and statesman*, Harrap, London, 1940

Wilson, Jeremy, *Lawrence of Arabia: The authorised biography of T.E. Lawrence*, William Heinemann, London, 1989

Yardley, Michael, *Backing into the Limelight*, Harrap, London, 1985

ARTICLES

Adelson, Roger, 'Review, *Lawrence of Arabia* by Jeremy Wilson', *The Journal of Military History*, vol. 55, no. 2, 1991

Anderson, Perry, 'Kemalism', *London Review of Books*, 11 November 2008

Bader, Rudolph, 'Lawrence of Arabia and H.H. Richardson', *Australian Literary Studies*, vol. 11, May 1983

Barrett, Roby, 'Intervention in Iraq, 1958–59', *The Middle East Institute*, no. 11, April 2008

Binyon, Michael, 'Wise Words Survived Desert but Not Change of Trains', *London Times*, 1 March 2004

—'Lawrence: The man and the mirage', *London Times*, 8 October 2005

Bou, Jean, 'The Palestine Campaign 1916–18: Causes and consequences of a continuing historical neglect', *Journal of the Australian War Memorial*, no. 40, <www.gov.au/journal/j40/bou.htm>

—'Cavalry, Firepower, and Words: The Australian Light Horse and the tactical lessons of cavalry operations in Palestine, 1916–1918', *The Journal of Military History*, no. 71, January 2007

Coulthard-Clark, Chris, 'Aborigine Medal Winners', *Sabretache: Journal of the Military Historical Society of Australia*, vol. XVIII, No. 1, January 1977

Daley, Paul, 'Straddling the Divide', *Sunday Times*, 3 August 2008

Day, Elizabeth, 'Legendary Lawrence of Arabia Made Up "Rape"', *Daily Telegraph* (London), 20 May 2006

Demirmen, Dr Ferruh, 'Oil in Iraq: The Byzantine beginnings', *Global Policy Forum*, 25 April 2003

Duffy, Denis, 'Lawrence of Arabia', *US National Post*, 7 January 2002

Ersavci, Murat (Ambassador to Turkey), 'The Gallipoli Legacy: A firm and abiding friendship', *Canberra Times*, 23 April 2007

—'Never Again', *Herald Sunday Sun*, 23 April 2006

Faulkner, Neil & Saunders, Nick, 'Archeology, Lawrence and Guerilla Warfare', *UK History Today*, August 2007

—'Logical Idea that Could Have Prevented Strife', *London Times*, 12 October 2005

Fromkin, David, 'The Importance of T. E. Lawrence', *The New Criterion* online, 10 September 1991

Furst, Barbara, 'Gertrude Bell and Iraq: Déjà vu all over again', American Diplomacy.org, 1990

Fyfe, Hamilton, General Sir Edmund Allenby, *War Illustrated*, 12 October 1918

Goldberg, Jeffrey; 'After Iraq', *The Atlantic* online, January/February 2008

Hill, A.J., 'Introduction', in Henry S. Gullett, *Official History of Australia in the War of 1914–1918*, Volume VII: *The Australian Imperial Force in Sinai and Palestine*, University of Queensland Press in association with the AWM, St Lucia, 1984

Hitchens, Christopher, 'The Woman Who Made Iraq', *Atlantic Monthly*, 29 May 2007

Hughes, Matthew, 'Review of M. Brown's *T.E. Lawrence*', *The Journal of Military History*, Brunel University, UK, No. 1232

Ireland, Phillip W., 'Reviews of *Lawrence of Arabia: The man and the motive* (Anthony Nutting); 'Lawrence of Arabia, a Triumph (Robert Payne)', *Middle East Journal*, vol. 18, no. 1, 1964

Irwin, Robert, 'Ecstasy in the Desert' (review, complete 1922 'Oxford' text of *Seven Pillars of Wisdom*), *Times Literary Supplement*, 2 April 2004

Kedourie, Elie, 'Colonel Lawrence', *Cambridge Journal*, vol. 7, 1954

Knightley, Phillip, 'Lawrence', London, *Sunday Times Magazine,* 2 October 2005

Kroupnik, Vladimir, 'Zhemchug, Emden and Sydney', <http://australiarussia.com/emdenforwebENFIN.htm>

Leach, Hugh, 'Lawrence in Arabia', *History Today*, October 2005

Mack, John E., 'Review of *The Secret Lives of Lawrence of Arabia*, (Knightley)', *Middle East Journal*, vol. 24, no. 4, 1970

Malvern, Jack, 'Lawrence of Arabia's Lessons on Fighting Iraqi Rebels', *London Times,* 13 April 2004

—'Lawrence's Vision of Arabia and Beyond', *London Times*, 12 October 2005

Paul, James A., 'Great Power Conflict over Iraq Oil: The World War I era', Global Policy Forum, October, 2002

Ryan, Peter, 'Lawrence Biography Worth Having' (review of *The Golden Warrior* by Lawrence James), *Age*, (undated)

Sacks, David, 'Private Shaw', *New York Review of Books*, 16 April 2000

'Saying It with Flowers', *The Jerusalem Post*, 30 April 2008

Singh, K. Gajendra, 'Iraq's History Already Written', *Asia Times*, 15 July 2003

Sluglett, Peter, *The Primacy of Oil in Britain's Iraq Policy,* Ithaca Press, London, 1976

Stewart, Rory, 'The Queen of the Quagmire', *The New York Review of Books*, vol. 54, no. 16, 25 October 2007

Syal, Rajeev, 'Letters Rekindle Lawrence Suicide Speculation', *Australian*, 2 September 1996

Tuchman, Barbara, 'History by the Ounce', *Harper's Magazine*, July 1965

Veitch, Alan, *Queen of the Desert* (Gertrude Bell), *Age*, 9 October 2002

Wilson, Jeremy, 'Sense and Nonsense in the Biography of T.E. Lawrence' (prologue to the authorised biography) see <http://telawrencestudies.org/telawrencestudies/general_biography/sense_and _nonsense>

—review comments on *Lawrence, the Uncrowned King of Arabia,* <www.telawrence.info>

DOCUMENTARY

The Battle for Zion, Daystar International, 1986

Index

Index

Index

Index

Index

Index

LAVINIA URBAN'S SEVEN DEADLY SIN SERIES

AVA MANELLO

Jeanette

Hope you enjoy wrath
It's in memory of a very
special lady.

love
Ava Manello
x.

Formatting Services Provided by Leanne Clugston
www.facebook.com/IrishInkPublishing

Cover Created by Phycel Designs
www.phycel.com

This story is dedicated to Lavinia Urban
The strongest, bravest and classiest warrior
in her battle against cancer

–

Lavinia Urban had a vision to write this series, yet her life was taken from her all too soon after a heart-wrenching battle with Metastatic Breast Cancer. Aside from her family's welfare, her last wish was for her friends to continue these stories about The Seven Deadly Sins. With her husband's well wishes, seven authors banded together to bring **Lavinia Urban's Seven Deadly Sins Series** to her fans and readers everywhere. All proceeds will go to Lavinia's loving husband and adorable children.

May she rest in peace with the knowledge we will never forget her.

FOREWORD

BY STACY MCWILIAMS

This novella is dedicated in loving memory to a dear friend, colleague and mentor, Lavinia Urban.

Lavinia was an inspiration to all who knew her. She was funny, kind and encouraging. She battled metastatic breast cancer, not once, but twice and the second time claimed her life.

She was completely obsessed with all things Harry Potter and the whole author/reader community will miss her wit, humour and enthusiasm.

She leaves behind a family: husband Ian and two children Josh and Kasey-Ray and she will be sorely missed by all who knew her.

These stories are her idea, but she never got to finish them, so we are finishing them in her stead. We all hope we can do them justice and, if there's one thing that Lavinia has taught us, it's *don't stop following your dreams because you never know which day will be your last.*

Lavinia had metastatic breast cancer. So please, ladies

please, check your breasts and report any changes to your doctor. If you are worried, get checked out.

The NHS website provides these guidelines, so please follow them and remember reporting is not a waste of time or silly. Even if you think it may not be something, just get it looked at and make sure.

How should I check my breasts?

There's no right or wrong way to check your breasts. But it is important to know how your breasts usually look and feel. That way, you can spot any changes quickly and report them to your GP.

Be breast aware.

Every woman's breasts are different in terms of size, shape and consistency. It's also possible for one breast to be larger than the other.

Get used to how your breasts feel at different times of the month. This can change during your menstrual cycle. For example, some women have tender and lumpy breasts, especially near the armpit, around the time of their period.

After the menopause, normal breasts feel softer, less firm and not as lumpy.

The NHS Breast Screening Programme has produced a 5-point plan for being breast aware:

1. know what's normal for you
2. look at your breasts and feel them

3. know what changes to look for
4. report any changes without delay
5. attend routine screening if you're 50 or over

Look at your breasts and feel each breast and armpit, and up to your collarbone. You may find it easiest to do this in the shower or bath, by running a soapy hand over each breast and up under each armpit.

You can also look at your breasts in the mirror. Look with your arms by your side and also with them raised.

Breast changes to look out for.

See your GP if you notice any of the following changes:

- a change in the size, outline or shape of your breast
- a change in the look or feel of your skin, such as puckering or dimpling
- a new lump, thickening or bumpy area in one breast or armpit that is different from the same area on the other side
- nipple discharge that's not milky
- bleeding from your nipple
- a moist, red area on your nipple that doesn't heal easily
- any change in nipple position, such as your nipple being pulled in or pointing differently
- a rash on or around your nipple
- any discomfort or pain in one breast, particularly if it's a new pain and doesn't go away (although pain is only a symptom of breast cancer in rare cases)

Always see your GP if you are concerned.

Breast changes can happen for many reasons, and most of them aren't serious. Lots of women have breast lumps, and 9 out of 10 are not cancerous.

However, if you find changes in your breast that aren't normal for you, it's best to see your GP as soon as possible. This is because it is important to rule out breast cancer. If cancer is detected, then appropriate treatment should be planned as quickly as possible.

Reference: https://www.nhs.uk/common-health-questions/womens-health/how-should-i-check-my-breasts/

Now might be a good time to go stock up on some tissues, before you turn the page...

... don't say I didn't warn you x

Love Ava

1
WRATH

I roll my shoulders, trying to ease the tautness between them. It's been a long day. The ache doesn't lessen, not that I really thought it would, I put my back into today's job and I'm feeling it now. The knot just to the side of my neck is solid against my hands. A hot shower should help, and if nothing else I need one to clean the splattered blood from my skin and hair.

Tossing my red chequered shirt into the trash can rather than the laundry bin I pause for a moment and take note of my reflection in the mirror. I barely recognise the dark lifeless eyes that stare back at me, hell, I barely recognise myself anymore. My dark hair is a little too long on top and has started to give in to the natural curl that I hate, although mum always told me it was a kiss curl and she loved it. The shaved sides are growing out and my beard needs a serious trim as well. I'm starting to look like a dark haired version of Santa Claus with a six pack instead of a belly, although there's nothing good and giving about me. I've been on the road for what feels like forever, looking through the door to my bedroom here in the clubhouse I have to ask myself am I really home? I'm more nomad than brother these days, a club enforcer hired out to the highest bidder to do the dirty work no one else wants or has the stomach for.

Constant anger fills my veins, fuelling the work I do. Every job takes away a little more of the humanity I once had, making it easier to become the numb shell that's staring back at me in my reflection.

I don't question the guilt of my victims, I trust that my Prez has done that already. I just mete out the sentence. I walk in, carry out the punishment asked of me, and walk out, leaving someone else to clean up behind me. This is what my life has become, I'm more machine than man, and I can't see that changing any time soon.

Life was good once upon a time, and I vaguely remember the sound of my laughter, but that's in the past. A twist of fate and that life was gone, leading me to become the man standing here today. A man without a soul or conscience.

My brothers embraced that change. I am filled with anger, hate and violence and I use that to fuel the vengeance they ask of me.

Easing off my leather boots I place them carefully on the floor, then remove the rest of my clothes, and grab a clean towel from the pile on the shelf placing it within reach of the shower door.

The steam of the hot water flowing from the shower head

fills the small ensuite, my skin turning red from the punishing heat, the water swirling around the drain deep scarlet from the blood washing away. It's not my blood, it never is. I'm too good at what I do. It's the blood of yet another soul found wanting and deserving of punishment.

Closing my eyes I hear the man's voice pleading for forgiveness, fake apologies that mean nothing to me. He means nothing to me. He's just another name on a piece of paper that needs to be crossed off before I can move onto the next one. I don't ask what he's done because I really don't care. I can hazard a pretty good guess that it involved taking or touching something that didn't belong to him though from the way I was asked to deal with it.

The heavy meat cleaver had been there waiting for me when I walked into the room, along with the victim strapped into a chair. The whole scene had been set to put the maximum amount of fear into him. The dim bulb had swung naked above his head, casting moving shadows around the room. There was no need for bright lighting or a clean environment, this was no surgical procedure I was about to carry out. The damp walls and dirt covered floor added to the nightmare ambience of the situation.

I don't know how long he'd been sat there, restrained and awaiting my arrival, staring at that cleaver working himself up into a state of terror, but I do know that he recognised me as I walked in. My reputation preceded me. I could see the resignation and fear in his eyes as soon as he noticed it was me. I'm an imposing figure in a normal setting, my six-foot four height often has me standing a full head and shoulders above my brothers. I'm not overweight, but I'm toned and solidly built. In this setting I looked like an avenging angel, and I guess that's what I am.

Feeling the heavy weight of the meat cleaver I turned it over in my hand. It was well used, the blade keenly sharpened and the hilt had the nicks and scratches betraying its age. Without looking at the man I stood there for a long moment just turning and inspecting the weapon I was holding, stretching out the anticipation and terror deliberately.

With one deft stroke my work was done, the strike was clean and his hand was severed from his wrist. Blood spattered everywhere. I turned my back on his high pitched screams and walked slow and steady away from him and towards the daylight. It wasn't often a victim's screams followed me as I left a scene, more often than not the silence of death filled the room instead. This guy was lucky, not that he'd see it that way for a while I suspect, but he'd been allowed to live. I often wondered why they brought me in for this kind of job, but my Prez had once told me it was the effect the sight of me walking into a room had on a victim. My reputation was enough to fill them with terror, suspecting I was there to snuff out the life they no longer deserved.

It didn't matter to me one way or another, I had a job to do and I did it. That was my life now.

The water is finally running clear so I pick up the shower

gel and liberally apply it to my body, working up the lather and cleaning off any remaining evidence of today's labours. When I'm done I'll grab something to eat from the kitchen as I realise I haven't eaten all day, then I'll go see my Prez and find out what vengeance I'll be dishing up next, because that's my job. This is my life, it's the only one I know, the only one I dare remember. I can't afford to remember a time before this, when compassion was a part of me, when I had a soul. I can't be that man anymore. Too much has changed, too much has happened that cannot be undone.

I am a Cardinal Sin.

I am Wrath.

2

WRATH

I'm pulled from sleep by the phone vibrating across the bedside table. I release a barely audible curse. When I'd put it on silent I'd forgotten to take that into account. I lift my head an inch then decide that sleep is more important than whoever is calling. I'm so tired. I feel like I could sleep for a week right now and as my bladder ain't complaining I'm staying put. It doesn't take much for my eyelids to droop and lose myself in dreamless bliss again.

It's not long before the nightmares kick in, I'd hoped I was too tired and that I'd be so out of it they would give me a reprieve, especially now I'm back in my own bed at the clubhouse. I've been away so long that this room feels alien. The familiarity and sense of home and belonging I'd been looking forward to are eluding me. I've spent too long on the road, wandering from job to job, too valuable a commodity to my club to be allowed a break or even a modicum of recovery time. I'm only here tonight as it's a convenient stop off on the way to the next target.

Images of the sins I've committed in the name of the club flash behind my closed eyelids, the punishments for minor infringements, the lessons that had to be taught, and the ultimate sacrifices where trust had been betrayed and a brother couldn't be allowed to live. There were even a handful of civilian deaths in there, paid for by the highest bidder. I have to trust that they were justified, although my gut tells me it's become all about the money for my club and less about the righteousness.

I've left a trail of destruction and misery in my wake, families broken apart as a result of my actions, lives forever transformed from the torture I've inflicted. Broken sleep seems a small price to pay for the acts I've carried out.

I don't believe in heaven or a God. I've seen too much suffering to be able to reconcile the two. I do believe in Hell though and I'm sure that's where my damned eternity will be spent. It's fitting for the atrocities that I've carried out.

The insistent vibration of the phone drags me from the nightmare I'm in the middle of, a welcome relief from the carnage that would have filled my dreams otherwise. Whoever is after me seems keen. Without lifting my head from the pillow I reach out and fumble with my hand, almost knocking the phone to the floor but rescuing   it just in time. My bleary eyes take a moment to focus before I can read the name on the screen.

Why is Bandit calling me? We've not spoken for a number of years since our last big argument. He's never been able to reconcile the boy he once knew with the man I've become. At one time he played a huge part in my life, then fate played her cards and I took the wrong path. A path I can never come back from. His disappointment in me hurts, or it would if I could allow myself to care.

Between reaching for the phone and finally being able to focus on the screen too much time has passed and the call has dropped. Cursing, I sit upright in the bed roughly rubbing at my eyes to try and clear my vision and my thoughts. Checking the screen again I see a number of missed calls from Bandit but no voicemail icon. If it's that important I'm sure he'll ring back. I can't bring myself to be the one to break our silence and call him back.

Dread fills me when I realise he must be ringing with bad news, "Please don't let it be his wife Smokey," I call out to the universe. That woman is a saint. I'd do anything for her, aside from make my peace with Bandit. I know I broke her heart with my refusal, but what she was asking was too much for me. What they were both asking was too much. The boy they wanted back no longer exists. He's a memory. You can't bring back something that broken. It's just not possible.

It's only eight am but I'm wide awake now, although judging from the muted sounds outside I'm in the minority. My brothers like to party hard and I suspect the majority of them won't have hit the sack before three am at the earliest. Grateful for the silence and hopeful that means no unwanted conversations I pull on my jeans and head to the kitchen for something to eat.

Living from one motel to the next means I take what I can, when I can, when it comes to meals. One of the club sluts, whose name I've forgotten, has a skillet of bacon and eggs on the go and I practically inhale the food that she piles on my plate. For some reason the whole situation reminds me of being in Smokey's kitchen. I shake my head, trying to dislodge the thought. I don't have time for sentiments today or any day. I need to pack and hit the road again, onto the next job, the next deliverance of vengeance.

No sooner have the knife and fork hit the empty plate than my mobile rings again. It's Bandit. Swiping to accept the call I answer with a non committal grunt.

"Is that you, Danny?" His voice sounds hesitant.

"Danny doesn't exist anymore, I'm Wrath now as you well know." My voice is gruff and unwelcoming in response.

"Sorry, Wrath." He pauses after acknowledging my road name. "I need to talk to you, it's important. Can you come visit?"

"You know I can't," I respond. "Just tell me on the phone and I'll decide if it's important or not." I know I'm being an arsehole but I can't help myself. That last blow up we had was tough, we both said things we can never take back or forgive.

"This isn't something I can do over the phone, I'm sorry Wrath. I wouldn't ask if it wasn't really important. I need you." There's a long pause before he continues. "Please?" He begs.

The line goes silent while he waits for my reply. I can't

believe I'm even considering it, but in my head I'm calculating where I can fit him in. If I get this next job out of the way then I suppose I could run by his place for a day, it's not that far from where I need to be.

"Are you still there?" His question breaks the silence.

"I'll be there in three days," I offer. "Take it or leave it."

"I'll see you then, thank you." The relief in his voice is clear, although he doesn't sound his usual vibrant self, then again I guess a lot of time has passed. We've all aged. "Take care of yourself, Wrath." He hangs up without saying anything else.

Damn, I didn't ask him if Smokey was okay. Surely he'd have told me if she wasn't. Wouldn't he? Yeah, I reassure myself. Of course he would. My curiosity wanes as the club starts to come to life around me, I'll find out soon enough what he wants me for.

3
WRATH

I pull up on the suburban street a few houses away from my intended target and look around. It's a decent area, there are kids bikes abandoned on driveways and the homes are just far enough apart from their neighbour to allow a little privacy. The house I'm looking for stands out from its neighbours thanks to its neglected state. The lawn out front is overgrown and full of weeds whereas either side the lawns are neatly trimmed. The wood lap walls have peeling paintwork as do the window frames, although the glass in the frames is clean. That tells me that the man of the house isn't keeping up his side of the work, whereas the woman is still house proud.

I have an advantage I suppose in that I know who lives inside. This is the home of Jack and Freda Livingstone and their two children Alex and Letitia. In a short while it will be home to fewer people. This is the nature of my role as enforcer. It's not a job that I take pleasure in, but I think the remaining family will be far better off as a result of my actions.

I normally avoid collateral damage, but in this instance

I've been asked to carry out the hit in a very specific way. I don't agree with it, but my job is to do as I'm told. A lesson needs to be taught, and a message delivered.

Jack Livingstone owes the wrong people money, a fuck load of money. He's a gambler who doesn't know when to quit and you can tell from the state of the house that his priority isn't his family. From the size of the debt it's likely it's been a long time since they were. That grates on me. A father is supposed to take care of his loved ones, to provide for them, nurture them and care for them. Not that I'd know, mine didn't hang around long enough to see me born.

The bookie who is paying us isn't the kind of guy to accept excuses. He doesn't care about the why, you pay him what you owe him or you suffer. If you owe him enough money and you don't pay then you will suffer in such a way that the message is clear for everyone else who was thinking of missing a payment. Don't do it.

The kitchen door is ajar, letting in the slightly cooler outside air, and now me. I'm not bothered about sneaking in quietly, although I'd prefer not to wake the children if possible. I only need to do this in front of one witness for the message to get through. They don't need that memory scarring them for the rest of their lives if I can help it.

The muted sounds of the TV are audible through the walls and I follow them to the lounge where I find my target. The selfish bastard is sprawled on the sofa with a beer in hand and stuffing his face with a pizza while his wife looks on. I stand my ground and watch him for a while. He grunts demands at his wife, gesturing at her with the remote control and then throwing the empty beer bottle towards her head, no please or thank you. I move back into the shadows as she goes into the kitchen to bring back a fresh bottle placing it in front of him without words then retreating to her chair.

Jack lets loose a large belch and laughs, congratulating himself on his show of crassness. What a guy. I'll definitely be doing this family a favour removing him from their lives. Freda makes an effort at conversation but Jack cuts her off.

"Hush your mouth woman, can't you see I'm trying to watch TV!" He shouts across the room, dismissing her with a wave of his hand. I've seen enough, it's time to make my presence known.

I step forward, the weight of my boots deliberately loud against the laminate flooring. Freda lets out a gasp, bringing the back of her hand to her mouth and drawing in a frightened breath. The mother hen in her overcomes her fear and she stands abruptly crying out "Please don't hurt my children, please don't hurt my children." It's telling that she doesn't beg for herself, almost as though she's accepted her fate, whereas her arsehole of a husband shows concern only for himself as usual.

He blusters, putting on a false air of bravado that quickly disappears when I pull the gun out of the waistband at the back of my jeans. His cowardice displayed in the wet patch around his groin. The fucking pussy has wet himself. He isn't the first to lose control of his bladder in front of me and he sure as fuck won't be the last.

"I think we should take this into the kitchen, quietly" I advise in a calm, quiet voice that obviously carries enough menace that Freda moves without question. Jack carries on being a dick.

"I'm sure we can sort this out, it's all just a misunderstanding," he whines.

"So not paying Larry the 200 grand you owe him is a misunderstanding?" I question. Freda blanches at the amount.

"Well... I... It's a misunderstanding..." he splutters, his legs shaking so much he can barely stand.

"You were warned, more than once as I understand. You know the rules, you know the risks. Time to pay up." I reply, my voice monotone and disinterested.

"I, I can't pay you now." He laughs, the stupid fucker actually laughs at me. "What the hell, do you think I have it hidden down the back of the sofa?" He sneers.

"Oh you will pay me now," I respond. "This is one debt you can pay." I assure him. "With compound interest there's only one way to clear this debt." I lift my hand containing the gun and aim it at him. "On your knees."

Freda is standing there silent, and a glazed look on her face. She's gone a deathly shade of white, but she's just about holding it together. She sees me looking over at her and a shiver runs through her as she gathers strength to speak to me.

"Promise me you won't hurt my babies, please don't hurt

my babies." A single tear tracks down her cheek. She's one tough cookie and I respect the heck out of her for that.

"Your babies will be fine," I reassure her. "Larry will consider the debt paid after I've finished here tonight."

"Thank you," she whispers. Looking me square in the eye she continues, her voice full of resolve and strength. "I'm ready." As she finishes speaking she closes her eyes, not wanting to see the bullet coming.

"Oh, no Freda." I offer. "There's only one life required to pay this debt." I reassure her.

Jack's ears pick up and the selfish prick thinks he has a way out. "If we only need one life to pay the debt then take hers." He suggests.   Freda doesn't even show surprise at his words. I guess she knows how little she means to him already.

"Jack, Jack, Jack," I taunt. "Don't be so fucking stupid."

Realising there's no way out Jack starts begging and crying, I can't even say he's crying like a baby, it's worse than that. He has snot hanging from his nose and his eyes are red from tears. No doubt about it, Jack is one hell of an ugly crier.

"Look me in the eye, Jack." I command. "At least be a man at the end." Jack has his head hanging low, refusing to look at me and shaking his head side to side as the begging continues.

When he shows no sign of manning up I lose my patience, lifting my gun and taking him out with a single shot. I pause for a moment to make sure the bastards dead then turn and head for the kitchen door.

"I'm sorry for the mess I made, Freda." I apologise as I close the door behind me. What happens next isn't my problem. I've done the job I was paid to do, and with the bonus that the kids slept through it.

Walking back to my bike I'm mentally planning the route I need to take to go visit Bandit and find out what he wants from me. If I ride all night I can be there for breakfast.

Sounds like a plan to me.

4
WRATH

I pull up outside the house and set the bike on it's kickstand. I don't get off yet, just stare at the house where so much of my growing up happened. I came to live here full of anger after my mothers illness took it's toll and she couldn't care for us both anymore. Bandit isn't my Uncle by birth, but in every other way he's my family. He and Smokey kept an eye out for my mum when her parents turned their back on her when she got pregnant with me. My mum was an independent woman who hated asking anyone for help, but she gratefully accepted a job with Smokey at the garden centre running the little coffee shop there and was okay with them being in our lives every now and then.

Bandit's the one who taught me how to ride a bike, he gave me the gift of freedom, there's nothing like being on a powerful machine on an open road. I'll forever be grateful to him for that. Both he and Smokey struggled with the angry teenager they no longer recognised, but never stopped showing me love and affection. It was easier for me to cut ties with them when I joined the Cardinal Sins, they were a reminder of a past I was trying so hard to forget. Bandit would rather I'd joined his MC, Hellion, but to me it seemed full of old men with no danger or challenge. I'd found plenty of that with Cardinal, but these days I was starting to question if I'd made the right choice.

Even though it's just past dawn there are signs of life in the house. Bandit always was an early riser. Memories swirl around me, playing catch in the yard with Bandit, helping Smokey tidy up the garden, then sitting on the back deck with my mum near the end. It's peaceful here, no neighbours for miles and it gave my mum comfort. She loved this house. Thoughts of mum draw out mixed emotions, the love I can never forget that shone constantly in her eyes and the never ending pain at her loss, and how unfairly life treated her. She was a good woman, she deserved a better hand than she got.

The front door gives it's characteristic creak as it opens and Bandit heads down the path towards me. He gives me a head nod in greeting, and seems to be able to sense the indecisiveness of my mood.

"You coming in for breakfast?" He questions.

"I haven't decided yet," I respond honestly. Part of me itches to switch the bike back on and take off, and part of me is drawn to this man beside me. Deep down I know that it must have cost him a lot to ring me and ask for my help. He's a proud man, and I hurt them both deeply when I   left.

Bandit just slowly nods in understanding, standing at the

side of me and looking across the yard to the field beyond. The silence isn't un-nerving, if anything it's comforting. We stay like that for a few moments until I draw in a deep breath and pull my shoulders back. However bad this is going to be, Bandit needs me and I owe him the courtesy of at least hearing him out.

A small, almost imperceptible smile crosses his face when he sees me dismount. When he turns towards the house no words are spoken, I just follow him like I've done so many times before. It's only when we enter the large hallway that he breaks the silence.

"Smokey will be down in a minute, I didn't tell her you were coming. Just in case..." he pauses, then turns back to me and draws me into a tight hug. I'm not sure if it's for his benefit or mine until I feel him shaking with emotion. "Sorry I had to call you back, but there was no one else I could ask." He finishes cryptically.

Before I can question him there's a high pitched shriek and Smokey flies down the stairs towards me.

"Oh I've missed you so much, Danny." She whispers in my ear, her voice breaking with emotion. She's holding me so tightly it's as if she's afraid I'm not real and might disappear in a puff of smoke if she lets go. I wrap my large arms around her back and kiss the top of her head.

"I missed you too," I admit.

When she pulls away I'm sure I see tears in her eyes but she turns quickly, trying to hide her face from me while she

29

pulls herself together. "Who's ready for breakfast?" She asks, her voice cheery but still betraying her emotions.

"Is there a Y in the day woman?" Bandit laughs.

The kitchen has barely changed since I was last here, it's still the heart of this home, just a fresh coat of pale yellow on the walls rather than the white that used to be there. It makes it look even cosier if anything.

I pull out a chair from the large pine table that fills the centre of the room and sink into it, although I'm quick to rise when Smokey admonishes me. "Did you wash your hands yet, Danny?" The look of disapproval on her face has me making quick time to the washroom down the hall. She didn't have many rules but one of them was washing your hands before sitting down to eat.

Returning to the table I'm greeted with a plate full of home cooked goodness. My mouth is watering just from the memory of it. There are fresh eggs from the chooks out back, smoked bacon, sausages, hash browns, baked beans, mushrooms, grilled tomatoes and toast. I raise my knife trying to decide where to start. Hidden under several rashers of bacon I find a slice of black pudding. I remember being disgusted when the ingredients were first relayed to me, but these days I shut that out and just enjoy the taste of it. I cut a piece along with some hash brown and dip it in the runny egg yolk.

Smokey looks over at me and lets out a loud guffaw. "Good to see you still enjoy your food." She grins at me. Damn, that groan of satisfaction in my head must have echoed in my voice the way she's looking at me.

I'm too distracted by the food on my plate to worry about conversation right now. That can wait until after I've eaten my fill as I suspect I'm not going to like whatever news I'm about to receive. It must be something serious for me to have been summoned back here. I sneak a glance at both Smokey and Bandit, seeing if there are any clues on their faces and realise that they look old, really old. I know as a teenager anyone over the age of 21 is considered ancient, but I guess I always thought of these guys as invincible. I'm not sure time has been kind to them as both of them look tired and drawn. Although they're putting on a bloody good act for me, I've known them too long to be fooled by it.

The comfortable silence around the table is broken by Smokey, it's as though she has to fill the silence and rattles on about Rebel, and something about her mother having turned up last year. I'm only half listening. I remember Rebel, we spent some time together when I moved in with Bandit and Smokey, but not much. Having been raised by the club she was their princess and off limits.   I'd been invited to her birthday party last year, but declined, not wanting to revisit the past. I'm not the guy I used to be when I was a part of her life, or theirs.

Smokey is chattering away, unaware I've only caught a word here and there. I pay attention when she starts talking about a ranch for abandoned and orphaned children that

Rebel has set up. Her eyes light up as she talks and it's obvious she gets a lot of pleasure from helping out there. Bandit looks at her with love in his eyes. "Smokey does a good job over there helping mother those poor souls." He says, his voice full of pride.

"You do your bit when you can," she responds, but there's an edge to her voice I can't quite make out, followed by a sudden and uncomfortable silence. She breaks it by offering me some more bacon, seeing I've eaten all of mine.

"We'll talk after breakfast," Bandit makes sure that Smokey has her back to us before he speaks in a hushed tone. My appetite takes a slight nosedive, whatever it is, can't be good, but then Smokey appears at my side, a hot pan in her hand and piles more delicious food on my plate.

"Later," I nod to Bandit as soon as she returns the pan to the range. We'll definitely talk later.

5
WRATH

Smokey clears the table after breakfast and refuses my help in washing up, instead ushering Bandit and I out to the back deck with freshly brewed coffee.

"I'm heading to the ranch as soon as this is done to help with lunches," she tells me. "You will be here when I get back won't you? Do you think you could visit with us old folk for a couple of days?" There's so much longing in her voice, and I realise that I miss these people. I've put off coming back because of my anger and my memories, but none of it was their fault. They're not to blame, and if I'm honest with myself, I've missed them.

"I'll be here," I reassure her. She rushes over and hugs me tightly, then hmph's at her display of affection and returns to the dishes in the sink.

"Go drink your coffee, young man. Bandit's been looking forward to seeing you."

I head out to the back deck and slump into the cushioned seat.

"So, are you going to tell me what's going on old man?" I turn to him.

Bandit draws in a deep breath, and several times looks as though he's going to say something, but stops himself. Looking back to the kitchen he pauses for a moment, as though deciding what to say. "We'll talk when Smokey's gone out," he responds slowly, turning his head back to the view of fields in front of us and sitting silently.

Many's the night we've sat out here like this, not talking, just enjoying each other's company and the silence around us. I'm easy with that. I'll give him time, and it's obviously not going to be something I want to hear if he's having so much trouble saying the words.

We must have been there a good half hour when Smokey comes out brandishing fresh mugs of coffee for us, and kissing us a cheery goodbye as she heads off to the ranch she was talking about.

"That place has been good for her," Bandit acknowledges. "Means she has less time to mother me."

"You know you don't need mothering, old man," I tell him fondly. "You may have lost your arm in that accident, but you certainly didn't lose your independent streak." I smile.

A flash of something crosses his face, and I sit up straighter, trying to read him.

He grits his teeth a moment then just comes straight out with it. "There's no easy way to say this lad, I've got cancer, I'm dying." He looks at me, waiting for a response.

I can't have heard him right. Not Bandit, that guy's as strong as an ox. Surely life wouldn't be so cruel as to take two of the most important people away from me because of that fucking evil disease. I close my eyes and draw in a breath, trying to centre myself. It feels as though my world is splintering apart around me. I can't lose Bandit. He's the closest thing I've ever had to a father. He was there for me, holding me up and keeping me right all the way through mum's treatment and losing her. "No,... you can't... I don't... you can't be," I finally splutter out. There's a physical pain in my chest and it feels like I'm struggling to breathe. The world doesn't make sense to me right now.

I'm looking at the ground at my feet, unable to look him in the eye, because I know if I see his face then it will all be true and I can't handle that.

"Danny... Wrath," he corrects himself, "look at me boy." I draw my head up slowly and face him. The pain in my chest becomes tighter as I see the truth of his words on his face.

"No!" I shout, standing so quickly from the chair that I knock it over. "It can't be fucking true, it can't be." I pace back and forth across the deck, shaking my head, willing the words to have gone unspoken. If I never heard them then they can't be true.

Bandit's voice calls softly to me, and I let go of the anger clouding my vision long enough to take in the pain in his face. No matter how much I'm hurting right now, it's got to be so much worse for him. I need to man up and help him, support him.

"Sit down," he gestures to the chair I knocked over. I right it slowly and move it closer to his chair, before doing as I'm told and lowering myself into it. I look across at him, scrutinising him, wondering why I didn't see it, why I couldn't tell. He just looks tired, a little thinner than I remember, but then I've been away for a long time. Too long I realise. I should have been here when he needed me.

"They can treat cancer nowadays," I rush out. "They have chemo, radiotherapy, drugs and all sorts of shit. It's not like it used to be." I bluster.

Bandit shakes his head and looks at me sadly. "I left it too late, stubborn old fool that I am."

"What type of cancer is it?" I ask, my voice shaking and betraying the hurt I'm feeling. What a stupid question, I think to myself. It doesn't matter what fucking type of cancer it is, just that it's killing him.

"Fucking breast cancer," Bandit lets out a guffaw and I look at him in shock. It's obviously written on my face as he answers the unspoken question. "It's rare, but yeah, guys can get breast cancer too. I found a lump and just put it down to a sprain or muscle tear as you do. It didn't even hurt, it was just this hard, bumpy lump that didn't move." He takes a sip of his coffee and I imagine he's remembering ignoring the symptoms, then he continues. "It was only when I noticed it was getting bigger that Smokey finally persuaded me to go to the doc's and get it checked out."

"She knows?" I ask, trying to reconcile the smiling woman from earlier with the news I've just been told. Right now, I don't think I can smile, even for Bandit's benefit.

"She knows, " he nods slowly as he says the words.

"All of it?" I question.

"All of it."

"And you're sure they can't do chemo or some other fucking treatment?" There's a hint of anger in my voice now, not at Bandit but at the unfairness of the situation.

"They could, but I told them not to," he admits. "It wouldn't cure it, just delay it and not long enough to make suffering the side effects of the treatment worthwhile. It's spread too far now."

"How long have you known?" I ask him, wondering how long he's kept this secret. "Who else knows?"

"About the cancer, a couple of months, about the prognosis just over a week." He takes another sip of coffee and I wonder how he can seem so calm. "No one else knows, and no one else is going to know." He tells me in that firm voice of his that means he's not asking me to keep it to myself, he's telling me.

"Why didn't you call me sooner?" Right now I feel so much guilt that I wasn't here for him.

"Because I didn't need you before," he pauses a moment then gets out of his chair to come stand in front of me. "I didn't need you before, but I do now. I know what you are Wrath, I know what you do. I need you to do it for me." He turns his

37

back on me, and looks out over the field before destroying me with his next sentence.

"I want you to kill me."

6
WRATH

I look at Bandit in shock, my jaw dropped. I can't have heard him right. He sees the look on my face and repeats himself.

"I want you to kill me, Wrath." He says it in the same tone he'd use to ask me what I thought of the game last night, not as though he's just destroyed my world.

I shake my head angrily in response as I can't seem to get any words out.

"Listen to me, I need this. I can't tell you how much pain I'm in constantly, and I can't go through what your mum went through, not only for me, but for Smokey. I just can't put her through that again."

I'm still sat there unable to utter a single word, shaking my head no. He can't ask this of me. I want to shout and rail at him, but when he reminded me of the hell that mum went through, I got it. I wouldn't have wished that on my worst enemy, and especially not on a guy like Bandit. He doesn't deserve this. Mum didn't deserve it.

"I can't do it on my own, Wrath," he pleads. "How the hell is a one armed man supposed to commit suicide other than with a gun?" He looks at me, his face so haggard now it's destroying my soul to hear him beg. "If I use a gun then the insurance won't pay out, it's got to look natural, I can't go knowing that Smokey won't be taken care of."

I know he's right, and I'm sure he's thought this through and examined all the options, but I can't do it. I know I'm an enforcer, it's my job, but Bandit isn't a job, he's one of the few people I give a shit about. I'd say I love him but I don't think I'm capable of love, I'm too broken for that. That emotion left me a long time ago when I held my mums hand as she took her last breath.

Unwelcome as they are the memories surge up and take over. I've kept them hidden away too long and they're demanding to be let loose. Putting my head in my hands I give in to the past.

The body in the bed looks so small and almost like a stranger to me. Without the drips and machines that crowded the bed at the hospital I want to believe that she's going to get better, she's just asleep and will wake up soon. In my heart I know that's not going to happen. She's come home to die. She'd begged us to bring her home so she could die in her own bed, whether she was at home or the hospital wouldn't change a thing, this ending was inevitable, no matter how much we railed against it.

The sedation means her breathing is more gentle, less

laboured although still slightly louder than normal. Watching her fight for breath was horrible, and hearing her describe the fear she felt that she wouldn't be able to draw the next breath was soul destroying. There were constant battles to get her put back on oxygen every time they discharged her, the Occupational Therapists telling us she could manage without it, but mum telling us she couldn't. The worst thing is we believed the OT's, why wouldn't we, they were the medical professionals. We pushed her and pushed her to try and carry out normal everyday tasks not realising until too late just how impossible it was for her. The last time we took her in to the ER her oxygen level was only 50, the OT's were wrong. She couldn't manage. I'm sure that losing that argument hastened the end for mum,. They'd said the cancer was treatable, she was just too weak right then to have the chemo and radiotherapy she needed, but they gave her steroids and were sure in a month or so she'd be strong enough. We never got the month.

At least in the hospital there were staff available to call on, someone who knew what to do when the machines beeped a different noise or she cried out in pain, needing more drugs to numb her back to sleep. Here at home, it was just us and a machine that pumped drugs in automatically that the community nurse topped up as required then locked behind her. Hidden away under the covers you wouldn't even know it was there. A small box no bigger than a house brick, if that, was all that kept her with us. Every day the dose was *increased to deal with her increasing levels of pain, the more she slipped away from us.*

I wanted to tear it out and have my mum back, but having seen several of the vicious pain attacks she endured I just didn't have the heart to do it. I couldn't bear to watch her suffer. The pain nurse had explained that even now, despite the technological advances we'd made, they still couldn't stop nerve pain. I'd expected morphine to magically ease the pain as it had in the past, but even the oral version had no more effect than a soda. It had taken a few days for the gabapentin to build up in her system and then she'd seemed to rally, more her old self, sat up in bed laughing and joking with us and hope had bloomed, despite the fatal prognosis received just a few days before. How could she be terminal when she looked so like her old self. It just didn't make sense.

It was all false hope, just days later, albeit almost a week after I'd been told she wouldn't last the weekend, she took a turn for the worse. We'd brought her home a few days earlier, the doctors unable to offer us anything that would convince her to stay in hospital.

The double bed drowned her, the weight loss evident by how little space she took up. We'd settled her slightly off centre of the bed so I could crawl on beside her, and lay there watching over her, careful not to get too close and trigger the pain any movement made. I refused to leave her side that last day, some inner knowledge telling me these few hours were all I would have with her and not wanting to waste a moment away from her.

Smokey came and went, checking to make sure the drug machine was working and she didn't need changing, occasionally dampening her lips with a small wet sponge. They looked so dry and cracked I was sure they must be sore, but she didn't seem to notice. That last day she didn't even know I was there. She'd been out of it the previous day, rousing only occasionally to complain of a figure standing at the foot of the bed. Smokey explained that the drugs were causing her to hallucinate, but for the most part they kept her pain free as far as I could tell.

It was early evening when the community nurse came for the last time, the look of pity on her face as she left the room almost destroying me. Refusing offers of food and ignoring the drink that Smokey kept refreshing for me on the side of the bed, I laid there beside her, gently holding her hand and just talking to her about inane things. Adventures we'd shared together, memories we'd made, but that would be all I would have left of her soon.

Several times throughout the long night she would draw in a breath and then pause just a moment, filling me with dread that this was it, this was the end, and then letting out a loud gasp as the next breath filled her depleted and damaged lungs.

When it came it was almost a non event, there was no pause, no gasp, she simply didn't take the next breath. It was as close to peaceful as you could get I guess, if you ignored the horror she'd endured the past few months. I laid there waiting for that next breath but it never came.

I'm not sure how long I laid there before Smokey came in to check on her, it felt like an eternity but probably wasn't. Looking at the bed she let out a small sigh and left the room, returning only moments later with the community nurse. From the hushed conversation between the two women it seemed the nurse had known it was coming and hadn't left. Bandit came into the room and leaned over to kiss mum on the forehead, calling her his angel. It took him several minutes to persuade me to leave her side so Smokey and the nurse could take care of her. I didn't want to leave, not willing to believe what I knew in my heart to be true. She was gone. The essence that was my mum wasn't with us anymore, all that was left behind was this empty shell. I wanted to hold her tight, tell her how much I loved her and needed her and have her back, but it wouldn't change anything.

"She's not suffering anymore, Danny, take comfort in that." Bandit offered. She had suffered, she had suffered more than anyone deserved or should. I knew that what he was telling me was true, but it didn't do a thing to stop the hurt in my heart right then.

Easing us from the room he paused as I turned to take a final look at the woman I would love with all my heart forever.

Recalling that night and the pain that I still carried with me daily brought everything to the surface. Turning to look at

Bandit I gave him the answer he didn't want to hear.

"I'm sorry, Bandit. I can't. I won't." Standing abruptly from the chair I turned my back on him and fled.

7
WRATH

I fire up the bike and speed off, the roar of the pipes instantly easing the tension that's tightening across my shoulders. Being on the bike is the only place I truly feel free. I've only had it a few months, having had to replace the old one when I crashed it after taking a bend too fast. It could have been repaired but when I saw the Harley Low Rider S in the showroom I had to have it. It's all blacked out which means it's understated, and the lower rake on the handlebars gives a more comfortable ride on long journeys. With the work I do for the club there are far too many of those.

When I'm on the bike I have to concentrate on the road, there's no room for the shit that constantly fills my head, I proved that when I trashed my last bike. Instead, I concentrate on that throaty Harley raw that screams out just how much power I'm controlling, alert always to what's happening around me, just waiting for a lazy car driver to pull out in front of me without looking or something similar.

The roads around here are pretty quiet though and the

bike handles flawlessly. Glancing down at the speedo I can see I'm way over the limit, but there's no indication that this baby can't handle more. Nevertheless, I ease back on the throttle, not needing some over zealous cop to chew my ass off as the mood I'm in it wouldn't end well.

I'd half expected to stay over with Bandit and Smokey tonight, but after what he's just asked me I can't go back. Not yet. I need time to process what I've just been told and to deal with the memories it's woken up. I won't abandon him, but right now I'm hurting so badly that I can't help him. There's no way I can do what he's asked of me, I know why he asked, but who I am with the Cardinal's is not the man they know nor the man I am around him and Smokey. They're my past and I can't let my present ruin what was. I won't defile the good memories.

I slow down a little more as I spot a sign for a bar that offers motel style accommodation. Right now a drink or several sounds like the perfect solution. The rooms don't look that great, but all I need is a bed to crash in so they'll do.

When I open the door to the room I've been given I almost groan, it's clean which is about all it has going in its favour, I don't think they've decorated since the seventies and it looks like the set of a cheap porno. The sheets on the bed are worn in places and the curtains and carpet clash in shades of brown and green. I've honestly slept in worse. I toss my pack on the bed and turn my back on the room, desperately in need of the solace from a bottle of bourbon.

The interior is dark after the bright light of day outside, but as my eyes adjust the gloom suits it. There's a bar along the back wall that looks well stocked, and a room full of booths and tables and chairs with a small stage and dance floor in one corner. It's empty now. I look at my watch realising I've no idea what time it is, and realise I must have ridden further than I thought as I've lost several hours. It's five o'clock already. An appetising aroma of burgers wafts near me and my stomach grumbles quietly reminding me I should eat.

Turning I see a waitress walking past with a tray of food, heading for one of the booths in the back. I take a moment to appreciate the tight fit of the jeans on her ass and the sway of her hips. The guy behind the bar notices me and calls over asking if he can help me. I pull my eyes from the waitress and head over, eying the selection of bourbons I spot on the back wall.

"I'll take a double Makers Mark on ice," I point at the bottle.

"Good choice," the barman agrees. "Want any food with that?" He reaches over to the side and grabs a plastic covered menu before offering it to me.

"What's good?" I ask, perusing the list. It's a burger and steak bar primarily, but I notice they offer a few vegetarian and gluten free options too. What the hell is wrong with meat? Why do they have to have this trendy shit on offer?

He recommends the double burger and fries with a side of onion rings and coleslaw, all homemade he assures me and

I go with it. We chat about nothing as he busies himself ringing up my order and making my drink. It's nice to have someone not look at me as though I'm trouble as soon as I walk in the door.

It's still early and the bar's quiet so it doesn't take long for my food to arrive. It's delivered by the same waitress I saw earlier and the front view is equally as good as her rear. She's got long dark hair that's pulled back in a pony tail and a strappy white vest that gives just a hint of cleavage between a pretty nice rack. She's just polite and friendly enough to merit a tip, but doesn't hang around for conversation.

The food's as good as it smelled and I wolf it down. One of the downsides of being on the road so often is the crap I often find myself eating, so it's a pleasant change to find this place. The bourbon is good and I'm being left to my own thoughts as the bar fills up around me. When I've finished my meal the waitress comes by and collects the plates, offering a selection of desserts and pies.

"Are you on the menu?" I joke, and watch a shadow cross her face.

"I'm disappointed in you biker boy, for a minute there I thought you were different," she huffs.

"I'm sorry," I find myself apologising. She's not the same as the usual bar bunnies I've encountered before who come across as desperate and cheap. "No dessert thank you, but do tell the chef that was one of the best meals I've eaten in a long time."

"You've obviously been eating in the wrong places," her laugh has a throatiness to it that makes my cock react. Before I can continue the conversation she's turned her back on me and gone.

"Shot down at the first hurdle, want another drink?" The barman is at my shoulder and enjoying my knock back. I don't blame him. He quickly pours me another bourbon and I resume my people watching.

There's something about people watching that I can't explain. I can do it for hours. It's something I'd do with my mum, sat in the diner or the park and we'd make up stories about the strangers we were observing, the crazier the better.

The guy in the corner in the cowboy hat, for example, was a secret billionaire, he'd invented some farming machinery that was going to transform the third world and was on the lookout for his next trophy wife. In reality I suspect he was just a simple ranch hand enjoying a rare night off.

The two young guys in the back booth looked like college guys, so less inventive here, I pegged them as football heroes just out to get wild and drunk. The dark haired men in the far booth I decided were drug dealers, discussing their next deal. Hey, I can't help it, the more bourbon I drank the less imaginative I became. Mum was always better at the game than I was.

Sadness fills me whenever I think of mum, and I lose myself in the memories of those last few days with her. I can't help it after what happened with Bandit this morning. As much as I don't want to remember her like this, it's always the first memory that comes to mind.

"Are you okay?" I didn't notice the waitress come up beside me. She's leaning over the bar handing in her apron. "I'll see you tomorrow, Mike. Have a good one." She turns back to me, concern on her face.

"Just a bad memory," I offer. "I'll be fine." She doesn't look like she believes me, and points towards my glass.

"Want another and tell me about it?" She offers.

"Thought you were heading out?"

"I've always got time for a stranger in need," she holds her hand out to me. "I'm Maeve, nice to meet you."

"Wrath," I take her hand and bring it to my lips, kissing the back of it. "It's a pleasure to meet you, Maeve."

She shouts across at the barman, ordering two more of whatever I was having and settles herself on the bar stool beside me.

"So tell me all about it, Wrath? What's brought the sadness to those lovely dark eyes of yours?"

"Wouldn't you like to know?" I laugh bitterly and down the drink Mike just placed in front of me. "Set them up again, Mike," I request. "Looks like it could be a long night."

8
WRATH

The door to the motel room creaks open slowly and Maeve giggles behind me. "That sounded like something out of a horror movie, are we going to get murdered in there?"

I still, does she know what I really am, and how plausible what she just said is? I have murdered women over the years, not just men. The only line I draw is children, I won't punish them for the sins of their fathers no matter how high the pay.

Maeve spent all night chatting to me, and although she's not drunk, she's definitely had a few more bourbons than is safe for her to drive home. She accepted my offer of a bed for the night, although I think we both know there's not going to be much sleeping. There's some weird connection here between us, but she's fully aware that it's not going to last beyond tonight. That's not who I am or what I do.

I'm not sure why Maeve agreed to this, but I'm not going to try and dissuade her. My cock is hungry for her, and I can't wait to sink into her sweet pussy and feel her wrapped around me.

"I'll keep you safe," I whisper in her ear.

"Not too safe," she laughs out loud, "I'm kind of hoping you're going to turn into the big bad wolf when we get in there and you're going to eat me up!" No sooner has she said the words than a blush fills her face, she's obviously not comfortable with talking about sex, no matter how much she wants it.

"Oh, I'm definitely going to eat you up," I promise, dragging her into the room behind me. I turn the key in the lock and out of habit pocket it. Her eyes raise in alarm at the action. "Force of habit," I confess. "I don't want anyone knocking the key out and retrieving it under the door."

"What kind of life do you lead, Wrath, that you have those kind of thoughts?" She genuinely looks interested.

"Not one you need to know about." I shrug. We've talked a lot tonight, but not about anything important. I know she grew up around here,   she's single and her favourite band is Shinedown. I don't need to know any more. "Come here," I command, my voice husky with desire and goddamn me but she does just that.

She's looking at me, and there's a combination of lust and wariness in her eyes. This girl doesn't do hook ups, that much is obvious. I trace a finger down her cheek and rest it on her lips. "No talking." She nods her head in compliance then surprises the fuck out of me when she draws my finger into her mouth and sucks on it.

My cock is straining in my jeans, but not for long as the

cheeky minx already has her hands working away on the buckle of my belt. She draws my jeans down at the same time she lowers herself to her knees. I'm lost for words when she takes my cock in her hand, wrapping her fingers around it just tight enough to grip without pain. She eases her hand up and down, massaging my length and drawing a groan of pleasure from me then leans forward and takes me in her mouth. Holy fuck! Her warm mouth feels amazing around my cock, and she teases the length with her tongue as she draws me in and out. Her slow, steady rhythm increasing until I'm fucking her mouth.

My hands tangle in her hair, holding her in place, so close to losing it, but enjoying the experience too much to tell her to stop. Her pace increases and I can't stop myself as I flood in to her mouth. She lowers her ass back onto her feet, still kneeling and looks up at me as she licks her lips. This is not how I expected this evening to go, I guess I'd thought that even as hot as she is, this would be a totally vanilla experience.

Maeve stands slowly and stalks towards me, lifting her vest over her head as she walks, revealing pert breasts in a simple white bra. "I think you still have too many clothes on," her voice almost purrs as she starts to undo the button on her jeans and slides them down her legs. She teases me with how slowly she removes her bra and panties.

"I think you're right!" I agree and make quick work of removing my boots, jeans and tee, although in a far less elegant way than she just did. We stand facing each other, naked and

I have to say I really like the view in front of me. Maeve isn't as confident as her words and actions led me to believe. Now she's naked there's a nervous air about her, and I know that what I say next will make all the difference. I'm not sure who caused this woman to doubt how beautiful she is, but he was a dick for sure.

"You look amazing," I place my lips on the top of her shoulder and leave a gentle trail of kisses in my wake as I move lower down her body. Her head falls back when my lips graze her nipples, but I have another destination in mind first, "I'll come back to these, but I seem to remember promising to eat you." Her body stiffens, but I carry on kissing my way down, and as soon as my hands reach for the crease between her legs she relaxes only to tense again when I start flicking my thumb against her clit. Her legs start to tremble so I pick her up and lay her back on the edge of the bed, my tongue now joining my thumb, as I lick across her wet slit. Her back arches in pleasure and I continue until I feel the climax fill her body.

She sags back against the bed, wasted. "I, I just can't…" she pants out. "That was fucking breathtaking."

It seems weird hearing Maeve swear, but the way she says it so naturally fills me with pleasure. In any other circumstance I could see myself with a woman like her, if I hadn't been leading the life I have. I'm only going to have this one night of escape with her so I plan on making it one I'll remember for a long time.

"Turn over," I command as I pull a condom from my

wallet and slowly wrap my length in it. "Let me see that gorgeous ass in the air for me." She does as I ask and I stand behind her, admiring the globes of her ass, running my palms against them. She shivers in anticipation and without a moments thought I raise my hand and slap her. She doesn't complain, and that turns me on even more. Lining up behind her I thrust into her quickly, taking a moment to appreciate how she feels wrapped around my cock.

"Oh, god, that feels so fucking good," she whimpers.

I slap her ass again and her pussy clenches tightly around me, squeezing me and it feels fucking amazing. I tease her by almost pulling out and when she lets out a moan of disappointment ram myself back in until I'm balls deep in her, repeating the motion as quickly as I can.

"Can I make a suggestion," she pants out. I pause mid thrust, curious to hear what she's going to say. She shimmies up so she's laid flat on the bed, her legs together. "Put your legs either side of mine and try that again." I do as she suggests and holy fuck, that's even tighter and deeper than it was with her laid over the edge of the bed.

"Fuck, yes!" She cries out at the sensations as I thrust in and out of her in this new position. My cock has never had it this good and I thrust harder and harder. This woman is a bloody enigma, but I'm not complaining.

It doesn't take long before she screams out her orgasm, and as much as I'd like to make this last all night I soon follow. Discarding the condom I flop on the bed beside her, breathless.

"That was fucking incredible," I tell her.

"You're telling me," she laughs softly. "I sure as hell didn't expect my night to end like this when I came to work this morning."

"Who said the night has ended yet?" She looks at me from the corner of her eye, her hair splayed around her.

"I like the sound of that."

As I thought, there's no sleeping getting done tonight.

9
WRATH

It was sunrise before we finally fell asleep, sated. We'd had hard and fast sex as well as slow and sensual, not to mention a bloody outstanding blowjob or two. We'd explored each others bodies with a familiarity that was lacking outside of the bedroom. When it came down to it neither of us really knew much about the other.

When I opened my eyes I half expected her to have gone, to have crept from the room. But there she still lay fast asleep, her lips slightly parted as she faced me, her dark hair framing her face. She made me wish I was a different man. This was the kind of girl you'd take home to meet your mother, not the kind you had a sordid one nighter with in a seedy motel room.

I felt guilty for how I'd treated her, that I'd encouraged her in to this, but I couldn't regret the night that we'd spent together. This would be a memory I could look back on without pain, and god knew, there were few of those in my life.

Reaching for my phone, trying not to disturb Maeve, I checked my messages. Prez was hassling me to check in, no doubt he had a shit load of contracts lined up for me. I'd contacted him yesterday when I got to the bar telling him I needed a few days to sort some family shit out. From the look of the messages on the phone he didn't give a crap.

Yesterday had highlighted how far I had fallen, how numb to the world around me I'd become. This isn't what my mum would have wanted for me. All she ever wanted was for me to be happy, and I was about as far from that as you could get these days.

I should never have moved away, never come across Cardinal MC, but as soon as I could I'd run away, thinking I could leave the grief behind me. The club welcomed me with open arms and slowly turned me into the weapon that I was today.

For too long I'd let anger rule me, and forced emotion and feelings as deep down as I could. If I wasn't around decent people then I had no need of a conscience. I'd had a good life once, I'd been happy. And then I'd lost mum to cancer and I couldn't get over the anger and hate that constantly flooded my veins.

Bandit and Smokey had tried to give me a home, and I knew deep down they loved me as though I were their own, their club Hellion MC had welcomed me, and I knew that Bandit hoped one day I'd patch in and become one of them. I couldn't. Being around any of them just reminded me of what I'd lost.

Hellion and Carnal were about as far apart as you could

get, chalk and cheese. The only common denominator being the bikes. Hellion were all about family and brotherhood, they'd even taken Rebel in and raised her as one of their own when she was abandoned at the club gates as a baby. Carnal on the other hand were all about money, and they didn't care if it was earned legally or not. They'd have sold Rebel to the highest fucking bidder if she'd been dumped on their doorstep.

That thought was pretty sobering. When you thought about it more closely none of the Carnal guys had old ladies or kids. I'd spent over a decade with them, slowly being poisoned by their greed and constant search for power. My wellbeing counted for nothing, only the contracts I could bring in.

Looking over at Maeve I knew that I could never have a life that would include someone like her, life expectancy with Carnal wasn't high and that alone was reason enough to walk away. Someone had hurt her in the past, and she deserved someone who would treat her like the princess she was.

She also deserved more than a one night hook up in a joint like this. I was curious about her, I'll be honest I wanted to know more about her, what made her tick, where she lived and how come she was working in a bar. I had no right to know these things though. I had no right to be around good people.

My thoughts went back to Bandit and what he'd asked me yesterday. As much as I didn't want to see him suffer, I couldn't be the one to end it for him. I realised that deep down I loved Bandit and Smokey as much as I'd loved my mum, but they were from my old life. Crossing the lines between old and new just wasn't something I could do.

Last night with Maeve was as close as I've got to the old me since I left. In order to do the job I do, I can't allow that version to surface at all.

She stirs slightly at the side of me, and part of me wants her to stay asleep, that way I can have just a little more time with her, live that illusion just a little longer.

"Hey," she greets me drowsily, sitting up and rubbing the sleep from her eyes. "Any chance of coffee?" Her eyes roam around the room in search of a coffee pot. I didn't take any notice yesterday so I'm not sure if there's one here either.

It looks like we're out of luck. "Well, I don't know about you," she stretches which causes her nipples to stand out even more, "but I think I'm going to head next door for coffee and toast."

Right now, coffee is the last thing on my mind. I'm captivated by those nipples and vaguely remember promising to lavish some attention on them last night but we kind of got distracted by all the sex instead.

"You sure you want coffee rather than a repeat of last night?" My cock is twitching in anticipation of her answer.

"I would love a repeat of last night," she sighs, 'but I think we broke my hoo ha." What the hell did she just call it? Her hoo ha? I sure as shit have never heard it called that before and break out in loud guffaws of laughter.

"I can kiss it better for you," I offer with a wink.

"I don't think so, biker boy, that's what got it in this state in the first place." Much to my disappointment she rises from the bed and heads for the bathroom, throwing me a kiss in her wake.

I hear the water come on in the shower and almost leave her in peace, but the memory of those pert nipples calls out to me. I can't resist the thought of them and decide to join her, her hoo ha may be off limits this morning but the rest of her body isn't.

Coffee can wait.

10
WRATH

Mike looks at me warily as we head into the bar for breakfast and coffee, but Maeve silences him with a shake of her head. It's good to see that she has someone looking out for her around here.

Unlike most of the bars I frequent this place actually looks okay in the daylight. Maeve leads me to a table close to the bar rather than a booth, and insists on going up to place our order herself. I let her as I'm sure she'll be getting the third degree from Mike and he'll serve her more civilly than me.

I feel bad that I've put her in an awkward position, but not that bad when I replay our shower in my head. Maeve comes back, her cheeks flushed with colour and I suspect that Mike may have called her out on her nighttime companion.

"Everything okay?" I gesture my head to the bar.

"It's fine, Mike's just looking out for me, but he forgets I'm a big girl now." She grins. She must have smoothed out whatever it was as Mike is smiling when he walks over with two mugs of freshly brewed coffee. I thank him and he nods at me in acknowledgment then heads back to the bar without uttering a word.

The breakfast is good, and so is the company. I feel an urge to have more of this in my life, but I know that I can't. Doing the job I do, I can't afford to show affection for anyone, it could be used against me. For now, I'll take this illusion and run with it.

"What time are you at work today?" I look at Maeve, who currently has a mouth full of bacon and can't reply. She quickly swallows it down so she can answer.

"I'm not, it's my day off. Why, what are you thinking?" She doesn't wait for my answer before she loads up her fork with the next mouthful. Got to love a woman with an appetite. That thought brings up the memory of her lips wrapped around my cock last night and I have to adjust myself before I reply. She notices and smirks at me.

"Just wanted to make sure you weren't going to be late is all." I pretend indifference. What I really want is to ask her to spend the day with me, I have a yearning for a day of normality before resuming my club life.

"You want to spend the day with me? There's a pretty cool place I go on my day off I'd like to share with you."

I'm intrigued to know more about Maeve's life and want to spend some more time with her, so I agree to her plan. She won't tell me where we're going and I kind of like that she's keeping me on my toes. When we head outside I eye up her truck with distaste. She chuckles softly and suggests that

64

maybe we should go on my bike instead. There's more to Maeve than meets the eye as she has no problem getting on the back of the Harley, looking as though she's been doing it all her life.

She wraps her arms confidently around my waist and gives me rough directions, agreeing to tap me on the shoulder when we come close to the turnoff, knowing the noise of the bike will be too loud to hear her words.

We pull off the road and head towards the Double D ranch, the name sounds vaguely familiar but I'm not sure why. As we come to a stop outside the ranch house I realise it must be the place Smokey was talking about yesterday.

A woman comes out to greet Maeve and looks me up and down with interest.

"Good to see you, Maeve, who's your friend?" She walks towards me and holds out her hand in greeting. "I"m Dee Dee, I help run this place."

"Nice to meet you, I'm Wrath." I offer in reply. She doesn't seem at all phased by my appearance or the bike but then I remember that this is Rebel's place so she's obviously used to having the Hellion guys over.

She leads us over to a barn at the back of the main house where a group of teens are gathered around an older looking guy who's showing them how to build a camp fire. One of the girls looks up and grins as she spots Maeve, waving her over and making room for her to sit beside her. The group welcomes her in, it's obvious she has a longstanding relationship with them.

The older guy looks at me with interest and Maeve rushes to introduce us.

"Jackson, this is my friend Wrath, he's just passing through but I wanted to show him this place. Wrath, this is my friend Jackson, his daughter Rebel runs the ranch."

It suddenly clicks that I know this guy, after all he hasn't aged that much since I last saw him, unlike me, and I can see a look on his face, he's trying to figure out why I look familiar.

"Nice to see you again, Jackson" I greet him, "it's been a while. You might remember me as Danny." Recognition lights up his face and he comes over and pulls me into a hug.

"Good to see you again, you've grown up a bit since I last saw you." His voice is warm with greeting.

We spend most of the day at the ranch, and I love it. I could have done with somewhere like this to come when I lost my mum, the majority of the kids here are orphans. I guess I was too, although I never really felt like one as I had Bandit and Smokey looking out for me. These guys have nothing, some of the stories Maeve tells me make me angry. These kids aren't just alone, a lot of them have suffered abuse at the hands of bad foster families. This place is giving them a second chance, and a safer more secure future thanks to the life skills they're being taught.

A lot of the guys from Hellion MC and their wives are involved, and I'm shocked to find out that the woman running the ranch is Rebel's mother who turned up out of the blue last year. She seems a decent woman though and certainly adores the kids under her care.

"So how come you ended up helping out here?" I ask Maeve. We're sitting around the camp fire that the kids have built, and enjoying the barbecue food that Maeve and Dee Dee taught them how to make.

"I heard about the work they do here and felt like I needed to, I had a tough time growing up and wanted to give something back, help someone else out so they didn't have to go through some of the stuff I did." She doesn't offer anymore and right now I don't question her, whatever memory she drew on cast a shadow on her face and I want my happy, smiley Maeve back.

"It's a good place." I tell her, it really is. You can see that some of the kids are still a little wary of strangers, but for the most they're a good bunch and learning to trust again. The ranch helps them by teaching them life skills, keeping them safe, giving them a loving environment and helping them get on their feet when it's time to leave the system. Rebel's done a great thing here.

"Thank you," Maeve looks up at me from where she's resting on my chest facing the fire.

"What for?"

"For last night and today, I know this isn't you, and I know you can't stay, but I wanted to say thank you." We never did get round to discussing me, other than how I knew Jackson and we definitely didn't discuss my past with Cardinal MC.

I pull myself back to reality, this isn't my life and it can't be. A little too brusquely I rise to my feet pulling Maeve up with me. "It's getting late, I'd better get you home."

Today was a nice interlude, but tomorrow I need to get back to being me. And as much as I don't want to, tomorrow I have to go and speak to Bandit.

He needs me.

11
WRATH

I dropped Maeve off at her truck, practically ignoring her once we got back. I know I looked like a cruel shit, but I had to leave her hating me, not wanting me. I can't be the man she wants or needs.

I decided to crash in the motel only because the room was paid for and it was late, although I was desperate to escape.

The bed smelled of Maeve, and it felt too big without her limbs wrapped around mine. Everywhere I looked in the room a memory of her was reflected. It was a long night of tossing and turning, not to mention the nightmares that haunted me from all the heinous acts I'd committed since I joined Cardinal MC. I realised I hadn't had a nightmare the previous night with Maeve. There was something about her that quieted the beast within me.

I'm sure I saw the light of dawn as it crept under the door and through the narrow gap in the thin curtains before I finally succumbed to sleep.

It was the vibrating of my phone that woke me, and I was

all set to ignore it when some sixth sense urged me to answer. Bandits number filled the screen and I accepted the call warily.

"Wrath." I stated, my usual one word greeting.

"Danny..." a woman's voice softly cried down the line. "I need you, Danny." I recognised Smokey's voice, but only just. She sounded like she was in pain. I'd never heard her so distraught.

"I'm on my way." Without thinking I dashed for the shower, moving as quickly as I could, not even drying off properly before I pulled my jeans, tee and boots on along with my leather jacket.

The ride to their house felt like it took forever, even though I knew that it was only a few miles. The day I'd left I'd taken a circuitous route, today I went in a direct line. The curtains were still drawn when I pulled up and it looked like the house was still sleeping. Warily I dropped my bike on the kickstand. The front door was slightly ajar, so I entered without knocking. I followed the sound of Smokey's crying to the kitchen where I found her slumped over the kitchen table, an empty box of tissues in front of her and the evidence of a long bout of crying crumpled all around it.

I slowly walked towards her and hesitantly placed my arm across her shoulders. She turned into me and if I thought she'd been crying before it was nothing compared to the torrent of grief she released on me, my tee quickly soaking through from her tears. She was taking huge gulping sobs and couldn't seem to stop herself. I did the only thing I could, I held her close and slowly stroked her back, whispering inane platitudes that I doubt she could hear anyway.

I looked around the kitchen but there was no sign of Bandit, it looked just as I'd expect first thing on a morning before breakfast. The house was silent so I assumed he was upstairs sleeping, probably having had a bad night.

Slowly Smokey pulled herself together, her sobs easing and her breathing less laboured, although I could feel the tears continue to fall. When she'd finally calmed enough to speak she sat back and apologised for making a mess of my tee.

"Don't be daft woman, that's what I'm here for." I reassured her. Many was the night she'd held a sobbing teenage boy against her chest, lost in his grief for his mum. It was the least I could do for her, knowing what lay ahead for her and knowing there was nothing I could do to fix it. She'd listened to me rail against the universe for the injustice of my loss. She'd held me tight and told me she'd always be there for me, then stayed with me as I cried myself to sleep.

Smokey was always so strong, or at least that's the memory I have of her. She hadn't had the easiest of lives and had gone through hell when Bandit lost his arm, but she was just grateful he survived the accident, she didn't care if what she got back wasn't the whole man she'd married, she'd take him any way she could have him. They were such a perfect match for each other and had been through so much, they were the strongest couple I knew. Looking at the broken woman in front of me, I wasn't sure that she'd be able to get through the journey ahead with Bandit. I knew that my place right now was here with her. I had to help her through what was coming. We'd both seen it firsthand with my mum, and as much as that had hurt her, there was a good chance that losing Bandit would destroy her. I couldn't take that risk.

Cardinal MC would release me, I'd served them well for the best part of my adult life, but I also knew that they'd never have me back. I was no use to them if I couldn't be the enforcer they demanded, and looking at Smokey I knew I couldn't go back. Right now I needed to be the man my mum would have wanted me to be, not the angry destroyer I'd turned into.

I felt guilty that I'd left Bandit and Smokey behind like I had, but my being here wouldn't have stopped him getting cancer, nothing would. All I could do now was be here for them both, and support Smokey when the inevitable happened.

"Did he have a bad night?" I ask, looking at the ceiling, knowing their bedroom was above the kitchen we were in and feeling bad that I didn't come to see him yesterday, instead selfishly enjoying my day with Maeve.

Smokey looks gaunt, tear tracks marking her face. She reaches for a tissue, unconcerned that it's obviously already been used and blows her nose loudly.

"I guess you could say he had a bad night," she almost whispers.

"I killed him."

12
WRATH

I look at Smokey in shock, I can't have heard that right.

"I killed him." She said it so matter of factly, so straight. I know it's not something she'd joke about, but I can't take in what I'm hearing.

"You wouldn't do it," there's a hint of anger in that statement which is aimed straight at me and I cringe. "I thought you loved him?"

"I do love him!" I shout back. "That's why I couldn't do it!"

"You did love him," she corrects me. "Past tense, he's gone now." The barrier breaks and she starts crying again. I want to reach out and comfort her, but I'm struggling to process what's happening here.

Just the day before yesterday we were all sat here laughing and smiling, I've not had time to process the news about Bandit's cancer so how can he be gone? It just isn't making sense to me right now. The world feels like it's spun on its axis, everything has changed and I'm off kilter here.

My legs are starting to tremble and I have to sit down, I pull the chair closer to Smokey and take her hands in mine, looking at her. It's like a stranger is looking back at me. I can't tell if her eyes are filled with grief, or if it's anger aimed at me for putting her in this position.

I'm patting her hands and realising how ineffectual that act is. What comfort can that possibly offer to a woman in her position, nevertheless my hands keep up the movement. Her crying eases off again, and her gulping breaths slow down.

"I don't understand, Smokey, what the hell happened?" I ask gently.

"I knew he'd ask you, and I knew you'd turned him down. I could tell that day when I got back from the ranch. He just sat out there, defeated." She looks up at me, pleading with her eyes for me to understand. "He was in so much pain, he hid it well, but I knew. We all watched your mother die, would you have had him suffer like that? It's bloody ridiculous, they'd never let an animal go through suffering like that, but for some reason they inflict that torture on people. I just don't get it."

Her shoulders are heaving as she starts sobbing again. Everything she's said is right. I still vividly remember watching my mum racked with uncontrollable pain and wondering why she had to go through that. I also remember the times she begged me to make the pain stop, and my heart would break that I couldn't do that for her.

Smokey's also right in that I wouldn't have seen an animal suffer like that without putting it out of it's misery, but

I just couldn't do it for Bandit. I couldn't. Hot drops hit the back of my hand and I realise that I'm crying as well. Smokey realises and despite her own pain pulls me into her, and comforts me. We sit there together, both mourning the man that we loved.

It feels like forever before we finally pull apart. Some element of sanity is coming back to me now, and I know that I have to fix this situation so that Smokey doesn't end up in trouble.

"How did you do it?" I ask her, my words soft and gentle so as not to alarm her.

"I mixed the sleeping pills they prescribed him into a hot chocolate, and then added the Nembutal in with it. He just went to sleep beside me as normal, and never woke up. I laid with him all night, I couldn't sleep myself, and I just held him close until he took that last breath." She looks up at me suddenly. "It was peaceful, he didn't feel any pain." She reassures me.

"I knew what was coming you see, from that first diagnosis. I couldn't watch him suffer like that, couldn't watch as he wasted away, became a shell of the man he once was, so I'd been doing my research. I know they're trying to pass a law to make it legal but god knows how long that would take, even if it would ever get through, and by then it would be too late. I spent hours researching the best way to do it, so he wouldn't suffer, so many of the drugs I found would have meant he'd have been in agony and I couldn't go there. I couldn't do that to him." She pauses a moment, trying to hold her grief at bay so she can continue to tell me how she killed her husband. My heart hurts listening to her, knowing how hard this must have been, how much thought she'd put into it.

"In the end I realised the only way to do it was the way they do it in those other countries, just give him some Nembutal and he'd just drift off to sleep."

"But you can't even get that stuff here?" I've no idea what Nembutal is, but it sounds like she's talking about euthanasia drugs and the last I heard they weren't available here at all.

"You want anything hard enough you can find it," she sighs. "And if you have enough money. A few weeks ago I came across someone who has it sent over illegally from china, it just looks like a powder in an envelope. All I had to do was mix it up and add it to his drink." I shudder at the thought of the kind of people Smokey must have been hanging around.

"They're not drug dealers," she reassures me, obviously realising what I'm thinking, "they're just people who've lost loved ones to this dreadful disease and can't face watching someone else go through it. The lady who helped me out was someone who's been through the same thing, although she didn't know about the drug at the time and had to watch the full hell of the illness take her husband from her. Now she keeps a small supply to hand to help others."

"But they'll find it in his system?" I say, shocked by how much thought she's put into this whole thing.

"The doctor was here a couple of days ago, he warned us

then that his heart wasn't great. According to my research into the drugs there shouldn't need to be a post mortem."

I hate that Smokey has had to go to these lengths, spend so much time researching how to do this, even knowing what would happen afterward. I should have been here for her, for them.

"I'm sorry," I pull her in tight. "I'm sorry I wasn't here for you, and that I couldn't do this for you." I start sobbing again. I'm the one that's supposed to be comforting her and I'm crying like a bloody baby.

I'm still struggling to take everything in. Smokey looks too calm, too accepting of what has happened whereas I want to rail and shout and let all this anger out, yet at the same time my heart feels as though it's breaking. I need to man up, I need to be here for her.

"Do you want to see him? To say goodbye?" She asks hesitantly.

Fuck, no I don't want to see him. What's left isn't Bandit anyway, just an empty shell, but I nod my head knowing that if I don't then I'll never be able to accept this is all real. Walking up those stairs is the hardest thing I've done.

She opens the door and stands back, allowing me to enter in front of her. He looks like he's sleeping, the creases on his face that were there the other day are gone. He's at peace now. I take a hesitant step towards the bed, and although I can tell from his colour I still have to reach out and touch him. It's too much and I sink to my knees, letting out an almighty wail of grief.

13
WRATH

I'm still on my knees and lost in grief when I'm startled out of it by the sound of items smashing around me. I look up to see that Smokey has lost it. She's picking up anything loose on the dresser and throwing it across the room, absolutely overwhelmed with grief and anger.

As much as I just want to let her be, knowing she needs this, I'm scared she's going to hurt herself. I was right, she launches a jewellery box against the far wall and it knocks over an oil lamp that was still burning. I barely have time to wonder why the hell she'd have an oil lamp in her bedroom, let alone lit, when the nets on the window catch alight.

Smokey doesn't even notice. I try and drag her from the room but she's refusing to come with me. She rushes over to the bed and curls up beside Bandit, crooning softly to him and holding him tight.

I'm torn between getting her out of here and putting the fire out. I choose the fire, knowing that right now she'd fight me every step of the way. She never had been able to persuade

Bandit to install an en-suite in their room so I rush to the landing and throw some towels in the bath soaking them with water. I drag them dripping wet back to the bedroom, throwing one over Smokey to keep her safe and using another to beat at the curtains in a vain attempt to put the flames out.

The fire has taken hold so quickly I know there's nothing I can do other than get Smokey out. I look at Bandit and hope that I have time to come back for him. Smokey kicks and screams as I drag her from the bed, refusing to let go of her husband. I have to remove her hands from where they are clawed in a vice around his arm.

The smoke is getting thicker and is black and acrid, something in here is fuelling the fire and I need to get her out of here now. In the end I forcibly lift her and throw her over my shoulder in a grotesque parody of a fireman's lift. She fights me all the way down the stairs, almost causing me to lose my footing. As we pass the kitchen I'm amazed to see flames already in there, the wooden structure of the house obviously working against us.

I stumble into the yard, collapsing to the ground and greedily sucking in lungfuls of clean air. Smokey is too quiet, and fear runs through me that I've lost her as well. It can't be. Tentatively I reach out, desperately feeling for a pulse, it's there thank god, but only just. I think she's just passed out. I'm trying to rouse her when I hear the roar of a bike approaching.

It screeches to a halt, crashing to the ground close by when the rider sees the scene in front of us. Smokey is just coming round so I'm concentrating on her when I feel myself being yanked back by the shoulder.

I look up into the face of a young biker I've never met. "Where's Bandit?" He yells at me. "Where's Bandit." Without thinking I look back at the house and am shocked to see how far the flames have taken over. He's followed my gaze and realising Bandit is still inside rushes off.

"James!" Smokey croaks out, her voice hoarse. "It's too late, please no James!"

The boy hasn't heard her and the last I see of him is him running in through the burning front door.

"You've got to stop him," Smokey pleads with me.

"I'm on it," I assure her as I'm already stumbling to my feet. I can hear sirens and the sounds of cars approaching. "Stay here!" I needlessly advise her, knowing she can barely get up as it is, but grateful that help is on the way.

The house is just a mass of fire on the whole of the left side as I follow James in. I can see him struggling to make it up the stair case ahead of me.

"It's too late!" I shout up after him, but my words are drowned out by the ferocious roar of flames around us. By the time I make it into the bedroom James is passed out on the floor, his clothes alight, one hand reached up towards Bandit.

"Fuck!" I'm struggling for breath, there's not enough time to get both of them out of here so I concentrate on James, knowing that that's what Bandit would want. I stumble back into the bathroom grateful to find another bale of towels and soak them quickly in the water still left in the tub. I use them to put the flames out on James and hear a groan of pain as I press a little too hard with the towel. Thank god he's still alive.

I hear voices downstairs and follow them down the smoke filled hallway. My throat is burning and I can't get any words out to let them know that we are here. As we reach the top of the stairs I finally see figures at the bottom. My legs are giving way and I know I won't make it down the steps so with every bit of strength I have left in me I lift James and throw him at the figures below.

With any luck I'll be able to crawl into my old room and escape via the window in there, I'm sure it's on the side of the house that isn't burning yet. I'm almost at my bedroom door when the fire finds the gas supply in the kitchen. There's an almighty explosion from behind me and hot timbers start to fall on my legs. With everything I have left in me I push the door open and drag myself in.

The last thing I see is the photo on the bedside table of me and my mum.

14
WRATH

One month later

I should be dead. I deserve to be dead. Somehow, and I'll never understand how, they managed to get the fire under control and found me collapsed in my old room. I can only guess that I had a guardian angel watching over me after all.

Smokey and I both needed treatment for smoke inhalation, but it was James, who I later found out was a prospect from Hellion MC, that took the brunt of it. His burns were severe enough to land him with a lengthy hospital stay. He's in for a long road of treatment ahead, but the good news is he'll survive. Smokey feels so guilty that he got hurt trying to save Bandit that I know he's going to be well looked after during his recovery. She'll take him under her wing, just as she did me when I needed her after mum's passing.

Everyone, the authorities included, accepted that Bandit had passed in his sleep, and that the fire was a result of a simple accident brought on by Smokey's grief. She's never going to be the same, because she's lost such a huge part of her life, they were by each others sides for over fifty years and I'm not sure you can ever get over that. She's a shadow of the woman she used to be, but I know her and I know that she'll come back to us little by little if we give her time.

The funeral was hard for all of us, Bandit had so many people who loved him, and they were all united in their grief. Smokey clung to me and wouldn't let go throughout the ceremony. How she got through the graveside service I'll never know. She seemed to draw on some inner strength.

She's begged me not to go back to Cardinal, and told me that she can't lose me as well. Every time I look at her I'm filled with guilt for what she had to do because I'd said no. That's going to haunt me forever. It should have been me. I should have taken that burden from her.

I'm renting a small house for us both, until she decides where she wants to be. The club have reassured her that she will always have a place with them but she's stayed away for now. There are too many memories and it's too painful for her to visit just yet.

Today is a new day though, and I've finally persuaded her to let me take her to the ranch to visit with the kids. She needs them because they need her. I know that spending time with them will be good for her, it will remind her she still has a purpose in her life.

When we pull up outside the ranch house she hesitates. For a moment I think she's going to back out on me then one of the kids comes running over and shouting her name.

She dismounts from my bike and walks hesitantly towards him where he pulls her into a hug.

"We've missed you, Smokey. It's so good to see you back."

She looks back at me for reassurance, I hate that this is how she is these days, but at my nod she smiles back at the boy and follows him to the barn where I know the rest of the kids are waiting for her. She's promised to run a craft session with them.

The door of the ranch house creaks open and I look over to see Jackson walking towards me.

"You got a moment?" He asks. I walk up to the porch and settle in front of him in a chair while he takes the porch swing.

"You did a good thing bringing her here today." He looks over at the barn, and I can see the sadness still in his face. Bandit was a close friend.

"It's what she needs," I reply not wanting to take credit for Smokey's strength in coming here today. That's all her.

"So what are your plans now?" Jackson asks.

"Whatever Smokey needs," I reply.

"And Cardinal?"

"Cardinal aren't interested unless I'm prepared to carry on as their enforcer, they've no time for me otherwise." I'm bitter at how easily they were prepared to let me go, but not surprised. I'd expected that would be their reaction. There was always someone younger, someone more eager at Cardinal.

Jackson nods his head in understanding. "You're a good

man deep down, Wrath. If you ever want it you've got a place with us in Hellion." He stands and touches my shoulder as he walks away.

I sit there slightly lost for words at his offer. I never saw that coming.

Right now I have no idea what my future holds, I know that Smokey won't need me this close forever, just until she gets her grief under control. That's the thing with grief though, it never goes away. It sits there out of sight, and festers away before popping up when you least expect it. I don't care what anyone says, you never get over grief. You just learn to live with it. One day it will be a scent or a song and grief stabs at you again, reminding you that it's always there just waiting to catch you out.

There's no cure for it, no magic fix. All you can do is try and remember the good times, the happy memories that you shared, the best bits of the person you lost. You have to remind yourself to be grateful that they're no longer suffering, lying to yourself that it's a blessing that they're gone, when in reality your life is less because they're no longer here.

Life is cruel, it's unfair and cancer is the most cruel and unfair of them all. Life is short, you need to embrace it and spend it making memories, spend it with the people you love and care for. Somehow, over the years since I lost mum I'd lost sight of that. I'd lost sight of the man she would have wanted me to become.

Losing Bandit has reminded me that life has to be lived,

not just survived. It's okay to fall on your ass with grief, to be angry, to miss them as though your soul is on fire. It's not okay to stop living.

I look over at the barn where I can hear the sweet sound of Smokey's laughter. It's a sound that heals a broken soul and a sound I hope to hear a lot more of in the future.

As he left, Jackson had handed me a slip of paper. I unfold it cautiously, curious to see what is written inside.

It's a phone number for Maeve. I look at the number and wonder if she wants to hear from me, although I suspect that Jackson wouldn't have given it to me otherwise.

I look at the number again and reach for my phone.

Life is for living after all.

The End

ACKNOWLEDGEMENTS

When you read a book you don't realise just how much work goes into it, particularly a book like this where you give up a part of your soul to write it.

It's not a solo journey, the writer may get the credit on the cover, but there's a whole team behind the writer who support them and encourage them as well as offering support.

This project generated a lot more pressure than normal. Because it was for Lavinia, it had to be right. It was her dream and in some small way was my way of honouring her memory.

I'd like to thank Heather Woodman for being an amazing alpha and beta reader and also the rest of my beta team: Nadia Debowska-Stephens, Yvonne Eason, Naomi Connor, Ann Walker, TL Wainright, Marie Pedrick, Nikki Costello and Margaret Hassebrock. They supported me through this tissue filled journey, corrected my spelling and grammar, and encouraged me every step of the way.

Thank you to you, the reader, for taking a chance on this book, and therefore supporting Lavinia's family and honouring her memory.

And lastly, thank you to Lavinia, for being so strong, courageous, honest and an amazing lady I was honoured to meet.

ABOUT

LAVINIA URBAN

Lavinia originally grew up in Cheshire and moved to a small village just outside of Edinburgh with her husband, two children, and two fur babies.

Writing had always been something that Lavinia had loved since an early age.

Over the years, Lavinia had faced many obstacles but that had only spurred her on. In 2017, Lavinia was diagnosed with Metastatic Breast Cancer. She chose to not let this define her. If anything it gave her the drive to do more.

Lavinia's intense battle ended all too soon, yet her legacy will forever be remembered.

For a list of Lavinia's books, please visit
https://smarturl.it/laviniaurban

Other places to find Lavinia:

https://www.facebook.com/LaviniaUrbanAuthor

https://www.facebook.com/groups/LaviniasUrbanLegends

www.laviniaurban.co.uk

ABOUT

AVA MANELLO

Ava is a passionate reader, blogger, publisher, and author who loves nothing more than helping other Indie authors publish their books be that reviewing, beta reading, formatting or proofreading. She will always be a reader first and foremost.

She loves erotic suspense that's well written and engages the reader, and loves promoting the heck out of it for her favourite authors.

As Ava says: "I took a chance and followed a dream when I wrote my first book. It was scary, challenging and hard work, but above all it was worth it."

http://www.avamanello.co.uk

Printed in Great
Britain
by Amazon

31673167R00057